UNITED STATES POLICY
TOWARD THE ARMENIAN QUESTION
AND THE ARMENIAN GENOCIDE

UNITED STATES POLICY
TOWARD THE ARMENIAN QUESTION
AND THE ARMENIAN GENOCIDE

Simon Payaslian

UNITED STATES POLICY TOWARD THE ARMENIAN QUESTION AND
THE ARMENIAN GENOCIDE
© Simon Payaslian, 2005.

First published in 2005 by
PALGRAVE MACMILLAN™
175 Fifth Avenue, New York, N.Y. 10010 and
Houndmills, Basingstoke, Hampshire, England RG21 6XS
Companies and representatives throughout the world.

PALGRAVE MACMILLAN is the global academic imprint of the Palgrave
Macmillan division of St. Martin's Press, LLC and of Palgrave Macmillan Ltd.
Macmillan® is a registered trademark in the United States, United Kingdom
and other countries. Palgrave is a registered trademark in the European
Union and other countries.

ISBN 1–4039–7098–X hardback

Library of Congress Cataloging-in-Publication Data

Payaslian, Simon.
    United States policy toward the Armenian question and
the Armenian genocide / Simon Payaslian.
        p. cm.
    Includes bibliographical references and index.
    ISBN 1–4039–7098–X
        1. United States—Foreign relations—Turkey. 2. Turkey—Foreign
relations—United States. 3. United States—Foreign relations—
1865–1921. 4. United States—Relations—Armenia. 5. Armenia—
Relations—United States. 6. Armenian question. 7. Armenian
massacres, 1915–1923. 8. Turkey—History—Ottoman Empire,
1288–1918. I. Title.

E183.8.T8P39 2005
956.6'20154—dc22   2005049181

A catalogue record for this book is available from the British Library.

Design by Newgen Imaging Systems (P) Ltd., Chennai, India.

First edition: December 2005

10 9 8 7 6 5 4 3 2 1

Printed in the United States of America.

Transferred to digital printing in 2006.

In memory of His Holiness Zareh I Payaslian
Catholicos of the Great House of Cilicia
(1915–1963)

Whose generation rebuilt

Contents

LIST OF TABLES

PREFACE

The advent of the United States as a global power coincided with the internationalization of the Armenian Question in the late nineteenth century. Since its early days, the United States had developed commercial relations with the Ottoman Empire, where it pursued expanding economic and missionary interests throughout the nineteenth century. The U.S. government functioned as the "promotional state," as its representatives in Constantinople and across the Ottoman Empire sought to maintain friendly relations with Turkish authorities. The Ottoman government, in turn, hoped its relations with the United States would lead to widening commercial and financial ties to improve the empire's economic and military capabilities. By the time the Wilson administration entered the White House in 1913, the American missionaries, commercial enterprises, and the Navy, with the support of the Department of State, were already shaping U.S. foreign policy toward the Ottoman Empire. President Woodrow Wilson cultivated close government-business relations by emphasizing the responsibilities of the "promotional state" abroad. This study examines the U.S. responses to the Armenian Question in general and the Armenian Genocide in particular within the context of the political economy of U.S. foreign policy. Wilson's rhetoric of moralism and humanitarianism notwithstanding, his administration refused to employ military intervention to stop the genocide being committed by the Turkish government against the Armenian people. Instead, the administration sought to maintain friendly relations with the Turkish government during and after World War I.

I am deeply grateful to Andrjez Korbonski, Michael Morony, Damodar SarDesai, and Jessica Wang, for their helpful comments on earlier drafts of this study while in its dissertation stages at UCLA. It is my great pleasure to have this opportunity to express my deepest appreciation and to acknowledge my intellectual debts to Richard G. Hovannisian. Without his encouragement and advice, this study could not have been completed. A brief summary of this study has appeared as a chapter in a volume, *Looking Backward, Moving Forward: Confronting the Armenian Genocide*, edited by Hovannisian

(Transaction Publishers, 2003). I am also indebted to the Kaspar and
Siroon Hovannisian Fellowship, the Movel Fellowship, the Mangasarian
Fellowship, and the Armenian Educational Foundation, for their
financial support that enabled me to complete this study. I would like
to thank the staff of the Houghton Library, Harvard University, for
their able assistance in researching the archives of the American Board
of Commissioners for Foreign Missions. Thanks to Leslie A. Morris,
Curator of Manuscripts at the Houghton Library, and the Reverend
Bennie E. Whiten, Jr., Interim Executive Minister of the Wider
Church Ministries, United Church of Christ in Cleveland, for their
permission to include material from the ABCFM papers. Thanks also
to Bruce Kirby, Manuscript Reference Librarian at the Manuscript
Division, Library of Congress, for his prompt assistance regarding
permissions for the papers of Henry Morgenthau, Sr., William
Jennings Bryan, and Robert Lansing. Special thanks to David Pervin
and the editorial staff at Palgrave Macmillan for bringing this book to
fruition.

I want to express my deepest gratitude to my wife, Arpi, whose
indefatigable energy and patience enabled me to complete the book
on schedule, and to my parents and family who as always encouraged
me with unswerving moral support.

CHAPTER 1

THE POLITICAL ECONOMY OF U.S. FOREIGN POLICY TOWARD THE OTTOMAN EMPIRE AND THE ARMENIAN QUESTION

The United States and the Ottoman Empire established bilateral relations during the early years of the founding of the republic. Even before independence, as Adam Smith noted, New England traded with the Mediterranean economies, exporting fish to these far away shores. He complained that, while previously British trade across the Mediterranean could sustain the "great naval power," by the 1770s American trade had surpassed its mother country.[1] Upon independence, commercial and geopolitical considerations constituted an essential component of U.S. foreign policy for the economic and physical survival of the new nation.[2] Policymakers in the United States expressed interest in cultivating trade relations with the Ottoman Empire in the 1790s,[3] but political difficulties in U.S.-British-French relations at the turn of the century, on the one hand, and extensive British, French, and Russian involvement in Ottoman affairs, on the other, prevented negotiations toward a treaty. Nevertheless, by 1811 American merchants had established a trading house at Smyrna.[4]

Although as early as 1801 it was believed that the Ottoman Empire was in process of disintegration,[5] U.S.-Ottoman trade relations continued to flourish. The Ottoman authorities favored close ties with the United States and promised protection for U.S. trade at Smyrna. The United States in turn requested guarantees for trade at Turkish ports under the principle of most favored nation, free access to the

Black Sea, and consent to appointment of consuls to Turkish ports.[6] In May 1830, the Jackson administration, urged by Secretary of State Martin Van Buren, the U.S. Navy, and influential merchants, signed the first formal treaty of commerce and amity with the Ottoman government, allowing for the exchange of diplomatic and consular offices.[7] In 1845, the Ottoman government sent its first consul to the United States at Boston.[8]

During the Civil War in the United States, the Ottoman government expressed its sympathies toward the Union, even when, as U.S. Minister to Constantinople Edward Joy Morris wrote to the Secretary of State William H. Seward, "some of the Christian powers of Europe seem to be indifferent to its fate."[9] For its part, the Lincoln administration instructed Morris to convey to the sultan the desire of the administration "to improve as far as possible the commercial interest of the two countries." "I am happy in thus being able to report," Morris wrote, "that the United States has a true and loyal friend in the sovereign of this great power." Accordingly, on February 25, 1862, the United States and Turkey signed a commerce treaty in Paris, and the U.S. Navy was permitted to navigate in Turkish waters without restriction.[10] After the Civil War, the availability of a large surplus of arms and ammunition as well as military men provided a new incentive to widen trade relations, led primarily by the Remington Arms Company.[11] A number of former Union and Confederate soldiers, some with experiences in wars against the Indians and Mexicans, went to work for the Ottoman government.[12] Further, in the 1860s, the Sublime Porte encouraged the distribution of American cottonseed in efforts to reinvigorate agricultural production.[13] During the Spanish–American War in 1898, Sultan Abdul Hamid II urged the Muslims in the Philippines to remain friendly toward the United States. U.S.-Turkish trade had grown substantially by then (the total volume for 1899 was more than $6 million),[14] and expanding economic relations contributed to the long-term strengthening of U.S.–Turkish relations well into the twentieth century.

After the depression of the 1890s, U.S. foreign policy decisively turned to commercial and military expansion with a missionary zeal, as demands for domestic economic stability and growth compelled political and business leaders to search for solutions abroad. Although not all of the public favored such expansionism, policymakers and manufacturers alike stressed the necessity of Open Door policy and freedom of the seas for greater international competitiveness and commercial supremacy.[15]

Contrary to claims that U.S. commercial interests in the Ottoman Empire prior to World War I were insignificant, confined to isolated or failed business ventures, U.S. commercial interests had expanded considerably by the turn of the century. Aiming to widen their international operations, companies such as Standard Oil, Singer Sewing Machine, International Harvester, the American Tobacco Company, the National City Bank of New York, and New York Life Insurance, as well as manufacturing associations such as the National Association of Manufacturers (formed in 1895), the American Asiatic Association (1898), the U.S. Chamber of Commerce (1912), and the American Manufacturers' Export Association (1913), lobbied heavily for government support for their ventures abroad. Each business interest was the dominant group in its specific sector, and they together exerted enormous influence in Washington.

In its annual report for 1900, the Treasury Department boasted that the total value of exports exceeded "by $163,000,750 those of any preceding year. While the increase in exports appeared in nearly every category of goods, manufactures registered significant gains, amounting to $94,259,610 over 1899." It noted that "new markets are being found for American products . . . in every part of the world, and especially in those countries to which all the great manufacturing and producing nations are now looking for an increased market."[16] In the early 1890s, the U.S. share of world trade in manufactures totaled 3.9 percent; by the end of the decade that figure had reached 9.8 percent, and 11.0 percent in 1913. By 1913, the United States accounted for about 30 percent of total world industrial production.[17] The expansionist thrust in the form of Open Door and Dollar Diplomacy was aimed at Latin America, East Asia, as well as the Ottoman Empire. Competing agricultural, manufacturing, and financial sectors shaped U.S. foreign policy, and securing stable markets and access to raw materials (such as oil) became one of the primary objectives of U.S. foreign policy in the Middle East. The administrations of William McKinley, Theodore Roosevelt, William Howard Taft, and Woodrow Wilson viewed U.S. economic expansion in both market and geostrategic terms in the region, widening U.S. ties with the Ottoman Empire.[18] Accordingly, the administrations during this period assumed responsibilities of the "promotional state" to facilitate greater access to international resources and markets and to enhance the nation's economic security.[19]

THE ARMENIAN QUESTION

The expansion in U.S.-Ottoman trade relations during the second half of the nineteenth century coincided with the rapidly deteriorating political and economic conditions for Armenians across the Ottoman

Empire. The diverging paths taken by the Ottoman determination to reverse the military and economic decline, on the one hand, and the cultural reawakening of Armenians, on the other, led to an intensification of government repressive measures against the Armenians throughout the six Armenian provinces of Van, Bitlis, Kharpert, Sebastia, Erzerum, and Diarbekir. The various administrative improvements promised under the *Tanzimat* (Reorganization) reforms from the 1830s not only proved elusive, but the authorities in Constantinople and in the provinces as well as the Muslim population in general perceived such structural changes as a threat to their status in society. After the Crimean (1854–56) and the Russo-Turkish (1877–78) wars, the close attention paid by the Western powers to the Eastern Question and the presence of foreign official representatives and missionaries in their communities gave rise to unrealistic expectations among the despondent Armenians that their grievances, long ignored by the sultanate, could now be addressed. Armenians hoped that the treaties of San Stefano and Berlin, both signed in 1878 in the aftermath of the Russo–Turkish war, would enable the major powers to intervene more directly in Ottoman affairs to alleviate their plight. Yet, none of the powers demonstrated a serious interest in the implementation of the promised reforms. German Chancellor Otto von Bismarck wrote in 1883: "The so-called Armenian reforms are ideal and theoretical aspirations, which were given an appropriate place in the ornamental part of the transactions of the [Berlin] Congress, so that they could be used for parliamentary purposes. Their practical significance, whatever the final outcome, is very doubtful."[20]

The "final outcome" was the intensification of Turkish hostilities toward the Armenians, who in turn responded by arming themselves rather than continuing to rely on the European powers for protection. Loosely organized groups formed in the 1870s and early 1880s (e.g., the Union of Salvation in 1872 and the Black Cross Society in 1878 at Van and the Protectors of the Fatherland in 1881 at Erzerum) to repel Turkish and Kurdish attacks, by the next decade became organized political parties espousing revolutionary ideologies and strategies: the Armenakan Party in 1885 in Van, the Hnchakian (Bell) Revolutionary Party in 1887 in Geneva, and the Hai Heghapokhakan Dashnaktsutiun (Armenian Revolutionary Federation) in 1890 in Tiflis.[21] Although each adhered to its own ideological predilections and *modus operandi*, which included cooperation with the growing Young Turk movement against Sultan Abdul Hamid II, all agreed on the common objective of protecting the physical security of their communities.

THE UNITED STATES AND THE ARMENIAN QUESTION, 1890s

In March 1895, several months after nearly 3,000 Armenians were massacred in Sasun,[22] U.S. minister to Constantinople Alexander W. Terrell warned the State Department that further bloodshed was expected and recommended that the U.S. Navy pay a "friendly visit" to the Turkish coasts on the Mediterranean. Terrell also demanded that Ottoman Minister of Foreign Affairs Said Pasha issue orders to "every portion of the Ottoman Empire where American missionaries are found" to secure their protection. Said Pasha countered that reports expressing apprehensions of massacres were "invented" by those "ill-disposed" toward Turkey and had "no serious foundation" and that the authorities guaranteed public order and tranquility, "so that no apprehension can be entertained by American citizens."[23] Convinced that the situation required action, Acting Secretary of State Edwin F. Uhl informed Terrell in early April 1895 that the Secretary of the Navy had directed two ships, the USS San Francisco from Palermo and the USS Marblehead from Gibraltar, to proceed to Turkish waters.[24] The Turkish minister to Washington, Mavroyeni Bey, protested the dispatch of ships to Turkey and claimed that news regarding the massacres were false. He requested that the State Department publicly deny reports that American ships had been ordered to Turkey, as such a policy would be interpreted by American missionaries and Armenian "revolutionists" as "an act unfavorable to Turkey."[25]

Within two weeks, Terrell changed his tone and reported that he saw "no cause to fear present danger."[26] In April, having visited Smyrna on the USS San Francisco, Rear Admiral W.A. Kirkland reported that it was not necessary to maintain a naval presence in Turkish waters, as American citizens were secure. "As far as apprehension of a massacre of Christians in this port is concerned," he observed, "I see no reason to believe in such incident in the near future."[27]

In early October, Sultan Abdul Hamid II launched massacres across the Armenian provinces, lasting for more than a year and resulting in the death of more than 100,000 Armenians.[28] In response, the U.S. Senate adopted, on December 4, 1895, a resolution requesting that President Cleveland submit to the Senate all information received by the State Department regarding "injuries inflicted upon the persons or property of American citizens in Turkey, and in regard to the condition of affairs there in reference to the oppression or cruelties practiced upon the Armenian subjects of the Turkish Government."[29] Despite a number of resolutions debated in Congress, neither Congress nor Cleveland was willing to antagonize the Sublime Porte on humanitarian matters.[30] A lengthy report by the Department of State informed the Senate that although several missionary properties were destroyed no injuries were caused to American citizens and that the *San Francisco*, *Marblehead*, and *Minneapolis* were dispatched to the Syrian and Adanan coasts to secure their protection.[31]

The McKinley administration demanded compensation for the loss of missionary property during the massacres, and in 1898 both governments agreed that the sultan could pay the compensation through purchase of a warship from an American company.[32] Thus, while the United States appeared to sympathize with "oppressed nationalities,"[33] the true beneficiaries were the missionaries (who were granted an *irade*, a decree, by the sultan to rebuild the missionary school at Kharpert), the shipbuilding Cramp Company of Philadelphia, and the sultan, who had insisted during the negotiations that he be allowed to "save face." The sultan promised that if the purchased cruiser proved a success, he intended to purchase three or four larger ships. Further, the sultan "expressed confidence in the rifles manufactured in America" and hoped to purchase them for the Ottoman Army in large numbers.[34]

THE U.S. NAVY, COMMERCE, AND MISSIONARIES

Reflecting the rapidly changing role of the United States in world politics, Alfred Mahan, writing in the 1880s, underscored the significance of the Mediterranean basin for U.S. commercial and geostrategic objectives. "The history of Sea Power," Mahan introduced his treatise, "is largely, though by no means solely, a narrative of contests between nations, of mutual rivalries, of violence frequently culminating in war." Nations strove to expand and to dominate commerce across the seas and engaged in wars to protect their commercial and strategic sea-lane communications. Sea power in general and the Mediterranean Sea in particular, Mahan added, had shaped world history since the Roman Empire, and the imperatives of geostrategic formulations prevailing then continued to be relevant in the late nineteenth century. The decline of the Ottoman Empire, Russian expansion across the Black Sea, and the competition generated between the Eastern and Western powers rendered naval power all the more important for commerce and strategy.[35] From 1900 the U.S. Navy witnessed enormous changes in policy orientation and technology.

President Theodore Roosevelt, who concurred with Mahan, sought to achieve naval parity with the European powers, especially Great Britain, and proposed to augment battleship capabilities.[36] Indeed, Congressional naval appropriations increased from $66.95 million in 1900 to $103.9 million in 1904, and to $143 million in 1913 before the Taft administration left office.[37]

In addition to the Navy, commercial enterprises also sought to maintain good relations with Constantinople. Business groups in the United States stressed the importance of avoiding conflict with Turkey and frequently criticized pro-Armenian organizations for their anti-Turkish activities and Congress for its humanitarian pronouncements with respect to the Armenian situation. Businesses played a particularly significant role in U.S.-Ottoman relations since the U.S. administration frequently relied on private individuals for the conduct of policy toward the Ottoman Empire. Since businesses were concerned primarily with the promotion of their interests, assistance to protect the Armenians in times of crises, as during the massacres of the 1890s, fell beyond the purview of their activities. Such concerns were left to U.S. charity organizations and missionaries, who collected funds and sent volunteers to aid the needy. Moreover, businesses and the U.S. government wished to avoid meddling in the "internal" affairs of the Ottoman Empire.[38]

The gradual conversion from coal to oil for purposes of industrialization heightened the awareness of policymakers in Washington concerning the potential threat depleting domestic oil resources would pose to the nation's economy. The conversion sharpened the interest of the U.S. Navy and businesses in Middle Eastern oil supplies. Accordingly, they sought to protect U.S. oil interests in competition with Russian, British, and French oil monopolies in the Middle East and the Caucasus.[39] The oil industry was among the most active groups lobbying the U.S. government for expansion abroad.

As early as the 1870s, U.S. refineries exported nearly 75 percent of their oil, particularly illuminating and lubricating oil products. The next two decades witnessed the growing confidence of American oil producers regarding their competitive edge in world markets. Europe was the largest market for U.S. oil products, followed by Asia, which received nearly 153,000 barrels annually, of which 50,000 went to Asiatic Turkey. By the mid-1890s, however, the economic depression, on the one hand, and growing competition in international markets, on the other, caused serious concerns for the U.S. oil industry. The formation of the Royal Dutch Oil Company in 1890 and the rapid development of Russian oil production, particularly in the Baku region, intensified international rivalry over resources and markets. The Russian construction of the Baku–Batum railroad in the 1880s facilitated greater access of Russian oil to international markets via the Black Sea, and the development of the Russian oil industry in the Caucasus invited intense competition from U.S. companies, especially since Russian production included illuminating oil as well, one area of U.S. market dominance.[40]

The Ottoman Empire, particularly Mesopotamia, was known to possess vast reserves of oil, while other areas such as Van, Trebizond, and the Gulf of Adalia needed further investigation.[41] In 1892, the U.S. chargé d'affaires at Constantinople encouraged John D. Rockefeller to pursue the advantages of Caucasian and Mesopotamian oil more aggressively and to thwart the expanding influence of Russian oil interests in Turkey and the Persian Gulf region.[42] In the meantime, Russian production of crude oil had surpassed that of the United States and at the turn of the century supplied over 30 percent of world oil.[43] The State Department noted in 1898 that the increasing international consumption of American products required greater diplomatic engagement on the part of policymakers and that the latter "can no longer afford to disregard international rivalries now that we ourselves have become a competitor in the world-wide struggle for trade."[44] Regarding U.S. oil interests in the Ottoman Empire, former U.S. minister at Constantinople Samuel S. Cox stressed to James L. Barton, secretary of the American Board of Commissioners for Foreign Missions (ABCFM), that "his chief business was to look after the interest of the two American imports, kerosene and missionaries."[45]

U.S. commercial ventures, having expanded throughout the nineteenth century, assumed a greater role in U.S.-Turkish relations, especially as the latter's domestic needs to combat both economic and military decline required capital and superior technology. By the turn of the century, the United States had become one of the major partners of Ottoman trade, and the early years of the twentieth century witnessed an enormous increase in their trade relations (see table 1.1). Ottoman tobacco was the principal export to the United States. The latter in turn exported a wide range of manufactured goods, including cloth, firearms, and machinery. In some cases U.S. products superseded their European competitors in the Ottoman market, as in the case of the Singer Sewing Machine, which undermined its principal competitor, Cornély de Paris.[46]

International commerce and diffusion of technology in the late nineteenth and early twentieth centuries bore certain advantages for Ottoman society, but they also caused economic dislocations and

Table 1.1 Annual value of U.S.-Turkish trade, 1900–21

Year	U.S. exports to Turkey	U.S. imports from Turkey	Total
1900	567,012	7,754,237	8,321,249
1901	587,120	7,284,636	7,871,756
1902	774,552	8,895,740	9,670,292
1903	773,107	10,570,006	11,343,113
1904	1,110,336	9,587,126	10,697,462
1905	888,260	11,195,128	12,083,388
1906	1,520,027	12,994,267	14,514,294
1907	1,753,815	14,606,188	16,360,003
1908	1,973,400	10,759,570	12,732,970
1909	2,518,142	12,429,128	14,947,270
1910	2,357,672	16,353,901	18,711,573
1911	3,940,053	17,690,812	21,630,865
1912	3,798,168	19,208,926	23,007,094
1913	3,313,821	22,159,285	25,473,106
1914	3,328,519	20,843,077	24,171,596
1915	994,120	12,228,707	13,222,827
1916	42,169	864,485	906,654
1917	167,515	335,590	503,105
1918	305,557	222,039	527,596
1919	25,231,722	37,003,002	62,234,724
1920	42,247,798	39,766,936	82,014,734
1921	23,947,110	13,246,638	37,193,748

Source: Annual reports of U.S. Department of the Treasury and Department of Commerce and Labor, Bureau of Statistics, *The Foreign Commerce and Navigation of the United States* (Washington, DC: Government Printing Office, 1900–21): 1900–18, Years Ending June 30; 1919–21, Calendar Years.

exacerbated gnawing political problems, with serious ramifications for the Armenians. The advent of the railroad, on the one hand, and shifting agricultural and manufacturing sectors, on the other, more closely integrated the Ottoman economy into the global economy but also rendered it vulnerable to fluctuations in global market demands.[47] The railroad not only accelerated commercial access to raw materials but also military mobility across the empire. As existing primitive forms of transportation were superseded by the railroad, certain regions and industries—for example, tobacco in the eastern provinces—benefited as they successfully competed in the world economy and experienced rapid economic growth. Other regions and industries, however, failed to compete with foreign products, such as wheat exports from the American Midwest. American goods, especially cotton and wheat, secured a greater share of world markets, thus undermining Ottoman competition.

Intensification of international competition and saturation of Ottoman markets by cheaper Western products caused domestic producers to change their production and marketing processes.[48] The Ottoman economy in general, however, failed to meet the challenges of world political economy, with detrimental consequences. Economic dislocation, coupled with the prevailing antagonism toward the *Tanzimat* reforms since the mid-1800s and the mass immigration by Muslims following the loss of Ottoman territories in the Balkans, led to growing animosity against the Armenians.[49] These hostilities transformed into state-sponsored mass violence, which in turn encouraged and legitimized hostilities in matters of market competition. Advertisements urged Muslims to boycott Armenian merchants:

> Why should we bow before these Armenians, who make of us a laughingstock though we never deserve it? The fortunes that they have made, the arts that they have grasped, are all generated from the fact that they have lived at our expense. Let's display zeal, let's roll up our sleeves. Do not have any kind of relationship with the Armenians; then the number of our merchants and artisans will increase as a natural consequence.[50]

The American Protestant missionary community became instrumental in the expansion of American commercial interests as well. Active in evangelical work in the Ottoman Empire since the early nineteenth century, missionary workers traveled with American merchants and the Navy and engaged in explorations throughout the region collecting "commercial intelligence" and serving as the eyes and ears of the United States.[51] An integral element in American nationalism at home and expansionism abroad, the American missionary community had established "missionary dynasties" by the late nineteenth century, with a genealogy of generations active in international work and with close ties to the commercial community.[52]

The American Board of Commissioners for Foreign Missions provided the organizational springboard for the expansion of missionary activities in the Ottoman Empire in the early decades of the nineteenth century. In its formative years, the American Board's membership roster included such prominent political figures as John Jay, Elias Boudinot, William Phillips, and Robert Ralston, who were among the wealthiest merchants in the United States and made large contributions to the missionary cause. U.S. businesses financially and morally supported the missionaries in the Ottoman Empire. When the first missionaries to the Ottoman Empire arrived at Smyrna in 1819, they were greeted by European and American merchants and businessmen. Commodore Porter and Henry Eckford, the American shipbuilding tycoon who at the time was working for the sultan, contributed generously to the missionary crusade.[53]

According to the authoritative *Encyclopedia of Missions*, by the turn of the century the American Board had created one of its most substantial missionary networks in the Ottoman Empire, accounting for nearly 25 percent of its total missionary fields in the world. In Asiatic Turkey alone the American Board had 12 stations and 270 outstations headed by 145 missionaries; 811 native workers; 114 organized churches serving 13,125 communicants and 48,000 adherents; and 1,266 schools at all levels with approximately 60,000 students.[54] The American Board raised approximately $81,600 annually, a substantial sum guaranteeing a healthy degree of self-sufficiency with respect to its expenditures in the region.[55] The principal missionary educational institutions in the Ottoman Empire included Central Turkey College at Aintab (established in 1874), Euphrates College at Kharpert (1876), Anatolia College at Marsovan (1886), College for Girls in Marash (1886), St. Paul's Institute in Tarsus (1889), American College for Girls at Constantinople (1890), and the International College at Smyrna (1902). The other two major American educational institutions not associated with the American Board but exercising enormous influence were Robert College at Constantinople and the Syrian Protestant College at Beirut. Under the direction of James L. Barton as secretary and its activists (including Robert Stapleton, Henry H. Riggs, Ernest W. Riggs, Mary L. Graffam, and Grace Higley Knapp), the American Board became the most active among the Western missionary societies in the Ottoman Empire, particularly among the Armenians, expending nearly 30 percent of its funds in that region.[56] Table 1.2 presents the figures for missionary staff and institutions before, during, and after World War I. These numbers indicate the increase in American missionary activities in the Ottoman Empire, but particularly revealing is the postwar drop in the number of students, most of whom were Armenian prior to the war.

The international image of the United States as a nation uninterested in imperial objectives had enabled American missionaries to pursue an expansionist course. As in the case of commercial competition, however, American missionaries dreaded the challenge posed by European and Russian missionaries in the eastern provinces. There, Armenians, isolated among Muslim neighbors, sought a reliable ally in Russians as Christians. American missionaries complained:

> Russia is always an ominous cloud on the missionary horizon. Its aggressions are political and religious. . . . Russian missionaries are

roaming among the Armenians, promising them that if they abandon the Gregorian to join the Russian Orthodox Church, they will be protected by the Czar against the Kurds and other Moslems better than they are protected by the Sultan. In the vilayet of Erzerum more than 5,000 Armenians have already passed to the Muscovite orthodoxy.[57]

American missionaries also expressed concern regarding equal treatment under Ottoman law and stressed the necessity of applying the Open Door principle to their institutions as well.[58]

Table 1.2   American Protestant missions in Turkey [a]

Years	Foreign staff	Residence stations of foreign staff	Native staff	Communicants	Educational institutions	Students
1903[b]	251	46	1,302	16,739	572	26,576
1911[c]	246	31	1,181	15,398	663	55,632
1916[d]	309	37	1,357	14,309	397	24,070
1925[e]	256[f]	29	373	3,987	50	5,731

[a] Data for combined Turkey-in-Asia and Turkey-in-Europe.

[b] 1903: The 1903 report lists two categories of educational institutions: day-schools and higher institutions. The number for day-schools is 527, and for students is 23,572; the number for higher institutions is 45, and for students is 3,004.

[c] 1911: Educational institutions include a total number of 313 Sunday schools with 31,454 students; kindergartens: 1, with 57 students; elementary schools: 278, with 18,567 students; boarding and high schools: 56, with 4,496 students; colleges and universities: 9, with 1,022 students; theological and Bible training schools, 5, with 36 students.

[d] 1916: Educational institutions include kindergartens, elementary and secondary schools, colleges and universities, and theological and Bible training schools. The number for kindergartens is 11 and for elementary schools 341; the figures for students are 453 and 18,650, respectively.

[e] 1925: Educational institutions include kindergartens, Sunday and elementary schools, higher and middle schools, industrial schools, teacher training schools, colleges and universities, and theological and Bible training schools. The number for kindergartens is 1 for Turkey-in-Europe and 0 for Turkey-in-Asia, and the number for students in both is 0. The number for elementary schools is 12, with 1,044 students. There were 5 elementary schools in Turkey-in-Asia, and 7 in Turkey-in-Europe, with 144 and 900 students, respectively. Moreover, there were 14 Sunday schools with a combined total of 2,159 teachers and students in Turkey-in-Asia; the figures for Turkey-in-Europe were 15 and 661, respectively.

[f] Includes 3 for foreign staff and 1 for residence stations in Transcaucasia (Armenia, Azerbaijan, and Georgia).

Sources: For 1903, see Harlan Beach, *A Geography and Atlas of Protestant Missions*, vol. 2: *Statistics and Atlas* (New York: Student Volunteer Movement for Foreign Missions, 1903 [1906]), pp. 19, 25. For 1911, see James S. Dennis, Harlan P. Beach, Charles H. Fahs, eds., *World Atlas of Christian Missions* (New York: Student Volunteer Movement for Foreign Missions, 1911), pp. 92, 107. For 1916, see Harlan Beach and Burton St. John, eds., *World Statistics of Christian Missions* (New York: Foreign Missions Conference of North America, 1916), pp. 66, 81. For 1925, see Harlan P. Beach and Charles H. Fahs, eds., *World Missionary Atlas* (New York: Institute of Social and Religious Research, 1925), pp. 87, 107, 131, 147.

THE METAMORPHOSIS IN MISSIONARY OPINION

American missionaries concentrated their energies mainly on the Armenians because Muslims were prohibited from conversion. Missionary views regarding the Armenians changed with the political and economic circumstances in the United States and the Ottoman Empire. During the larger part of the nineteenth century, the American missionaries showed little respect toward the Armenians and believed them to be "nominal Christians" in "a state of deplorable ignorance and degradation," an "illiterate population [who] lived in underground houses and worshiped in underground churches presided over by ignorant priests."[59] One missionary traveling through Kars to Tiflis, Erevan, Echmiadzin, the Mother See of the Armenian Church, and Tabriz reported that Armenians were

> ruled by unprincipled wine-bibbing priests, appeared of low moral character, notable for their dishonesty and ingratitude and addicted to concubinage. One bishop of good private character the Americans did find, but although expert in canonical doctrines and ceremonies, he, like all his compatriots, proved wholly ignorant of evangelical ideas. . . . Everywhere in the journey dishonesty and chicanery had proven major obstacles: if the Armenians, with their dominant love of money, cheated less than the Greeks, still they cheated plenty. . . . Everywhere there existed a general immorality, and a prevalence of natural and unnatural vice. . . . Yet nothing in the picture led to discouragement. . . . The need was to drive away the darkness.[60]

The influence of the missionaries extended beyond educational and religious activities, raising serious questions regarding its political implications for the Armenian communities in the Ottoman Empire. A small number of Armenians welcomed missionary activities as vehicles for intellectual renaissance and economic opportunities, and their support led to the chartering of the Catholic and Protestant *millets* (religious communities). Others, however, vehemently resisted their growing influence. Local religious institutions viewed the missionaries with suspicion and as a threat to their status in the Middle East.[61] Not surprisingly, Armenians, especially the Armenian Church, resented the condescending attitude exhibited by American missionaries toward them and believed that the missionaries intentionally disseminated dissension and divisions in their communities in order to weaken and eventually to usurp the authority of the Armenian Church.[62]

Most Armenians viewed Armenian conversions to the foreign faith as treasonous and suspected that those who converted did so primarily for financial rewards. In 1858, the renowned Armenian novelist Raffi (Hakob Melik-Hakobian) warned of the negative impact American missionary schools exercised on Armenian communities.[63] Another observer noted in the mid-1890s:

> This last blow did not come like its various precedents in the shape of tyrannizing force, but rather like a wasting disease which consumes one's vital strength and prostrates the victim gradually to sink and die. This blow was the one dealth by the missionaries of the American Board, who entered into the house of the Armenians like lambs, but tore them up like wolves. . . . They were going to create strife and conflict among the natives and then fish in the troubled waters. *Divide et impera* was their policy.[64]

Despite such difficulties, American missionaries, determined to conquer "pagan" hearts and minds, continued to arrogate to themselves the "divine right" to enlighten the "nominal Christians." Missionary schools taught English, arithmetic, and science, and soon provided employment for their Armenian pupils, a strategy "rationalized as teaching for the pupils the dignity of labor and the need to avoid the vice of idleness."[65] Under the direction of Cyrus Hamlin, for example, a number of factories were opened for the production of stoves, flour mills, and bakeries.[66] When local interests protested American investments, the latter found safe refuge under the Capitulations, which permitted foreigners to operate their companies in the Ottoman Empire according to their own laws. These missionary industrial operations, ostensibly designed to cultivate Christian-American habits of labor, developed into "big business," and their profits were reinvested in new churches, publications, and hospitals.[67] The rapid increase in such missionary enterprises eventually "provoked an examination of the nature and scope of 'Christian philanthropy,' " but missionary extracurricular activities continued to expand from their initial religious objectives to promoting modern agricultural machinery and household amenities.[68]

By 1900, missionary opinion with respect to the national characteristics of the Armenians in the Ottoman Empire had experienced a major metamorphosis.[69] As news of Turkish massacres of Armenians reached the United States, public opinion leaders and policymakers expressed outrage, particularly since the bloodshed and destruction also damaged American missionary institutions. American missionaries and community leaders began to organize Armenophile organizations and expended enormous energy to mobilize public support for the protection of Armenians and missionaries in Turkey. News of imminent expulsion of missionaries led Lyman Abbott to plead, in his progressive Christian magazine, *Outlook*, for government protection "and, if necessary, to spend its last dollar and call out its last soldier for that purpose."[70] No longer were Armenians looked upon as "nominal Christians." In sharp contrast to the condescending views previously expressed in missionary reports, Americans now exalted the Armenians as Christian martyrs. In an article titled "Armenian Characteristics," Alice Stone Blackwell identified the key characteristics of Armenians as portrayed by foreign officials and travelers. She wrote that Armenians were first among their neighbors in intellectual capacity, moral progress, physical strength, and energy. Their business acumen and enterprising spirit enabled them to hold prominent positions in the commercial affairs of Asia Minor. Similarly, Frances E. Willard, director of the Women's Christian Temperance Union, wrote that "Armenians physically resembled 'our Lord' more than any other race, were brave, chaste, simple in faith like New Testament Christians, earnest, unarmed, pastoral, peaceful."[71]

This change in missionary opinion, however, while heightening American sympathies toward the Armenians, did not translate into humanitarian military intervention for the physical protection of the Armenians during massacres.[72] Instead, it served to enhance the competitive advantages of the missionaries vis-à-vis their European and Russian counterparts, on the one hand, and market opportunities for American businesses, on the other. This transformation also reflected the social and economic changes and challenges American missionaries confronted in the United States. They exploited the Armenian crises to increase their budgets and "their presence and prestige in the United States as well as abroad."[73] As LaFeber has suggested, "churches were challenged by the new Darwinian science, and the church's social status came under siege by the secular demands (and profits) of the industrial transformation. . . . Expansion was as much a requirement for religion as it was for Carnegie's steel mills."[74] Isaac Taylor Headland, a missionary for decades, explained the role and impact of missions as follows:

> Indeed, if I were asked to state what would be the best form of advertising for the great American Steel Trust or Standard Oil or the Baldwin Locomotive Works . . . or the Singer sewing machine, or any one of a dozen other great business concerns, I should say, Take up the support of one or two or a dozen mission stations, an educational institution, a hospital, a dispensary, or a hundred native preachers or teachers. Every one thus helped would be, consciously or unconsciously, a drummer for your goods, and the great Church they represent at home would be your advertising agents.[75]

Accordingly, the missionaries believed that Christian evangelism could, as a civilizing force, contribute to the "increase of imaginary wants" as a prerequisite for the "passion for commerce."

> The spread of European habits of dress was hailed as an index of advancing taste and civilization; note was taken of the fact that in Turkey "those who do not read the Bible live on in their gloomy and comfortless abodes," while "chairs and tables, books and book-cases, Yankee clocks and glass windows, mark the homes of Bible-readers." . . . The first call of a convert from heathenism is for clean clothes and a better house. Clean clothing is suggestive of a long list of textiles, and a better house implies the importation of a vast cargo of industrial products. Races that accept Christianity almost invariably increase their imports.[76]

The interests of the U.S. commercial and missionary communities converged, as free trade and missionary evangelism posed to "unite mankind" in "the most happy state of public society that can be enjoyed on earth."[77] Whether the American missionaries exercised a negative or a positive impact on Armenian culture is a subject for debate, but one fact remains beyond any doubt: a by-product of their activities was the collection of vast amounts of information about the Armenian communities they had come to serve.

Encouraged largely by missionary activities in their home communities, Armenians in increasing numbers sought a safe haven in the New World. Armenian students from missionary institutions attended American universities at Princeton, Yale, and Columbia. The number of Armenian immigrants increased exponentially from the early 1890s as repressive Turkish rule and Kurdish brutalities spread fear across the Armenian Plateau and devastated Armenian social and economic life. The massacres of 1894–96 led to the emigration of approximately 60,000 Armenians across the Russian border and 6,900 to the United States between 1896 and 1898. Similarly, after the massacres of 1909 at Adana and as fear of another round of wholesale massacres in the Armenian provinces spread, about 3,100 Armenians emigrated to the United States in 1909, followed by about 5,500 in 1910 and 9,300 in 1913.[78]

In the meantime, several Armenian political and cultural organizations established branches in the United States to generate political support for their compatriots in the Ottoman Empire. The principal Armenian political organizations in the United States were the Dashnaktsutiun, the Hnchakian, and the Verakazmial Hnchakian (Reformed Social Democrat) parties. Despite the economic and cultural difficulties they encountered in their newly adopted country, and despite their lack of familiarity with its political culture and customs, they developed their communities, extended financial and political support to the fatherland through compatriotic societies, and organized various associations to lobby the government in Washington. They organized mass meetings, circulated petitions and pamphlets, and published newspapers and journals to disseminate information regarding Turkish atrocities against the Armenians. They urged their compatriots back home to remain loyal to the government even if repression and suffering could not be alleviated immediately.[79] Their efforts in the United States, however, registered little success in mobilizing public support for government policies favoring the Armenian cause. In fact, the State and Treasury departments may have been wary of the activities of Armenian organizations, and in 1906 the Secret Service office of the Treasury Department relayed a note to the Turkish minister in Washington reporting in some detail on the meetings of the Armenian organizations in the United States, the financial support transferred to their compatriots, and their activities in the Ottoman Empire.[80] The Armenian community in the United States, too small in numbers and too inexperienced in American politics, could not compete with the incomparably greater powers of missionaries, corporations, and bureaucracies.

U.S. foreign policy toward the Ottoman Empire was yet to experience unprecedented challenges in the coming years as the latter came face to face with the imminent threat of partition and dissolution. Thus far, the United States had successfully promoted and protected its commercial, geopolitical, and missionary interests across the Ottoman Empire. Neither the recurring tensions in U.S.-Ottoman relations nor persecutions of Christians had caused serious harm to their bilateral ties. Although in comparison to its British counterpart the U.S. Navy had achieved no more than a secondary status in the Mediterranean as of yet, it had nevertheless secured a comfortable position with growing interest in regional geopolitical and economic matters. Despite the growing Armenian community in the United States and the influence it sought to exert on domestic public opinion, the influence of domestic interests on the foreign policies of successive administrations at the turn of the century superseded calls for humanitarian engagement in the Ottoman Empire. The Armenian Question and the massacres proved inconsequential to those determined to maintain good relations with the Ottoman government.

It was in this context of naval, economic, and missionary expansion that the U.S. government elevated the office of minister at Constantinople to ambassadorship in 1906. In formally notifying

Ottoman Minister of Foreign Affairs Tevfik Pasha of this decision by the U.S. Congress, the American Chargé d' Affaires Peter Augustus Jay conveyed the administration's warm regards to the Ottoman government: "I am specially charged to state that the President is glad of this opportunity to testify fittingly the very high feeling of regard with which the United States is animated towards the Ottoman Empire, and thereby also to strengthen the ties of friendship that have always existed between the two nations."[81]

CHAPTER 2

UNITED STATES RELATIONS WITH
THE YOUNG TURK GOVERNMENT

Turks and Armenians alike as well as policymakers in Washington welcomed the Young Turk revolution that overthrew Sultan Abdul Hamid II in July 1908. The revolution, which led to the reinstitution of the 1876 Constitution, promised a political system premised upon principles of constitutional government, equality among Muslim and non-Muslim citizens, greater political stability, and economic liberalization. Armenians hoped that the revolution would finally provide the long-awaited opportunity to improve conditions under a new regime by introducing the desperately needed reforms but never implemented under the sultan.[1] Foreign and domestic problems, however, dashed all hopes for such reforms.

MASSACRES AGAIN

Crises in the Balkans, as in October 1908 when Austria-Hungary unilaterally declared annexation of Bosnia and Herzegovina, challenged the legitimacy of the new government,[2] which in turn responded with ideological extremism toward and severe repressive measure against real and imagined internal and external threats. The fact that along with democratic reforms the new leadership stressed Turkism as a national ideal and the Turkish language as the only official language was a significant departure from the well-rehearsed gestures for reforms previously witnessed during the reign of Sultan Abdul Hamid.[3] Nevertheless, Armenians and foreign observers expected conditions to improve. In March 1909, the British Ambassador to Washington, James Bryce, wrote that "the good relations between . . . the Armenians and the Young Turks are the best feature of the situation."[4] In April, however, as reactionary, counterrevolutionary forces attempted to recapture Constantinople, massacres broke out in the Cilician town of Adana and the neighboring villages, leading to the death of approximately 20,000 Armenians.[5] The Young Turk government regained control, and the restoration of stability was viewed favorably in the United States.[6]

Nearing the closing days of its tenure, the Roosevelt administration sought to cultivate closer relations with Ottoman officials and Turkish nationalists for greater access for American businesses to Turkey's resources and markets.

Similarly, the Taft administration, emphasizing Dollar Diplomacy[7] and protection of American commercial interests in the Ottoman Empire, accorded greater significance to issues of commerce (tariff, nondiscriminatory practices toward U.S. companies, extraterritorial jurisdiction) than to humanitarian concerns.[8]

All was not well in Washington regarding the political situation in Turkey, however. Responding to the Adana massacres, on April 21, along with the British, the French, and the Italians, to provide medical relief to the needy, Secretary of State Philander C. Knox informed Ambassador Leishman that the *USS Montana* and *USS North Carolina* were dispatched immediately to Gibraltar, there to wait for further orders.[9] Leishman requested that the two U.S. cruisers be stationed at Mersin and Alexandretta with permission for the embassy to dispatch them as necessary.[10] On April 29, Representative Irving P. Wanger of Pennsylvania introduced a joint resolution in the House of Representatives applauding the return to constitutional government in Turkey and congratulating the ascension of Sultan Mehmed V to the Ottoman throne. The resolution expressed hope that under his leadership the new government would eliminate "the appalling atrocities upon Christian missionaries and other non-Muslims which thrill with horror the civilized world."[11] "Young Turkey's revolutionary honeymoon is over," commented the popular journal *North American Review* in July 1909.[12] Unlike the public outcry during the massacres of the mid-1890s, however, the Adana massacres did not produce a strong reaction. In fact, in 1909, the year of the Adana massacres, the United States exported $84,574 worth of firearms and $38,466 worth of cartridges to Turkey; the following year, the figure for U.S. exports in cartridges to that country rose to $105,950.[13]

Turkification and Pan-Turkism

Despite the massacres at Adana and the ensuing repressive situation, the leading Armenian party in the Ottoman Empire, the Dashnaktsutiun, chose to maintain its political alliance with the Young Turks, and on August 24, 1909, both parties agreed to cooperate in efforts to strengthen the constitution and political institutions for the future of the empire.[14] Political crises in Constantinople and in the European parts of the empire, however, bode ill for the future of that cooperative spirit. Public celebrations ushering in the new era had masked the intentions of the extremist factions among the Young Turk leaders, who, after a brief period of toleration toward democratic practices, exhibited proclivities at variance with such principles. The Ittihad ve Terakki (Committee of Union and Progress, CUP), eventually monopolized and led by Mehmed Talaat, Ismail Enver, and Ahmed Jemal, increasingly relied on the nationalist propaganda of Turkification and pan-Turkism despite efforts by leading Armenian organizations to find a common ground for cooperation.

The issue of eliminating the Armenians throughout the Ottoman Empire was apparently discussed during two conferences at Salonika in August and October 1910, although it is not clear whether they did at this time explicitly adopt a policy to that effect. Talaat insisted on devising concrete steps, including the use of force, toward creating a homogeneous Turkish Empire.[15] British Vice Consul Arthur B. Geary reported that during a session, Talaat Bey demanded that the party leadership force "ottomanization" of the empire:

> It is essential that the Committee display to the world a solid and resolute front, for this alone can preserve our prestige in Europe and the maintenance of our power in our own country. . . .
>
> You are aware that by the terms of the Constitution equality of Mussulman and Ghiaur was affirmed but you one and all know and feel that this is an unrealizable ideal. The Sheriat, our whole past history and the sentiments of hundreds of thousands of Mussulmans and even the sentiments of the Ghiaurs themselves, who stubbornly resist every attempt to ottomanize them, present an impenetrable barrier to the establishment of real equality. We have made unsuccessful attempts to convert the Ghiaur into a loyal Osmanli and all such efforts must inevitably fail, as long as the small independent States in the Balkan Peninsula remain in a position to propagate ideas of Separatism among the inhabitants of Macedonia. There can therefore be no question of equality, until we have succeeded in our task of ottomanizing the Empire. . . . [16]

The ideological formulation justifying greater consolidation of power and etatization of culture had been propagated by such ideologues as Ziya Gokalp (alias for Mehmed Ziya), a member of the CUP Central Committee; pan-Turkist author Tekin Alp (alias for Moise Cohen); and Yusuf Akchura, founder of the *Turk Yurdu* (Turkish

Homeland) journal.[17] The nationalist Young Turk leadership was determined to pursue the strategy of "Turkey for the Turks," and as part of its widening plan, the Turkish government encouraged refugees and immigrants to begin settlement in Armenian towns.[18]

The Taft administration preferred to ignore such issues deemed matters of Ottoman internal affairs. Secretary of State Knox urged Ambassador William W. Rockhill, appointed to Turkey on June 1, 1911, to promote the "real and commercial rather than academic interests of the United States in the Near East."[19] And that year, with the support of the Department of State, the American Chamber of Commerce for Turkey established a new headquarters at Constantinople, with branch offices in major Ottoman cities and with its own publication, *Levant Trade Review*.[20] The journal aimed at promoting U.S.-Turkish commercial relations and accordingly presented the Young Turk regime as a democratically oriented government whose object it was to bring progress and economic development. The first issue, published in 1911, featured a report by George Ghevond, the journal's correspondent at Kharpert, informing the reader that the region was "developing very slowly" as transportation methods were extremely primitive. Construction of a railroad and efficient use of waterpower from the Euphrates River would stimulate economic development. The article estimated that Kharpert received approximately $600,000 from Armenians who had emigrated to the United States. The report encouraged American companies to cultivate their relations with the local merchants and to send them catalogues and samples promoting their products.[21]

Another lengthy report observed that Asia Minor presented enormous opportunities for trade, "a fact which is appreciated by the leading commercial nations of Europe, whose Governments are manifesting keen interest in the administration of affairs, and whose manufacturers and merchants have injected themselves into all the commercial and industrial activities" seeking "preponderance and control." It added:

> Under the new régime in Turkey a constitutional government has been formed, abuses and corruptions have been abolished, and steps have been taken to place Turkey in the march of progress as speedily as is consistent with a sound public policy and with due regard to the conservation of the public tranquility. . . .
> The awakening has begun that will bring many and valuable opportunities to the Occidents for the extension of old and the introduction

of new trade, and if the United States is to share in the distribution its manufacturers and merchants must bestir themselves.[22]

Yet, in December of that year, Rockhill reported from Constantinople that conditions across the empire were rapidly deteriorating and that the Turkish government had failed to stabilize the situation. In the Armenian provinces "murders of Armenians by Kurds and often of Kurds by Kurds are of daily occurrence, acts of brigandage have increased, while the authorities are showing the supineness as elsewhere." The Armenian deputies to the Ottoman Parliament had brought the gravity of the situation to the attention of the authorities, but such appeals had failed to affect policy. The ambassador warned that "nothing short of a catastrophe must soon overtake the present régime in Turkey."[23]

Meanwhile, a succession of military disasters threatened dissolution of the empire. In September 1911, Italy went to war against Turkey over Tripolitania (Libya), which Italy gained under the peace treaty signed in October 1912. The Italian–Turkish conflict was followed by the Balkan wars of 1912–1913, as a result of which Turkey lost its European territories except Adrianople, Scutari, and Janina.[24] With the outbreak of the Balkan war in October 1912, the chargé d'affaires at the Greek embassy in Washington, L.L. Caftanzoglu, informed the Taft administration that the failure of the Ottoman government to effectuate the reforms as promised in the Treaty of Berlin had compelled the Balkan states to resort to force. He appealed to the U.S. secretary of state "not to refuse it its benevolent neutrality in the arduous task it has just assumed."[25] As the Bulgarian army approached Constantinople, the Taft administration, at the request of Ambassador Rockhill and the diplomatic corps, after some hesitation ordered the *USS Scorpion* to Turkish waters to protect American lives and property, with the promise to send additional war vessels if necessary.[26] Secretary Knox informed Rockhill that the Navy had ordered two armored cruisers, the *USS Tennessee* and *USS Montana*, to Smyrna and Beirut, where they would await further instructions from the U.S. embassy.[27] In the meantime, the Turkish government appealed to the major powers for mediation or intervention.[28] The foreign ministry assured the U.S. embassy that the authorities could provide adequate protection for the American schools at Scutari and Robert College.[29] The *Scorpion* reached Constantinople on the morning of November 18, but with the conclusion of the armistice ending the hostilities, the vessel left the Ottoman capital on December 3 without any incident.[30]

DOLLAR DIPLOMACY

The Taft administration, true to its Dollar Diplomacy objectives, optimistically claimed in December 1909: "There is every reason why we should obtain a greater share of the commerce of the Near East since the conditions are more favorable now than ever before."[31] Accordingly, and much to the chagrin of European powers, immediately after the Young Turk revolution, the administration supported a group of American oil and railroad businesses, headed by Admiral Colby M. Chester, to acquire a concession from the Turkish government. In 1899, the McKinley administration had sent Admiral Chester aboard the battleship *Kentucky* to effectuate compensation for the properties of American missionaries damaged during the massacres against the Armenians in the mid-1890s. Chester later visited Turkey again, now as representative of U.S. financiers to contract concessions.[32] The Sublime Porte initially offered railroad and mining concessions across Asia Minor and historic Armenia to Mesopotamia, and the Department of State attempted to secure guarantees for railroad lines and concessions for Chester in the Arghana copper mines as well as gold and silver mines and oilfields.[33] Although Taft's first ambassador to Turkey, Oscar S. Straus, initially opposed the administration's Dollar Diplomacy, the Department of State nevertheless insisted that the ambassador press for U.S. commercial advantages, while all other pending issues, including reparations for damages incurred by the American missionaries during the reactionary uprisings in 1909, were relegated to secondary concern.[34]

U.S.-Ottoman bilateral trade experienced a rapid growth after the Young Turk revolution. As was shown in table 1.1, the total value of U.S.-Ottoman trade doubled from $12.7 million in 1908 to $25.5 million in 1913. The Young Turk government in turn saw a potential powerful ally in the United States to exercise greater diplomatic leverage against the European powers.[35]

The grand scheme for the Chester project failed, but it was seen as a major step by the United States toward a more "imperialistic course in Turkey," involving the government and such major companies as the J.G. White and Company, MacArthur Brothers, Laidlaw and Company, E.C. Converse and Company, and Charles A. Moore. The project was expected to open enormous investment opportunities for U.S. businesses, while challenging European commercial preponderance in the region. President Taft appointed F.M. Huntington Wilson as Ambassador Extraordinary on Special Mission to Turkey to show support for the expansion of U.S.-Turkish trade in general and for the

Chester concession in particular.[36] The Young Turk government, however, with whom Chester had solicited an agreement, became mired in domestic and foreign policy difficulties and did not ratify the new contract.[37]

While the Washington–Constantinople negotiations proceeded, Europeans viewed the project as a challenge to their interests. This was particularly true of Germany, whose eastward drive under the doctrine of *Drang nach Osten* rested on the Berlin–Baghdad railway for supremacy across the Middle East. Ottoman authorities eventually succumbed to European pressure and tabled the Chester project in 1910. The U.S. government and Chester made yet another attempt to revive the project, but withdrew in 1911. The Taft administration, perhaps embarrassed by this diplomatic defeat, reverted to the traditional policy of "noninvolvement in the Eastern Question."[38]

German financial and oil interests had gained greater access to the Ottoman economy and markets, undermining British capital and potential U.S. trade relations as well. Negotiations between the Armenian oil tycoon Calouste Gulbenkian and the Turkish authorities had led to the establishment of an office for Royal Dutch-Shell in Constantinople, and the Anglo-Persian Oil Company was founded in 1909.[39] Subsequently, Sir Ernest Cassel, advocating cooperation between Great Britain and Germany, had encouraged the formation of the Turkish Petroleum Company, comprised of the Deutsche Bank, the Shell Group, and the National Bank of Turkey.[40]

Such international commercial alliances did not bode well for American oil interests. U.S. exports in crude oil to Europe had dropped from 89 percent of total crude oil exports in 1900 to 14 percent in 1910, a situation exacerbated by the U.S. Supreme Court's anti-trust ruling in 1911 that forced the restructuring of Standard Oil. In 1911, the United States produced nearly 64 percent (30 metric tons) of the world's crude oil, while the figure for Russia was little over 19 percent (9.07 metric tons).[41] By 1914, the European oil combines were beginning to challenge Standard Oil in world markets,[42] and the U.S. oil industry responded by expanding research and marketing operations from northern Europe to the eastern Mediterranean. Williamson and Daum note that Standard Oil placed informants in U.S. consular offices and soon "Reports began to flow into 26 Broadway from all over the world, including those American consuls located at strategic points, some of whom were put on the Standard payroll. Company representatives were sent abroad to get firsthand information and to strengthen connections with foreign marketers."[43] John Worthington, for example, traveled from Russia to the Lake Van region in the Ottoman Empire in 1910 to study potential oilfields.[44]

Despite such efforts, however, Standard Oil began to lose market shares in the Ottoman Empire to European and Russian competitors, and European competitors such as Royal Dutch, Shell, the Nobels, the Rothschilds, and the German Deutsche Bank threatened the Standard Oil's attempts to establish oil production and distribution networks in the region.[45] The Deutsche Bank continued to pursue the Baghdad railway project into Mesopotamia, a concession incorporating oil rights along the tracks for more than 12 miles.[46]

In the interim, governments debated conversion of their navies from coal to oil. In the United States, the oil industry lobbied extensively for a larger share of the budget for the Navy's conversion.[47] In 1904, the U.S. Navy Fuel Oil Board had recommended conversion to oil, and by 1911 the superiority and efficiency of oil for naval operations had proved sufficiently convincing that the U.S. Navy became one of the most important consumers of oil.[48] In 1911, the Navy "purchased fifteen million barrels of oil for nineteen oil-burning torpedo-boat destroyers and for eight battleships using petroleum as an auxiliary fuel."[49] The political struggle over oil both at home and in international relations commenced in full force in 1911–12 as Western governments converted their navies to oil. Control over oil resources around the world became an essential component in the foreign policies of the major powers.[50] Soon thereafter, as the pro-Navy advocates gained political support, and concerned with the threat of depletion of oil resources at home, the U.S. government relaxed its anti-trust regulations and developed cooperative policies toward the oil industry for purposes of securing resources for the Navy. In 1914, Secretary of the Navy Josephus Daniels announced that the Navy had made the transition from coal to oil.[51] Americans could soon boast that U.S. "vessels were operating from the Murman Coast to the Adriatic, through all the Atlantic from the North Sea to the Azores, in the Pacific from Panama to Vladivostock."[52]

By the time the Wilson administration entered office in 1913, there had developed a mutually complementary triangular network of U.S. interests, consisting of Protestant missionaries, the Navy, and businesses in the Ottoman Empire. The missionaries continued to expand their evangelical operations in the eastern Mediterranean basin. Businesses sought opportunities to expand their operations for greater profit but also to counteract economic cycles of prosperity and depression at home. The Navy sought domestic and foreign political alliances for its own programs of modernization and expansion, and supported both the missionaries and businesses abroad. Further, the expected growth of these interests in the Ottoman Empire converged with the objectives of the Sublime Porte, which had been pursuing avenues to modernize its economy since the early nineteenth century.

The Ottoman economy and the polity in general, however, had decayed beyond repair as a result of mismanagement and misrule, and by 1913 the extremist nationalist leaders were posed to seize power and impose dictatorial rule and Turkification on the subject peoples in a desperate effort to revive the empire. On January 23, 1913, an Ittihadist clique led by Enver attacked the Sublime Porte in a coup against the government of the Hürriyet ve Itilaf (Freedom and Association, or Liberal Union)[53] and established a military dictatorship that ruled until the end of World War I. The reign of terror led to the murder of a number of leading government officials, including Minister of War Nazim Pasha during the coup, and subsequently Grand Vizier Kiamil Pasha as well as several members of his cabinet.[54] Once firmly in power, the triumvirate of Talaat, Enver, and Jemal, redoubled efforts to liquidate internal opposition and to check foreign interference in Ottoman affairs. They deeply resented Western geopolitical and financial designs with respect to the future of their country and influences on domestic public opinion, such as the European debates concerning the partition of the empire and humanitarian declarations regarding the Christians, which, the Ittihadists believed, encroached upon Turkish national sovereignty and priorities. Yet, wishing to recapture the bygone glorious years of Ottoman imperialism, they welcomed foreign investments and technical (including military) support in hopes of restrengthening the economic and political position of the empire at home and on the world stage. They hoped relations with the United States would improve the economy and expected U.S. Navy ships to visit its ports as a symbolic gesture of American good will and friendship toward the new government struggling to manage its affairs.[55]

Upon seizing power, the Ittihadists pursued two general policies to restrengthen the Turkish Empire: militarism and Pan-Turkism. They commenced the reorganization of the army with German advice. Former officials of the sultan were removed from office and in their stead "new proteges of the CUP, often men of worst type, took their places."[56] Despite some improvements in the military in the early stages of the reorganization program, the Turkish army continued to suffer from lack of ordinary appurtenances (e.g., decent transport and supplies) usually found in modern military. The long chain of Ottoman military disasters and particularly the Balkan wars had amplified the military weaknesses of the empire. Militarism required greater cooperation with Germany, and in 1913, the German military mission headed by General Otto Liman von Sanders and successive German engineering and financial envoys sought to rectify this situation. In addition, the Young Turk regime relied on the ideology of Pan-Turkism and instruments of propaganda to strengthen its own political legitimacy. The Turkish government began to pay greater attention to its Asiatic frontiers and emphasized Pan-Turkism to counter Russian-led Pan-Slavist objectives. Young Turk ideologues employed their propaganda campaign toward the Caucasus in order to mobilize Turkic sentiments of Muslim peoples from Turkey to Central Asia.[57]

Thus, by 1913, when the Wilson administration entered the White House, the Young Turk dictatorial regime and its ideological foundations of Pan-Turkism had been firmly established in Constantinople.[58] How would the United States respond to such changes and challenges in the Ottoman Empire? What priorities would determine the policies of the new administration? European interests in the Middle East involved geopolitical and economic considerations, and by the late nineteenth and early twentieth century the United States, as an emerging competitor in global politics, paid greater attention to the events transpiring in the region. British and French aggressive policies aimed to check German and Russian expansionism to the eastern shores of the Mediterranean Sea, the Suez Canal, and thence to the Indian Ocean, while seeking to control the Mesopotamian oilfields. As European commercial and naval predominance in the region had demonstrated for more than a century, so did the United States now increasingly appreciate the potential advantages to be gained through sea power, commerce, and evangelism.[59] The Armenian Question was of little importance to decision makers in Western capitals, as geopolitical and economic priorities weighed too heavily on their imperial agenda to effectuate obligations charged to their humanitarian pretensions. With respect to U.S. foreign policy toward the Ottoman Empire, economic and missionary interests entrenched in U.S.-Ottoman bilateral relations for decades provided the informal venues directing formal policies. Meanwhile, Armenians in the United States and in the Ottoman Empire, hoping to ameliorate conditions in their homeland, could seek to attract the attention of public opinion leaders, they could present their case to the principal policymakers, but they could not compete with the enormous influence naval, commercial, and missionary interests exercised in Washington and Constantinople.

CHAPTER 3

THE WILSON ADMINISTRATION
AND THE ITTIHADIST REGIME

The Wilson administration approached foreign policy through a bifurcated prism of principles and priorities that reflected the stress President Woodrow Wilson placed on morality, on the one hand, and the domestic and international considerations in matters of national political economy, on the other. Wilson the person opposed imperialism and the system of balance of power as practiced in the Old World, both of which he believed contributed to international conflicts and war; instead, he advocated free trade, self-determination, reduction of armaments, collective security, and international arbitration as necessary ingredients for peaceful relations among nations.[1] The Wilson administration, however, in general pursued policies at variance with such principles. Contrary to the principles of free trade, for example, the administration accepted the responsibilities of the "promotional state,"[2] committed to the growth of U.S. economic activities abroad. Wilsonianism soon became equated to "global corporatism."[3]

THE WILSONIAN "PROMOTIONAL STATE"

Wilson's convictions regarding government support for expansion of U.S. trade were evident prior to his assumption of the presidency. As a scholar, in an essay titled "Education and Democracy," he had categorically supported that role:

> Since trade ignores national boundaries and the manufacturer insists on having the world as a market, the flag of his nation must follow him, and the doors of the nations which are closed against him must be battered

down. Concessions obtained by financiers must be safeguarded by ministers of state, even if the sovereignty of unwilling nations be outraged in the process. Colonies must be obtained or planted, in order that no useful corner of the world may be overlooked or left unused. [4]

Wilson also advocated supremacy of the executive in matters of foreign policy,[5] and, although during his first presidential campaign he had criticized the enormous influence lobbyists exerted on policy,[6] as president he extended government support to commercial and missionary interests abroad so long as their activities concurred with his policies.[7] The administration thus operated within a power configuration comprised of symbiotic networks of private interests and official policymakers, reflecting the inextricably intertwined domestic and foreign policy priorities of the administration. In an address before the U.S. Chamber of Commerce, Wilson summarized his views on the government's promotional role:

> The Government of the United States is very properly a great instrumentality of inquiry and information. One thing we are just beginning to do that we ought to have done long ago: we ought long ago to have had our Bureau of Foreign and Domestic Commerce. We ought long ago to have sent the best eyes of the government out into the world to see where the opportunities and openings of American commerce and American genius were to be found. . . . We are just beginning to do, systematically and scientifically, what we ought long ago to have done—to employ the Government of the United States to survey the world in order that American commerce might be guided.[8]

Members of the administration agreed. Secretary of State William Jennings Bryan noted: "It is our intention to employ every agency of the Department of State to extend and safeguard American commerce and legitimate American enterprises in foreign lands."[9] Accordingly, the administration encouraged its cabinet bureaucracies, especially the Department of State and the Department of Commerce, to expand their operations in support of U.S. business interests worldwide, as it strengthened government-business ties effectively to compete with Europeans.[10]

Speaking before an audience of the Real Estate Exchange in Boston during the presidential campaign of 1912, Wilson underscored the necessity of expanding American businesses in international markets to maintain a healthy national economy. "The great trading nations of the world," he stated, "are not those who understand only domestic needs and tastes. They are those who understand the foreign needs and tastes." Wilson argued that, for example, the lack of a sufficient domestic market base for the cotton produced in the United States had deleterious consequences for that sector. Wilson asked the audience:

> what are we going to do with our surplus goods? . . . Stand pat when the world is changing? . . . We are facing a new age, with new objects, new objects of American trade and manufacture. . . . We are facing new objects with new standards, the standards of cosmopolitan intelligence instead of provincial intelligence, and with a new conception of what it means to produce wealth and produce prosperity.[11]

Wilsonian politics contained elements of both idealism and realism.[12] Upon entering the White House Wilson viewed political support for missionary interests at home and abroad as a vehicle to realize his ideals and political objectives. While characterized as a utopian visionary by historians, Wilson "was also a calculating politician,"[13] whose opinions and actions revealed both optimism and pessimism in matters of foreign policy. Progressive and missionary internationalism, coupled with global corporatist arrangements, necessitated a strong executive to expand the national interest into the international realm. While he had earlier criticized European imperialism, Roosevelt's "Big Stick," and Taft's Dollar Diplomacy,[14] as president he sought to expand the American way of life and the progressivism of the Social Gospel as guarantors against the political traditions of the Old World and its tattered systems of balance of power. The United States would protect and promote American religion and patriotism and in doing so fulfill God's will on Earth.[15] Wilsonian foreign policy therefore rested, according to circumstances, on the twin pillars of moralistic, idealistic rhetoric, on the one hand, and political realism, on the other.[16] In matters of policy, the administration pursued international expansionism to rectify domestic financial and trade problems associated with the recession of 1913 and 1914.[17] The Open Door policy as applied to the Far East by previous administrations extended to the Middle East as well, as the Wilson administration and U.S. commercial interests sought to gain the benefits of trade but without the attendant entanglements in the local affairs of trading partners.[18]

A.H. Baldwin, Chief of the Bureau of Foreign and Domestic Commerce in the U.S. Department of Commerce, expressed the Bureau's satisfaction regarding the commercial advantages gained in foreign markets. Its annual report stated:

> The foreign commerce of the United States in 1913 exceeded in value that of any preceding year. This is true of both imports and exports. The

imports aggregated $1,813,008,234, against $1,653,264,934 in 1912, the former high-record year in imports; the exports of domestic products aggregated $2,428,506,358, against $2,170,319,828 in 1912, the former high-record year in exports. . . . Exports for the first time averaged 200 million dollars per month, against an average of 100 millions per month in 1898; imports showed an average of 150 million dollars per month, against 50 million per month in 1898, exports having thus doubled and imports trebled during the period in question.[19]

As shown in table 1.1, the total value of U.S.-Turkish trade in 1913, when the Wilson administration entered the White House, was $25.5 million. Imports from Turkey totaled $22.2 million, including emery, licorice root, opium, dates, figs, raisins, shelled filberts, olive oil for manufacturing, and tobacco leaf.[20] Turkey was the primary source of emery, constituting 96.9 percent of the total 18,964 tons of imported emery; 83 percent of imported figs; 82.7 percent of opium; 80.1 percent of dates; 72.3 percent of filberts; and 50 percent of imported tobacco leaf.[21] U.S. exports of domestic products to Turkey in 1913, mostly in manufactured goods, totaled $3.3 million, including various cloths, glucose, boots and shoes, builder's hardware, firearms, metal-working machinery and tools, mining machinery, pumps and pumping machinery, sewing machines, pipes and fittings, stoves, barbed wire, leather, illuminating oil, lubricating and paraffin oil, cottonseed, rum, and starch.[22]

THE U.S. NAVY AND OIL

During the Wilson administration, as under the previous administrations, the Navy continued to be seen as the "agent of enlightenment."[23] Domestic support for naval power stressed the point that while the public did not desire rampant militarism for fear of undermining American democratic institutions, naval power would prove potentially less maligning.[24] Rear Admiral Bradley A. Fiske, echoing the doctrine of sea power advocated by Admiral Mahan and Theodore Roosevelt, maintained that a successful foreign policy necessitated naval strength and adequate preparation for war, as "the general welfare" of the nation required sufficient naval capability not only for military purposes but also to protect vessels transporting commerce across the free seas.[25] In a similar vein, Secretary of the Navy Josephus Daniels emphasized the significance of the Navy for the defense of the United States: "The American Navy is our first line of protection. It is the right arm of defense, the protector of the American home. . . . In this matter of preparedness in America, we shall, now that we are awake, go forward steadily, rapidly and earnestly, to repair the lack of building for the past dozen years, and we shall build a navy here of such size and strength as the American people need."[26]

On March 8, 1913, three days after the Senate confirmation of Daniels as Secretary of the Navy, the role of American naval power in Turkish waters was placed on his desk. Rear Admiral Austin M. Knight, who had led two ships to Turkey during the Balkan wars, informed Daniels that both vessels were no longer required in Turkey and requested that one be recalled. Upon conferring with Wilson, however, it was agreed that they remain in or near Turkey: one at Smyrna, while the other cruised off the coast of Asia Minor. "The Balkan war is not settled," Daniels entered in his diary, "how long will it be before Turkey is dismembered?"[27]

Sea power also necessitated the conversion of U.S. naval vessels from coal to oil. After a series of experiments with oil-burning engines during the late nineteenth and early twentieth centuries, relations of the Navy Fuel Board expanded with the oil and steamship industries, including, for example, the Oil City Boiler Works and Standard Oil. Their cooperation benefited both the Navy and the industries with respect to technological developments in oil engines and oil refinement. The United States possessed enormous petroleum deposits at home and its oil industry surpassed that of the Europeans in production, refining, and marketing. Although officials in the Wilson administration initially expressed concern regarding the long-term sufficiency of domestic oil supplies, the U.S. Navy, spearheaded by Secretary Daniels, decided, in 1913, that "its future battle fleet would burn oil."[28]

WILSONIAN POLICYMAKERS

As the Wilson administration assumed the responsibilities of the promotional state, domestic considerations of political economy heightened the incommensurability between idealism and globalism, to the detriment of the former. William A. Williams has put it most aptly:

By the time of World War I, therefore, the basic dilemma of American foreign policy was clearly defined. Its generous humanitarianism prompted it to improve the lot of less fortunate peoples, but that side of its diplomacy was undercut by two other aspects of its policy. On the one hand, it defined helping people in terms of making them more like Americans. This subverted its ideal of self-determination. On the other hand, it asserted and acted upon the necessity of overseas economic expansion in terms of markets for American exports, and control of raw materials for American industry, the ability of other peoples to develop and act upon their own patterns of development was further undercut.[29]

No sooner had the Wilson administration entered the White House than it became preoccupied with efforts to maximize the president's chances for reelection in 1916. The cabinet appointments, decided largely by Wilson and Colonel Edward M. House, the president's close adviser and "alter ego," aimed at satisfying the Democratic Party's constituency with little regard to foreign policy expertise, and the effective management of domestic public opinion became an integral component of the administration's foreign policy.[30] Although as scholar Wilson had unequivocally argued that the rise of the United States to the status of a world power required the appointment of "the best statesman we can produce . . . to fill the office of Secretary of State," he appointed William J. Bryan, toward whom he showed little respect, to that post largely because of his leading position within the Democratic Party but also because Wilson needed and relied on Bryan's cooperation in mustering congressional support for his policies. Moreover, Bryan's appointment as secretary of state bolstered the image Wilson hoped to cultivate of himself as a champion of international peace and democracy.[31]

As secretary of state, Bryan headed a department consisting of more than 440 diplomatic personnel, most of whom were ardent Democrats but, like the members of Wilson's cabinet, were inexperienced in international affairs and as a result invited severe public criticism. A progressive in ideological orientation, Bryan had established a reputation as a pacifist and was frequently criticized by realists for his idealism. He had little preparation in foreign affairs, however, and had to rely heavily on the department's legal counselor Robert Lansing and William Phillips, the head of the European desk, on matters of international law and diplomacy. Concerned primarily with domestic issues and party politics, Bryan soon realized he could exert little influence on the administration's foreign policy as the president assumed a central role in that area.[32]

Despite their differences, Wilson and Bryan agreed on the fundamental issue of economic expansion abroad as a means to address domestic economic problems. At a national convention of the National Council of Foreign Trade, Bryan asserted that the administration sought to "open the door of all the weaker countries to the invasion of American capital and enterprise." His views were shared by Secretary of Commerce William Redfield, who averred that "because we are strong, we are going out, you and I, into the markets of the world to get our share."[33] Robert Lansing, an international lawyer by training, came to the State Department as Bryan's counselor and succeeded Bryan as secretary of state after the latter's resignation in June 1915. Bryan was the consummate politician and moralist;[34] Lansing, the consummate legalist and realist. The son-in-law of former secretary of state John W. Foster, he had practiced law at Foster's law firm and had served as counsel in several international arbitration cases. His experience gained him the respect of Wilson and Bryan, and although he remained loyal to both, he did not share the moralistic views espoused by them.[35]

Secretary of the Navy Josephus Daniels, an active member of the Democratic Party, was initially slated for the position of Postmaster General because, House believed, he did "not size big enough for anything we could think of."[36] A leader of the progressive movement in North Carolina, Daniels was the editor of the *News and Observer* in Raleigh.[37] Although, as he himself admitted, he "didn't know a thing about the Navy" prior to assuming the post as secretary of the Navy,[38] he proved an effective executive in the Navy Department and was instrumental in its modernization.[39] Finally, to give another example, Secretary of Commerce William C. Redfield, wealthy businessman with close ties with the manufacturing sector, had served as president of the American Manufacturers Export Association and briefly in the House of Representatives as congressman from Brooklyn (1910–12). Redfield advocated close government-business ties and strong government support for business expansion in international markets.[40]

Cabinet members in the Wilson administration were not prepared for the task of leading the nation in matters of international political economy. Instead, their personal loyalties to the president and collective ideological predilections favoring economic expansion guided their decisions. As expected of elected politicians and political appointees, Wilson and his cabinet showed extreme concern with respect to domestic public opinion. For example, upon assuming his post Daniels entered the following comments regarding the Navy in his diary: "Conferred with Naval Board about the necessity of publicity—about the ways to secure accurate news to the people about the doings of the Navy."[41]

AMBASSADOR MORGENTHAU

Most members of Wilson's cabinet had little or no role in determining policy toward the Armenian Question. The implementation of that policy remained confined to Secretary Bryan and his staff and the U.S. ambassador to the Sublime Porte, Henry Morgenthau. The new ambassador, however, was hardly prepared for his post at Constantinople at the time of his appointment on September 4, 1913. Morgenthau had achieved financial success early in life and contributed generously to various organizations in New York, including the construction of the new building by the *New York Times*. Primarily involved in New York and Democratic campaign politics, he had no experience in foreign relations,[42] but his dedication to the Democratic Party and to Wilson's election earned him the confidence of the new president.[43]

On December 18, 1912, when Colonel House first suggested Morgenthau for appointment to Turkey, Wilson replied that "there aint going to be no Turkey"; "then let him go look for it," House responded.[44] Morgenthau initially declined the appointment. In a letter dated June 12, 1913, he wrote to Wilson that no post should be designated as a Jewish post and that appointments of Jews to ambassadorial posts should not be limited to the Turkish mission.[45] Morgenthau finally accepted the appointment largely at the urging of Rabbi Stephen S. Wise.[46] William G. McAdoo, Wilson's Secretary of the Treasury, wrote to Morgenthau that "Notwithstanding Turkey's reverses in the Balkan War, her importance in the East will continue to be great, and we need there, at this time particularly, a man of your force, intelligence and tact."[47] Similarly, Secretary Daniels prophetically wrote: "During the next few years you will be in the midst of one of the most historic theaters of action of our age."[48]

In September 1913, Morgenthau met with Bryan at the State Department to receive official instructions. Although he respected Bryan, this first formal meeting proved an illuminating experience: "I looked forward to this visit with great expectations. Alas for the illusions which a day can wreck! William Jennings Bryan was the Secretary of State. He knew no more about our relations with Turkey than I did."[49]

Prior to his departure, Morgenthau had an informative conference with several members of the American Board of Commissioners for Foreign Missions in New York, and in a follow-up letter Robert E. Speer of the Board communicated its concerns regarding protection of Christians in the Ottoman Empire, particularly in the eastern provinces. The letter noted that for centuries the Christians had lived in this region and struggled "with the burden of Kurdish oppression. . . . Our interest in the matter is close and intimate because our missionaries go to and fro through these mountains, endeavoring to keep the people at peace, opening schools and seeking to bring some enlightenment to races which are far aloof from the progress of the world."[50] The text of this letter also contained a lengthy quotation from a report submitted on May 9, 1913, by the Reverend E.W. McDowell about the increasingly dangerous situation the Christians found themselves across the eastern provinces and in the region of Urmia in northwestern Persia. McDowell wrote:

> [W]e have received word that the Kurds of Bohtan had taken Jezireh as a part of a plan to set up an independent government. The missionaries in Mosul had already written us that the Kurds were making an attempt to gain possession of Mardin, Midyat and Jezireh with a view to establish an independent Kurdish kingdom. It is a crazy idea. The government will send troops to break up this movement and in the resulting confusion the Christians will undoubtedly suffer. . . . God grant that something may be done to prevent a repetition of the massacres which so often have shocked the world. . . . If, however, precautions are not taken and the various factions are allowed to fight for the rule of what is left of Turkey, then Mexico will seem to have been a country school yard in comparison with what this country will be. I shrink from picturing to myself what will happen to the Christians of the land. May God avert such calamities.[51]

On the morning of November 1, Morgenthau, accompanied by James Barton and others, left New York on the *USS George Washington* for London and arrived at Constantinople on November 27. There he was greeted by more than twenty people, including the U.S. embassy's Chargé d'Affaires Hoffman Philip, the embassy staff, and Oscar Gunkel, head of Standard Oil operations in the Levant.[52] Within a week, he had his first conference with the Grand Vizier and Minister of Foreign Affairs Prince Said Halim Pasha and Minister of Finance Javid Pasha,[53] and on December 11, he paid his inaugural official visit to the sultan for the presentation of his credentials. Upon his arrival, the palace band played "My Country 'Tis of Thee." The sultan and Morgenthau exchanged salutary addresses, shook hands, and Morgenthau introduced the embassy staff. "It was all very impressive and agreeable," Morgenthau commented in his diary.[54]

IN CONSTANTINOPLE

Soon, Turkish officials frequented the embassy with proposals to encourage wider U.S.-Turkish economic relations. On December 8, Morgenthau met with a Turkish parliamentarian who had earlier supported the Chester project and now expressed an interest in reviving the scheme as his district, possessing little agricultural production, would benefit from industrial development. On December 22, Morgenthau and Talaat discussed the possibility of a U.S. financial loan to Turkey. Talaat spoke frankly of the poor economic conditions in his country, but he appeared "very anxious" to obtain an American loan not necessarily to ameliorate the situation but "to influence French financiers." Talaat invited Morgenthau to tour the empire and gain a first-hand knowledge of the economic condition, which the ambassador promised to do with the intention of "interesting American investors."[55] The next day, Morgenthau urged Standard Oil to loan 500,000 Turkish pounds to Turkey, and he cabled Secretary Bryan for approval to assist Turkey.

During his meetings with other officials of the Sublime Porte, Morgenthau was informed that the Turkish navy needed additional ships; the entire Turkish fleet consisted of 32 vessels, including 6 battleships, 4 cruisers, 3 torpedo-gunboats, 9 destroyers, and 10 torpedo-boats, while 2 Reshad-i-Hamiss class battleships were under construction and expected to be completed by 1915.[56] Minister of Commerce and Agriculture Suleiman al-Bustani, who had attended the Chicago World Fair in 1893 as Turkish commissioner, expressed an interest in securing an American loan and proposed that Americans "take entire charge of the reorganization of Turkish finance." Morgenthau subsequently recommended that the Department of State send Henry Bruère, a New York financier, to study the financial situation in Turkey. The Turkish leaders responded "favorably" to this suggestion, and the department immediately approved the plan. Instead of Bruère, as requested by the ambassador, however, C.K.G. Billings, an American millionaire, agreed to visit Constantinople.[57]

On December 27, 1913, Morgenthau briefly met with a group of Armenians, including the Armenian Patriarch Zaven Der Yeghiayan and Professor Abraham Hagopian of Robert College. They complained that the Armenians in the eastern provinces were "like vassals to the Kurds," who descended from the mountains "whenever they need anything—and when one of the Kurd chiefs hears of or sees a nice and young Armenian bride or wife—and likes her, he unhesitatingly takes her away and puts her in his house. . . ." They informed Morgenthau that the Armenian population in the entire region numbered "about 4 million, 2 in Turkey and 2 in Russia."[58] According to the 1912 estimates by the Armenian patriarchate at Constantinople, of the total 2,100,000 Armenians in the Ottoman Empire, 1,018,000 (48.5 percent) lived in the six Armenian *vilayets* or provinces of Van, Bitlis, Erzerum, Sivas, Kharpert, and Diarbekir.[59] Although Morgenthau, profoundly influenced by the Jewish experience in the United States, sympathized with the Armenian leaders as representatives of a minority group, at this early stage in his tenure he paid no particular attention to the plight of the Armenians. Events unfolding in the Ottoman Empire, however, as Secretary Daniels had predicted, would place the American ambassador "in the midst of one of the most historic theaters of action of our age."

THE END OF ARMENIAN REFORMS

In early 1913, after a lapse of several years the Armenian Question resurfaced as an international issue at the urging of Gevorg V Sureniants, supreme patriarch or catholicos of the Armenian Church from 1911 to 1930, who reportedly proposed annexation of the Ottoman Armenian provinces to Russia if the latter were so inclined. The tsarist government rejected this plan but promised instead to pursue effective reforms.[60] Having recovered from the Russo-Japanese War (1904–05) and the revolution of 1905 and now solicitous of Armenian cooperation for its geopolitical objectives in the Caucasus, the Russian government deemed the domestic and international environments conducive to greater engagement in the Armenian Question. As insisted upon by Russian Foreign Minister Sergei D. Sazonov, however, the Russian government could not employ the troops necessary for an outright annexation because of the potentially high costs such a policy would entail.[61] In fact, Russia appeared interested primarily in the settlement of the Turko–Persian frontier, on the one hand, and the prevention of German penetration into the eastern provinces, on the other.[62] The Armenian population situated across these regions could provide the pretext for a diplomatic excursion into a purportedly humanitarian reform platform.

By then, however, Armenian and Turkish orientation toward such reforms had so deeply diverged as to prove irreconcilable. Although most Armenians remained suspicious of European and Russian reform schemes, they nevertheless considered such international sponsorship as essential to restrain Turkish oppressive rule in the provinces.[63] The arrival of the German military mission of Liman von Sanders at Constantinople in December 1913 and the appointment of Enver Pasha as the minister of war in January 1914 did not bode well for the Armenian reforms.[64] Beginning in January 1914, official and unofficial persecution against Armenians intensified. U.S. Consul George Horton in Smyrna noted that the Ittihadists were determined to punish the Armenians. Horton wrote: "Peaceful agricultural laborers, against whom no accusation of any kind is brought, are cast into prison and shipped out of the country, and their families left to starve or subsist from charity."[65] Despite the uncertainties, the reform plan was finally signed by Grand Vizier Said Halim Pasha and Russian Chargé d'Affaires Konstantin N. Gulkevich on February 8, 1914. It provided for the consolidation of the Trebizond, Sivas, and Erzerum vilayets into a single de facto Armenian province, the Van, Bitlis, Kharpert, and Diarbekir vilayets into another, and the appointment of a European inspector-general for each province.[66] In mid-1914, Major Nicolai Hoff of Norway assumed his office as the inspector-general at Van, and Louis Westenenk of the Netherlands was expected to arrive at Erzerum soon thereafter.[67] Not surprisingly, the nationalist Ittihadist leaders opposed and sought to frustrate foreign interventions.[68] Jemal Pasha commented in his memoirs: "Just as it was our chief aim to annul the Capitulations . . . , so in the matter of Armenian reform we desired to release ourselves from the Agreement which Russian pressure had imposed upon us."[69]

THE WILSON ADMINISTRATION AND U.S. INTERESTS

The Wilson administration had remained aloof from the reform negotiations. Writing from Berlin, on May 29, 1914, House informed Wilson that having met with prominent leaders, including Minister of Foreign Affairs Gottlieb von Jagow and Grand Admiral Alfred von Tirpitz, the prevalent view in the German capital indicated little hope for improvement in European jealousies and hostilities. House stated that England would not want to see "Germany wholly crushed," as it would then have to carry alone the struggle against Russia.[70] Although increasingly concerned with respect to the political and military situation in Europe, the Wilson administration encouraged American businesses to gain greater access to foreign markets but to avoid geopolitical complications so long as they could advance their commercial interests.[71]

In Constantinople, Ambassador Morgenthau had his first direct contact with the Armenian people during a visit to a factory, which he characterized as "something awful." There, children as young as 10 years and women were working barefooted for 14 hours a day for 8 cents and 20–24 cents, respectively. "They can't stand thr [sic] work more than 15 years," Morgenthau wrote in his diary. In early February, he along with Talaat and other Turkish and Armenian dignitaries attended an Armenian concert, and another on February 22. The following day, Morgenthau met with Komitas Vardapet, the renowned Armenian priest and composer, whose twenty-four voice choir performed, on March 4, an Armenian concert before a host of Turkish officials and foreign diplomats.[72] Morgenthau increasingly grew more sympathetic toward the Armenian people, but in matters of official conduct he was the ambassador of the United States, appointed to promote and protect the national interest.

Morgenthau routinely held consultative meetings with representatives of various U.S. companies. On January 22, 1914, for example, he met with one Thomson, owner of copper mines in the interior, and on February 10 with the stock representative of McAndrews and Forbes, a licorice root company, to discuss import and export relations with Russia. On February 16 and 21, William Hills, Jr., of New York, called regarding commercial rights for the Smyrna Ice Company. On March 10, Morgenthau met with a representative of the Overland Company, and on the following day, with the president of Warwick Iron Company of Pottstown.[73]

In the meantime, Morgenthau sought to win the confidence of the Turkish authorities, and he was content that those in high command, such as Talaat, expressed their friendship toward him and believed that he was pro-Turkish.[74] Beginning in mid-January, however, he began to communicate his concerns regarding the gravity of the political situation. That month, Enver, now minister of war, expelled nearly 1,000 officers from their posts for failure to perform duties effectively during the Balkan wars, while ordering the imprisonment of others in the capital and the provinces suspected of conspiracy against him.[75] "There is a feeling here that there is something brewing and that it is likely to cause new trouble in the spring," Morgenthau entered in his diary. "The Young Turks are apt to be forced to action to maintain their hold on the Gov[ernment]. I fear a coup d'etat with Enver at its head."[76] Three days later, on January 20, during a dinner with a number of principal Young Turk leaders at Cercle d'Orient, a favorite restaurant frequented by Turkish officials and foreign emissaries, Morgenthau expressed "America's great sympathy" for, and his sincere desire to help, the rulers of the Ottoman Empire, and stressed the necessity of developing their commercial infrastructure. Sitting next to Morgenthau, Enver stated that "patriotism compels them to try everything to save the country from disintegration; if they fail and die they have done their duty." Enver was convinced that, given an opportunity, the Ittihadists could demonstrate their ability to govern and to establish an economically

and politically viable system. Talaat seemed less optimistic and emphasized the urgency of external financial support. Minister of Commerce
Bustani hoped that oil interests would contribute to the empire's economic reinvigoration, although bankers in general found the situation
discouraging.[77]

On February 28, 1914, Morgenthau made a carefully crafted
address as the guest of honor at a banquet of the U.S. Chamber of
Commerce before an audience of 220, among whom were Talaat,
Jemal, Bustani, President Caleb Gates of Robert College, William W.
Peet, treasurer of the Bible House in Constantinople, as well as foreign representatives.[78] Morgenthau opened his speech by offering the
economic development of the United States as a model for emulation
by Turkey. He stated: "What an achievement it would be if the Young
Giant of the West, who by strictly attending to his own business has
developed into one of the greatest and richest nations of the world,
could make others see the advantages and wisdom of following his
example." Identifying as key ingredients for national economic prosperity, he mentioned the successful completion of the transcontinen-
tal railroad, the significant role of educational institutions in the
nation's economic growth, the contributions of foreign investments
and immigration to industrial development, the willingness of the
people to "forget their past differences," and the protection of infant
industries "now managed by wonderful corporations that not only
stand alone but compete with the world." Morgenthau praised the
United States for having provided opportunities for native and immi-
grant Americans alike toward a better standard of living as they settled
across the land. "Gradually," he stated with some exaggeration, "they
acquired the almost luxurious surroundings in which they live to-day,
for there is hardly a farmhouse without an organ or piano, a sewing
machine, a small library and carpets on the floor, and most of them
own considerable agricultural machinery and a great many of them
their own automobiles."[79]

In his *All in a Life-Time*, Morgenthau identified four principal U.S.
commercial interests in Turkey: Standard Oil, Singer Sewing
Machine, tobacco, and licorice. Otherwise, he noted, "our interests
there were wholly altruistic," and "America's true mission in
Turkey . . . was to foster the permanent civilizing work of the
Christian missions, which so gloriously exemplified the American
spirit at its best."[80] U.S. commercial interests, however, involved far
greater number of goods than presented by the ambassador. For the
period June 1912–June 1914, the Department of Commerce
reported that U.S.-Turkish trade totaled about $50 million.[81]

Table 3.1   Principal U.S. imports from Turkey, June 1913–June 1914

Items	Quantity	Total $/Value	Comments
Tobacco leaf	15,616,543 lbs	4,800,284	29% of total pounds of tobacco leaves imported, second only after Cuba's 26,617,545 pounds (44% of the total)
Emery	13,804 tons	256,084	93% of total emery imports from abroad
Licorice root	56,355,101 lbs	921,520	49% of total imported volume of licorice root
Coffee	1,838,128 lbs	295,017	14% of total imported from Asia
Dates	28,858,381 lbs	519,132	by far the largest import in this category; 85% of dates imported from Asia and 76% of total dates imported from abroad, followed by 2,570,024 pounds of dates imported from England
Figs	13,160,786 lbs	719,021	the largest import in figs; 68% of total pounds, followed by 3,322,436 pounds (17%) totaling $115,617 (12%) imported from Greece
Raisins	2,730,338 lbs	119,046	60% of total raisin imports
Filberts	1,162,175 lbs	175,618	
Walnuts	1,683,121 lbs	288,473	ranking second after France. In fact, imports of shelled walnuts from France dropped from 9,707,520 pounds in 1913 to 6,684,566 pounds in 1914, while imports from Turkey-in-Asia increased from 353,387 pounds to 1,683,121 pounds for the same years.

Source: U.S. Department of Commerce, Bureau of Foreign and Domestic Commerce, *Foreign Commerce and Navigation of the United States for the Year Ending June 30, 1914* (Washington, DC: Government Printing Office, 1915), Table 3, pp. 21, 61, 75, 117, 118, 120, 125, 128, 262.

Table 3.1 shows some of the principal U.S. imports from Turkey. U.S. exports to Turkey included mowers and reapers, mining machinery, sewing machines, plumbing pipes and fittings, illuminating, lubricating, and heavy paraffin oil, and barbed wire.[82]

Clearly, Morgenthau had presented an overly simplified view of U.S.-Turkish commercial relations. His assessment of the political situation proved more accurate, however, as Turkish hostilities toward the Christian population increased. The authorities ordered a boycott of Christian businesses in Smyrna. On June 13, 1914, the grand vizier promised Morgenthau a delay of sixty days for the enforcement of the orders but insisted that the Greeks "had to go." Morgenthau protested to Talaat the deportation of 40,000 Greeks, but the minister of the interior complained that the various ethnic groups in the empire had caused its demise and requested that the ambassador urge American businesses "to employ only Turks." Subsequently, representatives of the Singer Company informed the ambassador that they would comply with the orders. " 'Turkey for the Turks' was now Talaat's controlling idea," Morgenthau observed in his *Story*.[83] In mid-June, Turks massacred Greeks at Phocia, while thousands of Turks from Macedonia forcibly displaced Greeks in Smyrna. The Turkish government had ordered the mining of Turkish territorial waters, including the port of Smyrna, which was closed to all ships. War between the two nations seemed inevitable. "I do hope I can help to prevent this war," Morgenthau entered in his diary for June 18, 1914. On June 25, the U.S. embassy received word that Secretary of the Navy Daniels had ordered the *USS Scorpion* to Smyrna, which arrived on June 26.[84]

The crisis was complicated by the Wilson administration's approval of the sale of two cruisers, the *USS Idaho* and the *USS Mississippi*, to Greece, in time before Turkey acquired its two new dreadnaughts, the *Reshadieh* and the *Sultan Osman*, which were under construction in English shipyards.[85] During a meeting with Morgenthau at the Pera Palace on June 15, Minister of Marine Jemal Pasha protested the sale of two cruisers to Greece, arguing that it would be viewed as an "unneutral act." Morgenthau in turn cautioned the State Department of the deleterious consequences the sale would exercise on U.S.-Turkish relations as it could instigate anti-American reactions in Constantinople, where the government lacked stable policy with friend and foe.[86] The Young Turk leadership, however, did not wish to brand the United States an enemy of the empire. On July 2, during a conference with Morgenthau, Talaat stated that while the Christian powers were more unified, the United States would not join the Entente in opposition to Turkey, although he expressed displeasure toward Wilson for the sale of the ships. Talaat insisted that U.S. enterprises were required to replace all Greek employees but refused to admit that his government bore any responsibility for the political discord. After another meeting with Talaat a week later, Morgenthau entered in his diary: "The more one talks with Talaat and others the more convinced one becomes that there is no security for property and no justice to be secured." On July 8, 1914, the U.S. Congress approved about $12.5 million toward the transfer of the *Idaho* and the *Mississippi*, now renamed *Kilkis* and *Lemnos*, to the Greek government.[87]

Such political difficulties did not appear insurmountable to American businesses, which solicited the support of the U.S. embassy for their interests in the empire. For example, an agent of the U.S. Rubber Company complained of the growing tendency on the part of Turkish authorities to implement discriminatory trade and investment policies favoring German companies, which had "ruined" the American tire business. Morgenthau and the company representative explored ways to widen the portfolio of U.S. exports in general and of the tire industry in particular.[88] Morgenthau also cultivated close relations with Standard Oil (in August, it transferred a company car to him). On June 30, 1914, he and a number of representatives of Standard Oil met with Turkish authorities to obtain oil concessions. Despite the difficulties confronted with the machinery of Ottoman bureaucracy, Standard Oil expected to secure avenues to transport oil to and across the region and to compete with Russian oil producers. The giant oil company must have been quite determined to bring this project to fruition; Morgenthau noted in his diary that the representatives of Standard Oil "prefer to submit to ill-treatment to secure this."[89]

By the end of July, having served as ambassador for six months, Morgenthau, now disillusioned with the Young Turk leaders, no longer seemed to enjoy his work and social events. After attending a bal-masque with about one hundred friends and diplomats, Morgenthau was easily irritable by those whose company he did not enjoy. "I am a fine hypocrite playing this society role," Morgenthau confided in his diary. "I doubt if I can do it much longer." As if with a premonition of the ominous events yet to unfold, Morgenthau on July 30, 1914, held a meeting with the embassy staff and "insisted that business must be kept up to date. . . . I am going to have weekly writings and keep track of everything."[90]

Chapter 4

War and Wilsonian Neutrality

Immediately after the outbreak of the war in Europe on July 28, 1914, the Wilson administration declared neutrality in relations with the belligerent powers largely to prevent entanglement in the European war before the 1916 presidential elections at home and to protect American interests abroad.[1] Concomitantly, to facilitate peaceful resolution of international conflicts, Secretary of State William Jennings Bryan launched his campaign for the ill-timed "peace treaties." Accordingly, he instructed Ambassador Henry Morgenthau at Constantinople to submit a copy of the "peace treaties" concerning international arbitration to the Turkish government for consideration. The Ottoman foreign ministry replied that current preoccupation with the Capitulations would postpone such considerations. Bryan did not force the issue; he and President Wilson hoped that Turkey would remain neutral "in the interest of humanity" and dissociate itself from German war plans, and Morgenthau attempted to influence the Turkish leaders, particularly the Grand Vizier Said Halim, Minister of War Ismail Enver, and Minister of Interior Mehmed Talaat, to that effect. The Turkish government, however, embittered by the sale of ships to Greece, informed Washington that the "only way to insure peace in that part of Europe was for Turkey to dominate the situation."[2]

Public opinion in the United States expressed anxiety over the situation in that part of the world, as the cruisers *USS Tennessee* and *USS North Carolina* sailed for Europe in August with nearly $8 million in gold provided by the Department of the Treasury and New York banks for the thousands of Americans caught in the war.[3] Unwilling to

trust the Ottoman banks, the Department of State solicited the cooperation of Standard Oil for the distribution of funds to organizations and individuals.[4] Robert Lansing, legal counselor at the State
Department, suggested that the company serve as a conduit for relief
funds. In response, R.P. Finsley, treasurer of Standard Oil, noted that
while the war had disturbed normal operations of banking facilities on
which the company relied to transfer home its profits in Turkey and
other parts of Asia, "we are glad to find that we can assist American
missions and other institutions, as well as many private enterprises and
individuals."[5]

THE TURN TO WAR

Such difficulties, however, paled in comparison to the rapidly escalating
hostilities toward Christians in general and Armenians in particular.
Reports from Constantinople, Smyrna, and other parts in Turkey
indicated in August 1914 that American lives and properties were seriously threatened.[6] Turkish authorities had issued explicit threats to
destroy Smyrna if invaded or bombarded, and the Muslim population
interpreted such declarations as a call to murder all Christians.
Morgenthau discussed with Turkish officials the threat made by
Governor General Rahmy Bey to burn Smyrna,[7] and on August 28,
Enver informed Morgenthau that it was meant for the Greeks in order
to prevent their alliance with Britain.[8] Some Americans, concerned for
their safety, preferred to leave and needed a safe passage. Turkish
authorities, however, refused permission for American ships to enter
the Gulf of Smyrna. Leland Morris, the U.S. vice consul general at
Smyrna, stressed the desirability of maintaining warships; otherwise,
he added, given the increasing difficulties encountered by Americans
"locally at least American prestige is greatly at stake."[9]

The American community in Smyrna anxiously awaited the arrival
of the *North Carolina* or any other U.S. vessel. "I am sure," James
Barton stated, "the State Department will take every necessary" measure for the safety of Americans and American interests in Turkey.[10]
Lansing assured Barton that the *North Carolina* and *Tennessee* were
in Turkish waters and that the secretary of the U.S. embassy found
"conditions there much improved."[11]

By the middle of August, political troubles indeed loomed large over
Constantinople and for Ambassador Morgenthau. Rumors traveled in
the Ottoman capital of a coup d'etat against Enver, who, it was feared,
would thrust the country into domestic turmoil and war with Russia.
On August 27, in response to a report by the London *Daily Telegraph*

in which Morgenthau had expressed serious concern regarding the lives of Christians and Jews in Turkey caught in political turmoil, Talaat wrote to Morgenthau: "This news so absurd and perfidious must not remain unanswered. I therefore appeal to your sentiment of justice, enhanced by your kindness, to oppose in the local press a most formal denial of this so calumnious news to be later reproduced abroad against us."[12] Morgenthau relayed this note to the State Department, adding that "Complying with Talaat Bey's request I sent the Press Bureau an unsigned statement of which I enclose a copy." Further, Morgenthau reported: "In reply to the inquiries of the representative of the Associated Press, I told him in an interview which I gave him yesterday that he could contradict the above mentioned statement of the 'Daily Telegraph' correspondent."[13]

Even before Turkey entered the war, various individuals and organizations in the United States expressed concern for the safety of Americans in Turkey. In September, O.B. Snyder of the Michigan Conference of the Mennonite Brethren in Christ urged the Department of State to secure the safety of ten missionaries in Hajin and Everek, as "Turkey is like a volcano ready to explode any day." The department replied that the missionaries were not "in any particular danger at the present time." But Snyder repeated his plea,[14] and Lansing relayed this request to the American consul at Kharpert with instructions to inquire as to the situation and to assist the missionaries "in every way to reach the coast" if they wished to leave Turkey.[15]

The American Board of Foreign Missions appealed to Washington on behalf of the U.S. colleges and institutions to send a cruiser or two to Turkish waters for protection. Although the *North Carolina* was expected to arrive soon at Smyrna, complaints were heard in political and missionary circles in the United States and in Turkey that the administration had failed to act quickly. Charles Arthur Reed, writing to Reverend Charles T. Riggs, noted that it was safe for American ships to enter Turkish waters and to reach Smyrna, and that "there are plenty of Americans who will risk going up, or down, or whichever way Turkish mines would send a war ship, by meeting the vessel outside and coming in on board her. The Turkish government seems adept at bluffing, and the American authorities splendid victims."[16]

On September 2, A.H. Burrows, a lawyer in New York, wrote to Lansing regarding the protection needed for American interests in Smyrna. According to Burrows, his client, MacAndrews and Forbes Company, had "an interest of two and one-half million dollars in Asia Minor and a great many Greeks and Turks employed with Americans and some Englishmen in management." Communications from

Turkey warned of imminent troubles, Burrows added, and the company inquired if the government would send war vessels to Turkish waters.[17] Lansing immediately replied that the Department of the Navy expected the *North Carolina* to arrive at Smyrna within eight to ten days.[18] As things stood, however, there was no sufficient cause to change U.S. policy of neutrality.

ABROGATION OF THE CAPITULATIONS

Meanwhile, the Young Turk regime launched a public opinion campaign against the Capitulations. In the evening of September 9, public demonstrations took place in Constantinople against the Capitulations, and on the following day the Turkish government formally notified all embassies of its decision to abrogate the Capitulations on October 1.[19] On September 27, the Young Turk government closed the Dardanelles, abrogated the Capitulations on October 1, and entered the war on the side of Germany on October 30.[20]

The Wilson administration immediately protested the abrogation of the Capitulations. Secretary Bryan instructed Morgenthau to notify the Ottoman government that the United States refused to recognize the authority of the Sublime Porte to possess such unilaterally applicable rights adversely affecting the privileges granted to foreign entities under the conventions.[21] While U.S.-Turkish disagreements concerning the Capitulations potentially could have proven injurious to U.S.-Turkish relations, the two governments also indicated their willingness to maintain good relations. Said Halim, Enver, and Talaat assured Morgenthau that Turkish authorities had no intention of mistreating American schools and missionaries, as they wished to remain on friendly terms with the United States.[22] In a similar vein, on September 21, Minister of Commerce Suleiman Bustani requested that Morgenthau inquire whether the Wilson administration would take charge of Turkish interests in Mexico and in the South American republics. The Department of State immediately notified of its willingness to represent Turkish interests in the said areas. Bustani in turn expressed an interest to visit the United States "to secure loan and revive Chester project."[23]

The abrogation of the Capitulations represented the ultimate expression of Turkish nationalism and served to remove any legal pretensions on the part of foreign powers to intervene in Ottoman domestic affairs, particularly as deportations and massacres were in progress on the eastern frontier of the empire. Morgenthau was aware of these events,[24] yet he failed to appreciate the full import of the stress the Young Turk regime placed on the abrogation of the Capitulations. As the Ittihadists moved to enter the war, they were also prepared to deal a final blow to the Armenian Question.

THE CALL TO JIHAD

On the morning of October 29, in a preemptive strike, the Turkish navy bombarded Russian ports on the Black Sea.[25] The Ottoman cabinet was divided regarding Turkey's entrance into the war, but the Ittihadist regime insisted on presenting an image of unity. Cabinet members opposing the war included Minister of Finance Mehmed Javid Pasha, Minister of Public Works Mahmud Pasha, Minister of Commerce Bustani, and Minister of Posts and Telegraphs Oskan Mardikian Effendi.[26] The extremist nationalists, determined to consolidate power in preparation for the proclamation of the *Jihad* (Holy War), encouraged resignation of the opposition.[27] The grand vizier offered to do so but was eventually persuaded to remain in office.[28] And immediately after Turkey entered the war, all Muslim subjects were, on November 14, called to *Jihad:* "O, true sons of Mohamed! abandon all commerce, business . . . and taking up arms march with all your belongings and lives against our enemies, because this is the only way to go to Paradise."[29]

Morgenthau observed that such government proclamations provoking Muslims to kill the infidels could prove disastrous not for the belligerent powers toward whom "the Turks have as yet manifested practically no signs of personal animosity," but in "the more remote parts of the Empire where latent fanaticism is far greater and is often able to profit by conditions of local disorder."[30] In his *Story*, Morgenthau noted that in addition to the official proclamation, the Turkish government distributed a secret pamphlet across the Muslim world with instructions for the believers. After enumerating the grievances of Muslims under European dominion, the pamphlet identified a specific outline as to direct action against the infidel. The *Jihad* would be carried out in three modes of activities: individual acts, killing by organized bands, and military campaigns.[31] On November 14, immediately after the proclamation of *Jihad*, a crowd attacked a French store, the Bon Marché, moved on to the British embassy, and attacked the Tokatlian hotel, whose owner was an Armenian. On that very day, Enver promised Morgenthau that no harm would come to the American institutions and "that there will be no massacres anyway."[32]

The Department of State sought to calm American public opinion by assuring those concerned that the *USS Tennessee* and *USS North*

Carolina were in Turkish waters.[33] U.S. Consul in Beirut W. Stanley
Hollis expressed a sigh of relief as both cruisers anchored at Beirut in
October. But conditions deteriorated rapidly, and in November he
advised that the protection of foreigners and local non-Muslims
would require U.S. "naval forces in these waters . . . be strengthened
by a number of small cruisers, or gunboats."[34] Morgenthau, however,
in a strictly confidential note to the secretary of state, communicated
his apprehension about "Hollis doing something rash," as the latter
was "very nervous" in Beirut and had antagonized Minister of the
Marines Ahmed Jemal, commander of the Ottoman Fourth Army
headquartered in Syria.[35] In one instance, when Hollis had criticized
Jemal Pasha, the latter had replied: "I do not authorize you to meddle
with my affairs. You have no official relation whatsoever with me. You
are free to write what you desire to your Embassy."[36] To avoid
tensions with the regime, Morgenthau insisted that if cruisers were to
be stationed at Turkish ports, no consul would possess authority over
such cruisers, and the captain at Beirut be instructed in no uncertain
terms that he "must not permit himself to become involved in
any incident by Hollis." The primary function of the cruisers should
be limited to providing "refuge and moral influence," and any misuse
would cause greater injuries than the protection they could
render.[37] Morgenthau reported that all Americans were safe in
Constantinople.[38]

On December 7, John Way, of Shopbell Dry Goods Company in
Williamsport, Pennsylvania, whose son was assistant treasurer of
Robert College, inquired whether press reports accurately depicted
the troubled situation of Americans in Turkey. The United Press
reported the Turkish seizure of foreign, including American, properties and warned that while Morgenthau may at times have been successful in protecting American interests, "there may come a time
when his demands will not be acceded to." Way cautioned that
"Fanaticism may break forth" and that "the world may be shocked by
Turkey's throwing off the veneer of Europeanism." Yet, Way noted,
contrary to the press reports, the letters from his son indicated no
such threats to Americans.[39]

The administration responded to such inquiries by stating that
conditions in Turkey were calm and that American citizens and interests received full government protection. Bryan wrote to Barton to
inform the missionary community that the U.S. ambassador, "with
hearty cooperation of Turkish officials," had secured protection for
Americans and that life was proceeding as normal. Acting Secretary of
State Lansing instructed the U.S. consuls to assist "in every way"

American missionaries who wished to leave Turkey. At the same time, however, Lansing informed Barton that reports from Smyrna indicated that conditions there were "much improved."[40] His and Bryan's replies to all such inquiries stated that latest news from the ambassador at Constantinople "indicate that everything is quiet and that American citizens are safe."[41]

Americans in Turkey possessing greater familiarity with Turkish modi operandi in matters of war and peace repeatedly demanded protection by U.S. warships. Their patience must have been tested when Turkish coastal guns fired blank shots at the USS *Tennessee* while it anchored at Smyrna.[42] As the crisis at Smyrna intensified, Wilson and Lansing met with Secretary of the Navy Josephus Daniels,[43] while Bryan instructed Morgenthau that he protest to the grand vizier. Morgenthau discussed the *Tennessee* incident with Talaat and Enver and urged them "to give this prompt attention to avoid public opinion in U.S. being aroused." In late November and early December, Smyrna and the security of American missionaries in Turkey remained a major concern for the administration, and Bryan and Lansing met with a number of advisors, including members of the military and foreign service personnel, to examine the matter.[44] In Constantinople, the Young Turk government promulgated an Imperial Rescript on December 16, 1914, nullifying the Agreement of February 8, 1914, which had promised administrative reforms and the creation of two Armenian provinces.[45]

By the end of his first year, better acquainted with the Ottoman political scene and "wholly disillusioned," Morgenthau warned in December 1914 that the Turkish government was "fast drifting into semi anarchy, promises are made one day and recalled the next, there is no fixed policy and the officials no longer rely on complete protection from Turkish government."[46] While Morgenthau could no longer rely on the Turkish government for the protection of American citizens, he nevertheless recommended no fundamental changes in policy.

On December 16, 1914, as Wilson and Colonel House met for a family dinner to discuss peace negotiations in Europe and relations with Latin American countries, they received an urgent dispatch from Morgenthau regarding the situation in the Ottoman Empire.[47] Concerned with reports of the troubles caused by Consul Hollis in Beirut as reported by Morgenthau, Wilson asked House whether "it would be advisable to warn all Americans out of Turkey." House "advised doing nothing for the moment, but to get a better insight into the true situation."[48] Wilson and Bryan agreed to warn the Americans in Turkey but without attracting public attention here at home. On December 20, concerned about public opinion, Bryan sent the following telegram to Morgenthau:

> The President approves the suggestion that Americans should be advised to leave Turkey wherever you think it would be unsafe for them to remain, but he suggests that to avoid frightening friends in this country and attracting public attention, it is better to handle the matter very guardedly and confidentially. Will you please send private word to all the inland missions and advise them to retire from Turkey as soon as they can conveniently do so, if they feel that there are grounds for serious apprehension, stating that in giving this advice you have the approval of the President, but ask them to regard the advice confidential and not to allow public mention to be made of it. If they send word to their friends at home they can simply state that they are intending to leave Turkey, without saying that they are advised to do so.[49]

Morgenthau informed the secretary that the missionaries, presently not in any danger, desired to remain.[50] Bryan thought the report encouraging and relayed it to the president.[51]

SARIKAMISH AND SINAI

Having entered the war on the side of Germany, the Turkish military was expected to defend the Caucasian front against Russian expansion. In late 1914, control over oil may have been one of the principal elements shaping Turkish military strategy regarding the Caucasus.[52] A military offensive into the Caucasus would secure the oil fields in the region and transform the Caucasus into a zone of Turko–German influence after the war. Further, a Caucasus campaign to conquer Baku and to march on to Central Asia would unite the Turkic peoples and thus accomplish the Pan-Turkist aspirations of the Ittihadist regime.[53]

In early November, Enver ordered Turkish troops stationed near the Aras (Araxes) River to the Russian front. While initially the Russian army thwarted the Turkish advance, the latter registered some military successes during the month. As the cold winter set in, no further military advances were expected. Enver Pasha thought otherwise, and in December, leading a force of about 95,000 strong, commenced a full-scale offensive against the Russian force of 65,000 troops along the Caucasus front.[54] Despite the earlier success, the campaign ended in total disaster. Enver's military operation was poorly organized and supplied (in fact, a map used during the campaign was highly inaccurate). The treacherous conditions of winter and insufficient logistical preparation quickly destroyed what military superiority the Turkish forces possessed. The decisive battle at Sarikamish was fought on December 29, 1914. By the middle of January, Enver's forces had been annihilated; no more than 18,000 had survived out of the initial 95,000. Russian losses were placed at 16,000 killed and wounded. Humiliated by this defeat, Enver departed for Constantinople.[55] In the meantime, reports had reached Constantinople of recurring attacks by Turkish soldiers and irregular *chete* bands on the Armenian villages near Sivas city, Shabin-Karahisar, Erzerum, Van, Bitlis, and Diarbekir.[56]

On his return to the capital, Enver publicly recognized the loyalty and bravery of the Ottoman Armenian soldiers during the Sarikamish campaign.[57] After welcoming him, Patriarch Zaven Der Yeghiayan requested permission to publish the minister's letters praising the Armenian soldiers. Enver agreed and noted that "had it not been for an unauthorized maneuver executed by a certain Sergeant Major Hovhannes, he would have been taken captive. For his valiant act, Enver told me [The Patriarch] that he promoted Hovhannes to the rank of Captain on the spot."[58] Enver wished to conceal the truth about his disastrous adventure. When Morgenthau met with him on January 23, 1915, the minister of war discussed the improved harvest since the previous year and about plans to build railroad tracks from Angora to Erzerum. He reported that Turkish troops had captured 2,000 Russian prisoners in Erzerum. His efforts to mask the Sarikamish affair could not last long, however, and rumors of a coup against him spread in the capital.[59]

In preparation for the conquest of Egypt, the Young Turks had placed Jemal Pasha at the head of the Ottoman Fourth Army centered at Damascus. Beginning in early November, British forces attacked Turkish positions at the Persian Gulf, occupied Shat al-Arab, and within a month advanced farther inland to control Basra. No sooner had the Sarikamish campaign ended than the battle for the Sinai Peninsula and the Suez Canal escalated in the last days of January 1915, as approximately 20,000 Turkish troops commenced the invasion of Egypt. Before long, however, British and French surveillance aircraft detected their movements. The British forces, about 70,000 strong, offered an unassailable defense. The Turkish army failed in this campaign as well. A report published in the London *Times* expressed doubt whether the Turkish high command had a clear objective in this engagement. Jemal Pasha and his German advisers had miscalculated British military capability and within two weeks the commander of Syria had been defeated.[60]

These military disasters undermined what little political legitimacy the Ittihadist regime possessed. Having usurped power through a military coup, its leaders now grew suspicious of their own institutions and population as rumors of various sorts of conspiracies against their rule spread. Indeed, in December 1914, Morgenthau noted in his diary that Chief of Police at Constantinople Ibrahim Bedri was "sending away all unemployed young men for fear that they might join an uprising" against the regime; "I think they are as much afraid of that as they are of bombardment." Yet, as was their custom, prominent Turkish leaders played poker daily at the Cercle d'Orient "and acted as though everything seemed OK."[61]

For the Armenian population in the eastern provinces, the Turkish military disasters suffered at Sarikamish and Sinai and the environment of conspiracies generated as a result had far reaching consequences. The fanatical rage, which the Ittihadist regime wished to vent against Europe and Russia but could not for military reasons, was unleashed against the unarmed Armenians, who, the Turkish authorities alleged, had become instruments of foreign subversion conspiring against Islam and Ottoman society. At the same time, Western indifference to the earlier massacres had amply demonstrated that the major powers involved in the regional conflicts and competition would not be particularly concerned about the security of the Armenians.[62] The military defeats in December 1914 and January 1915, therefore, caused the escalation of hostilities toward the Armenians, who were now blamed for the failures of the Ittihadist regime.[63] Talaat, Enver, and the other Ittihadist leaders viewed any efforts to discuss the persecution of Armenians as foreign interference in their domestic affairs. The abrogation of the Capitulations, they insisted, ended all justifications for such intervention.

Thus, as early as January 1915, when Ambassador Morgenthau complained about the treatment of Armenians, Turkish authorities expressed their annoyance that he showed such concern for their Christian subjects and, according to rumors, even threatened to request American warships for their protection. Morgenthau, however, denied such rumors. "The truth," he noted in his diary, "was that I had told [Johann] Pallavicini," the Austrian ambassador at Constantinople, "that if Germans encouraged massacres or if it took place, I feared U.S. would send ships to prevent it."[64] The Wilson administration was not prepared to take such a step, however.

ELECTIONS AND THE ECONOMY

For the administration, the year 1915 began with enormous political problems in other parts of the world, "the most serious" being, according to Bryan, "the situation in Mexico."[65] American public opinion was concerned primarily with the economic recession at home caused by the war. President Wilson enjoyed considerable domestic support for keeping the United States out of the war, and the administration deemed such public approval essential for securing a second term. Prepared to launch his campaign for the presidential elections of 1916, in his speech on Jackson Day, January 8, in Indianapolis, Wilson assumed a particularly partisan posture obvious during political campaigns; he criticized the Republican Party for not having "a new idea in thirty years" and not knowing "how to do anything except sit on the lid." Referring to the role of the United States in the world political economy, he stated: "Half the world is on fire. Only America among the great powers of the world is free to govern her own life; and all the world is looking to America to serve its economic needs."[66] Morgenthau, writing from Constantinople to Judge Abram Elkus of New York, also a friend of Wilson, noted with confidence that the president's "chances of re-election are improving."[67]

The administration worried, however, that the recession, if unchecked, combined with the uncertainties of the war, could diminish public support for Wilson. Reinvigoration of the national economy, Wilson believed, required promotion of foreign trade. Addressing a joint session of Congress in December 1914, the president had emphasized the negative impact the European war and insufficient shipping facilities exercised on trade, and had requested that Congress pass the ship-purchase bill proposed in the preceding session. Moreover, he had stressed the necessity of strengthening the nation's naval capabilities to meet the challenges of an increasingly hostile international environment and to safeguard commercial lines.[68] Undergirding the promotion of foreign trade, as the president saw it, was the willingness on the part of his administration to synthesize government-business efforts toward international expansion. Accordingly, in a speech before the U.S. Chamber of Commerce, Wilson encouraged closer government-business relations and reforms in anti-trust laws so as to afford American businesses greater legal flexibility in formation of corporate combines for the benefit of the commonweal and successful competition in global markets. Advocating a wider role for the U.S. government as the "promotional state," in a speech before the Pan-American Financial Conference in May 1915, he promised to propose the development of government-owned ships for commercial relations. "If private capital cannot soon enter upon the adventure of establishing these physical means of communication," he said, "the government must undertake to do so."[69]

In a similar vein, Secretary of Commerce William C. Redfield urged American industrialists and financiers to be prepared for further expansion of U.S. commercial relations after the war. As Europe was likely to lose its competitive edge vis-à-vis the United States as a result of the war, Redfield noted, it would necessarily be preoccupied to undo the destruction. "No one, I think, would be surprised to find the United States second in the world's competition, nor, if the war shall long continue, be astonished to find her first." Reflecting on the future of the Ottoman Empire, the role of Germany and Russia in the area, and the implications of regional developments for the United States, Redfield pondered: "Are we to see the release of Russia from the restraints that have hitherto always bound her? Are the Dardanelles and Bosphorus to be open doors, wide apart without restraint, to the commerce of the great Russian people? Are her wheat and oil and other products to be free from all hindrance henceforth by this route?" Moreover, he added, "what is to become of the Bagdad railroad? Something like a thousand miles of it have been built by German capital. Its eastern outlet on the Persian Gulf is now held by the British. Cyprus and Egypt, British possessions, are near its western terminal."[70] Redfield proposed that the United States be posed to assume a more leading role in the political and commercial relations of the region.

CHAPTER 5

POWER AND ITS PROMISES

The Ittihadist regime, now decidedly allied with Germany as one of the belligerents but confronted with the humiliations of the military defeats in Sarikamish and the Sinai Peninsula, was caught in the throes of fanatical nationalism and intense hostility toward foreign interference in their internal affairs. While expressing willingness to maintain good relations with the Wilson administration, the regime began to abuse American neutrality and threatened to close down American institutions in the Ottoman Empire. During his meetings with Minister of the Interior Mehmed Talaat Pasha, Ambassador Henry Morgenthau repeatedly requested that the Turkish authorities treat the American institutions in the empire as they would expect the U.S. government to treat foreign institutions in the United States.[1]

CRISIS OF POLITICAL LEGITIMACY

Increasingly, however, Talaat and the leadership of the Ittihad ve Terakki (Committee of Union and Progress, CUP) showed little patience for such foreign instructions in matters of domestic policy. Particularly troubling for the Young Turk leaders had been the close relationship developed between foreigners and the Armenian communities, and they were determined to disengage all such ties. Turkish nationalism was in large part a reaction to foreign diplomatic interventions, and Turkish nationalists viewed the activities of American educational and missionary institutions in local Armenian communities as challenging national sovereignty—a considerable point of vulnerability for them after the Sarikamish and Sinai campaigns, as the Ittihadists now felt threatened by the growing domestic political opposition as news of the military losses spread.[2]

Closely intertwined with the purported Armenian threat and simmering beneath the surface was the crisis of political legitimacy of the dictatorial regime as headed by the Ittihadist triumvirate of Talaat, Minister of War Ismail Enver, and Minister of the Marines Ahmed Jemal.[3] Their fear of imminent failure and collapse, national humiliation, and even the possibility of personal disparagement and physical attacks against them heightened their sense of insecurity. In February 1915 it was rumored that Talaat's bodyguard was killed as the two stepped out of their automobile in the capital, where also during the same night mass demonstrations were held against Turkey's involvement in the war. Since the middle of January, Talaat had slipped into a state of deep depression, as witnessed by the Italian Consul M. Garroni and Morgenthau. During a visit with the minister of the interior, the legal counsel of the U.S. embassy, Arshak Schmavonian,[4] found him depressed, continually referring matters to the ministry of war, as he felt that "he no longer asserts complete authority." Meanwhile, rumors spread of a plan led by Jemal, whose tensions with Enver were public knowledge, to oust Enver and the Germans. Enver, ever cautious not to offend Jemal, whose pro-Allied predilections threatened the regime's alliance with Germany, pretended that such challenges to his authority were mere British ploys to instigate rebellion within the military ranks so as to undermine his status in Constantinople.[5]

Determined to remain in power, the Ittihadists redoubled their efforts toward greater consolidation of power and targeted the Armenians as a potential source for anti-Ittihad revolutionary upheaval. On February 12, 1915, the authorities removed several Armenian officials from their government posts in the capital.[6] Enver also ordered the closing of the *Azatamart*, the principal organ of the Dashnaktsutiun (Armenian Revolutionary Federation) in Constantinople.[7] Talaat still assured Morgenthau that Christians had no cause for concern as they would be "properly protected."[8]

The Ittihadist government perceived foreign institutions, especially the American missionary buildings, as a center for political and religious agitation and repeatedly threatened with closure. Although the American hospital in Van, for example, treated Turkish soldiers, government harassment in various forms intensified. In one instance, the local authorities attempted to confiscate all medicine at the American missionary compound much to the chagrin of Dr. Clarence Ussher, the director of the medical section. Ussher met with the *vali* (governor) of Van province, Hasan Tahsin Bey, to protest such offenses against American institutions. The doctor contended that privileges of security and inviolability as accorded under extraterritorial rights guaranteed protection for the American properties. He noted that any violation of American premises would undermine U.S.-Turkish relations. "Poof!" the vali retorted. "We are not afraid of America. America has no army. She could not enforce her demands." Although the United States had no army when war was declared with Spain, Ussher responded, "when McKinley sent out a call for one hundred thousand volunteers, two million applied in one day. And there might be more next time."[9] Besides his protests, such a statement by a foreign consul represented an ominous threat. The vali was not impressed. The soldiers continued to demand medicine and hospital supplies, and when Ussher refused, they threatened to shoot him.[10] Ussher continued to insist on the inviolability of the American premises. The vali finally apologized for the conduct of the soldiers. Ussher later commented in retrospect: "Few American Consuls in Turkey dared to act boldly on their own initiative; could not count on support of their Government or on its prestige."[11]

On February 14, Talaat and Ziya Gokalp, a popular poet and one of the leading CUP ideologues, presided over a three-day conference of the CUP Central Committee at the Nuri Osmanieh headquarters in Constantinople. The conference resolved to expurgate the Armenian Question from the Ottoman political system during the war.[12] Attending the conference were the CUP elite, including Enver, Mehmed Javid, Behaeddin Shakir, Minister of Education Midhad Shukri, Dr. Nazim, and Hussein Jahid (editor of the CUP organ *Tanin*).[13] In a letter dated February 18, Abdulahad Nuri Bey conveyed to Jemal Pasha the views expressed and the decisions made concerning the Armenian people. Nuri Bey quoted Dr. Nazim as stating that the CUP had decided to shoulder the responsibility of "freeing the fatherland of the aspirations of this cursed race." Nazim added that the CUP, in hopes of establishing a better future for the nation, granted the government wide authority to eliminate all Armenians living in Turkey.[14]

The Turkish government, with the full backing of their German patrons, thus responded to the combined forces of external and internal challenges by declaring total war not only against their external enemies but also against those whom they identified as the internal archenemy, the Armenians.[15] Accordingly, the wartime policy of the Young Turk regime targeted the entire Armenian population, ostensibly as a matter of military security, for removal by all means necessary. In fact, beginning in January 1915, the central government had commenced attacks on Armenians in two regions: the Turko-Russian-Persian frontier near Lake Urmia and the Zeitun-Marash–Aintab region on the eastern edges of Cilicia.

LAKE URMIA BASIN

The Young Turk leaders encouraged the massacre of Armenians in several towns across the Caucasus region and stretching to Lake Urmia, where the Turkish and Russian military campaigns had created thousands of refugees since the outbreak of the war.[16] By the end of March, the Turkish forces had strengthened their position farther west in the Mush–Bitlis region, and in April, Halil Bey led his troops across the lands south of Lake Van to Urmia. Turks forcibly entered the American mission compound at Urmia, killing several Assyrian Christian refugees and attacking and insulting the missionaries. Halil Bey had forced the Russians to withdraw; however, within a few days, a successful Russian counterattack forced his retreat to Van. By the time the Russian operations had forced the Turks and Kurds out of the area, about 50,000 Christians had become refugees and thousands were killed.[17]

In one instance, Jevdet Bey, brother-in-law of Minister of War Enver, having failed in his military campaign against the Russian army at Khoy north of Lake Urmia, wrought his vengeance on unarmed civilians, killing nearly 800 people in the district of Salmas during his return to Van *vilayet* (province). Similar events followed in the outlying villages across the vilayet.[18] The more fortunate escaped across the Russian front to the region of Erevan. Mary E. Lewis, principal of the American School for Muslim Girls at Urmia, commented in her diary: "If it isn't Djihad (Holy War), it is very near it. It must have been planned beforehand, for there has been concerted action from one end of the plain to the other, though here and there some Moslems have been friendly throughout, have done many kindly deeds and saved many lives."[19]

CILICIA

The Turkish–Russian front was not the only area where Armenians faced such brutalities in late 1914 and early 1915. Years of government repression in Cilicia had sown a profound sense of mistrust among the Armenians toward the authorities and Turks in general. As a result, at the outbreak of the war, the Armenian leadership in Cilicia hoped that an Allied victory would lead to some form of regional autonomy.[20] In early January 1915, when a French warship bombed and destroyed the railway in Alexandretta (Iskenderun), the authorities, suspicious of Armenian collusion, gathered several hundred Armenians in Dort Yol and Hasan Beyli to rebuild the railway. The region of Zeitun, with a long tradition of resistance to Turkish repression, proved particularly troubling for the Young Turk regime, and hostilities escalated when about 5,000 Turkish soldiers converged on the town.[21]

In March, Catholicos Sahak Khapayan (Sahag Khabayan) of the Great House of Cilicia at Sis petitioned Minister of the Marines Jemal for protection of Armenian soldiers and deserters. Jemal promised that no injuries would be inflicted on Armenians loyal to the government; measures taken by the authorities would remain limited to the deserters. Similarly, in a letter to the vali of Aleppo vilayet Jelal Bey, the catholicos expressed his apprehensions about the crisis in Zeitun and requested that the vali investigate the situation.[22] The catholicos wrote to the Armenian patriarch at Constantinople, Zaven Der Yeghiayan: "How will this tragedy brought upon the Armenians of Cilicia be healed? We are told that appeals to Constantinople are useless, as Jemal Pasha is given absolute authority to arrange the matters as he deems fit. . . . Similar calamity is expected to occur in Hajin and Hasan Beyli."[23] While Turks and Kurds raided and plundered some of the Armenian houses and killed their inhabitants, deportations began in the Aintab–Marash region, with the expectation that more would follow.[24]

In early April 1915, Consul Jesse Jackson at Aleppo relayed to Morgenthau, to the secretary of state, and to the American Board of Commissioners for Foreign Missions, a report prepared by the Reverend John E. Merrill, president of Central Turkey College at Aintab, on the situation in the region stretching from Aintab to Marash and Zeitun. This 9-page document informed that the current conditions in the Marash region resembled the situation of the 1890s and 1909. As during the massacres of 1895–96, it noted, the Turkish government was spreading false rumors that the Armenians in the Marash region were threatening law and order. The local officials deceived the Armenians in Zeitun and in nearby Furnus into surrendering their arms in hopes of averting punishment, as during the Adana massacres of 1909, while causing the death of innocent women and children. Orders for conscription of young males for military service were followed by imprisonment, deportations, and massacres. Merrill concluded that the deportation of the educated Christian population from the Marash region was "a direct blow at American missionary interests, menacing the results of more than fifty years of work and many thousands of dollars of expenditure."[25]

On April 22, 1915, the supreme patriarch of the Armenian Apostolic Church, Catholicos Gevorg V Sureniants at the Holy See of Echmiadzin, appealed to President Wilson, the Russian Foreign

Minister Sergei Sazonov, and King Victor Immanuel of Italy to use their good offices with Constantinople to end the persecutions so that at least unarmed civilians were protected.[26] The following day, a small group of Armenian political leaders in Constantinople, including members of the Ottoman Parliament—Zareh Tilper (Dilber), Krikor Zohrab and Vartkes Serengulian—Harutiun Boshkezenian, and Hovsep Madatian, met at the Armenian patriarchate to discuss the gravity of the situation and appealed to the Sublime Porte to consider measures to stop the violence against the Armenians.[27] Rather than end the persecutions, the military command stationed soldiers throughout the capital on April 24. Constantinople, home to about 150,000 Armenians, seemed to be under martial law, and during the night of April 24–25, the authorities arrested and exiled more than 200 Armenians, mostly intellectuals and community and business leaders, including Komitas Vardapet, followed by an additional 600 soon thereafter.[28]

On April 30, Morgenthau dispatched an urgent message to the Department of State about the repressive measures and the conditions in Marash and Zeitun.[29] Morgenthau noted that the Italian ambassador, the Bulgarian minister, and the Armenian patriarch had made "strong representations" to Minister of War Enver. The latter justified the "movement against Armenians" on grounds that Armenian revolutionaries working under the banner of the Dashnaktsutiun in the Ottoman Empire as well as Russian Armenians were attacking government officials and buildings, especially in Van. In response, the government had decided to deport some of them. The grand vizier, the minister of war, and the minister of the interior promised that "excesses or general massacres" would not occur and that those imprisoned by mistake would be released.[30]

Secretary Bryan reported the conversations between Morgenthau and Talaat, Enver, and the grand vizier to George Bakhméteff, the Russian ambassador to Washington, who on behalf of the Armenian catholicos had requested that the United States impress upon the Turkish leaders to prevent persecutions of the Armenians. In successive messages, Bryan instructed Morgenthau to call on the Turkish government to end the violence.[31] Morgenthau replied that the secretary of state's instructions had been complied with, and Minister of the Interior Talaat had instructed the provincial authorities "to protect all innocent people from molestation."[32]

Yet, at the same time, a directive cosigned by Talaat, Enver, and Nazim ordered the provincial authorities to begin the deportations and massacre of the Armenians.[33] On April 26, an emergency conference at the patriarchate decided to meet with Grand Vizier Said Halim and Talaat. Accordingly, a delegation headed by the patriarch met with the grand vizier. Rejecting the notion that the Turkish government had no confidence in the Armenian people, Said Halim maintained that the arrests were primarily for security reasons. The meeting with Talaat proved equally futile. When Talaat and Morgenthau met immediately after the Armenian delegation left, the minister of the interior insisted that "he was determined to destroy all societies and combinations" deemed threatening to the state. Having once been the head of revolutionaries, Talaat noted, he was aware of the ability of such movements. Morgenthau commented in his diary: "It seems that they are determined to prevent their being displaced and seem to have considerable fears about a possible revolution."[34]

Representing a neutral power, Morgenthau remained the only foreign ambassador showing any interest in the safety of the Armenians. The Armenian patriarch expressed his utmost confidence in the ambassador but noted that Morgenthau "behaved with caution and did not want to invite suspicion by getting into direct relations [with the Patriarchate], but the legal counsel of the Embassy, Arshak Schmavonian, was a valuable intermediary between us."[35] On May 17, Komitas Vardapet, having been allowed to return to the capital, visited Morgenthau and informed him that of the Armenians arrested in Constantinople and sent into exile, only he and a handful of others had been released.[36]

Morgenthau also sought to convince the German ambassador to Constantinople, Hans von Wangenheim, to cooperate with him toward protection of Armenians. The German ambassador saw no such danger and changed the topic to discuss the U.S. delivery of $290 million worth of military hardware to the Entente powers during the past seven months. Wangenheim, however, emphasized that "if Constantinople were bombarded massacres were likely to follow."[37]

THE GALLIPOLI CAMPAIGN

At this juncture, one vital opportunity for Western military intervention that potentially could have altered the course of the war in the Middle East and perhaps prevented further deportations and massacres was the Allied attack on the Dardanelles. In December 1914, as Enver's forces attacked the Russian front, the tsarist government proposed an Allied action against Turkey so as to divert pressure in the Caucasus, a strategy that found growing support in London. As advocated by the First Sea

Lord, Admiral Fisher, and subsequently backed by Winston Churchill, the First Lord of the Admiralty, the principal object of the Dardanelles campaign was to neutralize Turkey and to free the Straits for transportation of oil from the Caucasus and Romania to Britain and France.[38] Churchill characterized the Dardanelles as "the great strategic nerve centre of the world war of 1915."[39] The price to remove Turkey from the war, he wrote to British Secretary of State for Foreign Affairs Sir Edward Grey, "would no doubt be heavy, but there would be no more war with Turkey. A good army of 50,000 men and sea power—that is the end of the Turkish menace."[40] Writing from London, Colonel Edward M. House, President Wilson's personal advisor, observed that the British thought the operation viable, requiring no more than two weeks. With the exception of Minister of War Enver, general opinion in Constantinople, as noted by Morgenthau, concurred, and the authorities made preparations to torch the capital to ashes if captured.[41] The Gallipoli campaign began on March 18, 1915, as Allied heavy artillery fired at the forts of Chanakkale and Hamidiye, and on April 25, the Allied troops, led by the British Mediterranean Expeditionary Force under the command of Sir Ian S.M. Hamilton, landed at Helles and Anzac. The Turko-German command headed by Otto Liman von Sanders dispatched reinforcements as Turkish troops fortified Constantinople.[42]

THE TURKO-GERMAN ALLIANCE

In the meantime the Turko-German alliance sought to capitalize on Muslim solidarity to counter the Allied Powers across the Middle East, as indicated by reports from the U.S. consuls to Constantinople and Washington on the conditions in the Ottoman Empire. Indeed, as early as November 19, 1912, U.S. Consul at Aleppo Jesse B. Jackson had reported that his consulate staff had brought to the attention of the foreign embassies in Constantinople that the Turkish government was using every pretext to place the entire vilayet of Aleppo under martial law. While Muslim deserters from the army were engaged in "depredations" in the province, the Turkish authorities accused the Armenians so that the latter "shall be at the mercy of the Moslems." Jackson requested the embassies to bring this matter to the attention of the Sublime Porte, so as to prevent atrocities against the Armenians "which, under the present strained conditions, would spread like wildfire, and likely engulf Christians of all denominations far and wide."[43]

By April 1915, the execution of that threat now more than ever seemed a reality. On April 8, Jackson dispatched to Morgenthau a copy of a 30-page "seditious pamphlet" printed in Arabic distributed by the Germans in Aleppo since late March. Jackson believed that the pamphlet was the work of Germans Mr. and Mrs. C.G. Koch and Oscar Flechsig and that it was printed either in Aleppo or in Constantinople.[44] Titled "A Universal Proclamation to All the People of Islam" and published by the National Society of Defense for the Seat of the Caliphate, the pamphlet stressed the duty of every Muslim to free the believers "in the Unity of God" from "the grasp of the infidels." Echoing advertisements urging Muslims to boycott Armenian businesses, it continued:

> The Muslims labored and toiled wearily and bore hardness of life that they might gain something with which to satisfy their needs, and the oppressive conquerors of the Christians subdued them and robbed them of that which was in their hands of the means of living. And they spend this booty in the West upon churches and upon the priests and places of shame and iniquity, in short, the Muslims work and the infidels eat, the Muslims are hungry and suffer, and the infidels are satiated and live in luxury. The Islamic world sinks down and goes backward, and the Christian world progresses and is exalted; and the sum of it all is, that the Muslim is enslaved and the infidel is the grand ruler. . . .
>
>   And now, O people of Islam, and O beloved brothers . . . rise up, awake, this weakness and this subjection has reached its limit, and this humiliation and this belittling has arrived at its end.[45]

Jackson warned that the Germans, in circulating this pamphlet, were attempting "to stir up a massacre here." He added: "Surely something should be done to prevent the continuation of such propagandas in the future, or one day the result sought will be obtained, and it will be disastrous."[46]

Armenian communities across the Ottoman Empire sank into hopelessness as their leaders, political activists, intellectuals, teachers, and clergy were imprisoned or murdered in increasing numbers. Turkish and Kurdish public opinion, as prepared by the *Teshkilat-i Mahsusa* (Special Organization), was mobilized against the Armenians, for long pejoratively labeled as *giavurs* (infidels) and now maliciously besmirched as collaborators with the enemy. Mounted irregular *chete* bands complemented the state bureaucracies and military at the service of the Ittihadist dictators for the implementation of the deportations and massacres.[47]

In response, Armenians in a handful of towns resorted to organized self-defense. In Van, for example, they established a committee (the Military Committee of Armenian Defense).[48] Fighting broke out in Van city on April 20 and lasted for about a month.[49] The overwhelming

Turkish forces, however, eliminated the initial Armenian resistance, while Jevdet Bey's *kesab taburi* (butcher battalions) murdered Armenian women and children. The American missionary Dr. Clarence Ussher saw the village of Shushants on Varak Mountain three miles south of Van burning, "and Varak Monastery, with its priceless store of ancient manuscripts, going up in smoke."[50] Not to jeopardize American neutrality in the conflict, Ussher recounted in his memoirs, a "foreign relations committee" established by the American mission prohibited Armenian soldiers from entering the compound "unless they were willing to leave their arms outside."[51]

The Russo-Armenian army to liberate Van was the only response from the outside. In early May, 10,000 strong Turkish troops under the command of Halil Bey pressed the Russians from Urmia and Dilman across the Salmas plain and destroyed Armenian villages on their path. Enver informed Morgenthau that word had arrived from his uncle Halil stating "all was well" in Urmia.[52] Having lost his advantages within a few weeks, however, Halil withdrew westward across the southern shores of Lake Van. Successful campaigns in the Urmia–Dilman–Tabriz region enabled the left flank of the Russian army led by General Trukhin to move toward north of Lake Van, and from there, finding that the Turkish troops and Kurdish irregulars had abandoned the area, he pressed forward to Bitlis. Trukhin and the Armenian volunteer units, led by Andranik, Hamazasp, and Dro, advanced toward Van, entering the city on May 19.[53] The Russian occupation led to the formation of an Armenian government in Van headed by Aram Manukian. The prospects of liberation from the brutalities and repression suffered under Turkish rule reinvigorated the Armenians, who turned their energies to the defense of their homeland.

Responding to news that Americans were in danger in the city of Van, Secretary Bryan sent an urgent telegram to Morgenthau:

> [The] Department [has been] informed on reliable authority of message said to have been sent by American Consul at Van that there is a general insurrection in Van [and] that Turks threaten to bombard [the] city and that [the] American colony is in danger. Please bring this to immediate attention of Turkish Government and urge necessity of taking immediate action to safeguard American lives and property.[54]

Morgenthau informed the secretary that "There is no American Consul at Van," and that he had discussed the issue with the minister of the interior, who promised to "take every possible measure to protect American citizens and institutions."[55]

The Petrograd Plan

Posed to capitalize on successes registered on the battlefield, Dr. Hakob Zavriev, assistant commissioner of the Russian government in Van, meanwhile submitted a secret document titled "The Petrograd Plan" to the Russian embassies in London and Paris. In May, he delivered a copy of the document to Boghos Nubar Pasha, who had been appointed by the catholicos at Echmiadzin to head the Armenian National Delegation to secure European support for the Armenians in the Ottoman Empire. The proposed plan outlined the conditions necessary for the protection of the Ottoman Armenians and for the envisioned postwar Armenia:

1. The creation of an autonomous Armenia within the borders of the Ottoman Empire;
2. The preservation of Turkish sovereignty, to be restricted to the conservation of the flag and the nomination by the Sultan of the governor general to be elected by the Allies. It would be unacceptable to interfere in the internal affairs of Armenia, and no Turkish military presence should be necessary in Armenia;
3. The protection of Armenia by Russia, England, and France;
4. Armenia's borders (excluding the western and southern regions, which are populated almost entirely by Moslems) will include the six vilayets, together with Cilicia and Mersin as its seaport on the Mediterranean (also excluded are the Bay of Alexandretta and Yumurtalik);
5. A plan for autonomy, along the initial lines of the Russian reform proposals introduced in the summer of 1913 in Constantinople, but modified according to the changing political conditions of the times.[56]

Only a small circle of Armenians led by Boghos Nubar in Europe and the catholicos at Echmiadzin had knowledge of this plan. Engaged in negotiations in European capitals for a postwar Armenia free from Turkish rule, a subject perhaps beyond his mandate, Boghos Nubar accepted the Petrograd Plan with great satisfaction, especially since unlike the Agreement of February 8, 1914, the new plan proposed the unification of Cilicia with the six Armenian provinces.[57] British and French representatives with whom Boghos Nubar discussed this plan expressed no more than a lukewarm support. Their first object was to ensure victory in the war, and only then could they entertain such schemes.

The Petrograd Plan assumed the presence of the Armenian inhabitants in their historic homeland, but events unfolding across the Armenian communities soon rendered such plans irrelevant. The entire region of Zeitun, considered strategically significant for wartime communication lines from Alexandretta on the Mediterranean to the interior yet again became the target of Turkish wrath. The authorities needed little incentive to accelerate the removal of the Armenians in the area, and the deportations from Zeitun, which had already begun in early April, resumed during the first half of May.[58] Consul Jackson reported that thousands had been sent to Aleppo and thence to Deir el-Zor. "The misery these people are suffering is terrible to imagine," Jackson wrote. "The Armenians themselves say that they would by far have preferred a massacre, which would have been less disastrous to them."[59]

Dr. Fred Shepard of the American hospital at Aintab submitted to Morgenthau and the secretary of state a similar report. The residents of Zeitun and neighboring villages, nearly 26,500 people, were deported, 5,000 of whom were sent to Konia, 5,500 to Aleppo, adding to the 32,000 refugees already in the Aleppo region from Hajin, Sis, Karsbazar, Hassan Beyli, and Dort Yol, and to the thousands of refugees scattered from Aleppo to the desert towns of Deir el-Zor, Rakka, and Baghdad. The report warned that if aid failed to arrive "until they get established in their new surroundings, two thirds or three fourths of them will die of starvation and disease" within the next few months.[60]

On May 5, Secretary Bryan instructed Morgenthau to use his good offices with the Turkish government to prevent further atrocities. The ambassador reported that since the declaration of Jihad, the authorities have continued to exhort Turks and other Muslims to kill as many infidels as possible.[61] In late May, he sent a lengthy report on the Armenian situation in the Ottoman Empire. He explained that since the Young Turk revolution in 1908, persecution of Armenians had intensified, as the government no longer considered them loyal. It was not surprising that the Armenians, along with other non-Muslim communities in the empire, hoped to see a change in the government. Because of the small number of Armenian revolutionaries, Morgenthau added, the government "cast suspicion on the peaceful Armenian communities elsewhere and notably in the capital." Yet, even at this stage in late May, Morgenthau failed to assess the situation accurately: "I do not believe that as yet there have been any massacres on a large scale, but the repression and the coercive measures employed have undoubtedly been responsible for some loss of life."

Morgenthau nevertheless acknowledged that the Armenian soldiers in the Ottoman army were disarmed and relegated to forced labor, while the Armenian population was ordered to surrender their weapons to the authorities "under penalty of death" even though the Muslims could retain theirs. He concluded: "Short of the actual taking of life, of which there appear as yet to have been but few cases, the period we are traversing is one of very severe repression."[62]

The Destruction of Historic Armenia

On May 29, 1915, the Ittihadist regime adopted the "Temporary Law of Deportation," authorizing the military to oversee the wholesale deportation of the Armenian population.[63] It was ironic that five days earlier, on May 24, the Allied Powers had issued a public declaration that they would "hold personally responsible [for] these crimes all members of the Ottoman government and those of their agents who are implicated in such massacres."[64] Such declarations of condemnation, however, failed to deter the Ittihadists from pursuing their policy of annihilation. On May 26, Talaat Pasha wrote to the grand vizier that the security of the Imperial Ottoman Army on the front required that "rebellious elements" among the Armenians be deported from the zones of military activities, as from the vilayets of Van, Bitlis, and Erzerum.[65] The Young Turk leaders responded to the declaration of May 24 by stressing the right to national sovereignty and self-defense. They insisted that the Entente powers were to be held responsible for their organization and support for the Armenian revolutionaries.[66] When, on June 7, Morgenthau met with the grand vizier regarding the deportations, the latter expressed extreme anger toward the Entente governments.[67] He resented such outside interference with the sovereign rights of his government concerning their Armenian subjects.[68]

Boghos Nubar Pasha, in a letter to Lieutenant Colonel G.M. Gregory, president of the United Armenian Association in London, expressed satisfaction that the Allies "seriously" considered the Armenian cause.[69] Boghos Nubar perhaps expressed the opinion of most Armenians in and outside the Ottoman Empire, but there were those who maintained a more realistic assessment of the geopolitical and military situation and the political will of the Allied Powers. In a letter dated May 28, 1915, Levon Meguerditchian wrote to Boghos Nubar: "Unfortunately, at the moment, we cannot rely upon the Allies for their help, since they have focused their attention on Gallipoli."[70] In fact, neither the belligerent nor the neutral states were prepared to intervene on behalf of the Armenians. The United States, adhering to the policy of neutrality, continued to rely on ambassadorial presentation at the Sublime Porte. In the absence of military threats, however, such protests were futile.

While the Allied governments were preoccupied with the conduct of the war, and the Wilson administration with priorities of neutrality, the Armenians across the Ottoman Empire were in danger of total annihilation, from Cilicia on northeastern shores of the Mediterranean Sea to the plain of Erzerum in the northeastern frontiers of historic Armenia, from the port town of Rodosto on the Sea of Marmara to the Lake Van basin, from the port cities of Trebizond on the Black Sea to Sivas, Kharpert, Diarbekir, and to the Mesopotamian desert.

Consul Jackson relayed to Morgenthau a report dated June 14, 1915, by the Reverend F.H. Leslie on the conditions in Urfa, a city with a population of 100,000, of whom 35,000 were Armenian.[71] Under direct orders from the Ittihadist *mutasarrif* (county governor) Ali Haidar,[72] the local authorities conducted daily searches for weapons in Armenian houses but unable to find any they nevertheless imprisoned the leading members of the community. The chief of the gendarmerie issued orders that unless Armenians surrendered all their weapons and revolutionaries, the military would remove the entire Armenian population from Urfa, as had been done in Zeitun.[73] Aware of the treatment of the refugees from Zeitun at the hands of the soldiers as their caravans passed through Urfa, the Armenians refused to surrender so easily. "Four weeks ago," Leslie noted, "they exiled fifteen men and their families sending them to the desert city of Rakka, three days journey south of here." If the government had ordered the Muslims to deliver their weapons as well, the Armenians would have gladly delivered theirs. But the government did not issue similar orders for the Muslims. As well, the report added, Urfa was never a center for revolutionary activities, and the Armenians were loyal to the government "even when they were butchered like sheep." Atrocities compelled some of the victims to resort to armed resistance, in turn provoking a "general massacre." Leslie urged Jackson to inform the U.S. embassy of this matter, so that the German and American embassies could exert sufficient influence in Constantinople to alter the attitude of the authorities toward the Christians.[74]

In a report dated June 30, U.S. Consul at Kharpert Leslie A. Davis, who frequently sent reports to Constantinople and Washington regarding the conditions in the Kharpert region, informed Morgenthau that the Turkish authorities were deporting virtually all Armenians, totaling about a million, from the six Armenian vilayets.[75]

Kharpert, one of the central regions of historic Armenia, became known as "the Slaughterhouse Province"[76] because it, particularly the town of Malatia, served as a central clearinghouse for the hundreds of thousands of Armenians deported from the province of Erzerum on the Russian front, from the southern shores of the Black Sea in the province of Trebizond, to Sivas and Kharpert, and to their ultimate destination, Deir el-zor.

CHAPTER 6

THE PRIMACY OF REALISM AND
LEGALISM

While the political atmosphere in the Ottoman Empire putrefied and the land bloodied, the policy of neutrality governed the agenda undergirding the position of the Wilson administration. Meanwhile, U.S. military preparedness became an increasingly contested issue in domestic politics. A growing number of anti-preparedness organizations, such as the American Union Against Militarism, led by the socialist Eugene V. Debs, clashed with conservative internationalist organizations—the National Security League, the Navy League, the American Defense Society, and the League to Enforce Peace—which criticized President Wilson for not doing enough to defeat Germany. Wilson repeatedly rebuffed the advocates of a strong, standing army. On May 7, 1915, when a German submarine torpedoed the *Lusitania* off the coast of Ireland, killing more than a hundred Americans among the passengers, the policy of neutrality as stressed by the administration appeared to have come under direct challenge. Public opinion in the United States grew hostile toward German propaganda and subterfuge, but despite such antipathy most Americans still preferred to avoid participation in the war.[1] "The situation not yet fully developed but need not if wisely handled involve a crisis," Wilson stated in a letter.[2]

As to the U.S. response, the president received contradictory advice from Colonel Edward M. House and Secretary of State William J. Bryan. House contended that the United States could ill afford to continue on the neutral course as adopted thus far. But more importantly, he argued, the administration's reaction to this crisis "will determine the part we will play when peace is made, and how far we may influence the settlement for the lasting good of humanity."[3] Bryan, on the other hand, ever so confident that his peace treaties, premised upon moral concordance, could prove amenable to cooperation based on just resolutions of international conflicts, emphasized the fact that the *Lusitania* carried ammunition. He pointed to the advantage gained in relying on peace: "Our people will, I think, be the more thankful that a believer in peace is in the White House at this time." He advised Wilson to formulate a response bearing in mind its impact not only on German policy but also on American public opinion. Wilson, Bryan, and Robert Lansing prepared drafts of a note protesting German aggression. The president approved the final draft expressing in harsh terms the administration's position on the *Lusitania* disaster, but Bryan thought it tantamount to an ultimatum to war. Disagreements between Wilson and Bryan, which had persisted for some time between the obstinate president and his equally stubborn secretary of state, proved insufferable in the aftermath of the *Lusitania* crisis and led to Bryan's resignation on June 9, 1915.[4]

It was expected in Great Britain that German aggression at sea and on land coupled with reports of egregious violations of humanitarian principles by Turkey would give rise to sufficient outrage in American public opinion to compel the Wilson administration to enter the war.[5] In early May, Lord Bryce sent an urgent note to Boghos Nubar recommending that the Armenians appeal to President Wilson, as the leader of a neutral state, to warn the Turkish government against the deportations and massacres of the Armenian nation.[6] In fact, under Bryan, the Department of State had continued to express concern regarding the grave situation in Turkey, although it offered no concrete measures to end the massacres. After the Allied declaration on May 24, Bryan forwarded the declaration to Ambassador Henry Morgenthau, noting that the Turkish leaders should be aware that they will be held responsible for lives and property in case of massacres.

Upon Bryan's resignation, Robert Lansing, who succeeded him as secretary of state, no longer mentioned in his communications to Morgenthau the issue of Turkish responsibility for the atrocities committed against the Armenians. Morgenthau did not know Secretary Lansing personally, but he was convinced "that he is the right man in his place and will make a fine Secretary of State." Bryan, on the other hand, Morgenthau thought, would be a political liability, "a great handicap," as he put it, for Wilson in the fast-approaching presidential campaign.[7]

But the question of whether the death of the American citizens on the *Lusitania* would bring the administration into the war remained suspended in the balance between the presidential election of 1916

and the political support Wilson had marshaled based on his promise
to keep the United States out of the war, on the one hand, and giving
in to the growing anti-German sentiments and taking the political risk
of losing that election by entering the war, on the other. Writing to
Bryan days before the secretary's resignation, the exasperated president commented: "I wish with all my heart that I saw a way to carry
out the double wish of our people, to maintain a firm front in respect
of what we demand of Germany and yet do nothing that might by any
possibility involve us in the war."[8] It must have hardly occurred to
Wilson that the settlement of the conflict and the maintenance of
peace were inextricably intertwined. As Lloyd Ambrosius has pointed
out, contrary to the more positive evaluations of Wilsonian statecraft,
"the goals and methods of his foreign policy were too frequently
unrelated to each other. He failed to coordinate political aims with
military strategy except in general terms."[9]

ROBERT LANSING

Robert Lansing formally accepted appointment as Secretary of State
on June 23, 1915.[10] Prior to his resignation, Bryan had advocated
international arbitration as the principal formula for resolution of
international conflicts and preservation of peace. Lansing disagreed.
He contended that governments jealously guard their sovereignty and
employ all means at their disposal, legal or otherwise, to protect their
territorial integrity and political legitimacy. As the war across Europe
continued, Lansing became all the more convinced that belligerent
nations could not maintain international legal standards regulating
normal affairs of states. Modern communication and transportation
systems and new military technologies, he observed, had fundamen-
tally altered military and naval strategies, thus rendering established customs and conventions of war obsolete. The European war transformed,
if not shattered, international standards, as the warring nations
abandoned old rules. Lansing underscored the mutually beneficial
bilateral commercial relations between a neutral and a belligerent, the
German policy of submarine warfare notwithstanding. Interruption of
that bilateral relationship deprived the belligerent the benefits of
commerce, but, he noted, the negative consequences for the neutral
partner should also be considered.[11]

Lansing held that a neutral nation, such as the United States, must
exercise patience toward the belligerent powers but notify them that
they would be held responsible for their injurious acts when their
conduct violates international law. Such notices, however, Lansing

maintained, would serve as little more than a "reservation of rights," as the belligerents would seldom be inclined to amend their policies simply to conform to the laws of conduct. "It is just as well to understand this at the outset and not build false hopes on so weak a foundation."

In addition, Lansing wrote, a nation enveloped with the agonizing struggle for survival would be easily annoyed when a neutral nation, failing to appreciate fully the urgency of the situation, also disregarded the legitimacy of its cause. A belligerent state therefore was likely to reject suggestions by a neutral one involving sacrifices in advantages over the enemy. Lansing maintained that in times of war, when the bellicose temperament of the warring nations and military priorities overshadow all other concerns, insistence on respect toward the rights of Americans would only exacerbate a difficult situation. "You might as well try to drive with an ox-whip a bull, which has been maddened by the bandrilleros and stands in the bullring dripping with blood." Moreover, it was necessary to explore opportunities for compromise, essential for maintenance of trade. Lansing concluded:

> None of the governments, which are depriving Americans of their rights, are going to change its policy because of diplomatic pressure however strong it may be. Unless this government is prepared to back up its threats with force it is useless to make them. No one believes that we should go as far as that, if it can be honorably avoided. There is only one way to avoid the issue, and that is to adopt a conciliatory and amicable tone. Even that may fail to give partial relief, but it is the only way to obtain any relief under present conditions.[12]

In another set of notes, titled "Cruel and Inhuman Acts of War," entered in his diary on May 25, 1915, a day after the Allied Powers issued their public condemnation of the Turkish atrocities against the Armenian people, Lansing observed that since time immemorial force has served as the ultimate vehicle for control over human affairs. Centuries of intellectual progress have failed to alter this reality in nature. "When it comes to the supreme test physical might dominates." The strong, not the just, imposed their will on others.[13] Accordingly, Lansing argued, "no nation at war, whose national safety is menaced, will permit or should be expected to permit obligations of justice, morality, humanity or honor to interfere with acts which it considers necessary for its self-preservation." An individual might accord fundamental values as liberty and justice a higher consideration; however, matters differed in case of nations, for they operated at a "lower plane," always according primacy to national existence and independence over national honor and morality. "I do not recall a case in history," Lansing added, "in which a nation surrendered its sovereignty for the sole purpose of being right." In times of war, not humanitarian ideas but the imperatives of national security and self-preservation motivate "bringing the war to a successful issue."[14]

Lansing thus justified the U.S. policy of noninterference on behalf of the Armenians on two legal grounds. First, the United States could not interfere in the domestic affairs of Turkey unless the lives and properties of U.S. citizens were threatened. The Armenians were Ottoman subjects, and the United States could only protest their treatment by the Turkish authorities and population. As noted above, however, Lansing admitted that mere protests could not "alleviate the condition." Second, related to the first was the principle of national territorial sovereignty. Lansing considered national interests and sovereignty superior to international law and international standards. The principal object of national security superseded all other, including humanitarian, considerations. Atrocities committed in the name of national security and self-preservation, therefore, could be justified on grounds of national sovereignty. Accordingly, he maintained, it was difficult to render direct support for the Armenians in Turkey as "large bodies of Armenians are in armed rebellion against the Turkish Government," and the Turkish government claimed to have employed measures necessary for self-preservation.[15]

Not all agreed with Lansing. Colonel House aptly pointed out: "Lansing exhibited one curious mind. He believes that almost any form of atrocity is permissible provided a nation's safety is involved," and that "the military authorities of the nation committing the atrocities" should determine whether such measures were necessary for national security.[16] Nevertheless, Lansing expressed the views held by the Wilson administration in general on matters of war, commerce, and peace.

Significantly, the opinion articulated by Lansing on matters of national security and the imperatives of national self-preservation, domestic stability, and noninterference, like the administration's policy of neutrality in general, directly converged with the position taken by the Young Turk regime on similar grounds as the latter sought to annihilate the Armenian people across the empire. Lansing was well informed of the nationalist views prevalent in Constantinople on foreign interference in their domestic affairs, as indicated through numerous reports relayed by Ambassador Morgenthau, the U.S. consuls, missionaries, reporters, and individual citizens. In an interview with Henry Wood, staff correspondent for the United Press, Enver Pasha insisted that the principal objective of the Turkish government was, as in the case of the European powers, to reestablish complete freedom and independence.[17]

A central concern for Lansing as pertaining to a U.S. response to the Turkish atrocities was the protection of American citizens and properties in Turkey. This concern, however, did not stem from anxieties regarding the safety of American lives nor from humanitarian considerations; instead, it arose from considerations regarding American public opinion. His diaries contained daily entries of meeting with newspapermen. Since Wilson repeatedly promised to keep the United States out of the war, Lansing feared that threats to American lives in Turkey would compel the administration to take military action, thereby creating a situation that could potentially jeopardize Wilson's reelection. It was therefore necessary for Lansing to manage public opinion and public perceptions of U.S.-Turkish relations, especially since articles on Turkish atrocities against Armenians repeatedly appeared in the American press. So long as Americans in Turkey remained unharmed, Lansing was not particularly interested in Armenian affairs.[18]

THE END OF HISTORIC ARMENIA

In Turkey, by the middle of June 1915 a conservative estimate of the death caused by the deportations and massacred stood at about 240,000. During the second half of June, Armenians were deported from across the vilayets far and wide, stretching from Trebizond on the shores of the Black Sea and Marsovan and Amasia in the northern edges of Sivas vilayet, to Erzerum near the Ottoman–Russian front, to Izmid and Brusa in the west, to Mardin in the southern edges of Diarbekir province, to Cilicia on the Mediterranean Sea.[19] Patriarch Der Yeghiayan informed Bishop Ghevond Durian, the prelate of the Armenian Church in Bulgaria:

> One after the other, populations from Samson and Gesaria all the way to and including Dikranagerd and Edessa [Urfa] have been put on the road. The Armenian populations of Trebizond, Sepasdia, Kharpert, Paghesh, Van, and Dikranagerd, from the oldest to the youngest and excepting not a single person, have been driven to the deserts of Mesopotamia—from areas south of Aleppo to Mosul and Baghdad.[20]

THE CILICIAN GATES TO DEATH

In early June, U.S. Consul Jesse Jackson reported that "a living stream of Armenians" was pouring into Aleppo from Marash, Zeitun, Adana,

Hajin, and other localities. Each group consisted of 300–500 old men, women, and children, as the young and the middle-aged had been ordered into military service. Thousands were scattered across the desert to starve or die of disease. Jackson estimated that more than 25,000 Armenian refugees were in northern Syria and that "in the interior a perfect reign of terror exists." It was clear, Jackson concluded, that the Turkish government had carefully planned the thorough extinction of the Armenians, and all appeals were ignored.[21] On June 8, Jemal Pasha wrote Catholicos Sahak of Sis, who had been exiled to Aleppo, claiming that the authorities had taken every precaution to provide for the safe journey of the Armenians. When Catholicos Sahak met with Jemal Pasha a few days later, he pleaded with the minister to consider the persecutions thus far committed sufficient to torture a people.[22]

Until mid-June, Morgenthau was not sure whether he should send a full report regarding the Armenian massacres. On June 17, he and legal counsel of the embassy, Arshak Schmavonian, discussed the advisability of sending such a report, and both agreed that "it will do no good and might hurt and therefore shall not send a full telegram."[23] After again consulting with Schmavonian, he cabled Washington about the massacres. Morgenthau reported on the growing hostility toward the Armenians and their leaders arrested and "hanged on ostensible charge of separatist conspiracy." His efforts to assist the Armenians may in some cases have mitigated the hardships but failed to convince the authorities to stop the bloodshed, which the latter justified on grounds of security.[24]

On June 19, Enver presented to Morgenthau the most detailed rationale for the massacres to date. The minister of war stated that three months ago he had warned the Armenian patriarch that if Armenians engaged in revolutionary activities or aided the Russian war aims, the government would not be able to prevent hostilities toward them. Enver argued that the government could not tolerate internal troubles while struggling to defend the Dardanelles and that it would employ all means necessary to control the situation. Enver maintained that while he was not opposed to the Armenian people and held "the greatest admiration for their industry etc., . . . they would have to be destroyed" because of their alliance with the enemies, as in Van. Russia, France, Britain, and the United States were "not doing them any kindness by encouraging them because he remembers that his party rec[ieve]d all its moral encouragement from the outside world when they attacked Abdul Hamid, and he said that the Armenians would give up all efforts to oppose present

Gov[ernmen]t, if they were not encouraged by outside countries. . . ." Finally, Enver promised that "there would be no more massacres of Armenians."[25]

On July 12, the *New York Times* reported: "Throughout the vilayets of Erzerum, Van, Bitlis, Diarbekir, Harput, Sivas, and Adana, the Armenians have been pitilessly evicted by tens of thousands and driven off to die in the desert near Konia or to Upper Mesopotamia. . . . It is safe to say that unless Turkey is beaten to its knees very speedily there will soon be no more Christians in the Ottoman Empire."[26] The Armenian population was disarmed of what little weapons they possessed, its leadership was decimated, its officials removed from government posts, and its youth and soldiers slaughtered to preclude any resistance against the genocidal scheme.

MILITARY CLASHES

Military engagement by an external power could have provided the desperately needed leverage to save some of the surviving Armenians. Thus far in the war, Russia alone had direct military involvement with the Armenian refugees on Ottoman territory, but abrupt shifts in fortunes on the battlefield led to vacillations in maneuvers of strategy and oscillations in movement of troops. Conditions on the battlefield would afford the Armenians neither protection nor liberation. The Russian military command, preoccupied with operations on the Russo-German front, did not intend to confine men and hardware in the Van–Bitlis–Erzerum region for long. In the month of June, Turkish forces regained military advantages against the Russians. Early in the month, they had advanced to Olti, 55 miles west of the city of Kars, and defeated the Russian troops stationed near the city. In the meantime, Russian troops marched toward Bitlis, where Turkish forces had concentrated, and the Russo-Turkish struggle in the region of Lake Van continued during the month of July.[27]

The region of Sasun in Bitlis province was especially troubling for the Turkish military. Perhaps somewhat too simplistically, the historian Arnold Toynbee characterized Sasun as "a federation of about forty mountain villages," living independently of the authorities at Bitlis or Diarbekir; they "held their own against the equally independent Kurdish tribes that ringed them round."[28] The ensuing military clashes seemed inevitable, especially given the hostile sentiments of the leading figures toward the Armenians in Bitlis: the *vali* (governor of province) Mustafa Abdul Halik Bey, brother-in-law of Talaat Pasha; General Halil Bey, uncle of Enver Pasha; Servet Bey, the *mutasarrif* (county governor) of Mush; Turhan Bey, commissioner of police; Colonel Yusuf Zia; and Jevdet Bey, the vali of Van, who fled to Bitlis during the Russian occupation of Van.[29]

Upon receiving orders to surrender their arms, the Armenians in Sasun, led by Haji Hagop Godoyan (Hakop Kotoyan), Misak Bdeian (Pteyan), Goriun (Koriun), Ruben Ter Minasian, and Vahan Papazian (Goms), while proposing alternative responses to the government, ultimately refused to comply with the orders.[30] While the Armenian defense at Sasun lasted until early August, longer than the Ottoman army expected, their insufficient supply of weapons and diminishing manpower were no match to the Turkish army, and nearly all of the Armenians were killed.[31] Arnold Toynbee aptly summarized the genocidal massacres in Bitlis, Mush, and Sasun:

> The extermination of the Armenians in these three places was an act of revenge for the successful resistance of the Armenians at Van and the advance of the Russian forces to their relief. There was no pretense here of deportation, and the Armenians were destroyed, without regard for appearances, by outright massacre, accompanied in many cases by torture.[32]

During the first week of July, 20,000 Turkish troops attacked Mush, a town that had been under siege for months since the Russian engagements in the Urmia–Dilman region in March–April and more recently in Tutak, Malazkert, and Bulanik (Kop) north of Lake Van. General Oganovski ordered the Russian troops under the command of General Charpentier to advance from Adiljevaz to Akhlat on the northwestern shores of Lake Van, while General Trukhin moved from south of the lake toward Tatvan. As the Turkish soldiers scrambled to defend themselves, the entire region of Mush seemed open for a Russian advance.[33] But the struggle in the region continued until August. The Russians, having changed their strategy, withdrew from the area and did not return until March 1916.[34] The Turkish army pressed toward Van, forcing the American and other foreign missionaries, beginning in early August, to depart from Van with the Russians. Thousands of Armenians left their houses and fields, stores and schools, and followed the Russian army to the border.

In the Middle East, the Allies moved northward from Egypt across Mesopotamia along the Tigris and the Euphrates rivers. They expected that the Mesopotamian campaign, in sharp contrast to their experiences at Gallipoli thus far, would prove more successful. Their forces captured Amara on June 3 and Nasiriyeh a few weeks later. In early July the Turkish army attacked Aden, but British forces easily pressed them to Lahej.[35] Turkish efforts to attack the British from the rear at Amara in September failed at the cost of 6,650 men. The British troops under General Townshend advanced to Kut and prepared to take Baghdad. The Turkish troops, despite greater human losses, retaliated and forced the British to withdraw. No sooner had the demoralized soldiers regained strength at Kut than 30,000 Turkish forces under the command of Field Marshal von der Goltz attacked the city.[36]

The operations at the Gallipoli, which commenced in March 1915, showed no signs of relief. In August, the Allies, determined to end the deadlock at the Dardanelles, landed additional forces at Sulva Bay and at Karachali north of the Gulf of Saros. By early October 1915, however, the campaign had cost more than 96,000 men on the British side, without registering significant advances. On November 22, Field Marshal Lord Horatio Herbert Kitchener recommended withdrawal, and the Allied troops began evacuation from Anzac and Sulva, finally abandoning the Gallipoli Peninsula on January 9, 1916.[37]

An Allied victory at the Straits, Morgenthau wrote, would have brought the government of the Young Turks to "a bloody end." For immediately after the campaign began, placards appeared in the streets denouncing the Ittihadist leadership as responsible for the problems in the empire.[38] The Allied failure, however, mollified public criticism of the Turko-German alliance, strengthened the position of the pro-German faction led by Enver in the CUP, and enhanced the legitimacy of the Young Turk regime.[39] The catastrophic consequences of the Turkish victory for the entire Armenian people had become apparent, as Ambassador Morgenthau commented in his *Story*.[40] Lewis Einstein, appointed by Secretary Bryan as a special agent at the embassy in Constantinople at the time, later noted:

> As soon as the Turks felt confident that the Dardanelles could not be forced, they saw before them an unexpected opportunity to destroy the Armenians, who were the real victims of the naval failure. No other government except the Turkish, while at war against some of the most powerful nations in the world, would have dared to carry out the deliberate extermination of an important though almost helpless minority.[41]

Whether the United States would enter the war and whether such a policy would benefit the Americans in the Ottoman Empire remained a hotly contested subject. During a meeting with American missionary physician Dr. Herbert Atkinson in Kharpert, local Turks believed that even if all of the American missionaries were killed, the United States would not enter the war.[42] Expectedly, as Morgenthau observed, the Ittihadist leaders felt invincible, as they had mobilized an army of more than one million men and forced Britain and France to employ thousands of troops in vain to secure the Dardanelles. The Young Turks claimed with much pride that they had demonstrated the vulnerability of the English naval power, while the Russians had failed to join their allies in carrying out their threat to punish the rulers of Constantinople.[43] The Turko-German alliance had withstood the Allied military offensive.

CHAPTER 7

AMBASSADOR MORGENTHAU'S
POLICY RECOMMENDATIONS

Ambassador Henry Morgenthau estimated that between April and October 1915 more than a million Armenians were deported from their homeland to the Syrian desert, the primary destination for the refugees.[1] Aleppo served as the clearinghouse for the Armenian refugees from Anatolia on their way to the desert, while those closer to the Russian front escaped to Alexandropol (Gumri), Echmiadzin, and Erevan.[2] The more fortunate were spared from Deir el-Zor and either remained in Aleppo or were moved farther south.[3] U.S. Consul Jesse Jackson at Aleppo estimated that by August, approximately 350,000 refugees had converged at Deir el-Zor,[4] and more than 500,000 Armenians had been killed.[5] A large number of the survivors were pressed farther south to Hama, Homs, Damascus, and as far away as Amman. Jackson estimated that provision for their "barest existence" would require about $150,000 a month, or a dollar a day per capita.

On the morning of July 10, 1915, Morgenthau prepared a telegram to the Department of State, indicating for the first time that the deportations involved more than mere transfer of Armenians from their homes to the interior:

> Reports from widely scattered districts indicate systematic attempt to uproot peaceful Armenian populations and through arbitrary arrests, terrible tortures, wholesale expulsions and deportations from one end of the Empire to the other accompanied by frequent instances of rape, pillage, and murder, turning into massacre, to bring destruction and destitution on them. These massacres are not in response to popular or

fanatical demand but are purely arbitrary and directed from Constantinople in the name of military necessity, often in districts where no military operations are likely to take place.[6]

The ambassador submitted another report dated July 16, 1915:

> Protests as well as threats are unavailing and probably incite the Ottoman government to more drastic measures as they are determined to disclaim responsibility for their absolute disregard of capitulations and I believe nothing short of actual force which obviously the United States are not in a position to exert would adequately meet the situation. Suggest you inform belligerent nations and mission boards of this.[7]

Secretary of State Robert Lansing responded that the Department of State approved Morgenthau's efforts and procedure in attempting to end the Armenian persecution and to enlist the support of the German and Austrian ambassadors to that effect. "The Department can offer no additional suggestions relative to this most difficult situation other than that you continue to act as in the past."[8]

In late July, Morgenthau and Arshak Schmavonian, the legal counsel at the U.S. embassy, called on Minister of the Interior Mehmed Talaat to urge him to send a telegram to Marsovan to secure the safety of Americans at Anatolia College and better treatment for the Armenians. Talaat promised to do so and inquired whether Morgenthau would like to take all the Americans out of Turkey. Morgenthau concurred; in fact, he added, he would also "organize a movement" to transport all Armenians to California by way of the newly opened Panama Canal. Talaat suggested that the ambassador discuss this issue with Minister of War Ismail Enver.[9]

On August 5, Morgenthau received word that Talaat wished to see him regarding Armenian matters but that he should come without Schmavonian.[10] During his visit with Talaat a few days later, the minister of the interior told Morgenthau that "he greatly preferred" that the ambassador "always come alone" to discuss any Armenian matters. Talaat presented his justification for the Young Turk policy toward the Armenians thus: (1) the Armenians had "enriched themselves at the expense of the Turks"; (2) they sought to dominate the Turks and to create an independent state; and (3) they "openly encouraged their enemies." The Young Turks therefore, Talaat stated, had arrived at the "irrevocable decision to make them powerless" before the conclusion of the war. Morgenthau for his part attempted to explain the negative consequences of the deportations for the national economy and commerce. "There was no use," the minister of the interior replied. The authorities had "already disposed" of 75 percent of the Armenians, leaving none in Bitlis, Van, and Erzerum, and the Young Turk leadership was determined "to finish it." The government in Constantinople, Talaat noted, did not care about the economic consequences of the deportations. The authorities would take care of the Armenians at Deir el-Zor and elsewhere, but "they did not want them in Anatolia." Morgenthau wrote in his diary: "I told him three times that they were making a serious mistake and would regret it. He [Talaat] said: 'We know we have made mistakes, but we never regret.' "[11] The military setbacks of the Turkish troops at Sarikamish, Van, and other places on the Russian front "were all due to the Armenian volunteers and the Russian troops," Talaat insisted.[12]

The situation in the capital seemed particularly precarious as persistent rumors of organized and unorganized violence against the Ittihadist regime threatened the leadership of Talaat and Enver. They even pursued the possibility of some sort of peace to exit the path of total destruction. In April 1915, Grand Vizier Said Halim had requested a formal statement by Berlin recognizing the abolition of the Capitulations,[13] and in late July negotiations had commenced between the Turkish and German governments with regard to the postwar peace. The Sublime Porte had dispatched representatives to Berlin to survey German intentions for their Turkish allies after the war. The envoys returned bearing a terse response: the German high command found it "inopportune" to dwell upon such questions at this juncture in the war. The Turks, Morgenthau commented in his diary, expected to be certain of German postwar plans toward their government and to secure explicit guarantees for their "absolute independence."[14] A related issue was that the Young Turks suspected the former Ottoman ambassador at Berlin, General Mahmud Muhtar Pasha, of collusion with opponents of their regime, and they replaced him by General Ibrahim Hakki Pasha, a loyal Ittihadist.[15] As the American Ambassador to Berlin, James Gerard, observed a few months later, the German government kept Mahmud Muhtar "in stock in case the Young Turks go out of power—also possibly to stir up trouble in Egypt as his wife is a daughter of one of the Khedives."[16] The leaders of the Ottoman Empire appeared desperate to sue for peace.

The empire seemed at peace neither with the outside world nor with itself. Serious tensions had developed within the Young Turk cabinet. Morgenthau observed that relations between Talaat and Enver had grown strained. Enver had confided to the German and Austrian ambassadors that Talaat was responsible for the extreme measures taken against the Armenians and that he had opposed them. Further, it was Talaat who had placed his own "henchmen" in positions of power in the provinces, with orders to ignore all other instructions except his own. The local authorities therefore, Enver had stated, paid no attention to orders from other departments. Eventually, as the provincial governments became accustomed to ignoring orders from the capital, they also learned to disregard instructions even from the interior ministry. Such unintended decentralization in the chain of command Enver thought injurious to the "best interests" of the central government.[17]

The Ittihadist regime would prefer to end the war at the earliest opportunity to revive the nation's economy. According to Morgenthau, the Turkish leaders eventually realized the deleterious consequences of their policies for the economy. Ineptitude and malice had devastated production and depleted profit as they uprooted the "earning power" of their nation. "They have drawn from the fields the male population and thereby destroyed their agricultural communities. They have annihilated or displaced at least two thirds of the Armenian population and thereby deprived themselves of a very intelligent . . . and useful race."[18]

At this juncture, on August 11, 1915, Morgenthau identified three options for a U.S. response to the situation in the Ottoman Empire:

1. That the United States Government on behalf of humanity urgently request the Turkish Government to cease at once the present campaign and to permit the survivors to return to their homes if not in the war zones, or else to receive proper treatment.
2. If our present relations permit that an official appeal be made to the Emperor of Germany to insist on Turkey, his ally, stopping this annihilation of a Christian race.
3. That a vigorous official demand be made without delay for the granting of every facility to Americans and others to visit and render pecuniary and other assistance they may desire to Armenians already affected by Government deportations.[19]

Morgenthau recommended the third option, without elaborating upon the first two. The first option would necessitate heavy involvement in Turkey. The United States would be faced with two equally undesirable options: either to intervene with direct military force and shoulder the responsibility of saving the Armenians, or not to intervene and lose international prestige and credibility. Instead, Wilson preferred to act as the peacemaker among the European powers.

Nor was the second option practicable. Germany was not inclined to antagonize its ally to prevent the massacres. On several occasions, Morgenthau had discussed the issue of Armenian massacres with German Ambassador Hans von Wangenheim.[20] The latter was concerned about public opinion in Great Britain and the United States. He approvingly reiterated Talaat's view that the task had to be completed prior to the conclusion of the war. If the United States was so humanitarianly inclined, however, the German ambassador would support removal of the Armenians to the United States. Morgenthau now vacillated. He replied that the number of ships required to transport the Armenians could not be organized at present time nor would there be sufficient coal for the purpose. The United States could not undertake such a plan without assurances that the Armenians could leave. Morgenthau remained convinced that Wangenheim "was the one man, and his government was the one government, that could have stopped these crimes," but, as the German ambassador had mentioned, the government in Berlin pursued single-mindedly one objective: "*to win this war.*"[21] Morgenthau later told Wangenheim that public opinion in the United States "was much aroused and that it was ridiculous for the Turks and the Germans to think that the knowledge of the atrocities committed against the Armenians could be suppressed; that crimes like these that cry to heaven will certainly be heard of in America."[22]

There was no reason to believe that the German kaiser would show greater interest than his ambassador in the safety of Armenians in Turkey. During the massacres of the 1890s, Kaiser Wilhelm II had visited Constantinople and decorated Abdul Hamid II, the "bloody tyrant's breast, and kissed him on both cheeks."[23] The kaiser condemned the atrocities committed under the sultan's rule but would not jeopardize German national interests and influence in Turkey for humanitarian principles.[24]

With respect to the third option, Morgenthau contended that under the circumstances assisting the Armenians would be the "most acceptable" course of action, and that immediate relief action would also register the administration's "protesting attitude."[25] The Ittihadist government, however, viewed the American missionaries and their institutions as one of the key elements—in addition to European and Russian influences—contributing to Armenian cultural Westernization and nationalism.[26] While the Ittihadists deemed it necessary to maintain good relations with the United States, they also emphasized that such relations were predicated upon the assumption of respect for Turkish sovereignty. This option, however, was most acceptable to the U.S. government, as it reflected the Wilson administration's preference for neutrality and noninterference. Equally importantly, Morgenthau's recommendation indicated a willingness on the part of the U.S. government to accept a *fait accompli*, the fact that nothing would be done to prevent the Armenian massacres, and that the primary focus of U.S. policy would be limited to the provision of financial and other assistance for the survivors.[27] Moreover, U.S. policymakers and companies hoped that U.S.-Turkish relations would develop greater commercial activities. Within days after Morgenthau dispatched his recommendations, Enver indicated to Morgenthau his willingness to revive the Chester project as part of their efforts to strengthen Turkey's independence from foreign interference.[28]

THE FORMATION OF U.S. RELIEF

The influence of the American missionaries in the United States had led to the establishment of the Dodge Relief Committee (named after Cleveland H. Dodge, vice president of the Phelps Dodge Corporation) early in 1915. In July 1915, an American Armenian Relief Fund had begun collection of aid money for the refugees in Turkey.[29] Based on the recommendation received from Morgenthau, a relief network began to take shape in the United States. James L. Barton, former president of Euphrates College at Kharpert and now secretary of the American Board for Foreign Missions, was the principal organizer of the effort. In late August 1915, he invited representatives of the Presbyterian Board and college boards with interests in the Middle East to a conference at Cleveland Dodge's office to examine the condition in Turkey. As the group met, Barton wrote, it became apparent that while "no one had very definite information as to what was taking place in Turkey," nevertheless "all had grave apprehensions." During the meeting, a cable was received from Morgenthau, through the Department of State, reporting the deportations and massacres of Armenians and suggesting immediate relief.[30]

Barton and Dodge called a second conference in the latter's office to decide on concrete steps. On September 16, representatives of several philanthropic, missionary, and educational interests in the Middle East responded favorably. Although not familiar with the details of the situation in Turkey, they supported the idea of founding an organization to raise relief funds, the Armenian Relief Committee, with an office at 70 Fifth Avenue, which was Dutton's office as secretary and treasurer of the Constantinople Women's College. Barton was elected chairman, and Charles Crane treasurer. They set $100,000 as the target amount to be raised and granted the officers authority to that effect, the amount to be forwarded to Morgenthau in payments of $25,000. The members subscribed some $50,000 at this first meeting, while Dodge pledged to pay for the office and clerical expenses.[31]

The committee decided to send Barton to the Department of State in Washington to collect the necessary data on the events in Turkey. Accordingly, less than a week after the above meeting, Barton traveled to Washington on September 21 with permission to examine all the despatches received from Morgenthau and the U.S. consuls during the past year. "Permission was unhesitatingly granted and I was given a guide to the office of the Assistant Secretary, Mr. [Alvey] Adee, who was in charge of all of the files of the Department." Back in New York, Barton set in motion the process of mobilizing public support for relief funds. He prepared the press despatches and reports about the situation in Turkey.[32] In November, the Armenian Relief Committee joined the Syrian–Palestine Relief Fund and the Persian War Relief Fund under the name of the American Committee for Armenian and Syrian Relief (ACASR).[33]

Closely related to the humanitarian endeavor was the protection of American economic interests negatively affected by the deportation of the Armenians. In a *note verbale*, the U.S. embassy at Constantinople brought to the attention of the Ottoman foreign ministry the concerns of the Singer Sewing Machine Company regarding its operations in Asia Minor in the aftermath of the deportations of the Armenians. In towns where the agents of the company were Armenians, the deportations had led to the closing of the shops and the keys transferred to the local authorities. Accordingly, the embassy maintained, the local authorities had "assumed all responsibility for the protection of the company interests" and that therefore positive steps were necessary to "safeguard the property of the company which has thus been forcibly abandoned by its employees and agents." The note asserted that the embassy reserved to itself all rights to submit future claims for any losses sustained by the Singer Company. Irked by this curt affront, the Ottoman foreign ministry replied that the interior ministry had sent instructions to the provincial governments to secure "the safeguarding of the merchandise" in the agencies of the company, "which were entrusted to Armenians who have been sent to other localities." The foreign ministry, however, felt obliged to note that the Ottoman authorities could "not assume any responsibility for losses" which the Singer Company suffered "from circumstances independent of their will." Adee informed the Singer Company of the response received from the Ottoman government. The Department of State notified Morgenthau that it approved his action in this matter.[34]

In Adana, during the deportations the authorities confiscated the firm of Avedissian and Kechichian, which represented the interests of a number of American exporting companies such as the International Harvester Company (Chicago), the Ohio Cultivator Company (Bellevue, Ohio), Rumsey and Company, and the Goulds Manufacturing Company (both of Seneca Falls, New York) in the region. Consul Edward Nathan at Mersin wrote to the Department of State on November 2, 1915, to notify the above companies of the situation "with a view to recovering any possible outstanding indebtedness." Accordingly, the Department of State informed the companies, noting that, as the firm of Avedissian and Kechichian had been dissolved, "the goods remaining in their store have been taken possession of by the authorities and the creditors of the firm." This was brought to the attention of the companies, the letter added, "so that you may be enabled to take such steps as you deem necessary and advisable to protect your interests, if any there are."[35]

Three months later, Nathan reported that he had received the necessary documents from the Goulds Manufacturing Company for its claims against the firm of Avedissian and Kechichian, and that he had submitted the case to the Deutche Orientbank at Mersin for collection. The said bank, the consul reasoned, enjoyed a favorable status and its competent lawyers would undoubtedly secure the collection out of the assets of the dissolved firm. The fee for their legal services was set at only 5 percent on all collections, and, the consul noted, "I understand that the assets are sufficient to cover the claims."[36] The management of the Goulds Manufacturing disagreed. R.S. Allen, head of its export department, had communicated to the Imperial Ottoman Bank for securing the claims against the Avedissian and Kechichian firm. At the same time, Allen informed Consul Nathan that since the Ottoman Bank held the drafts covering the company's account, the collection of its assets be made through that bank. The consul was advised to inquire as to the feasibility of leaving the account with the Ottoman Bank or with the Deutsche Orientbank.[37]

Finally, Consul Nathan in turn informed the Department of State that the claims against the firm of Avedissian and Kechichian had been submitted by three American companies—Goulds Manufacturing, Ohio Cultivator, and International Harvester. As the latter alone claimed $15,000, the consul stated, the firm was not likely to pay since its assets could not now total more than $5,000 or $6,000, of which $3,000 would be required to pay a claim of the Deutsche Orientbank where the assets had been deposited. Efforts would be made, however, "to collect as much of these claims as is possible."[38]

THE ITTIHADISTS' RESPONSE TO RELIEF AID

The founding of relief organizations in the United States to assist refugees in the Ottoman Empire failed to impress upon the rulers in Constantinople the desirability, if not the necessity, of termination of the atrocities against the Armenians. Having nearly completed by the end of 1915 the task they had set up for themselves to accomplish before the conclusion of the war, combined with their military successes at the Dardanelles and Mesopotamia, which they considered a face-saving redemption for their earlier failures at Sarikamish and Egypt, the Ittihadists had grown too confident to entertain such proposals as distribution of foreign relief aid directly to their victims. Paradoxically, their arrogance also constituted an integral part of their fears, permeating their entire machinery of despotism and destruction, of an internal revolt against their government.

Minister of War Enver Pasha informed Morgenthau that "they had made up their mind positively that no relief should be given" to the Armenians except through the central government. Insisting that foreign humanitarian aid strengthened Armenian resolve to resist, the regime adamantly opposed such intervention in its internal affairs. Attempting to reason with the minister of war, Morgenthau pointed out that while the current measures against the Armenians might be useful for military purposes, such policies were destroying the economy of the country. Enver replied that "they have nothing else in their mind just now but to win the war; that economic conditions are unimportant; if they win the war, everything will be all right; while if they lose, everything will be wrong anyhow." Enver admitted that he was fully aware of the fact that the orders emanating from Constantinople had resulted in "a great deal of harm." The minister of war would not, however, blame the authorities of lower rank but was prepared to accept "full responsibility himself as Cons[tantino]ple had ordered the deportation and felt that they were fully justified owing to the inimical condition of the Armenians." Enver pointed out that "it only took twenty to make a revolution and that the Armenians at the wrong time had displayed their friendship for the Russians and their enmity to the Turks." Morgenthau, for the first time, intimated to Enver at this meeting that perhaps he would soon be recalled to the United States. Enver, though not surprised, appeared dissatisfied. The ambassador's departure, Enver said, would benefit no one in Constantinople, as Turkish confidence engendered toward the American ambassador for the past years would be difficult to imitate

by a new ambassador. Changing the subject, Enver reminded
Morgenthau that the Ittihadist leadership welcomed foreign investments in Turkey as the economy of the nation was pressed for
improvements. At the same time, however, in an effort to Turkify the
nation's economy and enterprises, the government instituted new
laws requiring all domestic and foreign operations in Turkey to keep
their records in Turkish and to employ only Ottoman subjects
and preferably Muslims. Representatives of the American business
interests opposed such regulations and hoped that Morgenthau could
convince the authorities to repeal them.[39]

Despite their initial negative reaction to American involvement in
distribution of relief aid to the Armenians, the Ittihadist leaders eventually granted permission before the year 1915 had ended. By the end
of 1915, William W. Peet, treasurer of the Bible House, had received
$100,000 from the United States for distribution in the Ottoman
Empire. Peet transferred on weekly basis 500 Turkish pounds to each
Aleppo and Konia and similar amounts to other areas in the empire.
At Konia, the representative of the Bible House, William S. Dodd,
distributed the relief funds in the region. Commenting on Peet's contribution to the distribution of relief funds to the Armenians in the
empire, Patriarch Zaven Der Yeghiayan wrote that Peet, "a venerable
American" and as the Treasurer of the Bible House, "had been very
helpful during the 1895–96 massacres. During this war, too, he was
extremely helpful to us . . . [as] he brought his precious contribution
to the work of alleviating the condition of the unfortunate Armenian
refugees and earned our Nation's gratitude."[40]

On November 12, meeting with the new Ottoman Minister of
Foreign Affairs Halil Bey at the U.S. embassy, Morgenthau pointed to
the gravity of the "serious mistakes" by the Turkish government with
regard to the Armenian Question; while "the harm was already
done," he noted, the situation should nevertheless be remedied. The
ambassador did not wish to interfere in the internal affairs of Turkey
nor did he mean to criticize its leaders. As a friend, Morgenthau said,
he hoped "to see such a serious error corrected."[41] Halil Bey agreed:
the "tragic results" of the "excesses and violations" were deplorable.
He wished, however, to present the government's point of view.
According to the minister, immediately after the declaration of war,
Arshak Vramian, a leading member of the Dashnaktsutiun and a
deputy from Van, had presented to the *vali* (governor) of Van a
memorandum concerning local administration. The document, Halil
said, suggested that the Dashnaktsutiun intended to commence
"an independent action." At first, Halil Bey recounted, the Committee

of Union and Progress (CUP) sought "cordial harmony with the Armenians and believed that they had succeeded in doing that until Nubar Pasha started the agitation in the European Cabinets for the so-called reform in the Eastern provinces. From the action of the Armenian committees, backed by the Armenian press, even by newspapers published in Constantinople, it was clear that the Armenians had national ambitions which, at least in the Government's opinion, were not compatible with Ottoman interests." As the Speaker of the Chamber of Deputies at the time, Halil Bey had discussed the memorandum with Deputy Vartkes Serengulian and had warned that if the Armenians desired independence, "they should await a propitious moment." In times of war, however, if the Armenians acted against Ottoman troops, then the military would in self-defense "deal with those in the war zone" but also "dispose of all Armenians who happened to be on the rear of the army" by sending them "to a safe distance to the south." Halil stated that he offered this as an explanation of the "extenuating circumstances of the severe measures taken against the Armenians and not as a justification." After Halil left the embassy, Morgenthau commented that this explanation "was the pleading of a clever lawyer who was defending a bad case."[42]

Predictably, the Ottoman economy began to experience acute inflationary pressures as prices doubled. When Morgenthau met with Assistant Minister of Foreign Affairs Rashid Hikmet, the topic of their conversation quickly centered on the economy. The ambassador emphasized "the evil results of Turkish chauvinism" and the "absolute" necessity of bringing foreign experts to the empire in order to acquire the requisite technological know-how "to manufacture their own goods." Morgenthau pointed to the progress achieved by Japan as it initially pursued such a policy and then learned how to "do it themselves." He noted in his diary: "I told him about locomotives that had been sent there and taken apart and copied." Less optimistic than the American ambassador, Hikmet maintained that lack of sufficient resources such as gold and iron in the Ottoman Empire would impede industrial development and therefore Turkey could not "become a large manufacturing country." Morgenthau mentioned the vast oil fields that could replace coal as a principal source of energy for economic modernization. Hikmet, of course, was not only familiar with the oil fields pointed out by Morgenthau and with their uses, but also, as the ambassador commented in his diary, "mentioned a great many more oil fields than I heard of." Hikmet hoped that his government would send some of their men to the United States for education and training. Finally, Hikmet revealed the true purpose of his visit, a message from Halil Bey. The message, originally sent by Minister of the Marines Ahmed Jemal to Enver, who in turn relayed it to Halil, stated that Morgenthau must "stop" the U.S. consuls in Syria "from busying themselves about Armenian affairs." Jemal Pasha argued, as it had become so familiar to Morgenthau by now, that the Armenians, whose "great organization" and "ramifications reached all over the country," had demonstrated their disloyalty to the empire while the nation fought a war, and therefore "had made a great mistake." Since "the Turks could not stop to distinguish between the guilty and the innocent," they "had to punish them all." Having conveyed the message, Hikmet returned to the subject of economic development. The Ottoman economy, he held, would remain essentially agricultural; they had no choice but to export "large quantities" of their goods to outside markets and to import needed products. They could thus generate sufficient revenues for the government. Further discussions on economic and Armenian matters with Ottoman and foreign officials convinced Morgenthau before he left Constantinople that "it is impossible to do business with the Turks."[43] Policymakers in Washington thought otherwise.

AT THE WHITE HOUSE GATES

In July 1915, Catholicos Gevorg V at Echmiadzin sent a telegram to President Wilson informing that reports from Cilicia had established that the atrocities and massacres committed against the Armenian people resulted from orders of the Turkish government. "Those horrors appeal to the seat of God," the catholicos wrote, "and again constrain me to call on the generous sentiments of Your Excellency and the great American nation and beg in the name of humanity and our holy Christian faith for mighty intervention of the United States and high protection of your Excellency in order to put an end to said atrocities and massacres."[44] In a similar vein, at the request of Lord Bryce and intended for President Wilson, U.S. Ambassador at London Walter Hines Page relayed to the secretary of state a translated and abridged copy of a letter, dated July 13, 1915, by Patriarch Zaven Der Yeghiayan on the situation in Turkey. In writing a series of letters to the Armenian prelate in Bulgaria on the Turkish atrocities, the patriarch had sought to move public opinion in Western societies. The letter, as transmitted to the Department of State, related the extent of suffering inflicted on the Armenians by the Young Turk regime as a result of the deportations and killings. The ultimate object of the Turkish leadership was to render "Armenia without the

Armenians," he wrote. The letter ended with a somber note: if the Armenians in foreign lands failed to stir "the pity of neutral countries," soon only a few Armenians would remain. "The annihilation of our people will thus become inevitable."[45] A facsimile of the letter was submitted by the Armenian bishop of Cairo to U.S. Consul General Olney Arnold, who in turn sent it to Secretary Lansing. Bishop Torkom Kushakian explained that a translation of the patriarchal letter was sent to Arnold to "invoke" the "kind intervention" of the U.S. government "on the score of humanity and justice, to put an end to this horrible state of things."[46]

The Armenian communities in the United States petitioned the Wilson administration and Congress to pay greater attention to the atrocities committed against their compatriots and families in their homeland. Among the leading figures engaged in these efforts was Vahan Cardashian, representative of the Turkish pavilion at the international exposition at San Francisco in the summer of 1915, and who later, along with such activists as Mihran Sevasly, organized the Armenian National Defense Union of America in Boston. In a letter to Secretary Lansing, Cardashian stated that the Young Turk regime had resorted to massacre and destruction of the Armenian people in the empire, a policy inaugurated by the Hamidian regime. As Russia and Turkey were consumed by their clashes across historic Armenia, the two million Armenian inhabitants of the land had since the start of the war been subjected to wholesale deportations and massacres. Cardashian wrote: "I know it to be the fixed policy of the Turk to dispose of the Armenian question by the extermination of the Armenian. Will Civilization tolerate the perpetration of crime so ghastly and so sweeping as the obliteration of a whole race?" Asserting that President Wilson "will sympathize" with his sentiments, Cardashian recommended that the U.S. government consider the matter with Berlin, as policies emerging from Constantinople were being shaped under direct German control. Rather than rely on representation by the U.S. ambassador at the Sublime Porte, therefore, Cardashian concluded, "if the President would find it proper and opportune to convey a personal message to the Emperor on the subject, a larger measure of success can be reasonably expected in the right direction."[47]

Lansing for his part relayed this letter to the German ambassador at Washington, Count J.H. von Bernstorff. More than a month later, Bernstorff replied with an enclosed report from the German consul at Trebizond detailing the situation in that city and the failed promises by the vali for the safety and protection of the Armenians. If German influence would alleviate the condition, policymakers at the Department of

State reasoned, then greater effort should be made by the German government. Morgenthau reported in August that even the German government had protested the Turkish measures against the Armenians but such protests had failed to produce the desired effect, although the German government had instructed its embassy at Constantinople "to demand from the Sublime Porte that the horrible deportations cease and all possible reparation be promptly made." Such an effort, Morgenthau noted, joined by others might ease the crisis.[48] International principles of national sovereignty, however, as Lansing had emphasized, would not permit direct engagement in matters of internal policy decisions in Turkey or in Germany. When in early November Congressman Ira Copley of Illinois inquired whether the Department of State had urged the German government to exercise its leverage over the Young Turks "to save the remnants of the Armenian people," Lansing admitted that the department had not.[49]

Similarly, on September 23, Congressman Richard Austin of Tennessee relayed to the Department of State a letter from the executive committee of the Armenian National Defense Union of America, describing the pitiful condition in the Ottoman Empire and the annihilation of the Armenian people. Regarding their expectation of the congressman and of the Wilson administration, the letter with a mixed sense of confidence, trepidation, naiveté, and flattery stated:

> The United States is the only great neutral power that can bring to bear the weight of its influence to restrain the murderous hands of those who have decreed the extinction of a whole people from the land of their sires. We think it is in harmony with the noble traditions of the Land of the Free to raise its voice at this juncture in such a potent way as to render its action effective. We venture to hope and we are confident that you will do the needful in your sphere of influence and strengthen the hands of our illustrious President and of the State Department by any means that you may dispose for the purpose of bringing about some tangible results, for the matter is most pressing. . . . Our President and the State Department are already in touch with the situation and there is absolutely no desire to embarrass them in any steps they may think fit to take.[50]

Frank Polk, Acting Secretary of State, repeating the administration's policy on the Armenian matter since the beginning of the crisis a year earlier, responded that "the Department has used and will continue to use its good offices to the fullest extent consistent with the position of the United States as a neutral country, in behalf of the Armenian Christians in the Turkish Empire."[51] In a similar vein,

Alvey Adee replied to Sevasly that from the beginning Ambassador Morgenthau had "continued to remonstrate with the Turkish Government against their treatment of the Armenians, and that such remonstrances have been followed by orders by the Turkish Government modifying and ameliorating to some degree the orders previously issued relative to the deportation of the Armenians from their homes." Adee repeated almost verbatim Polk's statement concerning the neutrality of the United States, but added that the department had instructed Morgenthau to inform the Sublime Porte that reports of the Turkish treatment of the Armenians had "aroused general and unfavorable criticism among the American people, which is destroying the feeling of good will which the people of the United States have held towards Turkey."[52]

As Barton and Dodge organized relief aid for the Near East and distributed information regarding the crises in the region, reports on the Armenian Genocide appeared more frequently in the newspapers.[53] Lansing informed Morgenthau that the newspapers in the United States were publishing reports about the Turkish atrocities, and that letters from private citizens indicated that events in Turkey "have aroused a general and intense feeling indicative of the American people." The secretary encouraged Morgenthau to continue to use his good offices and inform the Turkish government that the persecutions were— repeating verbatim Adee's statement—"destroying the feeling of good will which the people of the United States have held towards Turkey."[54]

The volume of requests for information became so overwhelming for the Department of State that on October 26 Lansing sent a "form letter" to Joseph Tumulty, secretary to the president, with instructions to distribute to persons requesting information or urging action regarding the Armenian situation. This 1-page letter stated:

> The Department acknowledges the receipt of your letter of—————, relative to the present condition of the Armenians in Turkey and to the attitude of the United States Government relative thereto.
>
> In reply the Department begs to state that from the beginning the American Ambassador at Constantinople has continued to remonstrate with the Turkish Government against their treatment of the Armenians, and that such remonstrances have been followed by orders by the Turkish Government modifying and ameliorating to some degree the orders previously issued relative to the deportations of the Armenians from their homes.
>
> The Ambassador will continue to use his good offices, to the fullest extent consistent with the position of the United States as a neutral country, in behalf of the Armenians in the Turkish Empire.

> The Department has recently instructed the Ambassador to notify the
> Turkish Government that the reports of the treatment of the Armenians
> have aroused general and unfavorable criticism among the American
> people, which is destroying the feeling of good will which the people of
> the United States have held towards Turkey.[55]

These sentences, in whole or in part, although egregiously deceptive
with respect to the "ameliorating" effect the Young Turk orders exercised on the authorities in the provinces, appeared repeatedly in the
responses communicated by the Department of State and the White
House to individuals seeking information.

The White House received numerous letters from individual
citizens as well as those in official capacity. Confronted with the
specter of the total annihilation of his people across the Ottoman
Empire, Catholicos Gevorg V again entreated the Allied Powers to
intervene, as Christian states and in the name of humanity, to end the
atrocities against the Armenians.[56] "I am wondering," Colonel House
stated in a letter to Wilson, "whether this Government should not
make some sort of protest over the Armenian massacres."[57]

The responses related by President Wilson might have seemed
reassuring to those who wished the United States would become "the
Moses of the Armenians."[58] Upon closer examination, however,
particularly within the overall context of the domestic and international economic and geopolitical priorities pursued by the administration, his responses were vacuous and evasive at best. For example, in
late September 1915, an Armenian delegation from New Jersey
requested a meeting with Wilson concerning the Armenian massacres
and possible efforts for assistance. While at first he agreed to meet
with them, a few days later he changed his mind. Haigazoun
Hohannes Topakyan, a prominent businessman and former Persian
consul general at New York, in a letter to Wilson appealed for
U.S. assistance to end the massacres and the starvation. He noted that
the records of the Department of State provided more than sufficient
documentation for the massacres being committed against the
Armenians. Topakyan implored: "We pray your Excellency will use
your noble influence to help so dire a need in a colossal international
calamity, in a cause even of simple humanity, were all other considerations set aside, and this one act will stand out in the pages of history
for all times, a great luminous vision of human kindness and
compassionate mercy." A week later, in reply Wilson stressed his
"deep interest in the whole subject" and repeated the phraseology
found in the "form letter" prepared by Lansing: The Department

of State employed "every endeavor" to change the policy of the Turkish government, and "you may be sure that this Government will continue to do everything possible for it to do through diplomatic channels."[59]

On December 7, 1915, in his State of the Union address, President Wilson explicated the necessity of neutrality, the desirability of Pan-Americanism, and the imperatives of loyalty and good citizenship, of national prosperity and international peace. He justified his administration's policy of neutrality as a "manifest duty" to avert the collapse of world economy and industry and therefore a "universal catastrophe."[60] He presented Congress with a 5-year program for strengthening the naval capabilities of the nation. Wilson also stressed the pressing need for a "great merchant fleet," which he considered the essential ingredients for independent economic development and commerce. Private capital alone could not accomplish such a task, he argued, for "it is evident that only the government can undertake such beginnings and assume the initial financial risks. When the risk has passed and private capital begins to find its way in sufficient abundance into these new channels, the government may withdraw." Government support was necessary, he noted, so as to ensure that the nation's goods did not "lie piled up at our ports and stored upon side tracks in freight cars which are daily needed on the road; must not be left without means of transport to any foreign quarter."[61] The president thus reaffirmed his position on neutrality and his determination to pursue promotion of commercial relations with the outside world to overcome the economic difficulties at home.

U.S.-TURKISH TRADE RELATIONS

In his annual report the Secretary of Commerce pointed to the calamitous consequences of the war and, expecting heightened competition in international trade after the war, he recommended modification in anti-trust laws to permit American businesses greater freedom to form combinations as they engaged in international trade. For the year 1915, exports exceeded imports by more than a billion dollars despite the decline of nearly $83,000,000 in exports to Germany. Trade relations between the United States and Turkey suffered an enormous setback because of the war. While in 1913, U.S.-Turkey trade totaled about $25 million, that figure declined to $13 million in 1915.[62] U.S. opium imports from Turkey, the only commodity that saw an increase in volume among the principal imports, constituted 83 percent and 89.4 percent of the total opium imported by the United States in 1914 and 1915, respectively. In 1914, Turkey was the largest source of imported raisins, followed by Spain's 1,691,383 pounds ($179,021). In 1913, the United States imported from Turkey 63,882,480 pounds of licorice root worth $1,042,093; in 1915, it dropped to 47,076,323 pounds ($793,594). Asiatic Turkey was by far the largest source of figs for U.S. imports. In U.S. exports to Turkey, only wheat flour saw a significant increase, from 2,969 barrels ($11,461) in 1914 to 40,405 barrels ($166,019) in 1915. Tables 7.1 and 7.2 show the data for the U.S.-Turkey export and import of a number of goods.

For the Wilson administration, relations with the Young Turk regime would bring the benefits of rebounding trade ties upon returning to peace. For now, as Europe and the Ottoman Empire were engulfed in the war, it was imperative for the administration to attempt to save as much goodwill as possible.

Table 7.1   Principal U.S. imports from Turkey, 1914–15

Items	1914	1915
Licorice root	56,355,101 lbs $921,520	47,076,323 lbs $793,594
Coffee	1,838,128 lbs $295,017	398,840 lbs $66,337
Dates	28,858,381 lbs $519,132	19,374,505 lbs $278,209
Figs	13,160,786 lbs $719,021	12,372,312 lbs $746,276
Raisins	2,730,338 lbs $119,046	1,056,574 lbs $51,969
Almonds	166,090 lbs $44,012	123,412 lbs $14,080
Walnuts	1,712,209 lbs $290,050	16,135 lbs $2,875
Tobacco leaf	15,616,543 lbs $4,800,284	6,714,654 lbs $1,847,617
Opium	383,489 lbs $1,500,355	440,529 lbs $2,185,001
Manufactured carpets	286,704 sq. yds $1,404,987	118,752 sq. yds $612,360

Source: U.S. Department of Commerce, Bureau of Foreign and Domestic Commerce, *Foreign Commerce and Navigation of the United States for the Year Ending June 30, 1916* (Washington, DC: Government Printing Office, 1917), table 3, pp. 19, 59–60, 61, 73, 117–18, 120, 122, 127, 199, 258, 282.

Table 7.2   Principal U.S. exports to Turkey, 1914–15

Item	1914	1915
Wheat flour	2,969 bbls $11,461	30,405 bbls $166,019
Cottonseed	5,033,103 lbs $362,443	363,220 lbs $26,367
Starch	2,719,958 lbs $67,530	219,841 lbs $5,517
Meat/dairy products	3,252,217 lbs $321,773	478,943 lbs $45,465
Cloths	5.2 million yds $384,836	636,933 yds $39,889
Boots and shoes	46,471 prs $110,721	985 prs $2,121
Illuminating oil	6,371,490 gls $619,506	2,402,250 gls $219,773
Lubricating/heavy paraffin oil	473,604 gls $63,383	163,291 gls $19,724
Mining machinery	$4,043	$20,855
Pump/pumping machinery	$32,649	$4,266

Source: U.S. Department of Commerce, Bureau of Foreign and Domestic Commerce, *Foreign Commerce and Navigation of the United States for the Year Ending June 30, 1916* (Washington, DC: Government Printing Office, 1917), table 5, pp. 375, 381, 383–84, 425–27, 430, 521, 544, 545, 546–47, 549, 591–93, 598–622, 626–28, 646, 647, 648, 653–54, 709–10, 754–55, 759.

THE DEPARTURE OF AMBASSADOR MORGENTHAU

On the afternoon of January 14, 1916, the Armenian relief committee, headed by James Barton and Cleveland Dodge, met in New York to discuss possible means to improve distribution of aid in the Ottoman Empire, Persia, and Russia. Meanwhile, Barton had met with Mrs. Morgenthau in New York to discuss the possibility of a leave of absence for Morgenthau from his duties in Constantinople. The ambassador consented and on January 27 received word that he had been granted a leave of absence.[63] Morgenthau prepared to devote his energies to Wilson's reelection in the presidential elections of that year. When on February 1 he left Constantinople, on the train he was accompanied by a German admiral, who discussing the Armenian deportations, maintained that the Germans considered the expulsion of the Armenians from their homeland a military necessity.

"Of course," Morgenthau recorded in his diary, "he did not try to justify the massacres and deportation of the women and children."[64]

Ambassador Page informed the Department of State that, based on reports from the ecclesiastical leader of the Armenian people, Lord Bryce had inquired whether the department could do more in relief work or even the termination of the Turkish atrocities committed against the Armenians. Washington replied with the response rehearsed so well by now: the "Department has done everything it could in behalf of the Armenians and is continuing its efforts."[65]

CHAPTER 8

BETWEEN REALISM AND PHILANTHROPY

Ambassador Henry Morgenthau arrived at the port of New York on February 22, 1916, and the following day visited Washington for conferences with President Wilson, Secretary of State Robert Lansing, and Secretary of the Navy Josephus Daniels. In preparation for the presidential elections of that year, Morgenthau expressed the desire to work for the president's reelection campaign. Wilson complained that "some members of the Congress were indifferent to the fate of democracy as long as their reelection was assured." In matters pertaining to the Armenian situation, according to Morgenthau, Wilson discussed "at some length about the Armenian matters, and said that if necessary Americans should go to war for humanity's sake." The conversation quickly turned to the appointment of a successor to Constantinople, and Morgenthau recommended Samuel Untermeyer, a New York lawyer with expertise in finance, or Abram Elkus, a mutual friend and a judge in the state of New York.[1] Whether or not Wilson had ever seriously contemplated to take Americans "to war for humanity's sake" to protect the Armenians, he must have been aware of its implications. The power to maintain international peace and to punish violators of international law in times of war necessitated direct military engagement to prevent human catastrophes as experienced by the Armenians in the Ottoman Empire. In the end, however, humanitarian instincts had to be checked by short-term and long-term political and economic considerations. Morgenthau had not returned to the United States to mobilize public support for a war but for Wilson's reelection. There is no evidence that Wilson and Morgenthau further pursued this option during their meeting or thereafter, their humanitarian pronouncements notwithstanding.

PRESIDENTIAL ELECTIONS AND PUBLIC OPINION

The upcoming presidential elections made the administration—particularly Lansing—anxious about public opinion. On February 9, Lansing and Third Assistant Secretary of State William Phillips had discussed whether greater publicity should be given to the atrocities committed against the Armenians.[2] Although the result of their conversation was not recorded, Secretary Lansing discouraged public appearances on the subject. He had expressed concerns regarding public opinion before Morgenthau had arrived in the United States. In a letter to the ambassador, Lansing had noted:

> While I realize that a large number of our fellow citizens will wish to offer you testimonials as a recognition of the splendid work which you are doing, it would seem to me that, in view of the international situation a public meeting, however carefully arranged, might have unhappy results.
>
> Please pardon me for this suggestion, and also in giving you a word of warning in regard to newspaper reporters, who may misrepresent you and whom it is well to avoid as far as possible. I am looking forward greatly to the pleasure of meeting you when you come to Washington.[3]

Morgenthau too was at first cautious in this regard. When the renowned geographer Herbert Adams Gibbons returned to the United States bearing the felicitations of the Armenian catholicos to the U.S. government and to thank the ambassador for his assistance to the Armenian people, Morgenthau "urged him not to do so publicly," and Gibbons agreed.[4] Soon thereafter, however, as the political alliance between Wilson and the missionaries could not be neglected in an election year, in cooperation with James L. Barton, secretary of the American Board of Commissioners for Foreign Missions, on the one hand, and in support of Wilson's reelection campaign, on the other, Morgenthau began to make public appearances. He had decided not to return to his post in Constantinople; in his letter of resignation he stated that while he had not considered resignation, now he believed that he could best serve his country in the United States. He proposed his resignation to Lansing on March 8, 1916, and formally submitted his resignation to Wilson on March 23. Wilson accepted it immediately. When criticized for this sudden change, Morgenthau responded that he was "convinced that my assisting the President, when known in Turkey, will be of great help to my proteges out there."[5] He thus became heavily involved in Wilson's reelection campaign, and, if his diary is any guide, for the rest of the year he rarely discussed the Armenian situation with policymakers in Washington.

HOFFMAN PHILIP AT THE EMBASSY

During Ambassador Morgenthau's absence, the Chargé d'Affaires Hoffman Philip managed the affairs of the U.S. embassy. Morgenthau believed Philip a "fine gentle-man" and had enjoyed his company at the embassy, although the ambassador did not hold much confidence in his abilities. In political matters, Morgenthau commented in his diary, his "mind seems weak at times unable to grasp and hold a thought."[6] Be that as it may, Hoffman Philip continued to relay dispatches regarding the deportations and massacres of Armenians, but his reports no longer contained the detailed information submitted by Morgenthau in 1915. Nor was he successful in gaining the same degree of respect and cooperation Morgenthau had enjoyed from the Turkish leadership. His relationship with the authorities was further complicated when, in February 1916, the government began to withhold all communication privileges between the U.S. consulates and the embassy.[7] In a message to Morgenthau in March 1916, Philip complained that while the embassy continued to receive an enormous amount of correspondence, "letter writing has been beyond me." The embassy could finally enjoy a respite from correspondence, he added, since the Turkish government prohibited sealed dispatches. Philip noted that he had been able to maintain good relations with Turkish officials, but that the Armenian issue and the missionaries' close association with it complicated matters. "I have frequently wished," Philip confided, "I had the missionaries in the interior on a string and could pull them all in." The situation for the Armenians had not improved, Philip added, as the embassy had been informed about further deportations from the region of Aleppo.[8]

The Turkish abrogation of the Capitulations remained the primary concern for the United States. In a *note verbale* dated February 19, 1916, Philip reiterated the position recommended by Morgenthau earlier and confirmed by the Department of State that the United States could not recognize unilateral abrogation. In matters of extraterritorial rights, the note stated, the grantee "cannot relinquish . . . its manifest duty" to protect its citizens in the territory of the grantor. The U.S. government, therefore, reserved the right, "upon the establishment of judicial and administrative reforms in Turkey," to determine whether to surrender the extraterritorial rights of American citizens in the Ottoman Empire. The note warned that the United

States would hold the Ottoman government responsible for injuries to the United States or to its citizens, "through any interference on the part of the Ottoman authorities, with the extraterritorial rights possessed by the United States and its citizens in the Ottoman Empire."

In reply to this ominous warning, the Turkish foreign ministry insisted that the Capitulations had been "definitely and irrevocably abolished."[9] Relations, however, needed not be troubled, as the Turkish government would ensure the safety of American citizens. On April 24, 1916, Philip reported that the minister of foreign affairs, along with the minister of the interior, had instructed the provincial authorities "to avoid in all matters friction with Americans," and that he in turn instructed the U.S. consulates in the Ottoman Empire to maintain friendly relations with the local governments. The consulates at Beirut, Kharpert, and Smyrna had already informed the embassy of their "entirely friendly" relations with the local authorities.[10]

REMNANTS OF A PEOPLE

The deportations of the Armenians continued in 1916, and major massacres occurred in areas where the refugees had been gathered for several months. Thousands of the deportees were killed in Ras ul-Ain, Entilli, and Deir el-Zor. At Ras ul-Ain, convoys of Armenian refugees had arrived from the various provinces, particularly from Cilicia, on train and on foot. At first, they had been gathered at Islahiye, Katma, and Azaz but were soon sent to Ras ul-Ain to make room for the new arrivals. By the end of February 1916, an estimated 300,000 refugees had arrived at Deir el-Zor, 100,000 at the Damascus-Ma'an area, 50,000 at Ras ul-Ain, 20,000 at Homs, 12,000 at Hama, and 10,000 at Rakka, all totaling more than 480,000.[11] In March, Abdulahad Nuri Bey, the deputy administrator of refugees in Aleppo, informed his superiors that about 35,000 Armenians were dead in the region of Bab and Meskéné; 10,000 at Katlik near Aleppo; 20,000 at Tibsi, Abuharrar, and Hamam; and 35,000 at Ras ul-Ain. In April, those deported from Ras ul-Ain were massacred by Turkish and Kurdish bands who were pursuing them out of town.[12]

Meanwhile, in the region of Aleppo city, the local Aleppine Armenian community had established a committee for refugees. Led by the Reverend Harutiun Esayan, the committee included such local luminaries as the Mazlumian brothers (owners of the famed Hotel Baron), T. Shetikian (Shedigian), and pharmacist Rupen Ezajian. The committee received funds from the Armenian patriarchate and the U.S. embassy at Constantinople, the Armenian General Benevolent

Union, and European charitable organizations.[13] As reported by the local Armenian prelacy in January and March 1916, the committee supervised three orphanages housing about 800 children. The government expropriated one of them and placed the building and its 300 orphans under the direction of Miss Beatrice Rohner, a German missionary with previous experiences in Huraniye and Marash. The financial situation was untenable, the prelacy noted, as the meager resources currently available could provide for the daily sustenance of neither the arriving refugees nor those deported to the desert. One of its reports warned: "If we do not receive 5,000 liras by the end of this month, not even one-eighth of these refugees will survive the summer."[14] Typhus and hunger plagued a large number of the refugees. The authorities, including the local police chieftain, Feyzi Effendi, at Bab ul-Faraj, a section of Aleppo where one of the police headquarters was located, removed the refugees and murdered an unknown number of the Armenian residents in the city. One evening, Feyzi Effendi dragged an Armenian clergy from his house in the Jideyde quarter of the city and shot him in cold blood. Other refugees gathered in Aleppo were sent to different directions—to Ma'ara farther south, northeastward to Mumbuj and Ras ul-Ain, and eastward to Bab, Meskéné, Abuharrar, and Rakka on the road to Deir el-Zor.[15]

At Deir el-Zor, Armenians, exiled from their homes and ancestral homeland, from Trebizond and Erzerum and Sivas, from Rodosto and Angora and Konia, from Kharpert and Bitlis and Mush and Van, from Adana and Marash and Zeitun and Diarbekir, met their death through starvation and murder. Those surviving the carnage were ordered to march farther east to Mosul, but no longer able to continue they succumbed to hunger, to physical and mental exhaustion, their emaciated, skeletal frames, coiled and contorted, finally affixed to the arid sands of the desert of Deir el-Zor.[16]

Having eliminated the Armenian people, the Ittihadist regime turned its attention to the task of destroying the Armenian Church, the principal institution accorded legitimacy for representation of the Armenian nation in the Ottoman *millet* (religious communities) system. In January 1916, the patriarchate was informed of the nullification of the Armenian National Constitution, which had been in effect since 1863. Responding to news that the central government also intended to confiscate all bank accounts of Armenian organizations (e.g., Dprotsaser, Azganver, Zavarian Fund, and Help Sasun fund), the patriarchate decided to transfer their funds to its own account, and moved documents of neighborhood councils and charities as well as two pictures by the renowned Russian Armenian painter Hovannes

(Ivan) Aivazovsky (1817–1900) to the U.S. embassy.[17] The Turkish government, on July 19, 1916, issued a directive to combine the patriarchates of Jerusalem and Constantinople with the Catholicosate of Aghtamar, permitting the Catholicosate of Sis a permanent house at Jerusalem under the title of Catholicos-Patriarch.[18] In August, the chief of police at Constantinople, Ahmed Bey, who had replaced the infamous Bedri Bey some months earlier, and Beha Bey, the Superintendent of Religions, arrived at the patriarchate with an official statement, dated July 28, 1916 (n.s. August 10, 1916), from the Ministry of Justice and Religion abolishing the Armenian Patriarchate. The letter, addressed to Patriarch Zaven Der Yeghiayan, stated that, based on a new statute, "the Catholicosates of Sis and Aghtamar have been merged and the Patriarchates of Constantinople and Jerusalem also joined to this new Catholicosate. Consequently, your position and the structure of the Armenian Patriarchate have come to an end." Thus the patriarchates of Constantinople and Jerusalem were attached to the Catholicosate of Cilicia, which in turn became the newly established seat of the Armenian Catholicos-Patriarch at Jerusalem. A few weeks later, Patriarch Der Yeghiayan was exiled first to Baghdad and then to Mosul, where he remained until the conclusion of the war. The bishops and the students at the Armash Seminary at Constantinople were sent to Jerusalem.[19]

Catholicos Sahak II Khapayan (Sahag Khabayan) of the Great House of Cilicia at Sis, the catholicosal seat for centuries, had been exiled to Aleppo. Within days, he was ordered by the authorities to move to the Patriarchate of Jerusalem until further notice.[20] He remained at the St. James Monastery from October 31, 1915, to August 29, 1916. Upon his arrival at Jerusalem, the catholicos, as had been his practice, continued to send reports to the Armenian patriarchate about the conditions. "The road from Aleppo to Damascus," he wrote in one letter, "was lined with thousands of Armenian refugees. Some were living in tents and others in the open air, begging for bread and water and asking for news about their friends."[21] In May 1916, Minister of the Marines Ahmed Jemal Pasha notified Catholicos Sahak II of the decision by the central government regarding the restructuring of the Armenian Church. In doing so, the government limited what little legal protection and privileges the Armenian Church had retained during the preceding years. Further, the government hoped to separate the Catholicosate of Sis from what it viewed as the growing Russian influence in the Armenian provinces.[22] In October 1916, during the annual congress of the Committee of Union and Progress, Minister of the Interior Mehmed

Talaat presented the accomplishments of his government. The Young Turk leaders congratulated themselves for their successes.[23]

Relief Work at Home

In March 1916, James Barton communicated to Morgenthau the desire of the American relief committee to accelerate its fund-raising activities as encouraged by Jerome D. Greene, secretary of the Rockefeller Foundation, which had maintained close ties with the missionaries. According to Barton, in April 1902, John D. Rockefeller, Jr., had requested to discuss with him the general condition of the foreign missions. Rockefeller reportedly had complained that "the family were not doing all they should do for the non-Christian people of the world; that their wealth came from all countries, but operating through but one Missionary Society they could reach only a limited area. He also declared that they were giving as much as they could to the Baptist Missionary Board without having that Board appear to be a Rockefeller concern. . . ."[24] In December 1904, Rockefeller had agreed to contribute $100,000 to the American Board. Now in March 1916, Barton proposed to meet at Morgenthau's house to discuss "a practical plan of aggression in order to secure larger funds at once for repatriating the Armenians as soon as the opportunity arises."[25] This "practical plan" must have mystified Morgenthau, for the magnitude of the existing needs was so great across the Ottoman Empire, Persia, the Caucasus, Syria, and Palestine, that it would hardly seem pertinent at this juncture to contemplate the repatriation of the Armenians. To be sure, as noted by Barton, American relief aid was not intended solely for the Armenian refugees, and while initially American relief committees were formed in response to Christian appeals (Armenians, Syrians, Assyrians, Nestorians, and Greeks), relief was soon provided "to all suffering peoples on the basis of need and not creed, and included the Kurds, the Turks, the Tartars, the Arabs and the Persians."[26] Accordingly, the relief operations encompassed Greece, Bulgaria, Turkey, Armenia, Georgia, Azerbaijan, Russia, Persia, Iraq, Syria, Palestine, and Egypt.[27]

On April 7, 1916, Cleveland H. Dodge, Greene, Barton, and others held a conference at Morgenthau's office, and raised $50,000 for the relief fund. The American Committee for Armenian and Syrian Relief subsequently organized numerous public appearances for Morgenthau in several cities. These gatherings aimed at informing the public about the conditions of Armenians and Jews and about American relief efforts in the Ottoman Empire and Persia. Not all events attracted large numbers. On April 24, 1916, when Morgenthau gave a talk on the Armenians, the meeting, he commented in his diary, "was slimly attended." Not discouraged, on May 4, 1916, he informed President Wilson that during the month of May he would be visiting a number of states to "please the Armenian Relief Committee and some Jewish organizations, and to do some political work."[28] Now preoccupied with public relations campaigns, Morgenthau expected his successor immediately to assume the post at Constantinople so as not to jeopardize relations between the two governments.

ABRAM I. ELKUS

Colonel Edward M. House informed Morgenthau of the view prevailing in the Department of State that it was not necessary to appoint a successor immediately. Morgenthau disagreed. In May 1916, Morgenthau wrote to President Wilson that "it will displease some of our very good friends (Dodge, Charles Crane, etc.) who are interested in the American Institutions in Turkey, if the appointment of my successor is delayed much longer." Moreover, Morgenthau added, the Department of State ignored the fact that "our representative also takes care of the interests of eight other countries, and we certainly should have an Ambassador and not a Charge there."[29] After further delays by both governments, Abram I. Elkus was finally appointed ambassador to Constantinople on July 21, 1916. Eight months had passed since Morgenthau departed from Constantinople before the new U.S. ambassador arrived in the Ottoman capital in September 1916. He presented his credentials at Constantinople on October 2, 1916, and served as ambassador until Turkish–American relations were severed in April 1917.[30]

The appointment of a new ambassador provided an opportunity to both the Wilson administration and the Ittihadist regime to renew their commitment further to cultivate their bilateral relations. Despite the enormous respect Morgenthau had enjoyed in Constantinople, his growing opposition to the Ittihadists on account of the Armenians could have potentially threatened their relations. Ambassador Elkus was expected to avoid similar problems, and the press encouraged better relations. Prior to his arrival at Constantinople, the daily newspaper in Constantinople *Hilal* ran an editorial on September 1, 1916, titled "The Miracle." It referred to a talk given by Morgenthau at the New York Chamber of Commerce, where the former ambassador had praised the Turkish nation for its "force and capacity" as evinced thus far in the war. "The Turks," Morgenthau stated, "show a patriotism, which does not give way to any sacrifice." "Thus," the editorial noted, "the American diplomatist has paid a brilliant homage to our people who was admired by all for the gigantic effort, which it is making since two years as well as for the extent of the sacrifices, to which it has gaily consented for the safeguard of its honor, and for the preservation of its existence." The editorial added that Morgenthau was present at "our national resurrection, after having seen us in a state of lithargy [*sic*] from which as a rule one cannot recover. It was for him to see, occurring under his own eyes a real miracle, the happening of which nothing could fortell [*sic*] to him." Immediately after war was declared, the editorial continued, "a wave of enthusiasm animated and raised up Turkey. The Turkish people who hardly got rid of the most disagreeable experiences, was trying to organize himself, notwith-standing the verdict of death, which was pronounced against him, without allowing himself to be mortified by the new attempts which were prepared in the shade; . . . This war has shown to the world many surprises," the editorial concluded.[31]

While in Berlin on his way to Constantinople, Ambassador Elkus reportedly stated during an interview: "The United States are animated with the friendliest feelings towards Turkey. No disputes on political questions exist between the two countries." When asked whether the United States intended to expand its economic relations in Turkey, Elkus replied:

> This question does not interest the American Government . . . but private capitalists. I share your opinion as to the extraordinarily brilliant field which is open to capital in Turkey and I believe that this is also the opinion of many powerful American capitalists. American capital is already interested in many Turkish undertakings. I think after the war many people at home will desire to create new and large undertakings in Turkey. Turkey is a country very richly endowed by nature. I have the conviction that American capital can be very advantageously used especially in the Asiatic provinces of the Ottoman Empire.[32]

The reports dispatched by Elkus from Constantinople indicated that the Armenian situation in the Ottoman Empire had not changed since the departure of his predecessor, except that by now the deported had in large numbers been killed, or had died of exhaustion, starvation, or disease, or had become refugees in unfamiliar lands. In October 1916, he recommended that the Department of State exert greater pressure on the governments of Germany and Austria-Hungary to force the Young Turk regime to stop the annihilation of the Armenian people. In case of failure to enlist their support, he suggested that President Wilson personally appeal "to the two emperors and give full publicity to the exchange of notes between the heads of state."[33] By then, however, domestic political considerations had taken precedence over matters pertaining to deportations and massacres in faraway lands. The Wilson administration would pay attention to such issues only if they bore relevance to public opinion at home, particularly as he had to overcome opposition to his proposed league of nations.

DOMESTIC POLITICS: ELECTION YEAR

Wilson began earnestly to place the issue of a league of nations on the national agenda in the spring of 1916, although not all of his advisors concurred with him. In a letter to Wilson, Colonel Edward M. House argued that it was not practical to expect the formation of an international judicial tribunal or an international force to maintain peace. Such an international regime, House noted, could evolve only over time.[34] Secretary of State Lansing was more adamant in his opposition to a league. Confined to his bed by doctor's orders, Lansing sent a memo to Wilson regarding the proposal of the League to Enforce Peace. Stating that while "to an extent" he agreed to the League's proposal to establish an international board of conciliation to settle issues not amenable to "diplomatic adjustment," he nevertheless found it impracticable "to apply it in case of a continuing invasion of fundamental national or individual rights unless some authoritative international body has the power to impose and enforce an order in the nature of an injunction, which will prevent the ag[g]ressor from further action until arbitration has settled the rights of the parties." Matters of national sovereignty and national interests, he added, render such proposals, particularly as they would apply to the United States, rather unacceptable.[35] Wilson saw no inconsistencies in his approach to world affairs as promoter and protector of American economic interests and international peace. He had been proposing the elimination of anti-trust acts to free businesses from the constraints of burdensome regulations so that they could expand their operations abroad. He was also proposing an international organization for peaceful relations among nations. While he hoped to remain aloof from the Old World, he also "anticipated a global role for the United States."[36]

On May 27, 1916, Wilson gave a brief but a monumental speech before the League to Enforce Peace, where he presented the case for a league of nations.[37] Noting the harm caused by the war, Wilson emphasized the necessity of concordance among nations with respect to diplomacy, peace, and war. "If this war has accomplished nothing else for the benefit of the world, it has at least disclosed a great moral necessity and set forward the thinking of the statesmen of the world by a whole age." Further, he added, "In the dealings of nations with one another, arbitrary force must be rejected and we must move forward to the thought of the modern world, the thought of which peace is the very atmosphere." Wilson continued to enumerate three "fundamental" principles:

> First, that every people has a right to choose the sovereignty under which they shall live. . . .; Second, that the small states of the world have a right to enjoy the same respect for their sovereignty and for their territorial integrity that great and powerful nations expect and insist upon. And, third, that the world has a right to be free from every disturbance of its peace that has its origin in aggression and disregard of the rights of peoples and nations.

Wilson concluded by stating that "the United States is willing to become a partner in any feasible association of nations formed in order to realize these objects and make them secure against violation."[38] This speech served as the opening shot for his reelection campaign. Equally important, while Wilson could satisfy some of the progressives with the promise of keeping the country out of the war, the nation's economy required immediate action. The railroad strikes in June 1916 posed a particularly serious challenge for the administration. In the months of July, August, and September, Wilson worked toward the passage of legislation in support of the workers, and accordingly he won ample praise from socialists and liberals.[39]

On July 10, 1916, Congress adopted a concurrent resolution urging President Wilson "to designate a day on which the citizens of this country may give expression to their sympathy by contributing to the funds now being raised for the relief of the Armenians in the belligerent countries." Responding to this congressional initiative, on August 31, President Wilson proclaimed two days, Saturday and Sunday, October 21–22, 1916, "as joint days upon which the people of the United States may make such contribution as they feel disposed for the aid of the stricken Syrian and Armenian people."[40] In doing so, Wilson sought to stymy the critics of his administration on a variety of pressing domestic and foreign policy issues, most prominently labor unrest and the Mexican crisis.[41] The proclamation of August 31 was to assure his progressive supporters that despite his military engagements in the affairs of Mexico, he had not abandoned his humanitarian ideals. The president hoped to convince the public of his determination to defend his policy of neutrality and to keep the nation out of the war. He did not expect to face serious challenges from within the Democratic Party but nevertheless had to gain the full support of its leadership and, most emphatically, had to regain the support of his former secretary of state William J. Bryan. Wilson feared that Bryan and the peace progressives would become his most influential critics if he failed to make a strong commitment to peace.[42]

Wilson formally accepted the Democratic nomination on September 2, 1916. In his acceptance speech, Wilson highlighted the achievements of his administration in promoting U.S. commercial relations abroad. He pointed out that the administration had revised the tariff laws and established a Tariff Board to encourage foreign trade. Accordingly, "American energies are now directed towards the markets of the world." Further, the administration sought to revive an American merchant marine to strengthen the nation's commerce with other nations. The administration also enabled the Department of Agriculture, in conjunction with financial reforms introduced with the passage of the Federal Reserve Act and the Rural Credits Act, to promote the interests of the farmers. With respect to the European war, Wilson emphasized the policy of neutrality as "the fixed and traditional policy of the United States to stand aloof from the politics of Europe" and "because it was manifestly our duty to prevent, if it were possible, the indefinite extension of the fires of hate and desolation kindled by that terrible conflict and seek to serve mankind by reserving our strength and our resources for the anxious and difficult days of restoration and healing which must follow, when peace will have to build its house anew."[43] The proclamation of October 21 and 22 as Syrian and Armenian relief days immediately prior to the presidential elections in November served to amplify his humanitarianism.

Wilson won the presidential election in November. Knock contends that "strengthened by the electoral mandate for peace, [Wilson] was now determined to force a compromise in Europe." Having secured the reelection, the Wilson administration appeared ready to enter the war. Knock notes that most scholarly accounts of the League have viewed the congressional election of 1918 as "infusing intense degree of partisanship into the debate over American membership in the League of Nations." Such interpretations, he correctly argues, must be revised, as the League of Nations became a deeply divisive issue during the presidential campaign of 1916. Prior to his reelection, the president had fashioned his party platform to stress progressive internationalism, and during the campaign he had won praises from internationalists for his alignment with them. Wilson sought to expand the Democratic Party's political base, still a minority in 1916, in order to win the White House. Knock concludes: "Certain aspects of the president's performance were thus shaped by expedience."[44] The administration's response to the Armenian Question until the presidential elections of 1916 proved to be one such policy.

ALLIANCES, AIMS, AND RESPONSES

In November 1916, Ambassador James Gerard in Berlin requested that the German government attempt to improve the situation for the Armenians in the Ottoman Empire.[45] Viewed from Washington, however, Secretary Lansing expected no advantages in such a course of action. In a personal letter to Wilson, Lansing presented a comparative analysis of the German deportation of the Belgians and the French at Lille, on the one hand, and the Ottoman deportations of Armenians, on the other. He prefaced his letter by arguing that "the deportation of civilians" from an area by military authorities in and of itself was not "reprehensible." Military necessity would serve as "ample justification" for such a measure. With respect to the Armenians, he wrote: "It was not to my mind the deportation which was objectionable but the horrible brutality which attended its execution. It is one of the blackest pages in the history of this war, and I think we were fully justified in intervening as we did in behalf of the wretched people, even though they were Turkish subjects."[46] Similarly, he noted, military necessity required the removal of the French population from the region of the battle lines near Lille. The "ruthlessness and inhumanity" demonstrated by the German military toward the people at Lille "caused needless distress by the separation of families and deportation without due regard to age or sex and without opportunity to prepare for departure." Lansing added: "Of course in the case of the Armenians the Ottoman Government is by nature and training cruel and barbarous and could not be expected to conform to so high a standard of humanity as the enlightened Government of Germany, which makes the conduct more criticizable."[47]

U.S. Ambassador to London Walter H. Page disagreed with the policy of mere communication of protests as predicated upon the policy of neutrality by the Wilson administration since the outbreak of the war. On November 24, 1916, in a letter to the president, he wrote: "Only some sort of active and open identification with the

Allies can put us in effective protest against the assassins of the Armenians and the assassins of Belgium, Poland, and Serbia and in a friendly attitude to the German people themselves, as distinguished from their military rulers. . . . There can be no historic approval of neutrality for years, while the world is bleeding to death." As a first step, Page proposed the "complete severance" of diplomatic and eco-nomic relations with Turkey and Germany. A month later, Page sent another note to Wilson, stating that the Allies agreed that the Turks be "cleaned out of Europe" and that the Christians of the Ottoman Empire "be set free." President Wilson held little respect for Page and his opinions, however, and when the ambassador offered his resigna-tion he indicated that he was prepared to accept it immediately.[48]

In December 1916, the Wilson administration began preparation for entrance into the war. Colonel House recommended several authors and publicists for the task of mobilizing public support as the adminis-tration neared its decision. House proposed that the United Press and Scripps-McRay, the major newspaper chain, along with Ray Stannard Baker, George Creel, and Lincoln Steffins be brought together to form a committee for public propaganda. House wrote confidently: "The United Press together with the Scripps-McRay—(which are really one concern) did more in the election than any single factor. In Ohio, in Minnesota, in North Dakota and in California it was the most potential influence you had." He added that Cleveland Dodge and his associates were planning "to coordinate all the foreign relief societies . . . [and] believe they can raise something like a hundred million of dollars for European relief now and after the war."[49] President Wilson expressed his support for their foreign relief programs but, as House noted in his diary, was not inclined to take an active role in such projects.[50]

The economic mobilization for the U.S. entry into the war led the administration to cultivate government-business cooperation and closer relations with the oil industry. The administration placed the leading figures of Standard Oil in key positions within the command structure. Walter Teagle, president of Standard Oil, was appointed president of the U.S. Shipping Board, created by an act of Congress in 1916. The purpose of establishing the Shipping Board was not only to prepare for the potential entrance into the war but also to facilitate commercial expansion after the restoration of peace. A.C. Bedford, chairman of the board of directors of Standard Oil, became the presi-dent of the Petroleum Committee, which was established two weeks before the declaration of war. They brought their expertise to the operations of the war, but they also protected the interests of the oil company against British and French competition. The French, for example, under the leadership of Georges Clemenceau and through Henry Bérenger, concentrated their energies to maintain oil rights in Mesopotamia secured in the Turkish Petroleum Company agreements of March 1914 and in the Transcaucasus "to reclaim the extensive Rothschild holdings that had been sold to the Shell group in 1911."[51] Further, the Council of National Defense, established by Congress in April 1916, created an advisory committee comprised by "leading businessmen," including Bernard Baruch, followed by another advisory committee specifically on petroleum procurement.[52]

Representing the oil industry, the advisory committee on oil worked closely with the administration and Congress on various aspects of delivery and distribution of oil to the Navy and War departments. In an urgent appeal to Wilson to safeguard Navy oil reserves, Secretary Daniels stated that since the conversion to oil-burning battleships, the Navy relied heavily on oil reserves. He pointed out that according to estimates by the Secretary of the Interior, the oil fields in the United States contained supplies for no more than 28 years at the rate of current consumption. An effective Navy, he added, would require 4.8 million barrels of oil per year. Colonel House agreed. He advised the president to insist on a strong Navy, as effective naval power would enhance U.S. influence in Europe and around the world. House argued that "we must impress foreign governments with our ability to carry out our purposes. They know our latent strength, but unless we put it in concrete form, or indicate an intention to do so, we cannot make them give serious consideration to our aims."[53]

The predominance of the south in the administration and in Congress also compelled the administration to pay close attention to agricultural interests. Of the ten members on Wilson's cabinet, six, in addition to the president, were born in the south. The leaders of the Democratic Party in Congress were mostly southerners. Thus, the emphasis the administration placed on international economic expansion would benefit the industrial sector in the north and the agricultural interests of the south.[54] Endorsing government support for these interests, the Democratic Party platform of 1916 stated that the party favored measures "necessary to restore our flag to the seas and to provide further facilitation for our foreign commerce . . . [and] to remove unfair conditions of competition in the dealings of American merchants and producers with competitors in foreign markets . . . to promote and foster the orderly and efficient development of the industry and commerce of the nation, both at home and abroad."[55]

The administration's position toward Turkey reflected a combination of these influences when on April 2, 1917, Wilson formally requested a declaration of war, and Congress on April 6 declared war on Germany. Soon thereafter, a presidential order created the Committee on Public Information (CPI), headed by the journalist George Creel. The primary objectives of the CPI included censorship of the news to publicize only the positive aspects of the American engagement in the war and to "arouse ardor and enthusiasm" throughout the country for the Allied cause. Significantly, Wilson did not request a declaration of war against Turkey. In fact, in his address of April 2, he directed American opinion against Germany but made no references to Turkey, although in January during a conference with House he had opined that "Turkey should cease to exist." In his subsequent addresses, he presented Turkey as a victim of German geopolitical designs and the political upheavals in Turkey as instigated by machinations of German imperialist objectives.[56] The conventional view—as expressed by Robert Daniel, for example—held that the U.S. Congress did not include Turkey in its declaration of war because of the absence of hostilities between the United States and Turkey. The real reason involved the established missionary influence and the growing U.S. corporate interests in the Ottoman Empire and their lobbyists in Washington, on the one hand, and the determination of the Young Turk regime to capitalize on their good relations with the United States for postwar gains, on the other. As prior to the U.S. declaration of war against Germany there existed a convergence of interests in the continuation of amicable relations between the Wilson administration and the Young Turk government, so did protection of American missionary and corporate interests during the war and their further expectations to enhance their position in the region after the restoration of peace preclude such action. In February 1917, Talaat Pasha, now the grand vizier and foreign minister, had related to Ambassador Elkus the sultan's desire to maintain friendly relations with the United States. Talaat assured Elkus that in case the United States went to war with Germany, there was no reason why Turkey and the United States should not continue their cordial relations.[57]

James Barton and Cleveland H. Dodge lobbied in Washington to avoid a declaration of war against Turkey. Barton stated later in his book, *Story of Near East Relief*, that "President Wilson, sympathetically interested in the American institutions, the American personnel and American influence in the Near East, withheld a formal declaration of war against Turkey and Turkey simply broke off diplomatic relations." Individuals associated with relief work, Barton noted, "consistently refused" to act in ways that could elicit charges of interference. "When the question of declaring war on Turkey, after

America's entry into the conflict on the side of the Allies, was a matter
of deep concern to the relief workers, the educational institutions and
the missionaries, it was not discussed in the meetings of the Executive
Committee, although there were widely divergent opinions on the
subject." "Strict neutrality" was necessary, he argued, so as to gain
"the confidence of each and every one of the countries and secure the
fullest possible cooperation of the people and the government officials."[58] Dodge similarly stressed the necessity of neutrality toward the
Ottoman Empire to assure protection for the American missionary
and other institutions and colleges and the continuation of relief
work. President Wilson promised to manage the affair so as not to
jeopardize American interests in the Middle East.[59]

On April 21, 1917, under German pressure Turkey severed diplomatic relations with the United States. Newspapers and humanitarian
groups in the United States expressed concerns regarding not only the
safety of Americans but also regarding the Armenian situation in the
Ottoman Empire. Humanitarian organizations criticized the Turkish
persecutions and massacres committed against Armenians, and some
even advocated immediate action. The Department of State sought to
calm public opinion to prevent serious frictions between Washington
and Constantinople. The prevailing view in official policymaking
circles remained unchanged: that the United States, at least by official
policy, would not interfere in the domestic affairs of Turkey. As James
Gidney put it: "Since no disaster or even serious inconvenience
resulted from the absence of policy, presumably none was needed."[60]
Although the Young Turk regime for its part severed diplomatic ties
with the United States, it carefully avoided any conflicts with the
Wilson administration.[61]

As with business, the U.S. entrance into the war changed the government's relations with organizations involved in international relief
and technical assistance. On August 10, 1917, Wilson by executive
order established the U.S. Food Administration as a wartime agency
to be headed by Herbert Hoover, whose appointment the president
had announced on May 19, 1917. Although created to meet the
needs of the public and the military, the Food Administration also
served as an instrument of policy to supplement and strengthen the
Department of Agriculture, whereby the White House would, as a
wartime measure, directly manage the pricing, distribution, imports,
and exports of agricultural goods.[62] In April 1917, writing from
Europe, Hoover had issued a statement describing the great need for
food in the war-torn continent and urged the American public to
reduce consumption of wheat by 30 percent as a patriotic duty.

Women were encouraged to volunteer for the Food Administration. Their ability to save one pound of bread per capita in a single week, they were informed, would lead to an export surplus of one million bushels. Thereafter, the Food Administration met with representatives of various sectors of economy, including the sugar industry, the canning industry, the Fruit and Vegetable Growers of the United States, the Potato Association of America, the International Milk Dealers Association, as well as clergymen, and launched a major propaganda campaign to rally public support for its policies.[63] Speaking at a conference of the Educational Directors organized by the Food Administration on February 28, 1917, Alonzo Taylor stated:

> In order to induce the people to reconstruct their internal lives and add thirty or forty per cent of energy, on top of what they are doing, they must be convinced that the situation is one that demands, practically and imperatively, this reconstruction of the internal life and this putting forth of every ounce of energy. The people are never going to do that unless they are convinced that it is absolutely necessary.[64]

In May 1917, the Publicity Bureau of the American Committee for Armenian and Syrian Relief launched a major publicity campaign, distributing information about its relief work in Armenia, Syria, Caucasus, Persia, Mesopotamia, Egypt, and Palestine, all designated on maps specifically prepared for this campaign for later dissemination. The letters stated: "Give the map a place in your columns. It will be sent you without expense *for release June 3*, if you fill out and return the enclosed post card. It comes in widths of two columns and three columns respectively—electro, matrix, or proof."[65]

The disruption of U.S.-Turkish relations did not lead to the termination of distribution of relief aid, and representatives of the American Committee for Armenian and Syrian Relief (ACASR) continued their work. In some regions, Swiss and German missionaries assumed the responsibility for distribution. While U.S.-Turkish relations continued to remain on friendly terms after the U.S. declaration of war against Germany, there were concerns that the Turkish masses could become hostile toward Americans. The U.S. embassy in Constantinople advised American women and children to leave Turkey, and instructed the consulates similarly to prepare for departure. As instructed by the embassy, Consul Davis at Kharpert, for example, burned the cipher codes and some of the official correspondence. At first, the acting *mudir* requested no more than lowering the American flag at the consulate. Within a few days, however, the Turkish government closed the granaries and seized all the food supplies stored in the American missionary compound.[66]

Davis remained in Kharpert for three additional weeks after the break of U.S.-Turkish relations. On April 25, 1917, he received instructions from the embassy to depart for Constantinople as soon as possible, taking with him "all the Americans who wished to leave and who were permitted to do so." The missionaries vacillated at first; yet, as Davis reported, "the work of the missionaries would undoubtedly [have] been so restricted if they had remained there that they would have been unable to accomplish anything either of an educational nature or in the way of relief work." On May 17, Consul Davis, Henry Riggs, and the rest of the American community in Kharpert left for the United States. By August, more than one hundred Americans, including the U.S. consuls with their families, had departed from Constantinople.[67]

CHAPTER 9

SEPARATION AND PEACE

As the Americans journeyed from Constantinople to Europe, the Wilson administration prepared a plan for a separate peace with Turkey. On May 16, 1917, Henry G. Alsberg, "a lawyer and editorial writer for the New York *Evening Post*" and the private secretary of Ambassador Abram Elkus, held a meeting with Secretary of State Robert Lansing on "the desperate situation in Turkey," as Lansing described in his diary.[1] The secretary of state requested information specifically regarding the economic conditions in Turkey and the nature of the relationship between Turkey and Germany.[2] Alsberg informed Lansing that the economic conditions across the empire were extremely difficult and the "industries were at a standstill." Alsberg estimated that "200,000 persons were starving in Constantinople and he was sure that in the interior conditions were much worse." These conditions, Alsberg noted, caused a considerable degree of hostility among the people toward the Turkish government; however, lack of leadership had rendered the opposition impotent against the ruling Ittihadist triumvirate—Minister of the Interior Mehmed Talaat Pasha, Minister of War Ismail Enver Pasha, and Minister of the Marines Ahmed Jemal Pasha. The Turkish leaders were concerned that Germany "designed to rule Turkey after the war," that such a possibility raises the specter of open rebellion against the triumvirate, and that to counter such a rebellion the triumvirate felt compelled to rely on German military support.[3]

AN "EXTRAVAGANT" PROPOSITION

The Turkish government, Alsberg stated, maintained a most friendly attitude toward the United States but was forced to sever diplomatic relations under German pressure. They would prefer to resume relations with the United States as soon as circumstances permitted "because they felt that after the war Turkey would have to look to the United States for financial aid, which Germany could not furnish." Lansing inquired as to the reasons why the Turkish leaders felt compelled to "obey Germany." According to Alsberg, the principal cause was their fear of the German cruisers, the *Goëben* and *Breslau*, "anchored before Constantinople with their guns trained on the city." The Turks considered bombardment of Constantinople the greatest disaster. "I believe," Alsberg said, "that, if someone could place bombs on those two ships and blow them up, the Turks would be willing to defy Germany by making peace."[4]

At first, Lansing was surprised by this seemingly "extravagant" proposition. In the afternoon of the same day, May 16, 1917, however, Morgenthau called to discuss his own "fantastic and visionary" proposition to make a separate peace with and to win over Turkey and made a similar recommendation regarding the bombing of the two German cruisers.[5] Talaat and Enver, Morgenthau believed, would welcome an opportunity to free themselves of German control. The former ambassador argued that he could use his close relations with Talaat and Enver to ensure a separate peace. He proposed to visit Switzerland to meet with two former members of the Turkish cabinet in order to arrange a secret meeting with Talaat or Enver. He would promise "generous peace terms and by 'any other means'," by which, Lansing wrote, "I assume that he meant money." In the meantime, Morgenthau continued, he would "arrange with his Turkish friends, if they favored the general plan, that they allow three or four Entente submarines to enter the Dardanelles secretly and torpedo the *Goëben* and *Breslau*, it being understood that no Turk should be in any way involved but it should appear as an act of daring by the submarine commanders."[6]

Lansing informed President Wilson of his meetings with Alsberg and Morgenthau regarding a separate peace. Both agreed that the plan warranted a serious attempt and that, as suggested by Morgenthau, Lansing discuss the matter with Arthur J. Balfour, who led a delegation to the United States to contract Allied agricultural purchases to alleviate food shortages in Europe. On May 22, Lansing and Balfour met at the former's office and discussed the plan. Balfour, according to Lansing, believed that the plan deserved a consideration. The British would prefer that Morgenthau visit Egypt instead of Switzerland "which was simply overrun with spies." Morgenthau agreed to the change and also agreed to conceal the true nature of the mission from public scrutiny by presenting it as an effort "to alleviate the conditions of the Jews in Palestine."[7] On June 1, Lansing again discussed the plan with Wilson. As agreed, the Morgenthau mission prepared to depart for Gibraltar, where it would secretly meet with representatives of the British and French governments as well as the dragoman of the U.S. embassy at Constantinople now in Switzerland. Morgenthau would secure the release of a high-ranking Turkish official imprisoned at Malta, who would serve as a "peace offering" to Talaat and Enver but also transmit a message to them from the former ambassador. On June 15, Lansing signed their "special passports," and the party left on the following day.[8]

The policy of a separate peace with Turkey revealed a strategic advantage for the Wilson administration. Capitalizing on the growing weakness in the Central Powers, Wilson put his ideals to practical use: dividing the enemy.[9] The March revolution against Tsar Nicholas II had provided Wilson an opportunity to place the European conflict within a context of a "struggle between the forces of democracy and the forces of autocracy." The United States was among the first to extend official recognition to the Russian Provisional Government.[10] U.S. relations with Russia, however, clashed with British and French interests in the region, particularly after March 1917, when the British recaptured Baghdad, and British–French competition for Mesopotamian oil intensified. Nevertheless, in his address on Flag Day, June 14, 1917, Wilson denied that the United States would pursue similar economic advantages in the region. Instead, he maintained that American soldiers would be required to fight against the "military masters of Germany," who had compelled the United States to abandon neutrality. German militarism had imposed its colonial objectives on Turkey as a part of "a plan which encompassed Europe and Asia, from Berlin to Bagdad." The German military had subjugated to its will the local populations across these lands—"Czechs, Magyars, Croats, Serbs, Roumanians, Turks, Armenians"—all of whom desired independence. "The Turkish armies, which Germans trained, are serving Germany, certainly not themselves, and the guns of German warships lying in the harbor at Constantinople remind Turkish statesmen every day that they have no choice but to take their orders from Berlin. From Hamburg to the Persian Gulf, the net is spread." Wilson thus proclaimed a "People's War, a war for freedom and justice and self-government amongst all the nations of the world, a war to make the world safe for the peoples who live upon it and have made it their own."[11]

While Wilson's speeches promised civilization for the Old World, in reality, writes Ambrosius, "Wilson projected American ideals overseas and hoped that propaganda and eventual military victory somehow would facilitate this reformation of the Old World." Theodore Roosevelt captured best the essence of Wilson's thought. In a letter to a friend in England, he wrote: "Wilson is at heart a pacifist; he is not pro-German, but neither is he pro-Ally or pro-American—he is purely pro-Wilson. . . . Moreover, he is a rhetorician pure and simple, and an utterly inefficient administrator. He is a very adroit demagogue, skilled beyond any man we have ever seen in appealing to the yellow streak in people."[12] Lansing for his part remained skeptical of the promises made by Wilson. The secretary confided in his diary that insistence on self-determination in matters of colonial territories would lead the United States into enormous difficulties, as peoples in these lands consisted "chiefly of savages too low in the scale of civilization to be able to reach an intelligent decision."[13]

For now, the administration would rest satisfied with dividing the enemy as an intermediary step toward grander schemes of world peace and civilizational reforms. Morgenthau traveled to Europe in June, July, and August 1917 with the mission to explore the possibility of a separate peace. The ambassador held conversations with British and French officials, including Painlevé, Cambon, and Steeg of the French cabinet, and Generals Sir Douglas Haig, Sir Arthur Currie, Joffre, Pershing, Sibert, and Biddle. While visiting Paris, he discussed the Armenian Question with Boghos Nubar, who expressed his gratitude to the ambassador on behalf of the Armenians. Morgenthau returned to the United States with a report, drafted as he journeyed across the Atlantic, for submission to President Wilson, but he changed his mind and presented its contents in person on September 19, 1917.[14]

The several drafts of the report prepared by Morgenthau varied to some extent; however, they indicated that he was convinced of the near impossibility of a separate peace with Turkey at this juncture. The Committee of Union and Progress thought it neither necessary nor desirable. The Young Turk leaders believed that Germany would emerge victorious from the war; further, they personally "enriched themselves through the continuation of the war." In one of the drafts of the report, Morgenthau emphasized that those in power in Constantinople were still the same leaders who had "usurped power" and forced "the Sultan to assent to the execution of their wishes." They were "the same men whom we notified, at the request of the British, French and Russian Foreign offices, in the spring of 1915, that they would be held responsible for their misdeeds." "The Turks," Morgenthau commented in this draft, "should undoubtedly be punished for the wholesale murdering of hundreds of thousands of innocent Armenians, Syrians, and Arabs." The other drafts of the report did not mention the issue of punishing the perpetrators but stated that the Turks should not be allowed to govern non-Turks. The Turkish government, however, could not realistically expect German successes on the battlefield, as the Allied military victories at Verdun, Ypres, and Lens since the early months of 1917 had weakened German positions and exposed the vulnerabilities of the German army. The Allied Powers, in turn, hoped to see the Wilson administration assume a wider military role in concluding the war, but also a wider diplomatic role in the mediation of postwar negotiations. Morgenthau noted that the European powers were "receptive to American ideas and ready, as far as possible, to meet our wishes." He encouraged Wilson "to give this matter your very serious thought. The need for a disinterested leader is absolutely imperative," particularly as pertaining to public opinion. The Allies hoped President Wilson, irrespective of the unprepared state of the U.S. military, would "take immediate control of the situation," as they needed his "guiding and universally trusted hand now at the International Helm."

Morgenthau recommended that a "special commission" be stationed in Europe to represent Wilson "in all civil and political matters." The proposed commission, Morgenthau argued, would, guided by the president, maintain close relations with political and military authorities as well as the press so as to influence public opinion. The commission would "collect all possible information, especially of a political nature" and report the findings to Wilson. The Allied nations would reconfirm their unity against German autocracy, the "menace to the welfare and rights of self government of surrounding nations." With a touch of self-affirmation of his own identity as a loyal American citizen, Morgenthau added: "No one feels this more keenly than the Germans and their descendants in the United States. They left Germany to escape this monster and enjoyed the privilege of living anew and becoming an indissoluble part of this great liberty-loving nation. Alexander II emancipated the Russian serf; Lincoln freed the poor Negro; and it is your privilege to extricate the Germans from their miserable thraldom." The crucial difference between Alexander II and Lincoln acting as leaders of their respective countries, on the one hand, and the proposed role for President Wilson at the "international helm," on the other, seemed irrelevant to Morgenthau. According to the ambassador, Wilson "was deeply impressed with the earnestness and solemnity of this message"; the president appeared "overpowered at the thought of the stupendous responsibility that it thrust upon him." Morgenthau observed: "he seemed perplexed, he seemed

almost to despair. 'They want me to lead them!' he exclaimed. 'But
where shall I lead them to?' " [15]

ON THE DOMESTIC FRONT

The issue of a separate peace, and the Armenian Question along with
it, receded from further consideration as the mid-term congressional
elections of 1918 drew near. Having secured the reelection of Wilson,
Morgenthau was less sure of the fortunes of the president's party in
the approaching congressional elections. The U.S. involvement in the
war created difficulties for the Democrats regarding public opinion.
Wilson had reneged on his promise to keep the country out of the
war, and now as the midterm elections approached, he and his party
felt compelled to remold public opinion into accepting the administration's justification for entering the war.

The Democratic leadership and George Creel had been working
to counter antiwar sentiments across the country, and Morgenthau
contributed his share for the mobilization of public support for the
Wilson administration. On November 26, 1917, a year before the
congressional elections, in a letter to Wilson he expressed concern that
antiwar and increasingly anti-Wilson sentiments might cause losses for
the Democratic Party in the midterm elections. Morgenthau wrote:

> It has occurred to me that someone should undertake a very specific task
> which now presents itself to me as necessary. This task is to concentrate
> the public mind upon certain facts leading up to the war with a view to
> rallying the indifferent and winning those who oppose us. The situation
> requires that the story of Germany's intrigue and perfidy be adequately
> set down in a way to be perfectly comprehended by our people.[16]

To educate the public, Morgenthau stated, "I am considering writing
a book in which I would lay bare" German schemes to conquer not
only Turkey and the Balkans, but the entire world. Such a book, he
wrote, would "appeal to the mass of Americans in small towns and
country districts as no other aspect of the war could, and convince
them of the necessity of carrying the war to a victorious conclusion."
Morgenthau expected the book to be "published simultaneously over
the whole country in the important daily newspapers, and in some of
the larger agricultural publications" in early summer. He inquired
whether President Wilson would approve of the project, the profits of
which, Morgenthau proposed, would be donated to a congressional
campaign committee, which in turn would assist "all Congressional

candidates of whose loyalty and support to the Administration, there can be no doubt."[17] Having received Wilson's approval, Morgenthau, with the assistance of Hagop S. Andonian and Arshak Schmavonian,[18] set out to complete the task as quickly as possible. Andonian in fact was to be drafted into military service, but Morgenthau intervened because, Morgenthau wrote to Third Assistant Secretary of State Breckenridge Long, Andonian possessed "intimate knowledge of the East" and therefore "could render greater service to his country by assisting me than by performing such functions as may be assigned to him as private in the army."[19]

As sections of the book were published in installments in the popular *World's Work* the following year,[20] Morgenthau toured the country giving public speeches on the subject and received letters of congratulations for his efforts to inform American public opinion about the brutal leaders and events in Germany and Turkey.[21] One reader was so impressed by the quality of the first installment that he recommended Secretary of the Navy Josephus Daniels to use parts of the article in his speeches.[22] Vartan Malcom, an Armenian attorney in Boston, congratulated Morgenthau for his articles on the Armenian massacres.[23] Encouraged by the overwhelmingly positive reviews of his work, Morgenthau proposed Wilson a production of a film based on the book. Wilson, however, rejected the idea as "a matter of principle." Moreover, he wrote, "There is nothing practical that we can do for the time being in the matter of the Armenian massacres, for example, and the attitude of the country toward Turkey is already fixed. It does not need enhancement."[24] The book, titled *Ambassador Morgenthau's Story* and dedicated to Wilson, was published in early October 1918, in time for the public to read before the congressional elections in November.[25]

The Wilson administration did not intend a military engagement in Turkey, as indicated earlier in the year when the president requested a declaration of war against Germany. The Bolshevik revolution in November and its promises to secure peace with Germany could have changed that policy.[26] In his annual message of December 4, 1917, Wilson, as before, condemned German aggression. He also emphasized the lack of "sympathy and enthusiasm" on the part of the Russian people toward the Allied cause. The Bolshevik revolution, he believed, had "poisoned" the Russians, now left "in the dark" and unable to comprehend the significance of an Allied victory for world peace. He portrayed Austria-Hungary, Bulgaria, and Turkey as the victims of "Prussian conquest and the Prussian menace." "We shall hope," he declared, "to secure for the peoples of the Balkan peninsula and for the people of the Turkish Empire the right and opportunity to make their own lives safe, their own fortunes secure against oppression or injustice and from the dictation of foreign courts or parties." Austria–Hungary, Wilson stated, "is for the time being not her own mistress but simply the vassal of the German Government," and therefore the United States felt compelled to use force to secure its freedom. He added: "The same logic would lead us to a declaration of war against Turkey and Bulgaria. They also are the tools of Germany. But they are mere tools and do not yet stand in the direct path of our necessary action. We shall go wherever the necessities of this war carry, but it seems to me that we should go only where immediate and practical consideration lead us and not heed any others."[27]

Wilson thus requested a declaration of war against the Austro–Hungarian Empire, and on December 7, 1917, Congress declared war. Some members of Congress advocated a declaration of war against Turkey as well, but, according to historian Robert Daniel, "there was no organized effort to bring about a declaration of war" on that country.[28] As it happened, there was in fact an organized effort to exclude Turkey from the declaration of war. The reasoning as presented by Barton to Senator Henry Cabot Lodge, the Republican leader from Massachusetts, provided an evidence as to the justification for the absence of such a policy. In December 1917, in his letter to Lodge, Barton stated that the atrocities committed by the Turks against non-Muslims was not unique to the Young Turk government presently in power but that it was the result of "Mohammedan law" applicable by any such government. After conversing with "from fifty to one hundred Americans" who had been active in the Ottoman Empire, Barton noted, he had come to the conclusion that the Turkish leaders, particularly Minister of War Enver Pasha, had served as agents of the German government. Nevertheless, Barton argued, Turkish officials were "increasingly friendly toward the United States" and that "they regard America as an ally rather than as an enemy." Moreover, a declaration of war by the United States against Turkey would lead to the immediate German confiscation of "the large plants of American colleges and institutions in Constantinople, Smyrna, Beirut, and elsewhere" for their military purposes, and would give Germany added justification to insist that Turkish authorities continue and even intensify their brutalities against non-Muslim populations, particularly those perceived as potentially jeopardizing German geopolitical aspirations in the region.

As a matter of military strategy, Barton noted, the United States must concentrate its energies in France and Italy, which therefore would not permit direct and sufficient military engagement in Turkey as to exert pressure on the Turkish leadership to change course, but would in fact "stir up new disturbances within the country, and would jeopardize American life and American interests as well as the lives of millions of helpless non-Muslems for whose protection nothing whatever could be done."[29] Barton and Cleveland Dodge thus continued their campaign to avoid any declaration of war on Turkey. A war with Turkey was militarily undesirable because the United States could not mount an attack on Turkey without undermining its efforts against Germany in the European theater, and it would bind Turkey and Germany diplomatically closer at a time when they seemed to be drifting apart. To these arguments was added the humanitarian consideration that a declaration of war would halt American relief work and subject American properties in Turkey to destruction and expropriation. Similar arguments were employed both by other opponents of war with Turkey, most notably President Wilson and Lansing. During a meeting with Lansing, Wilson expressed his approval for a declaration of war against Bulgaria, but not against Turkey. Later, when Consul Jesse Jackson reported from Aleppo that the missionaries now "favored war on Turkey if we struck hard," Lansing replied: "Tell them to get us the ships and then I will talk."[30]

On January 8, 1918, Wilson delivered his Fourteen Points address to a joint session of Congress.[31] His address sought to accomplish several objectives. With respect to the war, as Kendrick Clements has noted, the speech attempted to "encourage dissension within Germany and the Austro-Hungarian Empire and partly to seize control of the peace process from Russian Bolsheviks who were negotiating with the Germans at Brest-Litovsk and urging other belligerents to join in."[32] With respect to the Bolshevik revolution, Wilson hoped that his Fourteen Points would present the United States as a competitor against the promises advanced by V.I. Lenin for "the liberation of all colonies; the liberation of all dependent, oppressed, and non-sovereign peoples."[33] With respect to the Ottoman Empire, Point XII stated:

> The Turkish portions of the present Ottoman Empire should be assured a secure sovereignty, but the other nationalities which are now under Turkish rule should be assured an undoubted security of life and an absolutely unmolested opportunity of autonomous development, and the Dardanelles should be permanently opened as a free passage to the ships and commerce of all nations under international guarantees.[34]

Three points are worth noting regarding this oft-quoted paragraph. First, it is not clear how Wilson defined "the Turkish portions" of the empire. Second, and related to the first, it makes no reference to the fact that the Armenians, as one of the "nationalities," had been deported from their homeland and massacred. The establishment of "a secure sovereignty" for Turkey would, as dictated by the political reality on the field, render assurances for "autonomous development" irrelevant unless the administration was prepared to bear the responsibilities of repatriation. When on January 5 Wilson and House met to discuss the final draft of the speech, the president contemplated revising Point XII specifically to mention Armenia, Syria, and others, but House disagreed, "believing that what was said was sufficient to indicate this, and it finally stood as originally framed."[35] Third, in addition to the familiar proposition regarding the small nations, the Fourteen Points also contained principles of political economy, and Point XII underscored the necessity of keeping the Dardanelles open to international commerce, a central consideration of the Wilson administration for postwar economic development at home and abroad.[36] The Fourteen Points were therefore more than a statement on self-determination and democracy. The Wilson administration sought to address the "growing [domestic] economic concern toward the end of the war that the loss of war orders might bring about depression and unemployment. Moreover, Americans feared that Britain and France would institute economic restrictions after the war and greatly reduce America's overseas markets." Thus in Point III, Wilson advocated "the removal, so far as possible, of all economic barriers and the establishment of an equality of trade conditions."[37] As Carl Parrini has argued, this point "was directed at America's co-belligerents, not its enemies." The European Allies therefore rejected this postwar plan as proposed by Wilson, as their economies, devastated by the war, required mercantilist protections for effective reconstruction.[38]

In the afternoon of May 2, 1918, Lansing appeared before the Senate Foreign Relations Committee to present the administration's position on numerous issues pertaining to the war. He maintained that a declaration of war against Turkey would jeopardize U.S. commercial and educational interests and the lives of American employees, educators, and missionaries. Further, he argued, such hostilities would undermine the "powerful restraining influence exerted by American missionaries and relief-workers upon the Turks in their brutal conduct toward the Armenians and other Christians as well as the stopping of all charitable work for the suffering population." Once "the danger from the proposed declarations of war" subsided, Lansing expected the administration to maintain peaceful relations with Turkey until the conclusion of the war. During the postwar negotiations, he argued, the United States would support the expulsion of Turkey from Europe and freedom for the Ottoman subjects. Turkey, the secretary surmised, "would never then be able to disturb the peace of the world or have a voice in world affairs."[39]

Efforts to declare war on Turkey thus failed.[40] Senator Miles Poindexter of Washington, Chairman of the Committee on Indian Depredations, after expressing his support for the incorporation of the American relief committee by Congress, complained to Morgenthau that the policy pursued by the administration was "inconsistent" not only with respect to the Turkish government and the oppressed peoples within its dominion, but also "the wider issues involved in the war." Much would be gained by "the overthrow and reconstruction of the Turkish control," the senator wrote.[41]

RUSSIAN ARMENIA

As the genocidal policies of the Young Turks continued, about 300,000 Western (Turkish) Armenian refugees fled across the Russian frontier into the Caucasus, where approximately half of whom were to die of famine and ill health. As the situation in Russian Armenia during this period has been extensively studied, here a brief summary of the events and issues will suffice. On March 15, 1917, Tsar Nicholas II abdicated the throne, replaced by the Provisional Government headed by Prince G.E. Lvov. Russians and the subjects of the tsar, including Armenians, hailed the March revolution as a step toward democratization and modernization. With few exceptions, peoples throughout the Caucasus pledged loyalty to the new government.[42] The Provisional Government supported integration of Eastern–Western Armenian programs for repatriation and, in an effort to give greater latitude, assumed direct responsibility for the civil administration of Western Armenian lands. Under war conditions, however, effective administration would require military capability as well, but despite efforts by Hakob Zavriev, the Armenian envoy to Moscow; the famed General Andranik (Ozanian); Armen Garo (Garegin Pastermajian), the Armenian envoy to Washington; and U.S. consul at Tiflis F. Willoughby Smith to organize an Armenian military corps, the Provisional Government failed to effectuate such a policy. Mired in internal conflicts and struggles to check Bolshevik revolutionary activities, on the one hand, and the conduct of war at the hands of demoralized soldiers, on the other, the Russian government would not defer its urgent priorities to the Armenian Question.[43]

On November 7, 1917, the Bolshevik revolution ushered in a new cadre of leaders, headed by Lenin, who had criticized the Provisional Government for its continued involvement in the "imperialistic war."

Upon assuming power, the new cabinet, the Council of People's Commissars (*Sovnarkom*), chaired by Lenin, issued the "Declaration of Peoples' Rights," which, guaranteed national self-determination in addition to political and economic equality and development.[44] Bolshevik declarations of "peace at any price" encouraged the Turkish command to advance, and Colonel Kiazim Karabekir soon captured territories occupied by Russian forces, thus securing his prestige under the banner of Pan-Turkism across the Ottoman Empire and among the Caucasian Muslims. The Bolshevik government signed the Russo-German Treaty of Brest-Litovsk on March 3, 1918, and called for the total demobilization of the Russian army.[45]

As the Turkish army pressed forward to the Armenian town of Alexandropol, masses of refugees fled to Erevan.[46] In a letter to Catholicos Gevorg V, the editor of *Mshak*, Hambartsum Arakelian, proposed that the catholicos communicate to the German kaiser, as a last resort, to intervene on behalf of the Armenians to prevent further bloodshed.[47] No longer inclined to place hopes in the Western powers, the catholicos issued an encyclical on April 10, 1918, urging the Armenian leadership to find means of living in harmony with the neighboring Christian and Muslim peoples.[48] The geopolitical situation in the Caucasus was far from propitious when, in late May, the three Transcaucasian republics—Armenia, Azerbaijan, and Georgia—declared independence.

LANSING'S MEMORANDUM

In the meantime, as it became clear that the Central Powers could no longer sustain their war effort, Lansing prepared a 29-point memorandum on the postwar territorial arrangements in view of the turbulent situation in Russia. The memorandum stressed three fundamental principles: "the natural stability of race, language and nationality, the necessity of every nation having an outlet to the sea so that it may maintain its own merchant marine, and the imperative need of rendering Germany impotent as a military power." The current situation in Russia, Lansing maintained, offered hope to Pan-German aspirations to dominate the southern Russian zone so as to gain access to the Persian Gulf rather than rely on "the turbulent Balkans and unreliable Turkey." Within this geostrategic context, Lansing's memorandum stipulated, *inter alia*, the following points:

> *Fifteenth.* The Ottoman Empire to be reduced to Anatolia and have no possessions in Europe.

Sixteenth. Constantinople to be erected into an international protectorate surrounded by a land zone to allow for expansion of population. The form of government to be determined upon by an international commission or by one government acting as the mandatory of the Powers. The Commission or mandatory to have the regulation and control of the navigation of the Dardanelles and Bosphorus as international waterways.

Seventeenth. Armenia and Syria to be erected into protectorates of such government or governments as seems expedient from a domestic as well as an international point of view; the guaranty being that both countries will be given self-government as soon as possible, and that an "Open Door" policy as to commerce and industrial development will be rightfully observed.[49]

These points merely summarized, in general outline, the position of the administration prior to the Armistice. They failed, however, to identify the specific steps necessary as to their implementation. How would the Allied Powers reconcile the reduction of the Ottoman Empire to Anatolia and the creation of a protectorate over Armenia? Would the postwar conceptualization of "Armenia" be limited to the Republic of Armenia? To what extent would the Allies facilitate the repatriation of the Armenian refugees to their homeland, and what, if any, responsibilities would the United States assume in the process? The administration, it seemed, had not developed a clear policy with respect to such matters. What was clear, however, was the point that the "open door" policy would remain central to the promotion of American commercial interests regardless of the outcome of the post-war negotiations.

The speech Wilson gave for the opening of the Fourth Liberty Loan in New York, on September 27, 1918, failed to offer further clarification. The speech was largely designed to counter Republican charges of weakness in the conduct of the war under the Democratic administration and accusations of potentially rendering national sovereignty vulnerable to the proposed league of nations. Reiterating his condemnation of German militarism, he asked: "Shall the military power of any nation or group of nations be suffered to determine the fortunes of peoples over whom they have no right to rule except the right to force? Shall strong nations be free to wrong weak nations and make them subject to their purpose and interest?" He then identified five principles for the postwar peace scheme: impartial justice and equal rights, no separate settlements inconsistent with the common interest, no separate covenants outside the League of Nations, no exclusionary practices in matters of economy and commerce, and all international agreements and treaties be known to the world.[50] The content of the address was vague, interspersed with sprinklings of minor specifics. It mentioned neither self-determination nor the role of small states, neither Turkey nor Armenia.[51] A speech by Secretary Daniels two days later, on September 29, also proved mostly rhetorical, with little indication as to policy. He stated:

> a new entente, a new United States of the Near East, composed of the Arabs, the Armenians and the Jews, combining to give to the Orient a new culture, a new civilization, and making of it a guarantor of world-peace. And not only the spiritual rebirth of the Orient, but the rebirth of new ideals, of new ethical values, of new conceptions of social justice which shall spring as a blessing for all mankind from that land and that people whose law-givers and prophets and sages, in ancient days, spoke those truths which have come thundering down the ages, and which form the fabric and the foundation of modern civilization.[52]

If these public pronouncements were expected to garner political support for the Democratic Party in the congressional elections in November, they failed. As the elections neared, Lansing, too, became concerned about public opinion. In a memorandum referring to the "dangerous state of public opinion" and dated October 12, 1918, Lansing complained that "impulse rather than commonsense seems to control" public opinion which, he maintained, was easily malleable by public men with political agendas. "Today," Lansing wrote, "the voice of the American people is, judging from Congress and the press—not always the best proof however—relentless as that of the ancient Romans when they fiercely cried out that Carthage must be utterly destroyed. . . . There is one thing, however, that is only too obvious. It is that on the crest of this wave of passion which is sweeping over the country rides the malignant Roosevelt, the partisan Lodge . . . and all the lesser enemies of the Administration who have been seeking for a chance to bite."[53]

Morgenthau, also concerned about the election results, participated directly in public events organized for the Democratic campaign. He gave a speech at the Carnegie Hall and another at Cooper Union on Germany and U.S. policy toward that government.[54] The University of Wisconsin and the League to Enforce Peace requested that Morgenthau speak bearing in mind the opinion of "the mixed population in Wisconsin and adjacent states," in hopes of "remedying" the situation. "I consider the invitation one of the most important that will come to you this year, or at any time . . . [and] the meeting will be epoch-making in its influence," wrote William Short, secretary of the League to Enforce Peace, whose president at the time was William Howard Taft.[55] The Speakers Bureau of the United War Work Campaign, which included on its roster such luminaries as John D. Rockefeller, Jr., Albert G. Milibank, Cleveland H. Dodge, J.P. Morgan, and, as its letterhead boasted, was "organized at the request of President Wilson," thanked Morgenthau, its honorary chairman, for his "untiring zeal" for the campaign.[56] As Morgenthau and the American missionaries publicized the atrocities committed by Germany and Turkey against Belgians, Armenians, and Syrians, their activities conveniently coincided with the political interests of the Wilson administration and the Democratic Party in this election year. In the realm of foreign policy, the Democratic Party was to appear as the one posed to conclude the war to American satisfaction and the one engaged in humanitarian enterprises to feed and to clothe refugees across war-torn lands; at home, the party promised to effectively address postwar economic problems of recession and rising unemployment.

The problems confronting the president had deeper causes, however. His approach to leadership had not been conducive to facilitating debate on major policy issues in the Cabinet before but especially during the war. Further, while in his address to Congress in May 1918 he had invited members to avoid partisanship as the nation fought the war, he could not marshal support on the conduct of the war from, and was not inclined to cooperate with, the Republican leaders, most prominently Senator Henry Cabot Lodge. Nor were Democrats critical of his policies allowed a voice in matters of policy. The congressional elections of 1918 therefore hurt the Democrats in both houses, and the Republicans became the majority party in Congress. In the Senate, Lodge became the majority leader and chairman of the Senate Foreign Relations Committee.[57]

THE END OF THE WAR

On November 11, 1918, Wilson announced the terms of the Armistice to Congress. The Allied war with Turkey was concluded by the Mudros Armistice on October 30, 1918, and with the conclusion of the war also ended, it seemed, the Turkish Pan-Turkish aspirations. The Young Turk regime was defeated, and some of its leaders fled the country. The Allied Powers organized a new government headed by Grand Vizier Ahmed Tevfik Pasha and his successor Damad Ferid Pasha, while Sultan Mehmed VI remained on the throne. The postwar

Ottoman parliament repealed the Temporary Law of Deportations on November 4, 1918.[58]

During a Thanksgiving service in Buffalo, New York, Secretary Daniels spoke of the virtues of patriotism and the "forces of freedom" that secured Allied victory in the "war of liberation," crushing "the myth of Teutonic military invincibility." He added that the "Austrian mosaic has disintegrated, Turkey and Bulgaria are broken to pieces. New nations have sprung into life and ancient kingdoms like Poland are reshaping themselves in forms of freedom."[59]

The Allied Powers were in control of Constantinople, with troops in parts of Asia Minor. General Franchet d'Esperey in Thrace and General Allenby in Asiatic Turkey were in command of "ten times as many troops as would have been needed to occupy and disarm the whole of Turkey,"[60] but instead of forcing demobilization the victorious Allied Powers chose to canvass and court Turkish favor. General Allenby was in control of the southern portions of Anatolia, with particular attention to the Baghdad railway to Constantinople, but left the Armenian provinces in the east unoccupied. The Turks for their part greatly appreciated the disunity in object among the victors toward the Sublime Porte as manifested by the growing tensions with respect to the future power configuration across the eastern Mediterranean basin. Accordingly, the grand vizier manipulated the geopolitical jealousies and rivalries among the Allied Powers.[61]

With respect to Armenia, the Mudros Armistice provided for "the release of all interned Armenians, the demobilization of Ottoman armies except for a force sufficient to maintain order and guard the frontiers, and the immediate evacuation of North Persia and most of Transcaucasia. . . ." At the Mudros conference, while the Allies insisted on Turkish evacuation of Transcaucasia, they were mainly concerned with maintaining access to the Dardanelles and the Black Sea. The Turkish delegation was successful in keeping the province of Kars and sections of the Batum province as well as delinking "the status of Cilicia from that of the eastern vilayets."[62]

In the meantime, removed from the devastated lands of historic Armenia, the multitudes of Armenian refugees across the desert in Syria and Mesopotamia were dying of starvation and disease. By the conclusion of the war, Armenians regained hopes to return to their homes. The survivors had gathered in Aleppo, Kessab, Hama, Homs, Damascus, Tripoli, Beirut, Baghdad, and Port Said. The British Egyptian Expeditionary Force marching through Palestine into Syria found thousands of refugees in Damascus, Homs, Hama, and Aleppo in November and December 1918. Sir Mark Sykes estimated that there were 30,000 Armenian refugees in Damascus, 2,000 in Homs and the nearby villages, between 9,000 and 10,000 in the region of Hama, and 35,000 in Aleppo—and more continued to arrive from the rural areas. In Mumbij, Harran, Rakka, and Meskéné, the local Kurdish and Arab chieftains counted 650 Armenians in their tents and an additional 800 farther east. Women and children, uprooted from their homes and having lost their sons, brothers, husbands, and fathers to the *seferberlik*, to the "deportation" orders, and to the death marches, could now only hope to be rescued from the Muslim houses. When the Mesopotamian Expeditionary Force entered Deir el-Zor in January 1919, its soldiers found no more than 980 Armenians left alive in the desert. Relief agencies, including Armenian and Armenophile organizations, the American Red Cross, and the American Committee for Relief in the Near East as well as the British army, provided food and supplies, while they collected the Armenian women and children to reconstitute their apraxicated families. By the end of September 1919, about 450 Armenian children were rescued in villages within 50 miles of Aleppo.[63]

For the Armenians, organized community and culture and life as they had known before the war had been completely destroyed. Their patriarchate and prelacies, their political and cultural organizations, and their commercial and agricultural economies had been destroyed and lost. They had lost family, home, and land. The survivors welcomed the Mudros Armistice and expressed hopes that the return to peace would set them on the path to recovery.[64] While the Allied Powers were in control of Aleppo, the city served as one of the major centers for recovery and relief work, the other centers being Constantinople and Erevan.

In November 1918, as Congress debated the incorporation of the American Committee for Armenian and Syrian Relief under the new name, the American Committee for Relief in the Near East, ACASR prepared an investigative visit to Constantinople "to make a complete study of the problem of rehabilitation of the Armenians, Syrians, and other destitute people of the Ottoman Empire." The Committee had, by November 1918, "collected and administered through its agents in Western Asia about $13,000,000, $3,100,000 of which has come from the Red Cross, which uses this Committee as its agent in this area." The investigative commission to Constantinople (hereafter referred to as the Barton Commission) included missionaries and businessmen, James L. Barton serving as its chair. With the support of the Department of State, the ACASR planned to send between "100 and 300 experienced American workers, doctors, nurses, agricultural experts, sanitary engineers, mechanics and other technically trained men to assist in the work of rehabilitation." The Barton Commission hoped to raise $30 million between January 12 and 19, a substantial part of which to be made available for relief work in the Middle East. The Commission also invited the Rockefeller Foundation to send its own investigators.[65] Charles V. Vickrey, secretary of the executive committee of the ACASR, proposed that, given the lack of sufficient transportation, "a thousand or more" of the motor lorries acquired from Germany under the terms of the armistice be appropriated to the Committee for use in Armenia and Syria.[66]

In December 1918, while members of the Barton Commission prepared to depart,[67] President Wilson, as requested by the Committee, issued a proclamation designating the week of January 12–19, 1919, for contributions to the cause of international relief. Morgenthau also communicated the needs of the relief work to members of the Wilson cabinet. Secretary of War Newton Baker promised to provide the Committee with 100 Army trucks and supplies from the Quartermaster General and transportation of relief workers and supplies to Marseilles. Although encouraging, this left transportation to Constantinople, the Middle East, and the Caucasus uncertain. Morgenthau wrote an urgent letter to Secretary Daniels to arrange for transportation of relief supplies to the flagship *USS Scorpion* anchored at Constantinople. In his letter, he included several recent cablegrams from Americans and Armenians in the Ottoman capital and elsewhere in the region underscoring the urgency. One cablegram from Armenians in the Caucasus read: "Hundred fifty thousand refugees in hills dying by hundred daily from hunger and cholera. General starvation imminent." A cable from Dr. Harry Pratt Judson, of the University of Chicago and now visiting Turkey, stated: "Armenia looks to America for her salvation. Reply urgent." Morgenthau added that the ACASR could pay for the coal and necessary supplies for transportation.[68] He encouraged Wilson to make a public statement to the effect that the United States should assist the "poor, famishing, shelterless and scantily-clad people, deprived of nearly all of their breadwinners and presenting one of the most heart-rending problems in the world." Such a request from the president, Morgenthau noted, would produce "fine results which could not otherwise be obtained."[69]

Morgenthau in the meantime had continued his public engagements soliciting support for relief work. In September 1918, about 725 people had attended a dinner organized by the Liberty Loan Committee of the Department of the Treasury in Buffalo to hear him speak, followed by another talk sponsored by the Trust and Deposit Company of Onondaga in Syracuse. In December, his schedule included appearances, also on behalf of the American Jewish Relief Committee, in Cleveland, New Orleans, Nashville, Atlanta, Birmingham, and Montgomery.[70] Having attended an "Armenian Conference" in Montgomery, Leopold Strauss reported that the former ambassador was "the idol of conference" and that in Atlanta 10 percent more than the assigned $25,000 quota had been collected.[71] On January 4, 1919, however, when Morgenthau arrived at Boston to speak on the Armenian Question, he "was amazed that they had not advertised that I was to speak tomorrow. It seems their (Armenian Committee) publicity man had fallen down completely."[72]

These efforts further heightened public awareness of the Turkish atrocities against the Armenians and produced some positive results. In January 1919, the Oregon State Legislative Assembly passed Senate Joint Resolution No. 5 stating "that we, the Legislative Assembly, ask the United States . . . to assist in every way possible to help the cause of an United Armenian Republic. . . ."[73] Such declarations, however, had not prevented the deportations and massacres of Armenians. Nor were the proclamations of humanitarianism by Wilson sufficient to ameliorate their situation in the Ottoman Empire. What was needed was prevention of the genocidal policies of the Ittihadists, and the Wilson administration had failed to stop the process.

Had the Armenian leadership in Armenia and particularly in the United States paid attention to the speeches and events transpiring in the country, they would have realized that placing their hopes in the Wilson administration would likely prove futile. But neither the Armenian community in the United States nor the Armenian government in Erevan possessed the knowledge and the experience to understand the complexities of U.S. domestic politics and foreign policy objectives and their implications for the Armenian Question. The Armenians held a naive view of Wilson the politician and his administration and overestimated his capabilities.

CHAPTER 10

THE PERVERSION OF PEACE

By the time the war in Europe ended, the United States had emerged as the principal industrial and financial power in the world political economy. Its economy accounted for more than 50 percent of all manufacturing in the world. Its banks had lent some $2 billion to the Allies between 1914 and 1917, and during the next year and a half the U.S. government extended about $7.5 billion worth of credits to them. At home, war-time government spending had stimulated the economy to the advantage of corporations and the average citizen, as the manufacturing and agricultural sectors supplied goods for domestic and foreign markets. Immediately after the war, the Wilsonian corporatist, "promotional state," having successfully aided the Allies in securing victory, now prepared to compete against them for a greater share of the world markets and resources, a particularly pressing concern as demands for American goods in the Allied markets dropped.[1] U.S.-Turkish trade relations had, with the exception of a handful of products, virtually stopped after diplomatic relations were severed in April 1917, and both nations were determined to resume their economic ties. In the meantime, various interests at home competed to shape U.S. foreign policy toward the tattered Ottoman Empire. Armenian and Armenophile organizations, such as the American Committee for the Independence of Armenia, stood against the domestic and international priorities of the Wilson administration, Congress, the missionaries, and corporations. The Armenian Question, its claims to moral, humanitarian obligations notwithstanding, could not compete with the incomparably more powerful short-term and long-term domestic and international political and economic interests.

The Pursuit of Wilsonian Peace

The nation was in an optimistic mood about the future when, on December 4, 1918, President Woodrow Wilson and the American delegation left New York on the USS *George Washington* for the peace conference in Europe, scheduled to begin on January 11, 1919.[2] Prior to the peace conference, Colonel Edward M. House had believed that given the economic strength of the United States, the British and the French would easily acquiesce to American demands. Soon, however, as the Allies began to cancel "orders from American factories at the end of the war, it began to appear that the American economy was more in the grip of the British and the French than the other way around." While Wilson and the American delegation attended the peace conference, the American economy experienced a rapid decline. The year 1919 was marked by falling farm prices, a recession, an increasing number of labor strikes, and the Red Scare.[3]

Wilson's participation in the postwar peace conferences also gave rise to much controversy. He appointed House, Secretary of State Robert Lansing, General Tasker H. Bliss, and Henry White as members of the American Commission to Negotiate Peace, but excluded prominent Republicans in Congress. Further, both Democrats and Republicans complained that domestic reconstruction should be accorded a greater priority over international issues.[4] Wilson had decided to attend the peace negotiations for two reasons. Wilson's vanity was one explanation. He sought to play a central role in the construction of the postwar peace as he had been in the formulation of U.S. foreign policy since he entered the White House in 1913. Being on the side of the victors, he crossed the ocean personally to claim some of the credit for winning the peace. In addition, he "did not fully trust" Secretary Lansing and his close friend and adviser Colonel House, with whom relations had soured during the previous two years. Equally important, he refused to include in the American delegation members of the Republican leadership such as Henry Cabot Lodge; the only Republican accompanying the president was Henry White, a professional diplomat but not a member of the Senate. The congressional elections of 1918 had heightened the rivalry between the administration and Congress, where the Republicans now held the majority of the seats. Thus, relations between Wilson and the Republican leadership in Congress, particularly in the Senate, were already troubled when he journeyed to Europe.[5]

Nor did the peace conference prove amenable to the agenda proposed by Wilson. Although the European Allies were willing to make the League of Nations a priority, they rejected the suggestion that the peace conference be predicated upon the Fourteen Points. When House, who had been sent to Europe to commence the armistice negotiations in October 1918, had discussed the Fourteen Points with the British and the French, the former had refused to recognize freedom of the seas (Point II), while the latter had insisted on German reparations. Wilson in turn had responded that he could not participate in the peace negotiations unless they recognized the principle of the freedom of the seas.[6]

For the Wilson administration the principle of the freedom of the seas represented a central ingredient in the Fourteen Points, expected to benefit both the U.S. Navy and commercial relations with other nations. In Washington, commenting on a naval appropriations bill before the House Naval Affairs Committee, Secretary of the Navy Josephus Daniels urged the committee to support the development of a strong Navy. Enumerating the advantages of a large navy, he argued that the United States must have a powerful Navy "to realize her destiny" as an international leader "in the protection of small nations, the preservation of the freedom of the seas for them and for the world at large."[7] An effective Navy and freedom of the seas were intimately related to the health of the domestic economy and the postwar peace being constructed in Paris.

As the administration set about promoting the nation's economic interests, one of the principal sectors that stood to benefit from its close relations with government, as developed during the war, was the oil industry. Government-business cooperation in this area had, in late 1918, culminated in the establishment of the American Petroleum Institute to promote and protect U.S. oil interests abroad. Such cooperation seemed all the more essential as competition with European counterparts intensified and as the potential (and perhaps exaggerated) threat to the nation's economy by oil shortages became of paramount importance for policymakers in Washington, particularly for Secretary Daniels.[8] U.S. oil companies, most prominently the Standard Oil Company (NY), criticized the British for trying to monopolize the oilfields in the Middle East and expected the U.S. government to secure concessions from the Allies at the peace negotiations.[9] The Department of State, for its part, instructed American diplomats abroad to report on investment opportunities for oil interests and to assist citizens seeking oil concessions.[10] The ongoing Armenian catastrophe in the Middle East and in the Republic of Armenia remained peripheral to their grand strategic designs.

THE MIDDLE EAST

After the Mudros Armistice, Armenian refugees in Aleppo and its environs totaled between 50,000 and 60,000, although that number increased to about 100,000 by the early 1920s when the repatriated Armenians returned to Aleppo. Orphanages were established in Aleppo, in the Cilician towns of Hajin and Marash, and in Juné, Lebanon. In Aleppo, the refugees, gathered in camps made up of tents and "houses" built by tin cans and wood, lived in abject poverty for years until they moved to the city. The prelacy at Aleppo, serving as the Armenian "consulate," assumed official responsibilities of representation of the Armenian community before the authorities in matters of distribution of relief funds received from abroad, verification of the identities of individuals, and distribution of letters to the refugees most of whom lacked private addresses and used the prelacy in the city's Salibé quarter to receive letters.[11]

The prelacy also established various committees for the distribution of goods and services. The National Union, created in Egypt by the Armenian delegation headed by Boghos Nubar Pasha in Paris, coordinated the relief works under the direction of Dr. Aram Altunian. In addition, as in Constantinople, various compatriotic associations (e.g., the Marash Compatriotic Union, the Kharpert Compatrotic Union, the Sebastia Compatriotic Union) were founded to care for the refugees from their respective provinces. Further, the political organizations such as the Dashnaktsutiun and Hnchakian parties were reconstituted, as were cultural, women's, athletic, theatrical, and youth organizations.[12]

While the orphanages provided a safe haven for children, they were not conducive to effective personal development. The administrators, themselves survivors, lacked the necessary preparation and patience for their tasks. The teachers assigned for the children had no training in matters of pedagogy. The children received no encouragement to cultivate effective personal relations and little training in community leadership. They lived in miserable conditions, and were forced to work 8 to 10 hours during the day in factories established by their compatriots and the Near East Relief (NER) and to attend classes at night, threatened with beatings, abuses, and expulsion if they failed to comply. According to Levon Chormisian, secretary of the Armenian prelacy from 1919 to 1924, the orphans never recovered from the traumatic experiences in their shattered lives, and as they matured, they exhibited symptoms of timidity, hesitancy, and slavishness in thought and action, ill prepared for the challenges of life as individuals and as members of community. That generation of orphans produced no more than a handful of intellectuals and community leaders.[13]

French culture along with Catholicism gained greater influence among the Armenian survivors in Syria and Lebanon, as did Protestantism while the Near East Relief distributed aid to the refugees. This was particularly true in the case of the American missionaries, who, as in earlier Armenian catastrophes, attracted the poor and homeless Armenians in rapidly growing numbers to their fold in exchange for physical safety and pecuniary favors. Indeed, as noted in chapter 1, American missionary expansion abroad sought to reaffirm the position of the church against Darwinism and secularization at home, and the masses of Armenian survivors of the deportations and massacres provided an unprecedented fertile ground for such a philanthropic enterprise. Those of the Armenian Apostolic Church, constituting a large majority of the Armenian population, countered such cultural challenges by concentrating their energies on the development of "national" educational institutions, as in the case of the Haigazian elementary school in Aleppo and years later the Karen Jeppe Jemaran (secondary school) named after the Danish missionary who had dedicated her life to the rescue of Armenian orphans.[14]

CILICIA AGAIN

The Sykes–Picot agreement of 1916 had allotted to the French the area extending from Lebanon and Syria to Cilicia, Sivas, Kharpert, and Diarbekir, but unlike the British who were already in position across the Arab lands, the French army, in command in Lebanon and Syria, confronted the task of establishing control from the eastern shores of the Mediterranean Sea to the three Armenian provinces. Geopolitical and economic considerations had led the French to demand Cilicia and northern Syria, and Georges Clemenceau in exchange had agreed to British control over Mosul. The oil reserves proved less lucrative than expected for the French, however, and Turkish nationalist reaction led by the Kemalist army to foreign occupation of Turkey rendered French administration of Cilicia impossible.[15]

As Armenian survivors began to return to their homes, Turkish nationalists, led by Mustafa Kemal Pasha, urged the local Turks to arm themselves in defense of the Turkish fatherland. For the Muslim masses, now forced to vacate the Armenian houses they had occupied since the deportations, the Kemalist movement provided the needed leverage to halt the re-Armenianization of Cilicia and to undermine the French administration.[16] The British and French military command's hoped to gain the cooperation of the local Turkish officials,[17] while the Armenian republic, mired in domestic and external political, economic, and military difficulties, could not exert sufficient influence on the course of events to alleviate the situation. The republic fell too far in distance to extend support to the remnants of the Armenian people.

Would the United States remedy the situation? Writing to Morgenthau, Lord Bryce expressed hope that the American people would accept the League of Nations. Turkish atrocities against the Armenian people continued, however, necessitating deployment of British troops in the interior, while France expected to hold on to Cilicia as part of its mandate. The peace delegation in Paris ought to give these matters serious consideration, Bryce argued.[18]

Representing the Armenian nation at the long-awaited Paris peace conference were Avetis Aharonian on behalf of the Republic of Armenia and Boghos Nubar Pasha as head of the Armenian National Delegation.[19] Representation at the Paris conference was divided between the two: Aharonian's primary object was the protection of the republic, while Boghos Nubar insisted that Cilicia be included in any plans for an integral Armenia uniting Western (Ottoman) and Eastern (Russian) Armenia. The Armenian delegation at Paris was encouraged by the favorable official and public sentiments expressed in Western capitals. Particularly supportive seemed President Wilson, whose Fourteen Points supported autonomy for the Ottoman subjects. The American Commission to Negotiate Peace proposed an Armenian state whose boundaries would include not only historic Armenia and the republic, but also Cilicia, Trebizond, Akhaltsik, and Akhalkalak. The Western Asian Division even recommended inclusion of Karabagh and Alexandretta. When Aharonian and Boghos Nubar met with the Council of Ten on February 26, 1919, they presented the Armenian case along similar lines. Disagreements among France, Italy, and Britain soon weakened the Armenian position, however, as the European powers struggled to protect their interests after the expected partition of the Ottoman lands in the Middle East.[20]

On March 26, 1919, Morgenthau advised Boghos Nubar to "moderate" his demands and "give up Cilicia," or the Armenians would "lose all." When the two met again on April 19, Boghos Nubar admitted that Armenians in Cilicia constituted less than 20 percent of the population, and he feared that Turks would oppose an Armenian state in Cilicia. He inquired whether the United States would accept a mandate over the region. In June, after another meeting with Boghos Nubar, Morgenthau commented in his diary that Boghos Nubar Pasha "knew little" about the region.[21]

THE BARTON COMMISSION

The investigative commission headed by James L. Barton, secretary of the American Board of Commissioners for Foreign Missions, arrived in Constantinople in February 1919, bringing with it the first shipment of the American Committee for Relief in the Near East (ACRNE) in the Middle East and the Caucasus.[22] Upon arrival, the commission met with Admiral Mark L. Bristol, senior U.S. representative and later U.S. High Commissioner at the Ottoman capital (August 12, 1919–June 25, 1927).[23] That its relief work would confront enormous challenges became immediately apparent. When Theodore Elmer, a member of the Persian Commission, visited the Barton Commission, he reported of the miserable conditions witnessed as he traveled through the Caucasus to Constantinople. An estimated 500,000 refugees from Turkey and Persia, virtually isolated from the world, faced imminent starvation in areas of political instability. Nor was it clear whether the commission could travel through the areas in need of aid.

Members of the commission were sent to different directions. Barton, intimately familiar with the Ottoman Empire, visited the interior of Asia Minor; Stanley White, Syria; Walter George Smith, the Caucasus; and Rabbi Aaron Teitlebaum, Palestine. Barton reported that the local Turkish officials and population greeted Barton "everywhere with the fullest expression of oriental courtesy." Representatives of the commission visited Diarbekir, Malatia, Sivas, Amasia, Marsovan, and Samsun. When teams traveled to Van, Bitlis, Erzerum, and Trebizond, they "reported that there were no refugees in these areas, that they found no Armenians were left in the region and the country in general was depopulated owing to the repeated Russian and Turkish invasions and counter attacks." It was clear, Barton stated, that "there was no need of relief work east of the Mardin–Kharpert line."[24]

Before returning to the United States, the Barton Commission established an administrative body in Constantinople, comprised of Major Davis G. Arnold, who served as its managing director, U.S. Consul General Gabriel Bie Ravendal, Oscar Gunkle (regional director of Standard Oil), and William Peet, treasurer of the Bible House in Constantinople. The report submitted by Barton to the ACRNE stated that the members of this administrative body "had authority to approve contracts, to deal with governments, to approve appropriations to each relief stations, to secure monthly audits, to approve all orders for supplies and all requests for personnel." Orphans were to be provided with "shelter, food, clothing, medical care, education, and industrial, moral and religious training"; "rescue homes" were to be established for women and girls freed from Muslim harems; "industrial enterprises" were to be set up to train orphans and rescued women in trades and to enable them to assist themselves; and refugees were to be restored to their homes if possible, or else settled in new homes as permitted by funds.[25]

Such programs, however, failed to provide physical protection to a large majority of the Armenian orphans and refugees. Moreover, geo-economic considerations soon took precedence over humanitarian concerns. In the meantime, a series of oil negotiations in March and April 1919 between Britain and France culminated in the Long–Bérenger accord concerning oil policy toward the Mediterranean basin. Foreshadowing the San Remo agreement a year later, the Anglo-French accord stipulated that both powers would secure a share of the oil in the Middle East, Romania, and the Caucasus.[26]

THE POLITICAL ECONOMY OF RELIEF AID

Avoiding the difficult issues of mandate and recognition, policymakers found it easier to send to Armenia the surplus wheat left in the silos of the United States Grain Corporation, a government agency created by an executive order on May 14, 1919, to succeed the Food Administration.[27] U.S. charitable societies under the umbrella organization of the ACRNE sent assistance to the republic beginning in early 1919,[28] and by September of that year, over 30,000 metric tons of food and clothing arrived through the NER—now including ACRNE—supplemented by tons of flour and grain distributed under the supervision of the American Relief Administration.[29] Between January 1919 and July 1920 the Caucasus and Armenia received 135,764 metric tons of relief aid, with a total value of $28,795,426, the Near East Relief contributing $11,155,591 of the total. Armenia "eventually received 40,633.5 metric tons (475,043 barrels) valued at $4,813,744 from a total of 481,945 tons (5,430,896 barrels) valued at $57,782,000, or about 8 percent of the full [congressional] allocation."

Programs were also set up for the vocational education of the orphans. In the Caucasus, centered mostly at Tiflis, Erevan, and Alexandropol (Gumri), the orphans received agricultural training, while in the Middle East (e.g., at Antelias) they were instructed mostly in manual trades and industrial work as carpenters, shoemakers, tailors, mechanics, cabinetmakers, shipbuilders, and so forth. The orphanages cared for the boys until the age of 16 and the girls until a home could be found for their safe transition to adulthood.[30] In addition to rendering assistance to the Armenian orphans, the NER sought to inculcate the Armenian youth with American values. The Armenian orphans absorbed "American ideals of wholesome living and [grew] into useful manhood and womanhood according to American standards and by American methods." The NER had cause to feel proud in its accomplishments.[31]

At home, the NER continued its public campaign for collection of funds. Like its predecessor, ACASR, during the war, it disseminated information about the tragic situation in the Middle East, Turkey, and the Caucasus, and appealed for contributions for the destitute survivors of deportations and massacres. Its representatives organized public events, sent pictures and prepared letters to the newspapers, popular monthly magazines, and religious presses, and garnered the cooperation of various women's, labor, and religious organizations. The end of the war raised concerns that the American public would lose interest in the wreckage left behind and donor fatigue would diminish contributions. Barton wrote:

> As the conditions changed new slogans were coined and new pictorial presentations were prepared. Immediately following the armistice, when the American public could be expected to lessen their interest and reduce their giving the story of unsettled refugees was told by a picture of desolation with the words, "Hunger Knows No Armistice." During the underwriting campaign when the question was the completion of a moral responsibility to thousands of orphaned children the picture represented an American, personified by a Scout, standing somewhat elevated, extending a helpful hand to less fortunate little children from the Near East. This was titled "Don't Let Go, Lift."[32]

Some of the best artists in the nation were recruited to design the illustrations used in the publicity campaign. Among them were Charles S. Chapman, Frederick Madan, Douglas Volk, Carl T. Anderson, Dean Cornwell, Casimir Mayshark, and M. Leon Bracker. American tourists traveling to Athens, Constantinople, Beirut, Jerusalem, and Cairo also contributed to the publicity of the NER, as they returned with stories from their visits at the orphanages, refugee camps, industrial facilities, and hospitals. These travelers included newspaper reporters, authors, and representatives of religious, financial, and commercial institutions (e.g., Oliver J. Sands, the American Bank and Trust Company, Richmond, Virginia; George M. Reynolds, the Continental Illinois Bank and Trust Company,

Chicago; Felix T. McWhirter, president of the Chamber of Commerce of Indianapolis; and Frank L. Fay, president of Greenville Steel Car Company). The religious and philanthropic missionaries had maintained relations with the Turkish government and now sought to restrengthen the competitive position of the financial and commercial missionaries after the war. As the transportation and distribution of relief aid indicated, even after relations between the United States and Turkey were severed, funds had continued to be transferred to Constantinople through Sweden, as the Swedish minister at the Ottoman capital had assumed the responsibility of representing U.S. interests.[33]

The U.S. government continued its role as the "promotional state" in support of the relief campaign as well. It permitted relief workers and freight for food and clothing free transportation on railroads and granted "free warehousing for these commodities in Brooklyn, New Orleans and elsewhere." In 1919, the U.S. Navy provided ships, free of charge, to transport workers and supplies and access to its radio services for purposes of administration. The Department of War transported war supplies worth $632,669 in 1919 to the NER branch in France.[34]

Relief aid, however, involved more than mere distribution of charitable funds for humanitarian purposes. They also included plans to generate capital for the NER. Barton maintained that the relief funds accumulated through contributions were not sufficient for the magnitude of the task at hand and therefore representatives of the organization "insisted on labor, whenever possible, in return for the relief they were able to distribute." In principle, Barton pointed out, relief aid sought to alleviate the conditions "without destroying their courage and initiative and without making them chronic dependents." Distribution had to be done "in such a way as to provide a possible permanent solution, maintaining the morale and the self-respect of the refugees themselves."[35]

Armenian and Assyrian refugees from Urmia, numbering about 50,000, who had moved toward Baghdad and came under British protection, were employed to spin cotton and wool and to weave cloth for the British army. As the closing of the Dardanelles had prevented importation of manufactured goods to the region, including cloths, the NER organized weaving factories to produce material for the refugees and for profit in the market.[36] Known as the "Near East Relief Industries," such operations relied heavily on refugee women and girls, who, in their assigned "workrooms," produced embroidery, laces, table covers, handkerchiefs, dresses, and various garments for markets in the United States. The NER also shipped cloth and old clothes in bales from the United States to its industrial workshops where refugee women and children sewed and repaired them for sale. According to Barton, 13,000–14,000 pieces of clothing (50 bales) were processed per day. The Industries aimed at becoming "self-supporting" institutions, and its profits were credited to the NER.[37] In fact, relief aid for refugees and orphans provided an avenue for the export of surplus manufactured and agricultural products in the U.S. market. As many senators held personal interests in industries and agriculture, and as lobbyists advocated relief for their sectors, congressional support for foreign relief was accomplished with greater ease than marshaling votes for the burdensome mandate.[38] Barton wrote:

> The bulk of the Committee's supplies were purchased and shipped from America. The requests of these orphanage cities of hungry children were met by regular monthly shipments of flour, beans, cocoa, grits, milk, macaroni, rice, etc., to Constantinople, Batum, Beirut and Piræus. . . . But every day necessitated three meals and the quantity these children consumed yearly made a complicated purchasing and distributing problem for the supply department, both in America and overseas, best illustrated by a statement of the yearly requirements for one area, the Caucasus, where 25,000 were being fed: 1,175,040 pounds of beans; 146,880 pounds of cocoa; 5,702,400 pounds of flour wheat; 250,560 pounds of figs; 246,240 pounds of raisins; 708,480 pounds of grits; 905,940 pounds of milk; 146,880 pounds of oil; 259,200 pounds of macaroni; 648,000 pounds of rice; 432,000 pounds of salt; 518,400 pounds of sugar; 2,160 pounds of tea; 56,160 pounds of tomatoes; 56,160 pounds of vinegar; 518,400 pounds of beats; 1,058,400 pounds of cabbage; 259,200 pounds of carrots; 518,400 pounds of onions; and 1,080,000 pounds of potatoes, making a total of 14,688,900 pounds of supplies.[39]

Above all, the campaign for relief aid organized by the NER and supported by both the Wilson administration and Congress sought to address the difficulties confronting the postwar economy at home. Immediately after World War I, as demands in domestic and foreign markets dropped, American businesses found themselves holding enormous wartime inventories. While prices dropped sharply, cuts in production led to unemployment, which rose to nearly 12 percent. Farm industries were particularly affected by the drop in prices, and Congress sought avenues to combat the problem. In February 1920, Julius H. Barnes, head of the U.S. Grain Corporation, informed President Wilson that 500,000 tons of wheat had been accumulated in its silos as a result of the price guarantees instituted in March 1919. In the absence of a ready market for cash, "it was feared that some of this might spoil." Steps had to be taken therefore to avoid loss of capital. Wilson authorized Barnes to reduce the stocks on credit in consultation with the Departments of State and the Treasury.[40] In 1921, for example, in efforts to check declining farm prices, Congress appropriated $20 million from the funds of the U.S. Grain Corporation to the American Federated Russian Famine Relief Committee, with the stipulation that the funds be used toward the purchase of American surplus corn. "Philanthropy doubled as a farm subsidy."[41]

The United States had sank into its worst depression since the early 1890s. Policymakers in Washington and businesses identified the problem as a "disjuncture" between overproduction and under consumption and hoped to stimulate the economy through foreign markets and "by the systematic, permanent investment of our surplus production in reproductive works abroad."[42] Moreover, the corporations responded to various regulatory policies instituted by the federal government by looking for less restrictive environments abroad. The passage of the Clayton Act in 1914 and the subsequent attempts by the Department of Justice to dissolve such conglomerates as U.S. Steel and International Harvester goaded companies to pay greater attention to markets and resources abroad.[43] Relief aid for the Armenian survivors represented part of the solution to the domestic economic crisis.

POLICY RECOMMENDATIONS AND THE WILSON ADMINISTRATION

As events unfolded in Turkey in the aftermath of World War I, policymakers in Washington debated two issues pertaining to the Armenian Question: whether the United States would accept the mandate over Armenia, and whether the United States would deploy troops in Armenia. The American mandate over Armenia has received sufficient attention in the literature.[44] Suffice it to note that the mandate system, as proposed by the Allied Powers under the auspices of the League of Nations and advocated by Wilson, was predicated upon the principle of Open Door, whereby the geographical allocation of colonial territories was expected to assure international economic equality among the Allied Powers. On January 20, 1919, in one of his drafts for the Covenant of the League, Wilson commented that the "Mandatory State or agency shall in all cases be bound and required to maintain the policy of the Open Door, or equal opportunity for all the signatories to this Covenant, in respect of the use and development of the economic resources of such people or territory."[45] From both American and European perspectives, the mandate system nevertheless entailed territorial administration for regional stability and for the maintenance of effective control over resources and peoples.

The American Committee for the Independence of Armenia (ACIA), the leading organization in the United States promoting the Armenian cause, adopted, at a meeting in New York on February 8, 1919, a resolution advocating that the peace conference consider the integration of the six Armenian provinces in Turkish Armenia (Van, Kharpert, Erzerum, Sivas, Bitlis, and Diarbekir), Cilicia, Russian Armenia, and Persian Armenia into a single independent Armenian state.[46] In attendance were guest speakers Charles Evans Hughes and William Jennings Bryan, and the organizers had requested a message from Wilson on the future of Armenia. Wilson confided to Cleveland H. Dodge that he had decided against sending a message because doing so would "prejudice a question which the Peace Conference is to consider."[47]

On February 28, 1919, commenting on the U.S. acceptance of the mandate in his remarks to the Democratic National Committee at the White House, Wilson stated that "personally, and just within the limits of this room, I can say very frankly that I think we ought to."

> I think there is a very promising beginning in regard to countries like Armenia. The whole heart of America has been engaged for Armenia. They know more about Armenia and its sufferings than they know about any other European area; we have colleges out there; we have great missionary enterprises, just as we have had Robert College in Constantinople. That is a part of the world where already American influence extends—a saving influence and an educating and an uplifting influence. . . . And I am not without hope that the people of the United States would find it acceptable to go in and be the trustee of the interests of the Armenian people and see to it that the unspeakable Turk and the almost equally difficult Kurd had their necks sat on long enough to teach them manners and give the industrious and earnest people of Armenia time to develop a country which is naturally very rich with possibilities.[48]

Secretary of State Lansing thought the president quite unrealistic with respect to the mandate. He commented in his diary that a "very noticeable fact" concerning the issue was that the availability of profitable resources in a given mandate determined the decision of the

Allies to accept a mandate. The British, French, and Italians willingly assumed the responsibilities of a mandatory in areas rich in mines, oil fields, grain fields, or railroads. At the same time, they insisted that the United States accept a mandate over "poor territories" which would be no more than "a source of expense." The "unselfish governments" of the Allied Powers proposed that in the name of humanity the United States accept the mandates over Armenia and Constantinople, while they would administer such resource-rich regions as Mesopotamia. "We would get an unproductive jumble of mountains and a port with little or no commerce," Lansing wrote, "while they would have great productive areas, profitable ports and valuable railways."[49]

Although the actual parameters of the American mandate over Armenia remained unclear, the entire question directly challenged Turkish nationalist aspirations after the war. And Turkish territorial integrity found ample support among Americans with various interests in the region. The Association of Armenian Alumni and Former Students of Robert College, for example, wrote from Constantinople to inform Morgenthau that Caleb Gates, president of Robert College, favored maintaining the territorial integrity of the Ottoman Empire and intended in Paris to advocate a single American mandate over the whole of Turkey.[50] The Turkish approach of "pernicious intrigues and under-handed diplomacy," the message read, continued after the initial shock of losing the war. They had resumed "their old activity of gentle persuasion and of blowing dust into the eyes of those who do not know them well." While declaring friendship with the victorious Allied Powers, Turks had now endeavored to hold the Armenians responsible for "what happened." The letter expressed concern that some well-intentioned Americans "have fallen easy prey to this pernicious propaganda," and added that declarations by Gates insisting on the territorial integrity of Turkey "have produced a most doleful impression among Armenians and Greeks here." The letter begged Morgenthau to use his influence to negate such proposals. The destiny of Armenia remained in "the guiding hand of the United States of America."[51]

The debate on the mandate question soon turned into a struggle for spheres of influence between private philanthropy and government resources in the U.S. relief work. The NER, led by industrialists and missionaries, represented private philanthropy, operating with the blessings of the Wilson administration. Another nongovernmental organization involved in relief work was the American Red Cross, an affiliate of the International Red Cross. Organizations outside the

United States included the Lord Mayor's (Armenian) Fund organized in London in the autumn of 1915, the Armenian General Benevolent Union in Paris (established by Boghos Nubar Pasha in 1905), and a host of Armenian relief and orphanage societies organized by the Armenian Church and compatriotic societies in Constantinople, the Caucasus, and the Middle East. The American Relief Administration, headed by Herbert Hoover, was a government agency. The relief work that was thus divided between private and public sectors increasingly became wasteful. As resources diminished, the NER, on the one hand, argued that private organizations could not expend their resources on projects that preferably could receive government funds, while at the same time the organization sought to maintain as much control over the distribution of relief aid as possible.[52]

By June 1919, it seemed that efforts by the United States to mobilize and transport relief supplies to Constantinople and the Caucasus were in crisis, as indicated by a series of urgent messages exchanged between Hoover and Morgenthau in Paris, Barton and Bristol in Constantinople, and Charles Vickrey in New York.[53] It was deemed necessary to establish an independent organization in Tiflis to head relief work in the Caucasus, but such an operation would require an estimated $1 million per month. Morgenthau informed his colleagues in New York that unless there were guarantees for appropriation of that amount, it would not be possible to establish such an organization in Tiflis. Morgenthau believed that if private organizations could no longer finance further relief aid, the U.S. government should assume responsibilities of administration and distribution. He reported that the American Relief Administration under Hoover had sent 31,000 tons of supplies at a cost of $8 million to Batum, which was expected to suffice until the next harvest. Although Hoover was not inclined to assume "full responsibility" regarding the Caucasus, he recommended that a "comprehensive plan" should be undertaken to determine further steps. Vickrey concurred that private philanthropy thus far had collected $25 million ($12 million since January 1919), $2.5 million of which was appropriated for Constantinople and $2 million for the Caucasus. Continued work by the NER would require greater appropriations from the government, as the American public could not be expected to contribute large sums for long.[54] Yet, some individual representatives of the NER, most prominently Barton, were not prepared to hand over distribution of relief aid to the government.

In a confidential letter to Edgar Rickard of the NER Executive Committee in New York, Hoover expressed doubt that the NER had a clear understanding of the "Armenian problem" and whether the members of the committee possessed the managerial skills necessary for the task. He was convinced that the relief support by that organization could not continue to render effective assistance to Armenia and proposed placement of that country under an independent program. Concerned with domestic repercussions of a failure in policy, Hoover warned that if the public became aware of the "waste and incapacity" it would be "the greatest scandal in American charitable history." The situation could perhaps be saved if the NER would "separate Armenia" from its other activities directed from Constantinople and would guarantee 90 percent of the charitable receipts of the organization "in addition to our efforts." He added: "It is improbable that the loss of two hundred thousand lives can at this day be prevented but the remaining five hundred thousand can possibly be saved. I am indeed reluctant to touch a mess created from no fault of our own." Nevertheless, Hoover agreed to send an additional cargo of flour worth about $500,000 to Armenia. Morgenthau agreed with Hoover that relief administration in the Caucasus be separated from Constantinople and more capable administrators be appointed by Hoover.[55]

On June 25, 1919, Morgenthau communicated to General James G. Harbord his hope that the general would assume the responsibility of taking "direct charge" of the situation in the Republic of Armenia to alleviate the hardships experienced by about 750,000 Armenians. Morgenthau explained that the relief committees could no longer raise the funds necessary for such a task, which now required congressional appropriation. The government of the Republic of Armenia was ready to cooperate with the U.S. agencies if the latter were so inclined. "Your immediate problem," he wrote to Harbord, "would be to arrange for the migration of these herded people back to their old homesteads and farms in Turkish Armenia." The enormity of the task, Morgenthau added, required more than mere humanitarian programs. "What is really required in this country is an American Mandatory with an American at its head." The conditions required immediate attention and did not permit the luxury of debate and proceedings by peace missions. "Were you to accept this appointment," Morgenthau concluded, "I am authorized to say that you would be vested with full powers in directing the work on the American Committee for the Relief of the Near-East in all its operation in this territory."[56] Harbord's reply raised a host of questions, including, for example, whether his responsibilities would involve political matters or strictly execution of relief. Also, he inquired, "To what extent is the President a party to the undertaking,—enough so that he can count on getting the officers desired from Army and Navy and not have some distant agency in the War Dept. make his choice for him, for a free hand in that particular would be essential to success."[57]

On that same day, June 25, Barton and Peet, unwilling to separate the Caucasus from their jurisdiction in Constantinople, sent a telegram to Morgenthau expressing their uncertainty regarding Morgenthau's proposal that Hoover assume management of that region. They argued that the relief work in the region should be kept as a single unit as currently directed from the Ottoman capital. The plan proposed by Morgenthau, they maintained, would create more confusion for the care and repatriation of 600,000 exiles, equally divided between Syria and Russia, to their ancestral homeland in Turkey. "The Caucasus situation now well in hand and can be easily and satisfactorily directed from Constantinople," Barton and Peet concluded.[58]

In New York and Washington, Dodge and other executive officers of the NER as well as some members of Congress approved of Morgenthau's plan for a more direct role for the United States in the Caucasus.[59] In a letter addressed to President Wilson, prominent leaders such as Charles Evans Hughes, Elihu Root, Henry Cabot Lodge, and James W. Gerard urged "that as a first step in that direction and without waiting for the conclusion of Peace either the Allies or America or both should at once send to Caucasus Armenia requisite food, munitions and supplies for fifty thousand men and such other help as they may require to enable the Armenians to occupy the non-occupied parts of Armenia within the boundaries defined in the memorandum of the delegation of integral Armenia."[60]

Hoover immediately informed Morgenthau that Lansing had instructed him to prepare a response to this Hughes–Root telegram, and on July 1, 1919, he and Morgenthau met to write the draft. Hoover vehemently opposed an American mandate over Armenia and the mission by Harbord to the Caucasus, in whose stead he preferred one of his loyal supporters, Colonel William N. Haskell.[61] Hoover informed Morgenthau that President Wilson had intimated to Hoover at the station before leaving Paris that he, Wilson, would take up the Armenian matter in Washington.

Armenians everywhere must have found such sentiments as expressed in the Hughes–Root letter and statements by Wilson quite encouraging. A closer reading of the letter, however, would indicate certain fundamental problems regarding the practicability of the proposed schemes. The first part of the letter, perhaps reflecting the views held by most American public opinion leaders if not by most

Americans in general, affirmed sympathy toward the Armenians. The phraseology of the statement was familiar, as similar sentiments had been expressed repeatedly by the Western powers since the internationalization of the Armenian Question in the 1870s.

The difficulty lay in what the letter advocated—namely, that "either the Allies or America or both" take the lead in addressing the hardships. Contrary to the earlier massacres, the Armenian Question now was no longer a mere "humanitarian concern." The problem confronting the Armenians presented an unprecedented situation, as since the outbreak of the war they had been the victims of a policy of total annihilation, while neither the Allies nor America intervened to prevent that human catastrophe. Now it was too late for any "sacred duty" to reverse the process. Removed from their homeland, a large majority of the survivors of the deportations and the massacres had become refugees in the deserts of Syria. Survivors near the Russian frontier had fled to the Caucasus, where since May 1918 there had emerged a Republic of Armenia. The United States had not yet extended official recognition to the republic. Significantly, the letter said nothing about official recognition of the republic as a first step toward addressing the crisis. It was necessary to formulate a foreign policy vis-à-vis the government of the Republic of Armenia based on bilateral arrangements. Yet, the Allies and the United States were preoccupied with their own domestic and foreign policy priorities, and public statements by policymakers and missionaries favoring relief aid notwithstanding, they were determined to strengthen their international economic position but without assuming the additional burdens of humanitarian responsibilities. Moreover, in the turbulent environment of the disintegrated Ottoman Empire, any solution without the military component would seem unrealistic and impractical. The assistance of "fifty thousand men," as recommended by the Hughes–Root telegram, would hardly seem sufficient for the task, when the Republic of Armenia remained surrounded by hostile neighbors—Turkey, Georgia, and Azerbaijan—while no Armenians had remained in the "non-occupied parts of Armenia." The Allied Powers, including the United States, were not prepared for such ventures necessitating unpredictable financial and human sacrifices in the name of some abstract humanitarian principles.[62]

Harbord had these issues in mind when responding to Morgenthau on June 28 whereby he refused the role of the "dictator" of the new Armenia. It was understood, Harbord stated, that the repatriation of a large number of Armenians to their homeland would require the removal of people hostile to them. After repatriation, U.S. and Allied

military forces would be necessary, in cooperation with government
agencies of the Armenian republic, to protect them against further
persecutions and raids. "The reason these Armenians are where they
are today," Harbord wrote, "is that they were driven there by force.
It will take force—at least a display of force—to put them back into
Turkish Armenia and protect them there." In addition, guarantees
were needed for the transport of sufficient supplies and resources.
While at present Hoover had promised to allocate some funds, further
congressional funding would be required; in case such appropriation
for the campaign did not materialize, the ACRNE would assume
responsibility for raising the balance, an estimated $1.5 million per
month.[63]

The mandate issue was inextricably related to the question of
deployment of U.S. troops in Armenia. Wilson, however, was not
willing to send American troops to Armenia. Instead, in March 1919,
he recommended at the Council of Four (Britain, France, United
States, and Italy) that an investigative commission be formed to
report on the situation in the Middle East. Having secured the
approval of the Allied Powers, Wilson then appointed Henry
Churchill King, president of Oberlin College, and Charles R. Crane,
an industrialist and a close friend of the president, for the task.[64] The
King–Crane Commission visited Jaffa, Jerusalem, Beirut, Aleppo,
then traveled to Adana and Mersin, and thence to Constantinople. In
the process, the commission investigated local public sentiments toward
Allied policy in the region. Regarding Turkey, however, as Gidney has
noted, "no purpose would be served by interviewing the inhabitants
concerning their wishes, since the bulk of the Armenian residents had
been driven from their homes and had not been repatriated."[65]

CHAPTER 11

UNSUSTAINABLE DIVISIONS

President Woodrow Wilson had traveled to Paris in March and returned to the United States on June 28, 1919. No sooner had he returned to Washington than he realized the difficult task that lay ahead. There had gathered enormous opposition in the Senate against his policies. Wilson presented the peace treaty to the U.S. Senate on July 10, 1919. His address placed the controversial issues pertaining to the League Covenant, which now constituted the principal object of his foreign policy, in positive terms.[1] The Senate Republicans, led by Massachusetts Senator Henry Cabot Lodge, opposed ratification of the treaty as introduced by Wilson. Their opposition stemmed from partisanship and the demand to reassert congressional authority in the foreign policymaking process rather than, as the literature on the American mandate over Armenia suggests, from resurgent isolationism.

THE WILSONIAN DEBATE

Far from being an isolationist, Lodge had advocated a greater role for the United States in matters of winning the war and of international commerce and finance. He did, however, oppose commitments premised upon idealistic notions of peace and security. As he put it, Wilson's talk about "the moral force of the world" to secure world peace represented utter "nonsense," as only military "force or the threat of force could actually assure peace." He argued that "if we guarantee any country on earth, . . . that guarantee we must maintain at any cost when our word is once given, and we must be in constant possession of fleets and armies capable of enforcing these guarantees at moment's notice."[2]

To counter such opposition, Wilson proposed to make a speaking tour across the country to marshal public support for the League of

Nations. His advisers, partly concerned for his deteriorating health and partly about the political consequences of such a strategy, attempted to dissuade him from participating in a speaking tour. Insulated from public opinion, they argued, "the effect on the Senate would be negligible or even negative."[3] Despite their objections, Wilson began his tour on September 3, 1919. By then, however, public criticism of the domestic economic situation and hostility in Congress toward him had eroded his political base. Even his ardent supporters, the progressive internationalists, would no longer fend for him.[4] Thus, contrary to the conventional view that had Wilson continued his speaking tour he would have aroused sufficient public support to secure membership in the League of Nations, and therefore would have successfully defended his position on the acceptance of the Armenian mandate, his speeches in fact antagonized even his own political allies. As he passed through the midwestern states, his speeches, coated with layers of taunts and threats, assumed a more aggressive tone not only toward Congress, but also toward various segments of the American population. Above all, however, his speeches stressed the close relationship between the acceptance of the treaty and the promotion of U.S. commercial interests in the global political economy. This point is worth emphasizing here since Wilson's brief references to the Armenians in his speeches during the tour have commonly been seen as an indication of his desire and determination to assist the Armenians. Yet, when placed within the overall context of his tour, the Armenian Question appeared no more than a passing interest for the president.

Speaking in St. Louis on September 5, Wilson referred to Constantinople as "One of the centers of all the bad business . . . of the chess game," where the "little pawns" were located. "The shrewdest politicians in the diplomatic service of the several nations were put in Constantinople to run the game, which consisted in maneuvering the weak for the advantage of the strong." Criticizing the opponents of the peace treaty and the League, Wilson maintained that in promoting the ratification of the treaty, he was "looking after the industrial interests of the United States," while the naysayers were ignoring such concerns.[5] Rejection of the League, he warned, would leave the United States "frozen out" of international commerce, would require the maintenance of a standing army and a permanently "mobilized nation" with a "militaristic organization of government." If, on the other hand, the United States did join the League, the United States would "be the senior partner. The financial leadership will be ours. The industrial primacy will be ours. The commercial advantage will be ours."

The Covenant of the League, he argued, promised a more peaceful world premised upon discussion and arbitration of grievances and unburdened by commercial jealousies, the root cause of war. The League encompassed all the fighting nations of the world, except Germany and Turkey. "The only nations that will not be admitted promptly are Germany and Turkey, and I take it that we needn't discuss it. We can at any rate postpone Turkey until Thanksgiving."[6]

The following day, September 6, in Kansas City, Missouri, Wilson reiterated the advantages of accepting the Covenant and the dangers in case of failure to do so. The former promised to lead the world toward a democratically inclined peace, the latter to war and bloodshed amid military clashes of autocratically driven governments. In a world of "unscrupulous enemies and masters," he added, defenseless peoples would remain subjugated to tyranny, as in the case of the Armenians.

> Great peoples are driven out upon a desert, where there is no food and can be none, and they are driven to die, and then men, women, and children thrown into a common grave, so imperfectly covered up that here and there is a pitiful arm stretched out to heaven, and there is no pity in the world. When shall we wake up to the moral responsibility of this great occasion?

The League would protect the freedom of such peoples, he asserted, and would make them as free as the people of the Philippines under "the American spirit."[7] In subsequent speeches during his tour, Wilson called to public attention the difficulties confronting Poland, Czechoslovakia, Rumania, Yugoslavia, China, the close relationship between U.S. engagement in the promotion of international peace and promotion of commerce, the economic challenges confronting the United States since the conclusion of the war, the resumption of peaceful conduct of trade as facilitated henceforth by U.S. capital, the positive role of the Red Cross, and the deleterious influence of the international opium trade, liquor traffic, and arms transfers.[8]

His speeches on the tour gradually became more aggressive and offensive. On September 9, in St. Paul he labeled opponents of the treaty as "hyphenated" Americans, "the most un-American thing in the world." "The entrance examination," he added, "to use my own parlance, into my confidence is: 'Do you put America into your thoughts?' If you put it first, always first, unquestionably first, then we can sit down together and talk, but not otherwise." A few days later in Portland, Oregon, he accused the opponents of the League of Nations of allying the United States, through "pro-German propaganda," with

Germany against the Covenant and the "free nations of the world."
On September 25, in Pueblo, Colorado, he charged that "any man
who carries a hyphen about with him carries a dagger that he is ready
to plunge into the vitals of this republic whenever he gets a chance."
He claimed that "it is only certain bodies of foreign sympathies, certain bodies of sympathy with foreign nations that are organized
against this great document, which the American representatives have
brought back from Paris." He went on to clarify Articles X and XI of
the Covenant and the territorial issues in China.[9]

During his tour Wilson referred to Armenians only in two speeches
and only briefly: in Kansas City, Missouri, on September 6, and at the
Tabernacle in Salt Lake City, Utah, on September 23. He never
mentioned the Republic of Armenia, or the mandate issue, or the
possible dispatch of U.S. soldiers to Armenia.[10] He presented the
United States as sympathizing with the deported and destroyed
nations but placed the burden of addressing the crisis on the League
of Nations. Nor was he familiar with the history and geography of the
region. In his address in Bismarck, North Dakota, he remarked that
while in Paris he had received numerous delegations representing
small and unknown nations; he asked the audience: "Did you ever
hear of Azerbaijan, for example? A very dignified group of fine-looking
men came in from Azerbaijan. I did not dare ask them where it was,
but I looked it up secretly afterwards and found that it was a very
prosperous valley region lying south of the Caucasus and that it had a
great and ancient civilization."[11]

Prior to his reelection in 1916 and during the war Wilson had carefully cultivated good relations with such "hyphenated" groups and
stressed national unity. Now, he relied on scare-tactics to win popular
support for his policies, a strategy so commonly familiar during and
after the Cold War. Rather than secure political backing for the treaty
and the League, Wilson's speeches further antagonized the opposition
in the Senate.[12]

VISIONS AND DISILLUSIONMENT

While Wilson toured the nation, Senator John Sharp Williams, member
of the executive board of the ACIA, had sponsored Senate Joint
Resolution 106, which, in its original draft, introduced on September 9,
1919, proposed the independence of unified Russian and Turkish
Armenia and authorized the president "to use such military and naval
forces of the United States as in his opinion may seem expedient for
the maintenance of peace and tranquility in Armenia until the settlement of the affairs of that country has been completed by treaty

between the nations."[13] On September 16, Wilson instructed Third Assistant Secretary of State William Phillips to communicate to Senator Williams and the appropriate committees in Congress "with regard to our being authorized to send troops to Armenia. I am heartily in favor of such a course if the Congress will authorize it, but of course am still willing to defer to the French, if they are sending a sufficient number, or to join with them if they are willing to accept joint military action, and we can get the authority of Congress."[14] His position that sending troops to Armenia required authorization from Congress or that he would "defer to the French" simply reflected Wilson's unwillingness to effectuate such a policy. When in a letter Charles Eliot urged the president to order "troops and supplies to Armenia" on his responsibility as commander-in-chief of the armed forces, Wilson replied on September 24, from Ogden, Utah: "I deeply regret to say that I have no authority in law to do what you suggest in your telegram, though every consideration justifies it."[15]

Senator Williams soon changed his mind and removed the authorization for employment of military force in Armenia. He presented two arguments justifying the modification: the French willingness to dispatch troops to Armenia, on the one hand, and opposition in the Senate Foreign Relations Committee to the employment of U.S. forces in Armenia, on the other. Instead of deployment of U.S. soldiers, Williams would permit foreign governments to recruit U.S. nationals for the purpose and the transfer of arms and ammunition from the United States to Armenia. Wilson communicated his disappointment to Phillips. "I believe that it is of immediate humane necessity to take energetic action," he wrote, as the survival of the Armenian people depended upon military action.[16]

Phillips replied that although the French had, as stipulated by the Sykes–Picot agreement, sent troops to parts of Cilicia, they had refused to deploy troops in Russian Armenia. At the same time, the British prepared to withdraw from the region. Polk had advised that American arms and ammunition and volunteers could be transferred to Russian Armenia only if U.S. troops could control the Batum–Erevan railway. Nevertheless, Phillips added, the French unwillingness to send troops to Russian Armenia would eliminate one of the reasons mentioned by Senator Williams for the Senate refusal to dispatch American troops to the region, thereby strengthening the president's position on the matter.[17] By the time the Senate adopted the amended resolution on May 13, 1920, however, the document submitted by Williams had been so completely transformed as to render it a mere expression of sympathy, excluding the provision for the use of military force.[18]

The King–Crane commission submitted its report to the White House on September 27, 1919, a day after Wilson collapsed during his speaking tour across the United States. Having traveled throughout the Middle East during the month of August, the commission supported the joint-mandate approach. It stated that the Armenians could not be entrusted to Turkish rule, and that a separate Armenia was necessary to secure their survival and to prevent further massacres by the Turks. The commission noted that the boundaries of the Armenian state should extend to parts of Trebizond, Erzerum, Bitlis, and Van (those areas under Russian control in 1916–1917), but Armenian territorial aspirations aside, Sivas, Kharpert, and Cilicia should be part of Anatolia. In case of failure in management, future negotiations would determine the status of Analotia under Armenian rule. The report thus recommended a single mandatory over three separate states: an Armenian state (excluding Cilicia), the internationalization of Constantinople as an autonomous entity, and a Turkish state in the rest of the former territories in Asia Minor. The report apparently failed to impress the policymakers in the Department of State, where it remained classified as a secret document during the next three years.[19]

In the meantime, following the advice by Morgenthau, the Wilson administration had sent General James G. Harbord on an exploratory mission to Armenia to investigate the geopolitical terrain and to prepare policy recommendations for future action if necessary. Having completed his mission (September–October 1919), Harbord presented the findings to the administration on November 12, 1919. He had little hope, however, that President Wilson would see the report given the condition of his health.[20] It proposed to implement the unitary model advocated by Gates and Rear Admiral Mark L. Bristol, U.S. High Commissioner at Constantinople, whereby a single mandatory would supervise the entire region from Constantinople to the Caucasus. Such a mandate would require an army of 59,000 soldiers and a five-year budget of over $756 million. The report included a list of 14 reasons for and 13 reasons against a U.S. mandate. The reasons favoring a mandate stressed the humanitarian bases for such a policy but offered little tangible benefits for the United States. Point 7 noted that "The building of railroads would offer opportunities to our capital," and Point 13 cautioned that "Better millions for a mandate than billions for future wars."[21] The reasons against a mandate, however, acknowledged the domestic and international complexities arising from deepening U.S. involvement in the region. The first point captured best the essence of the problem: "The United States has prior and nearer foreign obligations, and ample responsibilities with domestic problems growing out of the war." With respect to moral responsibilities for justice and peace in the region, Point 9 countered: "Peace and justice would be equally assured under any other of the great powers." Despite the overall favorable tone of the full report with respect to Armenia and Armenians, the negative arguments raised serious questions concerning the political, economic, and geostrategic feasibility of a U.S. mandate. The Harbord report was shelved and was not submitted to the Senate until April 1920. On May 24, 1920, Wilson submitted his proposal for the Armenian mandate to the Senate, which rejected it on July 1, 1920, by a vote of 52 to 23.[22]

The mandate issue nevertheless remained on the national agenda. A small number of politicians, Armenophile organizations, and influential individuals (e.g., Morgenthau) continued to keep the issue alive. After Wilson's illness, Morgenthau urged Barton, who supported a U.S. mandate over Turkey, to join Harbord and Taft on a tour of the United States to inform public opinion regarding the mandate. On November 19, 1919, however, the Senate rejected the Treaty of Versailles, including membership in the League, and on December 9, the United States officially withdrew from the peace conference.[23] Clements has concluded: "The responsibility of the treaty's failure must be laid squarely at Wilson's door," as he "had rejected all efforts to work out a compromise."[24]

That political and economic support from the Western powers would not be forthcoming any time soon should have been obvious to the Armenian delegation at the peace conference by the simple fact that they refused to extend formal recognition to the Republic of Armenia. Even the most ardent advocate of self-determination, President Wilson, withheld recognition on grounds that the prevailing circumstances would not permit such a step at this juncture. Nor was he prepared to assume the responsibilities of the mandate. During a press conference in July 1919, when asked if he would request that the United States accept the mandate for Armenia, President Wilson responded: "Let us not go too fast. Let's get the treaty [ratified] first."[25] Recognition of the republic, the United States and the other Allied Powers feared, would invite politically, economically, and militarily unpalatable obligations.

Meanwhile, the Turkish government found support among the Allied military officials, most notably Admiral Bristol, who opposed Armenian claims to statehood and to whom proposals to extend Armenian boundaries from the Mediterranean to the Black Sea seemed "outrageous" at best. The protection of Armenia and Armenian survivors, critics argued, would require complete occupation of, and enormous military capability throughout, the Ottoman Empire, but none of the major powers as a mandatory expressed a willingness to shoulder the obligations of such a commitment. Each hoped to convince the other to assume this "humanitarian" responsibility.[26]

The Armenian government, as Armenians everywhere, expected the United States to be not only one of the principal powers extending recognition to the republic but also the mandatory power securing the protection of Armenia. In June 1919, the Supreme Council had decided to postpone a final decision on the question until the U.S. government could inform whether it would agree to a mandate in parts of the former Ottoman Empire. Yet the Wilson administration would not respond until after it could obtain Senate ratification of the German peace treaty and the League of Nations. The mandate policy had become inextricably intertwined with the Treaty of Versailles and U.S. participation in the League of Nations. In Congress, the proponents for a U.S. mandate presented the usual arguments emphasizing humanitarian and moral responsibilities for justice and peace. If the advocates for an expansive U.S. role were to succeed, far greater and systematic efforts had to be made to sell such a policy at home.

Yet neither Wilson nor the Armenophile organizations seemed to have been prepared for such a task. Both relied too heavily on the humanitarian dimension of the projected engagement, but sympathies alone were not likely to lead to desired policy outcomes.[27] By the time Wilson finally launched his campaign across the country in September, much valuable time had been lost. Moreover, the American public viewed the U.S. involvement in World War I as a moral mission, after which American sons and fathers were expected to return home. The opponents of the mandate, led by Senator Lodge, appeared to be on more concrete grounds; it was far easier to convince the American public that the United States must refrain from involvement in further "entangling alliances" and obligations abroad diverting resources needed at home.

Urgent messages between Barton and Morgenthau in late December 1919 indicated that they had accepted defeat in their campaign for the Armenian mandate, although Barton remained hopeful that something could be done. On December 24, 1919, he wrote to Morgenthau that Armenians and Americans alike in the United States "are disturbed by the turn affairs seem to be taking in Europe with reference to the future of Turkey." While the United States delayed the ratification of the Treaty of Versailles and the Covenant of the League of Nations, Barton added, pro-Turkish sentiments were revived in Europe. "One cannot but fear that under these conditions the future of Armenia may have little sympathetic consideration, while the Armenians and Greeks and other non-Moslem peoples living in Asia Minor and Anatolia may be left wholly to the tender mercies of the Turk himself. All this seems unthinkable to those of us who know so well what has taken place in that country in the last few years in the way of abominable misgovernment and atrocities perpetrated upon a defenseless people." No part of Armenia should remain under Turkish rule, and provisions should be made to establish a "self-governing Armenia" inclusive of Cilicia, Turkish Armenia, and Russian Armenia. European pro-Turkish policy could prove detrimental for the Armenian people, Barton warned, while the United States debated its position vis-à-vis the new international situation.[28] Barton urged Morgenthau to communicate these concerns to the leaders in England and France, including the cabinet of David Lloyd George, and to present American sentiments regarding Armenia.

Morgenthau, far less optimistic, vacillated. He responded that "it would be most inopportune for us at present to attempt to influence the British or French opinion on the Turkish question." "Now that the Senate has and still is refusing to ratify the Treaty," Morgenthau noted, "it ill becomes us to say to our former allies what they should do with Turkey. It is very strange how things reverse themselves." Morgenthau went on to explain that he had asked British Undersecretary of State for Foreign Affairs Lord Curzon if it would be possible to send some of the friends of Armenia in England to Washington to "persuade us to take the mandate and he thought America would surely resent or refuse such interference. Now you propose that we should try to influence the English and French governments and I am of the opinion that they would be more justified in resenting it than we would have been in refusing to listen to Great Britain's wishes in the matter." Efforts to pursue the mandate at present "would be wasted and uselessly expended."[29]

Barton now concurred: the U.S. Senate opposed the treaty, and it would be unwise for Americans to advise British and French policymakers on the matter. The United States would focus its energies on relief work, he replied, while keeping pressure on Congress to secure the ratification of the treaty and membership in the League. Barton noted that he had not advocated support for Armenia because of the Armenian community in the United States but because the United States appeared to be the only nation that could render protection to the Armenians. "We must not lose sight of that fact," Barton added, "and that being a fact, it puts upon us a responsibility which rests upon no other nation, and which we cannot avoid."[30]

Ever so sensitive to the political force of public opinion, Barton asked Morgenthau whether it would not be possible to "start immediately a propaganda in the form of a brief, pointed statement of the situation, calling for protest in the name of justice and humanity against such action, and send it through our New York Relief office to every religious leader in the United States? They have a tremendous mailing list at the New York office," Barton pointed out. Turkey had demonstrated its inability to "govern justly even Turks, much less non-Moslems." "No promise of reform on the part of the Turk is worth the breath required to make the utterance." The war had been waged against such "atrocious misrule," and to permit Turkey to rule would lead to repeated atrocities. "Present atrocities newly breaking out indicate that the old spirit of Turkey is living and vital, and seeking only the opportunity to vent itself against innocent and unprotected peoples." Feeling defensive, Barton added: "As trustees of the Near East Relief are we not under obligation to protest with all the strength we possess against the wanton destruction of the wards of our organization whom we have been keeping alive for four years and whose very existence is now threatened by the old enemy?"[31]

President Wilson disagreed. When Morgenthau inquired whether he would "find it embarrassing if I spoke at a protest meeting to be organized on behalf of the Armenians," the White House communicated that it would be best "to postpone speaking on subjects of this kind for the present." Morgenthau wrote to Barton that the United States was too late now to exert any influence on Great Britain and France and that it would be best if the NER committee concentrated its energies on relief work rather than be involved in political activities. Morgenthau maintained that "unless the United States comes out boldly and accepts a mandate for Armenia and Constantinople and possibly Anatolia, nothing will or can be done by her that can permanently save those poor Armenians." "We can't do anything," he added, "until the President and Senate get back on speaking terms."[32]

U.S. RECOGNITION OF ARMENIA

The actual resolution of issues related to Armenia ultimately depended on the direction of, and the Allied response to, the Russian civil war. Support for the territorial integrity of Turkey became one of the principal strategies to contain Bolshevik expansionism. Not to be outdone by a French rapprochement with the Nationalist Turks, in early 1920 the British India Office and the War Office, ever so cautious not to provoke their Muslim subjects, stressed the importance of

Turkish territorial integrity to the stability of the British Empire. Winston Churchill supported this argument and insisted that improved relations with a strong Turkey were necessary if Britain hoped to contain Bolshevik-inspired agitation and turmoil. On January 6, 1920, the cabinet decided that the sultan would remain in Constantinople and that the Straits would remain under international supervision. Thus, while the French controlled Cilicia, the boundaries of the Ottoman Empire "would extend along the Black Sea . . ., thence southward to the east of Erzinjan and Kharput (leaving most of the Taurus region and Diarbekir to France), around the Adana vilayet to the Mediterranean, and along the Aegean coastline to the Sea of Marmara."[33] To the Republic of Armenia would be attached the districts of Erzerum, Mush, Bitlis, and Van, with access to the Black Sea at Batum. There was little hope, however, that the government of Armenia could function as a buffer state against Russia. Given the deplorable conditions and the unstable situation in Armenia, the British and French governments returned to their prewar policy of supporting Turkish territorial integrity against Russia.

At first, the British Foreign Office had stressed the need to maintain a buffer zone between Russia and its southern neighbors and deemed it essential to extend recognition to the republics in the Caucasus as an initial step toward creating a *cordon sanitaire* against Bolshevism. The War Office countered this proposal, insisting that British support for Lieutenant General Anton I. Denikin, who led the Armed Forces of South Russia against the Bolsheviks, would incur fewer obligations while more directly and forcefully containing Bolshevik expansionism. The British brought both arguments before the Allied Supreme Council on January 19, and after a short but contentious deliberation, the Council agreed to send ammunition and food to the three Transcaucasian republics. Having granted recognition to Azerbaijan and Georgia on January 10, the Council finally extended recognition to the Republic of Armenia on January 19, followed, after two months of vacillation, by the United States on April 23, 1920.[34] In fact, nearly two years had passed since May 1918 when the Republic of Armenia had been declared independent.

LANSING'S RESIGNATION

In addition to the complexities and divisions plaguing the debate over the treaty and the League, by late 1919, disagreements on a variety of issues also had created a deep chasm between Wilson and Lansing.[35] Confiding to his diary, Lansing thought his position "almost impossible.

I do not see how I can continue in office."[36] On January 7, 1920, he began to prepare his letter of resignation. In a memorandum, he wrote: "I confess that I cannot fathom the President's mind. I have endured many mortifications only out of a sense of duty."[37] On February 7, Lansing received a letter from Wilson accusing him of attempting to usurp presidential power by calling a meeting of the Cabinet. Wilson, wrote Lansing, "sounded like a spoiled child crying out in rage at an imaginary wrong. It seemed the product of an abnormal vanity." "Woodrow Wilson is a tyrant," Lansing commented in his diary, "who even goes so far as to demand that all men shall *think* as he does or else be branded as traitors or ingrates. . . . Thank God I shall soon be a free man!"[38] Lansing submitted his letter of resignation on February 12, 1920, and within 24 hours he received the president's acceptance "to take effect at once."[39] Lansing was succeeded by the lackluster Bainbridge Colby. During lunch with Lansing the following day, Frank Polk showed Wilson's letter that proposed Colby's name and requested that Polk travel to London to deal with the Turkish question. Both agreed that Colby was not the right person for the post. Lansing wrote in his diary: "We discussed Colby and the tragedy of such a secretary."[40]

WILSON'S FAILURE

Lansing's resignation was symptomatic of the crisis enveloping the Wilson administration. Scholars have considered Wilson's illness between the time he withdrew from Pueblo on September 25, 1919, to December 1919, as the principal cause of his failure to win passage of the Senate's support for the League. Yet, as Thomas Knock has noted, the issue was far more complicated and had deeper roots. Wilson had lost the support of progressive internationalists. The conservative "irreconcilables" in the Senate, 16 senators who vehemently opposed his foreign policy, refused a treaty that would infringe on U.S. sovereignty, and two Democrats, Senators James Reed of Missouri and Charles S. Thomas of Colorado, sided with the Republicans.[41] As Kendrick Clements has pointed out, Wilson seemed to have misunderstood the ratification process. On June 27, 1919, the president stated in a press conference that "the Senate could only approve or disapprove the whole treaty, since modifying or amending it was a part of the executive's negotiating prerogative."[42]

In matters pertaining to Armenia, Wilson was not as strongly committed as he was to the League, and he was not prepared to expend much political capital on the Armenian question. Had Wilson seriously wished to render economic and military assistance to the Republic of Armenia and the Armenian people in the Middle East, he could have done so with little constraint from Congress. U.S. presidents since George Washington had been engaged in various agreements with foreign powers without prior congressional consent, and Wilson himself had ignored Congress in his military intervention in Mexico.[43] Senator Lodge mentioned to Barton that regarding the Armenian question the executive, "under the Constitution, has the sole power to negotiate and enter upon negotiations."[44] Wilson concurred: he believed it would be wrong to allow Britain or France to assume the mandate over Armenia, for it was the "clear duty" of the United States "to assume that mandate and I want to be left as free as possible to urge such an assumption of responsibility at the opportune time."[45] Yet, he also thought pursuing this course of action would require yet another "long fight with the Congress (both Houses this time)." He confided in a message to Polk: "I am disinclined to introduce new questions just at this moment if it is possible to avoid doing so fairly to ourselves and to the interests involved in the East."[46]

Here was the crux of the matter for Wilson the politician, the chief executive, and the head of state: the struggle over the Armenian mandate represented a clash between the president and Congress—the former seeking to maintain a free hand in the domain of foreign policy, the latter determined to reassert its legislative authority in that very same policy area. Contrary to the conventional view, the Senate rejection of the League and the mandate did not stem from a resurgence of "isolationism." U.S. foreign policy had shed all pretensions to isolationism at least as far back as the Spanish-American War two decades earlier. Instead, the Senate rejection signified an effort on the part of the Senate to guard its constitutional prerogatives against an executive branch that had accumulated enormous powers during the war. The constitutionally driven executive–legislative tug-of-war, so common in U.S. history after major wars, manifested itself in the conflict over the Treaty of Versailles, the League of Nations, and the Armenian mandate.

In the final analysis, as William Appleman Williams has pointed out, the debate over the League of Nations signified more than the mere acceptance or rejection of a document and an organization, and more than a personal struggle between Wilson and Lodge. Rather, it reflected the struggle over strategy, "over how America should sustain and extend its power and authority in a world of revolutions." Most public and private leaders, regardless of party affiliation, accepted the Open Door policy as the central principle in postwar U.S. foreign policy. For Wilson and his supporters, the League of Nations and its promises for collective security represented "the best means of keeping the world safe for the Open Door policy." Their opponents agreed but also insisted on separating the Open Door policy from the proposed system of collective security. Despite the apparent disagreements, there was a general consensus on the desirability of overseas political and economic expansion.[47]

Furthermore, the political alliance between Wilson and the missionary community, particularly the American Board, since his assumption of office as president had served both well before and during the war, and their cooperation continued after the reestablishment of peace. Catering to the interests of the missionary interests, Wilson had not requested a declaration of war against Turkey. And after the war, the same missionary community, now in a leadership position in the NER headed by Barton and Dodge, sought to support Wilson in his endeavors to protect his position against the Republican Party. The NER also wished Wilson would arrive at a compromise with the Senate and thereby avoid Democratic losses in the next congressional elections. On April 29, 1920, writing on behalf of the NER, Dodge proposed to Wilson a major propaganda campaign in support of the treaty and the Armenian mandate. The approaching congressional elections, Dodge noted, presented a propitious opportunity for such a propaganda drive, particularly since the Republican Party appeared divided. The Senate would prefer "to get the Treaty out of the way," and "it is possible that this may suggest a new departure" if the president would "consent" to modification to the treaty.[48]

Writing on behalf of the ACIA, on May 14, 1920, James W. Gerard relayed to Wilson a telegram from Avetis Aharonian, head of the delegation representing the Republic of Armenia in Paris, on the desperate situation in the republic, as the collusion between Bolshevik and Turkish troops threatened its very survival. Gerard reminded Wilson that had the administration furnished the Armenian republic with supplies and an army of 40,000 troops, "as we had repeatedly advocated that we should," the present situation could have been averted. Gerard emphasized that "unless we hasten to her rescue she will be wiped out by massacre and starvation." He further brought to the attention of the president Senate Resolution 359 of May 14, 1920, approving the deployment of U.S. Marines at Batum and maintaining control over the Batum–Erevan railway for the transport of the troops and equipment.[49] A few days later, Gerard also reminded the president of the messages sent to him by Hughes, Root, and Lodge a year earlier regarding the urgency of deploying about 50,000 American troops in Armenia, and the point that Wilson, as the president, had "the power to act in the present crisis."[50] President Wilson, however, would neither entertain recommendations regarding a "consent" to modifications to the treaty by the Senate, nor would he agree to the deployment of U.S. troops for the protection of the Republic of Armenia. Instead, Wilson felt more comfortable with accepting the arbitration of the international boundaries of Armenia.

SAN REMO CONFERENCE, APRIL 19-26, 1920

Meeting at San Remo in April, the Supreme Council eventually decided to invite President Wilson to arbitrate the international boundaries of Armenia.[51] In his message dated May 24, 1920, Wilson informed Congress of the request by the Supreme Council and, referring to Senate Resolution 359, he stated that it was "providential, and not as a mere casual coincidence" that at the same time he had received the invitation from the Supreme Council to arbitrate the said boundaries. Wilson used this opportunity to request from Congress to accept the mandate over Armenia.[52] The Senate resolution was no more than "a gesture," Henry Ashurst commented in his diary, and it was passed without appreciation of its full import: that acceptance of the mandate would imply acceptance of membership in the League of Nations and lead to the deployment of U.S. troops in Armenia. "Armenia will call upon us in vain," Ashurst concluded.[53] Be that as it may, Wilson subsequently appointed a team, headed by Professor William L. Westermann, of the University of Wisconsin, to prepare the boundaries for Armenia.[54]

Ironically, by the conclusion of the San Remo conference, the Armenian question was relegated to a secondary concern, superseded by economic and geopolitical priorities. Professor Sir John Cadman, representing British oil interests as director-in-charge of His Majesty's Petroleum Department, and Philippe Berthelot, director of political and commercial affairs in the French Ministry of Foreign Affairs, signed the San Remo agreement, dividing the Middle East between the two powers with the mutual understanding that they would prevent other parties from entering the oil-rich region for exploration.[55]

Such exclusionary policies led to a diplomatic conflict between the United States and Great Britain after World War I. The Department of State sought to secure concessions from the British in Palestine and Mesopotamia, insisting on its policy of the Open Door. Communicating the department's position to the British government, Secretary of State Bainbridge Colby, Lansing's successor, maintained that the mandate system should adhere to the principle of Open Door and guarantee equal treatment for all nations.[56] In the meantime, when on June 8, 1920, the Wilson cabinet discussed the issue of sending ships to Armenia, Secretary of the Navy Josephus Daniels pointed out that the U.S. Navy could not land troops in Armenia without sufficient land force. The meeting turned to the economic conditions in Europe; it also urged that an investigative team, headed by the Tariff Commission, be sent to survey the oil situation for the oil industry.[57] The Department of State instructed its consular representatives to collect comprehensive data on oil reserves and foreign mining concessions and operations.[58]

U.S. oil companies, which opposed British monopoly over the oilfields in the Middle East, growing impatient with the lengthy peace conferences urged the American peace delegation in Paris to take a more decisive stance on their behalf and to secure concessions from the British. Standard Oil of New York had surveyed the marketing opportunities in the Middle East before the war and was prepared to expand its operations in the region.

American officials in Turkey agreed. The Middle East was one of the principal regions attracting U.S. oil policy for the exploration of reserves. Oil was necessary for the industrial development of the nation, and oil companies, such as Standard Oil, as well as government agencies, most prominently the U.S. Navy, were eager to gain and maintain access to such reserves. The U.S. Navy had launched the program to convert its fleet from coal to oil. It was not surprising, therefore, that Admiral Bristol, as the U.S. High Commissioner at Constantinople, representing the interests of the Navy and, by extension, of the oil industry, would oppose the assumption of the American mandate over Armenia.[59] Bristol criticized the policies pursued by the former Allies with respect to their oil interests in the Middle East. The European powers, particularly Great Britain, he maintained, were determined to monopolize the oil fields in the Middle East at the expense of the American economic and security considerations.[60]

Reiterating his argument in a later report, Admiral Bristol stressed that American economic development necessitated closer attention by the U.S. government to the political and economic situation and markets in the Middle East. The postwar peace as designed by the European powers was predicated almost exclusively upon economic interests. Failure to protect American market interests in the region, he warned, would exclude the United States in the future, with negative consequences for the nation's economy at home. Pursuing its imperial and territorial ambitions in Palestine, Arabia, and Mesopotamia disguised as mandates under the League of Nations,

Great Britain would secure a commercial monopoly in the region. When American geologists sought to survey the land in Palestine and Mesopotamia, Bristol wrote, the British "most strenuously opposed" such activities. Americans failed to appreciate fully the situation in Turkey, the admiral argued, on account of "the most persistent propaganda on the part of the Greeks and Armenians" during the past six years. Americans, including workers for the Near East Relief, visiting Turkey recognized this reality and changed their minds. People in the Turkish Empire, he maintained, "absolutely do not know the difference between falsehood and truth . . . [and] people, who do not understand these races in the Near East, are constantly fooled by stories and information that come from this part of the world." Bristol urged "that Turkey, as it existed in 1914, be not partitioned and that no independent nationalities be established."[61]

By 1921, as the competition between Great Britain and France intensified, particularly regarding control over Mosul, the British decided to send Sir John Cadman, technical adviser to the Anglo-Persian Company, to commence negotiations between the United States and Great Britain. The discussions led to an "oil peace pact" between Standard Oil, the British government, and Royal Dutch-Shell, whereby Standard Oil secured 25 percent interest in the Turkish Petroleum Company, in addition to rights in Palestine.[62] The *Manchester Guardian Commercial* reported of the major "commercial victory in consequence of the political intervention of the United States Government."[63]

In addition to oil interests, the U.S. government sought to bolster the nation's merchant marine to facilitate expansion of foreign commerce while European shipyards struggled to recover from the war. Immediately after the return to peace, the American Shipping Board and Congress commenced the process of privatization of the fleet. The Bethlehem Shipbuilding Corporation, for example, had received orders in January 1920 totaling $232 million, $80 million of which was earmarked for 31 ships for private owners. This reflected a considerable confidence in the future of U.S. capacity for market absorption and commercial expansion.

Postwar U.S.-Turkish commercial relations developed in the context of rapidly expanding U.S. economic interests. U.S. bilateral trade relations with Turkey, very much like with most other countries, experienced a considerable increase after the war. Little bilateral trade had taken place between the United States and Turkey after relations were severed in April 1917; the total value of U.S.-Turkish trade had dropped to about $530,000 in 1918, but that figure increased to $62 million in 1919 and to $82 million in 1920 before the Wilson administration left the White House. Whereas U.S. exports to Turkey had dropped to mere $167,515 in 1917, that figure rose to $25 million in 1919 and to $42 million in 1920. Similarly, U.S. imports from Turkey increased from $335,590 in 1917 to $37 million in 1919 and to about $40 million in 1920. Some of the major U.S. imports from Turkey included emery ore, licorice root, opium, dates, and tobacco leaf. While the import of some products appeared relatively insignificant, they were nevertheless the primary products imported from Turkey. In 1919, the United States imported 8,302 tons of emery ore from Belgium, Canada, and Turkey, at the total value of $235,596; of that total 99.74 percent came from Turkey. The volume of opium imported from Turkey in 1919 represented 88 percent of the total of 730,272 pounds (valued at $8,279,653) of opium imported by the United States that year.[64] Thus, U.S.-Turkish trade relations quickly recovered from the diplomatic difficulties experienced during the war.

By November 1922, when the Lausanne Conference convened, U.S.-Turkish negotiations for the Chester concession were revived. On April 9, 1923, the Turkish government agreed to grant Admiral Chester his long-coveted concession, now named the Ottoman–American Development Company, for 99 years, consisting of railway, mineral, and oil concessions extending nearly 13 miles on "either side of a 2,400-mile right-of-way," stretching from Angora to Sivas, Kharpert, Diarbekir, and Mosul. The development concession encompassed construction of ports, public works, mines, and oil wells, totaling $1,500,000,000.[65] Unfortunately for Chester, his project became a victim of internal dissensions and opposition by Standard Oil, which was determined to control transportation networks.

The Armenian Question was thus submerged beneath layers of geopolitical and commercial interests dominating the world political economy. The Allies had formally recognized the Republic of Armenia in January 1920, followed months later by the United States. Congress debated the Armenian mandate in May and June 1920. The U.S. Senate voted to defeat ratification of the treaty and rejected the mandate, ending the tortuous debates on the issue.[66] Humanitarian considerations proved insufficient for the task. In December 1920, Wilson requested a loan from Congress for the Armenian republic, but Congress rejected this as well.[67] Instead, the United States, having attained victory in war and returned to peace, resumed its commercial relations with Turkey.

CHAPTER 12

THE REMNANTS OF WILSONISM

The Allies and Turkey signed the Treaty of Sèvres on August 10, 1920, nearly two years after the signing of the Mudros Armistice in October 1918 at the conclusion of the war. Discussion of the peace treaty with Turkey had not commenced until the conferences at London in February and March 1920 and at San Remo in April. According to M.S. Anderson, several factors contributed to this delay: preoccupation with the formulation of the Treaty of Versailles; the redrawing of the Balkan boundaries; the debate in the United States concerning the mandate issue; the complexity of the geopolitical situation in the Russian and Ottoman empires; the rivalry and mutual suspicions among the Allied Powers with respect to their spheres of influence in the Middle East; and Turkish nationalism and the ability of Turkey to reinforce its military. "Above all," however, Anderson writes, "The long delay must be attributed . . . to the delusive hope that the United States might accept a mandate under the newly-created League of Nations for the Armenian state. . . . Wilson refused . . . to send American troops to help in the occupation of Turkey. . . . [and] never made it clear to the European allies how deeply American opinion was opposed to the acceptance of any responsibilities in the Near East."[1] The delay in the Allied decision with respect to the Ottoman Empire provided the Nationalist army under the leadership of Mustafa Kemal and Kiazim Karabekir, the commander of the XV Army Corps at Erzerum, ample opportunity to regroup the military ranks by capitalizing on the resentment the defeated and demoralized Turkish masses felt toward the Allies.[2]

The Treaty of Sèvres provided for an international commission to control the Straits and to maintain freedom of transport for ships and warships regardless of nationality; retention of the sultan at

Constantinople; an independent Armenian state with access to the Black Sea, with Wilson assuming responsibility to arbitrate the Armenia–Turkey boundary; termination of Ottoman rule in the former Arab provinces in the Middle East; Greek administration of Smyrna but within formal jurisdiction of Turkish authority until plebiscitary ratification of its status after five years; joint British, French, and Italian control of the Ottoman finances through the Council of the Ottoman Debt. The postwar Turkish government signed the treaty but also added its protest to the conditions.[3]

By the time Wilson presented his boundaries for Armenia to the Allies on November 24, 1920, the Republic of Armenia was on the verge of collapse. Incessant Turkish attacks and insidious Bolshevik machinations had exhausted the Armenian nation of its meager military and economic resources. The contradictory algorithms of European and American philanthropy and humanitarian declarations, on the one hand, and their geopolitical and economic considerations motivating vacillation and betrayal toward the Armenian state, on the other hand, had by now not only baffled the inexperienced Armenians but also rendered them vulnerable yet again to massacres and bloodshed. All the while, in the republic, in areas where the deported Armenians had been repatriated, and in the refugee centers across the Syrian desert, the loss of family and friends, the death marches, abductions and rape, wretched living conditions, poverty and homelessness, had enervated the Armenian nation. At first, victims of deportations and massacres, they had now become victims to misplaced hopes and misperceptions.

On November 22, 1920, the Assembly of the League of Nations adopted a resolution proposing to entrust the task of addressing the "Armenian tragedy" to a power and terminating the hostilities between the Kemalists and Armenia. Paul Hymans, president of the League Council, sent a letter to President Wilson informing of this resolution, which sought to identify a power willing to be engaged in the affair so as to "end as speedily as possible" the "terrible tragedy." Hymans stressed that the proposal did not represent an invitation to assume responsibilities of a mandate in Armenia. Nevertheless, he noted, the Council hoped that the United States would accept that "humanitarian task," given the great interest the American public had exhibited toward Armenia and the president had agreed to define its boundaries.[4] President Wilson replied that despite the Senate's rejection of the mandate, the United States continued to declare "its solicitude for the fate of and welfare of the Armenian people." However, Wilson added, he could not, without congressional authorization, "offer or employ the military forces of the United States in any project for the relief of Armenia," nor could he extend "any material contributions" without such authorization. Congress was not now in session, and its action he "could not forecast." Having placed the entire responsibility of U.S. policy toward the Armenian affair on the shoulders of Congress, Wilson then turned his attention to the European powers and the League. If the Allied Powers and the League Council would extend "moral and diplomatic support," he was prepared to appoint a personal envoy for mediation.[5] Speculations that Morgenthau would be the designated person proved true,[6] as President Wilson appointed the former ambassador to Constantinople to head a mediation commission. Intense lobbying was required in Europe and the United States, however, to grant the commission the force necessary to terminate Turkish atrocities against the Armenians and the military campaigns against the Republic of Armenia.[7]

THE COLLAPSE OF THE REPUBLIC OF ARMENIA

Hamazasp Ohanjanian, prime minister of the Republic of Armenia from May through November 1920, had accepted mediation of the Armeno-Turkish negotiations for peace by the Council of People's Commissars (*Sovnarkom*) chaired by V.I. Lenin.[8] Ohanjanian remained suspicious of Bolshevik intentions, however, particularly since the Red Army continued to cooperate with the Turkish forces. He believed that the Turkish Nationalists did not necessarily seek the total elimination of the Republic of Armenia but instead preferred to maintain a buffer with Russia, which, for its part, insisted on extending its dominion over the republic as a condition for support. Confronted with a drastically altered military situation by late November, the Bureau of the Dashnaktsutiun, hoping that the Bolsheviks would more favorably regard relations with Armenia, appointed Simon Vratzian, a socialist, as prime minister.[9]

On November 24, 1920, an Armenian delegation, headed by former Prime Minister Alexandre Khatisian, arrived at Alexandropol to conclude the peace treaty with General Karabekir. The latter rejected proposals for Soviet or any other third-party mediation since, he argued, both sides had already agreed to sign the agreement for truce. Karabekir demanded the nullification of the Treaty of Sèvres by the Armenian government, although his military campaigns during the past month or so had de facto accomplished that objective. Nevertheless, on November 26, Khatisian presented Karabekir the

Armenian declaration acknowledging that the republic "is disavowing the Treaty of Sèvres."[10] With respect to boundaries, Khatisian proposed to include Bayazit, Van, and Mush, as well as access to the port city Rize in post-Sèvres Armenia. Karabekir was amused: "If the Armenians claimed all these territories while they were sitting defeated in Alexandropol, there was no telling what would be left of Turkey if instead they had been sitting in Van."[11] Karabekir let it be known that the days for such fanciful cartographic illusions were over.

To avert another round of Turkish attacks, Vratzian discussed with Boris V. Legran, Soviet Plenipotentiary to the Caucusus, the potential sovietization of the republic, since only the Red Army was in position to stop a Turkish advance to Erevan. On November 29, 1920, as the Red Army advanced to Ijevan, Sevkar, and Dilijan, most of the Armenian soldiers either welcomed their arrival and sided with them or refused to fight. The following day, the Armenian Military Revolutionary Committee (*Revkom*) declared the sovietization of Armenia and made preparations for the transfer of power. While some Dashnakists insisted on defending the republic to the end, Vratzian and Minister of Military Affairs Dro (Drastamat Kanayan) saw no viable alternative to Soviet rule. Disillusionment with Western policies, constant destruction and bloodshed at home, the Turkish military victories since the fall of Kars in October, and Soviet–Turkic machinations, all had exhausted the Armenian leadership and sapped its resources and determination to fight. The Bureau of the Dashnaktsutiun appointed Dro to negotiate the transfer of power to Soviet rule and to accept the treaty with Karabekir. On December 1, 1920, the Armenian parliament voted in favor of sovietization, and Armenia was declared a "socialist soviet republic."[12] While the Bolsheviks assumed power in Erevan, the Khatisian–Karabekir negotiations in Alexandropol continued, culminating in the Treaty of Alexandropol on the night of December 2–3, 1920. The Treaty of Alexandropol was never ratified, and some Russian leaders, most prominently Soviet Foreign Affairs Commissar Grigorii Chicherin, insisted that having removed the "Dashnak menace," Soviet Russia should renegotiate the treaty to reincorporate Kars, Van, and Mush into Soviet Armenia. But the fact that Moscow supported the post-Sèvres boundaries in the Treaty of Moscow (March 16, 1921) and the Treaty of Kars (October 13, 1921) indicated that Soviet Russia, like the Western powers before, was not disposed to antagonizing Turkey and the Muslims within its borders on behalf of the Armenians.[13] The Turkish–Soviet boundary was further reconfirmed by the Treaty of Lausanne (July 24, 1923), granting Turkey complete sovereignty with the formal termination of the Capitulations and establishing the present boundaries.[14]

THE END OF THE WILSONIAN DEBATE

Meanwhile, the *New York Times* reported on December 3, 1920, that the British interception of the Italian steamer *Ancona* at Trebizond revealed that the Italian government was "regularly supplying" the army of Mustafa Kemal with military hardware. Armenophile organizations pleaded with President Wilson and Henry Morgenthau to address this issue.[15] Such pleas, however, no longer seemed relevant as the political situation in the Republic of Armenia had been radically transformed by the sovietization of the country. James L. Barton stated in a letter to Morgenthau that the question now seemed hopeless. Senator Henry Cabot Lodge, Barton reported, had suggested that the matter of Armenian loan be referred to the House of Representatives, but, Barton added, it was not possible to take such a step as "we certainly would not want to loan to a Soviet organization that is controlled from Moscow." Further, he noted, the situation in Cilicia was troubling as well. "The French are treating the Armenians horribly, evidently desiring to break the back of Armenian sentiment and force in Cilicia before the Turks came back to power." The entire Armenian situation seemed hopeless. According to Barton, Senator Lodge had suggested that the Speaker of the House and the Chairman of the Appropriations Committee take up the loan issue. However, Barton added, "I hardly feel, under the present circumstances, in a condition to press the loan because it is impossible to answer the question as to whether there is any Armenian government whatever."[16]

Soon, reports circulated that Morgenthau had been appointed diplomatic commissioner to head mediation on behalf of the Armenian people as recommended by the League of Nations. Stanley White, a member of the Organizing Committee of the Armenia America Society, congratulated Morgenthau for his appointment and assured him that the Society was ready to cooperate with him in supporting the Armenian people. "Our representatives have been in Geneva through the meeting of the League," White wrote in a self-congratulatory tone, "and their efforts have not been futile in speaking for the Armenians."[17] Henry W. Jessup, secretary of the ACIA, held that Morgenthau's "mission would have little chance of success, unless it were backed up by the influence of the *Entente*." Jessup and James W. Gerard had met with Senator Lodge and were convinced that if Wilson took a strong position on the matter and convinced the Allied Powers, the mediation would resolve the crisis, "provided he could receive some assurance that his successor was like-minded, and that the policy he might inaugurate would have continuity."[18]

To assess the disposition of the President-Elect Warren G. Harding, Jessup and Gerard on December 17, 1920, met with him in Marion, Ohio, with a memorandum prepared by the ACIA on U.S. policy toward the Republic of Armenia. The ACIA also hoped that President Wilson would send the document to London, Paris, Constantinople, as well as to Mustafa Kemal; doing so, Jessup wrote to Morgenthau, would now strengthen the position of the former ambassador to lead the mediation commission for the League. Bearing the signatures of James W. Gerard as chairman and Henry W. Jessup as secretary, the ACIA memorandum stressed that the situation in the republic had been one of constant struggle against Turkish and Bolshevik geopolitical objectives, as a result of which Armenia now remained divided between the two.[19] The memorandum warned: "We believe that nothing but a prompt moral intervention by our nation can rouse the civilized nations of the world to a realization of the terrible responsibility which rests upon them, jointly and separately, to prevent the otherwise certain obliteration of the Armenian race." The Armenian republic failed, the memorandum argued, largely because it "received no aid, material or physical, from any one of the Allied or Associated Powers, except that America sold it, through the Hoover Administration, flour to the value of $12,800,000, the Red Cross donated $2,100,00, and the Near East Relief Society donated $4,802,000, and that, in June 1920, Great Britain sold to the Armenian government 25,000 ill-assorted rifles."[20]

The memorandum charged that the long delay by the Allied Powers in negotiating the peace settlement with Turkey allowed sufficient time for the maturation and spread of the Kemalist Nationalist movement. What was more, the policies of the Allied Powers directly and indirectly facilitated the strengthening of the Kemalist military, as nationals of the Allied Powers provided munitions and matériel to the Turks, thereby encouraging the Kemalists to ignore the Treaty of Sèvres. The cumulative result as generated by these unfortunate circumstances, the memorandum stated, was the abandonment of Armenia. After two years of resistance, the republic was compelled to accept Bolshevism.

On June 22, 1919, the memorandum reminded, members of the ACIA[21] had communicated to Wilson in Paris the urgent need, without further delay, for food, munitions, and supplies for 50,000 men in the Republic of Armenia, along with sufficient assistance "to enable the Armenians to occupy the non-occupied parts of Armenia." The Committee, with the approval of Henry Cabot Lodge, had also recommended to Wilson that, instead of a mandate, the administration could propose to extend direct economic assistance to Armenia. Realizing the futility of such endeavors, the memorandum complained:

> It is respectfully submitted that this is a record of the betrayal of Armenia which is without parallel in history and which is in the plainest antithesis to the high ideals of international relationships so freely expressed at the Peace Conference and at the first session of the Assembly of the League of Nations at Geneva.[22]

On March 4, 1921, the Wilson administration left the White House, succeeded by Warren Harding. Disgusted with the "Senatorial cabal, Harding, Lodge, Hughes, and Hoover," and now preparing for the midterm elections in 1922 and for the presidential elections of 1924, Morgenthau urged former secretary of state Bainbridge Colby that a "startling address" be devised placing on their shoulders the full responsibility for the "conspiracy" to reject the League of Nations in 1919 while "maliciously" destroying the influence of Wilson.[23] As before, Morgenthau continued to receive invitations, as from the Army War College, to speak on the current issues in Turkey, the Greco-Turkish war now being of "immediate interest" to students studying world politics and military operations.[24]

On February 16, 1922, former secretary of state Robert Lansing wrote a lengthy commentary in his confidential notes on the general situation of U.S. foreign policy. Traditional principles of American diplomacy, he observed, required a fundamental reorientation toward serving the nation's business community in foreign countries. The Department of State should more vigorously aid and protect the operations of U.S. companies abroad so as to enhance their competitive edge in the international arena.[25]

Indeed, in the 1920s U.S.-Turkish bilateral trade so expanded that briefly the United States was the largest trader with Turkey. The primary beneficiaries were the tobacco and the licorice industries. Also, oil had assumed a far greater strategic significance in major power geopolitical competition in the region than ever before, and the Harding administration, like its predecessors, adhered to the Open Door doctrine toward the region for equal access to such strategic materials and demanded equal opportunity for investments by U.S. oil companies in the Middle East. Immediately after World War I, the Ottoman–American Development Company and its subsidiary, the Turco-American Corporation, were formed to promote mutual commercial interests between the United States and Turkey. U.S. companies and government officials worked in support of a unified Turkey.[26] During the Harding administration, Secretary of Commerce Herbert Hoover (a mining engineer who headed the American Relief Administration during the Wilson administration, the American Institute of Mining and Metallurgical Engineers in 1920, and the Federation of American Engineering Society in 1921) encouraged the seven oil companies (Standard of New Jersey, Socony, Sinclair, Texas, Gulf, Mexican, and Atlantic) to combine as the American Group and exercise their combined financial and political strength to influence not only U.S. foreign policy but also to weaken the influence of European oil companies in the Middle East.[27] The struggle over Mesopotamian oil, as Nowell has noted, "helped occasion even more Turkish brutality against the Armenians, whose claims to independence threatened control of oil-bearing regions. That oil had been coveted by Anglo-Persian and the British Admiralty since 1912. . . . That oil had been the object of Turkish decrees and intense negotiations in the Ottoman Empire since the 1890s."[28]

By the time the Lausanne Conference convened in November 1922, the American Group, the Chester railroad and oil group, and a third American group, headed by American attorney Samuel Untermeyer, whom Morgenthau had in 1916 recommended as his successor in Constantinople, now representing the interests of the heirs of Sultan Abdul Hamid, had the full support of the Department of State. At the Lausanne Conference, which was concluded by the signing of the Treaty of Lausanne in July 1923, the central question for the Department of State was not, to paraphrase Winston Churchill, whether American oil was thicker than Armenian blood, but how to represent American oil interests equally and to avoid the appearance of partiality favoring one group over another.

In 1923, the American Board of Commissioners for Foreign Missions, the august body that for decades had sought to Christianize the Christian Armenians, adopted a resolution favoring amicable relations with Turkey.[29] Accordingly, James Barton experienced a "conversion" from pursuing justice for the Armenian victims and refugees to advocating improved relations between the United States and Turkey. This "conversion" was similar to the metamorphosis in missionary opinion regarding the Armenians before and after the massacres of the 1890s. The growing U.S. economic interests in, and the American Board's changing policy toward, Turkey after World War I were more than a mere coincidence. For years the American Board had expanded its operations in Turkey because, its activists had maintained, the Armenians as Christians had proved more easily accessible than the Muslim population. After World War I, as reports by the Board indicated, there were no Armenians left in Turkey, but the Board now found the Muslim population more accessible, therefore warranting continued missionary activity in Turkey. The American Board was further encouraged by the reforms introduced by Mustafa Kemal promoting westernization, liberalization, and secularization. In July 1939, when Turkey issued stamps celebrating the sesquicentennial of the U.S. Constitution, the American Board, emphasizing the significance of the event, argued that "evidently there is some ground for asserting that Turkey seeks comradeship and cooperation with the great democracy of the West."[30]

A confidential report titled *Preliminary Report of the Near East Survey* conducted in 1926[31] recommended that the American Board tailor its educational policies to the national needs of the host countries, while missionary and relief agencies gained the confidence of the host government. The report also recommended that a new organization be established to succeed the NER.[32] With respect to Turkey, the report recommended that all activities in that country be conducted with government cooperation "however difficult the task may be." American missionaries should focus primarily on educational work in the villages, while Robert College and the American Women's College at Constantinople and the International College at Smyrna design their activities according to the needs of the local people.[33]

Section II of the survey, prepared by Frank A. Ross, C. Luther Fry, and Elbridge Sibley, presented two types of data: (1) background information on the social and economic conditions—for example, demography, political organization, education, and public health; and (2) information about relief agencies operating in the area.[34] The report stated that in the autumn of 1926 Armenian refugees numbering hundreds of thousands in the Middle East remained "in a precarious situation."[35]

In Turkey, the report continued, various infrastructural improvements in communications and transportation (roads and railroads) were necessary, while the industrial sector lacked trained mechanics and agriculture needed farm machinery and modern systems for water dissemination and irrigation. Institutions for health services were in serious disrepair, and efforts toward westernization required rapid social adjustments. According to the report, about 85 percent of the population could be classified as illiterate. American experts could lend assistance in all such areas at least in an advisory capacity. "Turkish authorities," the report added, were "becoming more friendly toward American enterprises. . . . So far as the agencies now operating in Turkey are concerned, the sensible course would seem to lie in the direction of bending every effort to further develop the confidence of the Turkish people about the value of American enterprises." The American institutions could no longer operate "on the basis of proselytizing for Christianity. This is an issue that must be frankly faced. No new work should be undertaken without the hearty endorsement of the Turkish Government." The situation was similar in Armenia. Its economy was in poor condition, in need of agricultural modernization and development of industries. Public morale remained low. "Armenia is the only national home for the thousands of Armenian refugees in other parts of the Near East," the report concluded, and the leaders struggled to solve the problems in the absence of sufficient funds.[36]

The forced evacuation and flight of Armenians from Kemalist Turkey continued.[37] In August 1922, an estimated 25,000 Armenians were again forced from Cilicia and Urfa to Aleppo and Beirut, while the Kemalist army forced the withdrawal of the Greek military deployed in Smyrna since 1919.[38] Mustafa Kemal declared the Republic of Turkey in 1923. George Montgomery, director of the Armenia America Society, lamented the fact that the Western powers had reneged on their promises toward the Armenians. The Turkophile elements governed policymaking circles at the expense of the nationalities previously under Ottoman rule.[39]

Dr. Clarence Ussher, who had served as a missionary physician in Van during World War I until the withdrawal of Armenians and Americans with the Russian army, expressed best the sentiment held in the United States regarding the relief aid extended to the Armenian orphans and refugees, on the one hand, and the pursuit of opportunities, on the other:

> So the hearts of the Turks are now open to Christian truth as never before in the history of Mohammedanism.
>
> When the war is over the future of the blighted country must be very largely in the hands of the Armenian children who have survived, for, as always hitherto, this Mohammedan country must owe its economic and intellectual development to the Christian. These children, these orphans, can be trained now for that stupendous task.
>
> Behold America's opportunity![40]

NOTES

1 THE POLITICAL ECONOMY OF U.S. FOREIGN POLICY TOWARD THE OTTOMAN EMPIRE AND THE ARMENIAN QUESTION

1. Adam Smith, *An Inquiry into the Nature and Causes of the Wealth of Nations*, gen. eds. R.H. Campbel and A.S. Skinner, textual ed. W.B. Todd, 2 vols. (Indianapolis: Liberty Fund, 1981), vol. 2, pp. 578, 598–99.
2. Thomas A. Bailey, *A Diplomatic History of the American People*, 2nd edn. (New York: F.S. Crofts, 1944), pp. 1–90 passim; Nicholas J. Spykman, *America's Strategy in World Politics* (New York: Harcourt, Brace, 1942); William Appleman Williams, "The Age of Mercantilism: An Interpretation of the American Political Economy, 1763–1828," *William and Mary Quarterly* 15 (October 1958): 419–37.
3. See Circular Letter, Congressman Abram Trigg of Virginia to James Preston, Philadelphia, February 25, 1799, Preston Papers, Virginia Historical Society; Congressman Robert Goodloe Harper of South Carolina to Jonathan Dayton, Philadelphia, March 20, 1799, Harper Papers, Maryland Historical Society, in *Circular Letters of Congressmen to Their Constituents, 1789–1829*, vol. 1: *First Congress-Ninth Congress, 1789–1807*, ed. Noble E. Cunningham, Jr. (Chapel Hill: University of Carolina Press, 1978), pp. 156, 172.
4. Leland James Gordon, *American Relations with Turkey, 1830–1930: An Economic Interpretation* (Philadelphia: University of Pennsylvania Press, 1932), pp. 43, 83–98; Howard A. Reed, "Yankees at the Sultan's Port: The First Americans in Turkey and Early Trade with Smyrna and Mocha," in Jean-Louis Bacqué-Grammont and Paul Dumont, eds., *Contributions à l'histoire économique et sociale de l'Empire ottoman* (Leuven: Édition Peeters, 1983), pp. 353–83.
5. Circular Letter, Congressman John Fowler of Kentucky to Alexander Hamilton, Washington, March 6, 1801, Alexander Hamilton Papers, Library of Congress, in *Circular Letters*, vol. 1, p. 269.
6. Charles O. Paullin, *Diplomatic Negotiations of American Naval Officers, 1778–1883* (Baltimore: Johns Hopkins Press, 1912), pp. 137–38.
7. Ibid., pp. 145–50; Gordon, *American Relations*, pp. 10–11.

8. James A. Field, *America and the Mediterranean World, 1776–1882* (Princeton, NJ: Princeton University Press, 1969), p. 175.

9. Despatch No. 1, Morris to Seward, Aug. 25, 1861, U.S. Department of State, *Papers Relating to the Foreign Relations of the United States, 1862* (Washington, DC: Government Printing Office, 1863), p. 786.

10. Despatch No. 4, Morris to Seward, Oct. 25, 1861; Despatch No. 5624, Aali Pacha to Morris, Feb. 28, 1862; Despatch No. 17, Morris to Seward, May 6, 1862, *FRUS, 1862*, pp. 786–89; Gordon, *American Relations*, p. 12.

11. Field, *America*, p. 388; Oral Sander and Kurthan Fişek, *Türk-ABD Silah Ticaretinin İlk Yüzyılı, 1829–1929* [The First Century of Turkish–U.S. Arms Trade, 1829–1929] (Istanbul: Çağdaş Yayınları, 1977), pp. 6–7; 24–26.

12. Field, *America*, p. 394.

13. Tevfik Güran, "Tanzimat Döneminde Tarım Politikası (1839–76)" [Agricultural Policy during the Tanzimat Period (1839–76)], in Osman Okyar and Halil İnalcık, eds., *Türkiye'nin Sosyal ve Ekonomik Tarihi (1071–1920)* [Social and Economic History of Turkey, 1071–1920] (Ankara: Mateksan Limited Şirketi, 1980), pp. 271–77; Suraiya Faroqhi, Bruce McGowan, Donald Quataert, and Şevket Pamuk, *An Economic and Social History of the Ottoman Empire*, vol. 2: *1600–1914* (Cambridge: Cambridge University Press, 1994), pp. 871–72.

14. Gordon, *American Relations*, pp. 13, 48, 50, 60, 65.

15. Alexander DeConde, *A History of American Foreign Policy* (New York: Charles Scribner's Sons, 1963), pp. 351, 360–92; Walter LaFeber, *The New Empire: An Interpretation of American Expansion* (Ithaca and London: Cornell University Press, 1963). On the opposition of women's movement leaders to imperialism, see, e.g., Judith Papachristou, "American Women and Foreign Policy, 1898–1905: Exploring Gender in Diplomatic History," *Diplomatic History* 14 (Fall 1990): 493–509.

16. U.S. Department of Treasury, Bureau of Statistics, *The Foreign Commerce and Navigation of the United States* (Washington, DC: Government Printing Office, 1900), p. 24.

17. Mary Locke Eysenbach, *American Manufactured Exports, 1879–1914: A Study of Growth and Comparative Advantage* (New York: Arno Press, 1976), pp. 38–52; W. Arthur Lewis, "International Economics: International Competition in Manufactures," *American Economic Review* 47 (May 1957): 579; William H. Becker, "America Adjusts to World Power: 1899–1920," in William H. Becker and Samuels F. Wells, Jr., eds., *Economics and World Power: An Assessment of American Diplomacy since 1789* (New York: Columbia University Press, 1984), pp. 175–76.

18. Bailey, *Diplomatic History*, pp. 494–609 passim; Becker, "America Adjusts," pp. 174–75.

19. On the "promotional state," see Emily S. Rosenberg, *Spreading the American Dream: American Economic and Cultural Expansion, 1890–1945* (New York: Hill and Wang, 1982), pp. 38–39.
20. *Die Grosse Politik,* IX, no. 2183, as quoted in William L. Langer, *The Diplomacy of Imperialism, 1890–1902,* 2nd edn. (New York: Alfred A. Knopf, 1951), p. 153. See also *Parliamentary Papers,* 1881, C (Turkey no. 6), pp. 748–49, in Akaby Nassibian, *Britain and the Armenian Question, 1915–1923* (London: Croom Helm, 1984), p. 17.
21. Louise Nalbandian, *The Armenian Revolutionary Movement: The Development of Armenian Political Parties* (Berkeley and Los Angeles: University of California Press, 1963), pp. 90–178.
22. Richard G. Hovannisian, "The Armenian Question in the Ottoman Empire, 1876–1914," in Richard G. Hovannisian, ed., *The Armenian People from Ancient to Modern Times,* vol. 2: *Foreign Dominion to Statehood: The Fifteenth Century to the Twentieth Century* (New York: St. Martin's Press, 1997), pp. 219–20; Christopher J. Walker, *Armenia: The Survival of a Nation* (London: Croom Helm, 1980), pp. 136–42; idem, "From Sassun to the Ottoman Bank: Turkish Armenians in the 1890s," *Armenian Review* 30 (March 1979): 227–64.
23. Despatch No. 53, Terrell to Said Pasha, March 12, 1895; Despatch No. 460, Terrell to Gresham, March 13, 1895; Despatch No. 462, Terrell to Gresham, March 15, 1895, encl., Said Pasha to Terrell, March 14, 1895, U.S. Department of State, *Papers Relating to the Foreign Relations of the United States, 1895,* pt. 2 (Washington, DC: Government Printing Office, 1896), pp. 1238, 1239, 1240–41.
24. Despatch No. 409, Uhl to Terrell, April 4, 1895; Despatch No. 414, Uhl to Terrell, April 8, 1895; Admiral Ramsay to Gresham, April 5, 1895, ibid., pt. 2, pp. 1242–43. See also Thomas A. Bryson, *Tars, Turks, and Tankers: The Role of the United States Navy in the Middle East, 1800–1979* (Metuchen, NJ: Scarecrow Press 1980), p. 35; Barbara J. Merguerian, "The American Response to the 1895 Massacres," in *Genocide and Human Rights: Lessons from the Armenian Experience,* special issue, *Journal of Armenian Studies* 4:1–2 (1992): 53–83.
25. Mavroyeni Bey to Gresham, April 5, 6, 7, 1895, *FRUS, 1895,* pt. 2, pp. 1248–50.
26. Despatch No. 512, Terrell to Gresham, April 21, 1895, ibid., p. 1244.
27. Despatch No. 476, Uhl to Terrell, May 18, 1895, encl., Herbert to Gresham, May 15, 1895, subencl. 1, Rear-Admiral Kirkland to Herbert, April 17, 1895, ibid., pt. 2, pp. 1245–46.
28. Armen Karo (Garo), "Aprvats orer" [Days Lived], *Hairenik Amsagir* 1:9 (July 1923): 94; Johannes Lepsius, *Armenia and Europe: An Indictment,* trans. and ed. J. Rendel Harris (London: Hodder and Stoughton, 1897); Richard G. Hovannisian, "The Historical Dimensions of the Armenian Question, 1878–1923," in Richard G. Hovannisian, ed., *The Armenian Genocide in Perspective* (New Brunswick, NJ: Transaction Books, 1986), pp. 19–26.

29. Sen. Doc. No. 33, *Congressional Record*, 54th Cong. 1st sess., Dec. 4, 1895; See also Senate Debate, *Congressional Record*, 54th Cong. 1st sess., Jan. 24, 1896, pp. 959–64; House Debate, ibid., Jan. 27, 1896, pp. 1000–16.

30. Merle Curti, *American Philanthropy Abroad: A History* (New Brunswick, NJ: Rutgers University Press, 1963).

31. Richard Olney, Report of the Secretary of State, Dec. 19, 1895, *FRUS, 1895*, pt. 2, pp. 1256–57; Bryson, *Tars, Turks, and Tankers*, p. 35; Merguerian, "American Response," pp. 53–83.

32. Alfred L.P. Dennis, *Adventures in American Diplomacy, 1896–1906* (New York: E.P. Dutton, 1928), pp. 451–52; Field, *America*, p. 446.

33. Field, *America*, p. 448.

34. Despatch No. 295, Griscom to Hay, Dec. 11, 1900, U.S. Department of State, *Papers Relating to the Foreign Relations of the United States, 1901* (Washington, DC: Government Printing Office, 1902), pp. 514–15; Lloyd C. Griscom, *Diplomatically Speaking* (Boston: Little, Brown, 1940), pp. 162, 169–74. See also Despatch No. 156, Griscom to Hay, Jan. 27, 1900, Despatch Nos. 162, 215, 322, Griscom to Hay, Feb. 6, May 29, Feb. 13, 1901, encl., Minister of Foreign Affairs to Griscom, Jan. 2, 1901; Despatch No. 363, Hay to Griscom, March 16, 1901, U.S. Department of State, *Papers Relating to the Foreign Relations of the United States, 1900* (Washington, DC: Government Printing Office, 1902), pp. 907, 909–12.

35. Alfred Thayer Mahan, *The Influence of Sea Power upon History, 1660–1783* (Boston: Little, Brown, 1890; repr. Mineola, NY: Dover, 1987), pp. 1, 13, 32–34. See also William N. Still, Jr., *American Sea Power in the Old World: The United States Navy in European and Near Eastern Waters, 1865–1917* (Westport, CT: Greenwood Press, 1980).

36. Theodore Roosevelt, *Addresses and Presidential Messages of Theodore Roosevelt, 1902–1904* (New York: G.P. Putnam's Sons, 1904), pp. 323, 326. See also Paul M. Kennedy, *The Rise and Fall of British Naval Mastery* (London: Ashfield Press, 1983).

37. Bryson, *Tars, Turks, and Tankers*, pp. 40, 42; Lewis L. Gould, *The Presidency of Theodore Roosevelt* (Lawrence, KS: University Press of Kansas, 1991), pp. 261, 265–67.

38. Ernest R. May, *Imperial Democracy* (New York: Harcourt, Brace, 1961), pp. 27–29.

39. At the same time, the Navy had to compete against advocates of strengthening the nascent air-power. Robert E. Peary, "Command of the Air," *Annals of the American Academy of Political and Social Science* 66 (July 1916): 192–99.

40. Harold F. Williamson and Arnold R. Daum, *The American Petroleum Industry: The Age of Illumination 1859–1899* (Evanston, IL: Northwestern University Press, 1959), pp. 488, 492, 511–12, 519, and on the competition in Europe, see pp. 580, 630–76; in France, see p. 584; Anton Mohr, *The Oil War* (New York: Harcourt,

Brace, 1926), pp. 32, 52. See also Boverton Redwood, *Petroleum: A Treatise on the Geographical Distribution and Geological Occurrence of Petroleum and Natural Gas*, 3 vols., 3rd. edn. (London: Charles Griffin, 1913), vol. 1, pp. 3–16, vol. 2, p. 158.

41. Redwood, *Petroleum*, vol. 2, pp. 134–35.
42. Gregory P. Nowell, *Mercantile States and the World Oil Cartel, 1900–1939* (Ithaca and London: Cornell University Press, 1994), pp. 50–51n12; Walter LaFeber, *The Cambridge History of American Foreign Relations*, vol. 2: *The American Search for Opportunity, 1865–1913* (Cambridge, UK: Cambridge University Press, 1993), pp. 37–38.
43. Williamson and Daum, *American Petroleum*, p. 632.
44. Rosenberg, *American Dream*, p. 40.
45. Papers of James L. Barton, Papers and Correspondence, Box 12, James L. Barton, "Autobiographical Notes," p. 70, ABCFM, Houghton Library, Harvard University.
46. Grabill, *Protestant Diplomacy*, p. 37; Field, *America*, pp. 150–75; U.S. Department of Commerce, Bureau of Foreign and Domestic Commerce, *Foreign Commerce and Navigation of the United States* (Washington, DC: Government Printing Office, 1900–1920), passim; Faroqhi et al., *Ottoman Empire*, vol. 2, p. 852; Donald Quataert, *Manufacturing and Technology Transfer in the Ottoman Empire, 1800–1914* (Istanbul-Strasbourg: Isis Press, 1992), pp. 22–25.
47. Immanuel Wallerstein, "The Ottoman Empire and the Capitalist World-Economy: Some Questions for Research," in Okyar and İnalcık, *Türkiye'nin Sosyal ve Ekonomik Tarihi*, pp. 117–22.
48. Faroqhi et al., *Ottoman Empire*, vol. 2, pp. 702–703, 772, 798, 844, 850, and chapters 31–34 passim; Donald Quataert, *Social Disintegration and Popular Resistance in the Ottoman Empire, 1881–1908: Reactions to European Economic Penetration* (New York and London: New York University Press, 1983), pp. 8–10.
49. Faroqhi et al., *Ottoman Empire*, vol. 2, pp. 875–77, 880–81. On the *Tanzimat* reforms, see Hagop Barsoumian, "The Eastern Question and the Tanzimat Era," in Hovannisian, *Armenian People*, vol. 2, pp. 175–201; Hovannisian, "Armenian Question," in ibid., pp. 203–38; idem, "Historical Dimensions," in Hovannisian, *Armenian Genocide in Perspective*, pp. 19–26.
50. Ulug, "Ermeniler," *Türk* 11, Oct. 21, 1905 (Cairo), as quoted in Elizabeth B. Frierson, "Cheap and Easy: The Creation of Consumer Culture in Late Ottoman Society," in Donald Quataert, ed., *Consumption Studies and the History of the Ottoman Empire, 1550–1922* (Albany, NY: State University of New York Press, 2000), p. 255.
51. Field, *America*, p. 119.
52. Arthur Schlesinger, Jr., "The Missionary Enterprise and Imperialism," in John K. Fairbank, ed., *The Missionary Enterprise in China and America* (Cambridge, MA: Harvard University Press, 1974), pp. 342,

353–54; Rosenberg, *American Dream*, pp. 43–44. On "missionary dynasties," see James A. Field, Jr., "Near East Notes and Far East Queries," in Fairbank, *Missionary Enterprise*, pp. 50–53.

53. M. Spooner and H.J. Howland, eds., *History of American Missions to the Heathen: From Their Commencement to the Present Time* (Worcester, MA: Spooner and Howland, 1840); Clifton Jackson Phillips, *Protestant America and the Pagan World* (Cambridge, MA: Harvard University, East Asian Research Center, 1969); Gustav Warneck, *Outline of a History of Protestant Missions* (New York: Fleming H. Revell, 1901); Thomas Otakar Kutvirt, "The Emergence and Acceptance of Armenia as a Legitimate American Missionary Field," *Armenian Review* 37 (Autumn 1984): 7–32. Grabill, *Protestant Diplomacy*, pp. 4–7; Field, *America*, pp. 93, 166–68.

54. Henry Otis Dwight, H. Allen Tupper, Edwin Munsell Bliss, eds., *The Encyclopedia of Missions*, 2nd edn. (New York, London: Funk and Wagnalls, 1904), pp. 27, 31, 754. The missionaries in Asiatic Turkey accounted for 26.42% of the world total; native workers, 22.65%; and communicants, 23.59%. (Author's own calculation.)

55. Warneck, *Outline of a History*, p. 241.

56. Rev. Charles C. Tracy, "The Outlook for Christ in Asiatic Turkey," *The Missionary Herald* 102:9 (Sept. 1906): 422–24; Dwight et al., *Encyclopedia of Missions*, p. 31; See also Aramayis P. Vartooguian, *Armenia's Ordeal* (New York: n.p., 1896); Beach, *Geography and Atlas*, p. 417; Warneck, *Outline of a History*, p. 241.

57. Beach, *Geography and Atlas*, vol. 1, p. 425.

58. See, e.g., Despatch No. 1300, Leishman to Secretary of State, Feb. 27, 1906, encl., Howard T. Bliss to Leishman, Feb. 23, 1906. See also, William R. Hutchison, "A Moral Equivalent for Imperialism: Americans and the Promotion of 'Christian Civilization,' 1880–1910," in Torben Christensen and William R. Hutchison, eds., *Missionary Ideologies in the Imperialist Era: 1880–1920* (Aarhus, Denmark: Aros, 1982), pp. 175–76.

59. Field, *America*, pp. 93, 156–57.

60. Ibid., pp. 160, 162; Warneck, *Outline*, p. 238.

61. Grabill, *Protestant Diplomacy*, p. 7.

62. Vartooguian, *Armenia's Ordeal*, passim.

63. Raffi (Hakob [Mirzayan] Melik-Hakobiants) to Hovhannes Avetisian, April 20, 1858, in Raffi, *Erkeri Zhoghovatsu* [Collected Works] (Erevan: Armenian Academy of Sciences, 1999), vol. 12, p. 152.

64. Vartooguian, *Armenia's Ordeal*, pp. 36–37, 39.

65. Field, *America*, p. 353.

66. William Ellsworth Strong, *The Story of the American Board* (Boston: Pilgrim Press, 1910; repr., New York: Arno Press and the New York Times, 1969), p. 199; Field, "Near East Notes," p. 49.

67. Grabill, *Protestant Diplomacy*, p. 23; Daniel, *American Philanthropy*, p. 54. See also John K. Fairbank, "Introduction," and Valentin H. Rabe,

"Evangelical Logistics: Mission Support and Resources to 1920," both in Fairbank, *Missionary Enterprise*, pp. 8, 63.

68. Daniel, *American Philanthropy*, pp. 68–69.
69. See Grabill, *Protestant Diplomacy*, pp. 43–44.
70. May, *Imperial Democracy*, pp. 27–29.
71. Alice Stone Blackwell, "Armenian Characteristics," *Armenia* 1:2 (Nov. 1904): 24–26; Grabill, *Protestant Diplomacy*, pp. 43–44.
72. Grabill, *Protestant Diplomacy*, p. 45.
73. Suzanne E. Moranian, "The Armenian Genocide and American Missionary Relief Efforts," in Jay Winter, ed., *America and the Armenian Genocide of 1915* (Cambridge: Cambridge University Press, 2003), pp. 201–02.
74. LaFeber, *American Search*, p. 99.
75. Isaac Taylor Headland, *Some By-Products of Missions* (New York and Cincinnati: Methodist Book Concern, 1912), p. 34.
76. Field, *America*, p. 189 and note 15.
77. Ibid., p. 92.
78. M. Vartan Malcom, *The Armenians in America* (Boston: Pilgrim Press, 1919); Robert Mirak, *Torn Between Two Lands: Armenians in America, 1890 to World War I* (Cambridge, MA: Harvard University Press, 1983), pp. 46–47, 54–55, 57.
79. See Manuk G. Chizmechian, *Patmutiun Amerikahay Kaghakakan Kusaktsutiants, 1890–1925* [History of American Armenian Political Parties, 1890–1925] (Fresno: Nor Or, 1930), pp. 66–67.
80. Notes to Turkish Legation, vol. 2, Robert Bacon to Turkish Minister, March 9, 1906. See Ralph Elliott Cook, "The United States and the Armenian Question, 1884–1924," Ph.D. dissertation (Fletcher School of Law and Diplomacy, 1957), pp. 105–06.
81. Despatch No. 1418, Peter Augustus Jay to Secretary of State, July 5, 1906, encl., Despatch No. 1418/736, Peter Augustus Jay to Tawfik Pasha, July 3, 1906.

2   UNITED STATES RELATIONS WITH THE YOUNG TURK GOVERNMENT

1. Richard G. Hovannisian, *The Republic of Armenia*, vol. 1: *The First Years, 1918–1919* (Berkeley and Los Angeles: University of California Press, 1971), p. 9; Simon Vratzian, *Hayastani Hanrapetutiun* [Republic of Armenia] (Paris: Armenian Revolutionary Federation, Central Committee of America, 1928; repr., Erevan: Hayastan, 1993), p. 4.
2. A.J.P. Taylor, *The Struggle for Mastery in Europe, 1848–1918* (Oxford: Oxford University Press, 1954), p. 451.
3. Haigazn G. Ghazarian, *Tseghaspan Turke* [The Genocidal Turk] (Beirut: Hamazkayin Press, 1968), pp. 13–14.

4. T.P. Conwell-Evans, *Foreign Policy from a Back Bench, 1904–1918: A Study Based on the Papers of Lord Noel-Buxton* (London: Oxford University Press, 1932), pp. 21–22.
5. Richard G. Hovannisian, *Armenia on the Road to Independence, 1918* (Berkeley and Los Angeles: University of California Press, 1967), pp. 29–30; Christopher J. Walker, *Armenia: The Survival of a Nation* (London: Croom Helm, 1980), pp. 182–88.
6. File Nos. 10044/139/179/141/142/169/170/172/250, Leishman to Secretary of State, April 14, 15, 16, 17, 20, 30, May 1, 20, 1909, U.S. Department of State, *Papers Relating to the Foreign Relations of the United States, 1909* (Washington, DC: Government Printing Office, 1914), pp. 562–76.
7. On Dollar Diplomacy, see Emily S. Rosenberg, *Financial Missionaries to the World: The Politics and Culture of Dollar Diplomacy, 1900–1930* (Cambridge, MA: Harvard University Press, 1999).
8. Thomas A. Bailey, *A Diplomatic History of the American People*, 2nd edn. (New York: F.S. Crofts, 1944), pp. 577–78. For a useful discussion on the foreign policy of the Taft administration, see Walter V. Scholes and Marie V. Scholes, *The Foreign Policies of the Taft Administration* (Columbia: University of Missouri Press, 1970).
9. File No. 10044/151A, Secretary of State to Leishman, April 21, 1909, *FRUS, 1909*, p. 568; Thomas A. Bryson, *Tars, Turks, and Tankers: The Role of the United States Navy in the Middle East, 1800–1979* (Metuchen, NJ: Scarecrow Press, 1980), p. 52.
10. File No. 10044/165, Leishman to Secretary of State, April 27, 1909, ibid., p. 569.
11. U.S. Congress, *Congressional Record*, 61st Cong., 1st sess., vol. 44, pt. 2, April 29, 1909, p. 1615.
12. [No Author] "World-Politics: Constantinople," *North American Review* 190 (July 1909): 132.
13. U.S. Department of Commerce, Bureau of Foreign and Domestic Commerce, *Foreign Commerce and Navigation of the United States* (Washington, DC: Government Printing Office, 1914), pp. 432, 496.
14. Gaidz F. Minassian, "Les relations entre le Comité Union et Progrès et la Fédération Révolutionnaire Arménienne à la veille de la Premiere Guerre Mondiale d'après les sources arméniennes," *Revue d'Histoire Arménienne Contemporaine* 1 (1995): 45–99; Hovannisian, *Armenia on the Road to Independence*, p. 29; Ghazarian, *Tseghaspan Turke*, pp. 15–16.
15. See Great Britain, FO 195/2359, folio 276; *British Documents on the Origins of the War, 1898–1914*, vol. 9, pt. 1, Doc. no. 181, Sept. 6, 1910, report, p. 207, eds. G.P. Gooch and Harold Temperely (London: H.M.S.O., 1928); FO 424/250, Annual Report 1910, p. 4; and French Consul Professor Mas Choublier's reports of November 1910, in Vahakn N. Dadrian, *The History of the Armenian*

Genocide: Ethnic Conflict from the Balkans to Anatolia to the Caucasus (Providence: Berghahn Books, 1995), pp. 179–80, 184, notes 2–5; idem, "Genocide as a Problem of National and International Law: The World War I Armenian Case and Its Contemporary Legal Ramifications," *Yale Journal of International Law* 14:2 (Summer 1989): 254; idem, "The Secret Young-Turk Ittihadist Conference and the Decision for the World War I Genocide of the Armenians," *Holocaust and Genocide Studies* 7:2 (Fall 1993), reprinted with revisions in *Journal of Political and Military Sociology* (*The Armenian Genocide in Official Turkish Records*) 22:1 (Summer 1994): 178. See also Ghazarian, *Tseghaspan Turke*, pp. 16, 17, 19.

16. FO 371/101. 33044/33044/10/44, No. 635, Lowther to Grey, Sept. 6, 1910; encl., No. 38, Geary to Lowther, Aug. 28, 1910, *British Documents*, vol. 9, pt. 1, pp. 207–09.

17. Stephan Astourian, *The Armenian Genocide: An Interpretation* (Glendale: ARF Shant Committee, 1995); Jacob M. Landau, *Pan-Turkism: From Irredentism to Cooperation*, 2nd rev. edn. (Bloomington: Indiana University Press, 1995); Taha Parla, *The Social and Political Thought of Ziya Gökalp, 1876–1924* (Leiden: E.J. Brill, 1985).

18. Ghazarian, *Tseghaspan Turke*, pp. 21–22; Leland James Gordon, *American Relations with Turkey, 1830–1930: An Economic Interpretation* (Philadelphia: University of Pennsylavania Press, 1932), p. 59.

19. Thomas A. Bryson, *American Diplomatic Relations with the Middle East, 1784–1975* (Metuchen, NJ: Scarecrow Press, 1977), p. 49.

20. Ibid., pp. 46–47; Gordon, *American Relations*, p. 58; John A. DeNovo, *American Interests and Policies in the Middle East, 1900–1939* (Minneapolis: University of Minnesota Press, 1963), pp. 41–43.

21. George Ghevond, "Conditions in Armenia," *Levant Trade Review* 1:1 (June 1911): 114, 116.

22. Major John M. Carson, "Trade in the Near East," *Levant Trade Review* 1:1 (June 1911): 16–17.

23. U.S. National Archives, Department of State, Record Group 59 (cited hereafter as RG 59), 867.00/358, Rockhill to Secretary of State, Dec. 12, 1911.

24. M.S. Anderson, *The Eastern Question, 1774–1923: A Study in International Relations* (London: Macmillan, 1966), p. 291; Taylor, *Struggle*, pp. 474, 489, 490; Bernard Lewis, *The Emergence of Modern Turkey*, 2nd edn. (London: Oxford University Press, 1968), p. 214.

25. File No. 767.70/44, L.L. Caftanzoglu to Secretary of State, Oct. 18, 1912, U.S. Department of State, *Papers Relating to the Foreign Relations of the United States, 1912* (Washington, DC: Government Printing Office, 1919), pp. 1342–43.

26. File Nos. 767.70/73/75/78, Rockhill to Secretary of State, Oct. 31, Nov. 1, 4, 1912; 367.11/7B/8, Adee, Acting Secretary of State to American Ambassador, Nov. 4, 6, 1912, ibid., pp. 1344–45.

27. File No. 367.11/29, P.C. Knox to Rockhill, Nov. 21, 1912, ibid., p. 1352.

28. File No. 767.70/83, Rockhill to Secretary of State, Nov. 4, 1912, ibid., p. 1344.

29. File No. 367.11/8, Rockhill to Secretary of State, Nov. 5, 1912, ibid., p. 1345.

30. File No. 767.70/190, G. von L. Meyer, Navy Department, to Secretary of State, Dec. 4, 1912, ibid., p. 1353.

31. The Annual Message of the President Transmitted to Congress, Dec. 7, 1909, *FRUS, 1909*, pp. xiii–xiv.

32. E.H. Davenport and Sidney Russell Cooke, *The Oil Trusts and Anglo-American Relations* (New York: Macmillan, 1924), pp. 24–25.

33. "American Railway Enterprise," *Levant Trade Review* 1:1 (June 1911): 6; John A. DeNovo, "A Railroad for Turkey: The Chester Project, 1908–1913," *Business History Review* 33:3 (Autumn 1959): 300–29; Henry Woodhouse, "American Oil Claims in Turkey," *Current History* 15:6 (March 1922): 953–59.

34. Naomi W. Cohen, "Ambassador Straus in Turkey, 1909–1910: A Note on Dollar Diplomacy," *Mississippi Valley Historical Review* 45:4 (March 1959): 632–42.

35. Bryson, *Tars, Turks, and Tankers*, pp. 50–51.

36. F.M. Huntington Wilson, *Memoirs of an Ex-Diplomat* (Boston: Bruce Humphries, 1945), pp. 223–24.

37. DeNovo, *American Interests*, pp. 58–87, 210–28; Gordon, *American Relations*, p. 259; Davenport and Cooke, *Oil Trusts*, pp. 24–25.

38. Gordon, *American Relations*, pp. 262–65; DeNovo, *American Interests*, pp. 68, 82–83; Cohen, "Ambassador Straus," pp. 640–41; Wilson, *Memoirs*, pp. 226–27.

39. Gregory P. Nowell, *Mercantile States and the World Oil Cartel, 1900–1939* (Ithaca and London: Cornell University Press, 1994), pp. 53–54, 65.

40. Davenport and Cooke, *Oil Trusts*, pp. 26–27.

41. Redwood, *Petroleum*, vol. 3, pp. 84, 94, 119; Williamson and Daum, *American Petroleum*, pp. 632–35.

42. Nowell, *Mercantile States*, pp. 70–71.

43. Williamson and Daum, *American Petroleum*, pp. 644, 658–62.

44. Ralph W. Hidy and Muriel E. Hidy, *Pioneering in Big Business, 1882–1911* (New York: Harper and Brothers, 1955), p. 586.

45. Williamson and Daum, *American Petroleum*, p. 662; Hidy and Hidy, *Pioneering*, pp. 509–12; Nowell, *Mercantile States*, pp. 58–61.

46. Nowell, *Mercantile States*, pp. 64–65.

47. John A. DeNovo, "Petroleum and the United States Navy before World War I," *Mississippi Valley Historical Review* 41 (March 1955): 643.

48. Davenport and Cooke, *Oil Trusts*, p. 3; DeNovo, "Petroleum," p. 645.
49. Hidy and Hidy, *Pioneering*, p. 454.
50. Anton Mohr, *The Oil War* (New York: Harcourt, Brace, 1926), p. 34.
51. S.N. Patten, "The Basis of National Security," *Annals of the American Academy of Political and Social Science* 66 (July 1916): 1–11; Gerald D. Nash, *United States Oil Policy 1890–1964* (Pittsburgh: University of Pittsburgh Press, 1968), pp. 1–2, 5.
52. John Wilber Jenkins, "Introduction," in the collection of speeches, Secretary of the Navy Josephus Daniels, *The Navy and the Nation: War-Time Addresses* (New York: George H. Doran, 1919), p. iv.
53. Lewis, *Emergence of Modern Turkey*, p. 224.
54. Ibid., p. 225; Feroz Ahmad, *The Young Turks: The Committee of Union and Progress in Turkish Politics, 1908–1914* (Oxford: Clarendon Press, 1969), pp. 116–20.
55. Bryson, *Tars, Turks, and Tankers*, p. 50.
56. W.E.D. Allen and Paul Muratoff, *Caucasian Battlefields: A History of the Wars on the Turco-Caucasian Border, 1828–1921* (Cambridge: Cambridge University Press, 1953), p. 228.
57. Ibid., p. 229; Ulrich Trumpener, *Germany and the Ottoman Empire, 1914–1918* (Princeton: Princeton University Press, 1968), pp. 13–14. See also Vahakn N. Dadrian, *German Responsibility in the Armenian Genocide: A Review of the Historical Evidence of German Complicity* (Watertown: Blue Crane Books, 1996), p. 20; idem, *History of the Armenian Genocide*, p. 204.
58. Landau, *Pan-Turkism*, pp. 32–45, 49–54; Uriel Heyd, *Foundations of Turkish Nationalism: The Life and Teachings of Ziya Gökalp* (London: Luzac, 1950).
59. Paul M. Kennedy, *The Rise and Fall of British Naval Mastery* (London: Ashfield Press, 1983), pp. 222, 258; Bryson, *Tars, Turks, and Tankers*, p. 40.

3 THE WILSON ADMINISTRATION AND THE ITTIHADIST REGIME

1. Thomas J. Knock, *To End All Wars: Woodrow Wilson and the Quest for a New World Order* (Princeton: Princeton University Press, 1992), pp. 36, 57.
2. Emily S. Rosenberg, *Spreading the American Dream* (New York: Hill and Wang, 1982), pp. 38–86 passim.
3. Thomas J. McCormick, "Drift or Mastery? A Corporatist Synthesis for American Diplomatic History," *Reviews in American History* 10 (December 1982): 318–30. For opposing views on the application of the corporatist model to U.S. foreign policy, see John Lewis Gaddis, "The Corporatist Synthesis: A Skeptical View," *Diplomatic History* 10 (Fall 1986): 357–62; Michael J. Hogan, "Corporatism: A Positive Appraisal," *Diplomatic History* 10 (Fall 1986): 363–72; Beth

McKillen, "The Corporatist Model, World War I, and the Public Debate over the League of Nations," *Diplomatic History* 15 (Spring 1991): 171–97.

4. "Education and Democracy," May 4, 1907, in Arthur S. Link, ed., *The Papers of Woodrow Wilson*, 69 vols. (Princeton: Princeton University Press, 1966–1994), vol. 17, p. 135; cited hereafter as *PWW*.

5. See his lecture notes, Sept. 19, 1889–Nov. 20, 1900, ibid., vol. 11, pp. 4–30; on the relationship between Congress and President in matters of foreign policy, see ibid., pp. 70–71; Wilson, "Constitutional Government," March 24, 1908, ibid., vol. 18, pp. 120–21.

6. Feb. 24, March 7, May 25, 1912, ibid., vol. 24, pp. 198–200, 228–300, 440.

7. Rosenberg, *American Dream*, p. 65.

8. Feb. 3, 1915, *PWW*, vol. 32, pp. 178–87.

9. See Rosenberg, *American Dream*, pp. 63, 65.

10. Ibid., p. 73.

11. Jan. 27, 1912, *PWW*, vol. 24, pp. 83–92. See also his speech before the General Assembly of Virginia and the City Council of Richmond, Feb. 1, 1912, ibid., pp. 101–17.

12. Lloyd E. Ambrosius, *Wilsonian Statecraft: Theory and Practice of Liberal Internationalism during World War I* (Wilmington: Scholarly Resource Books, 1991), p. 1; William E. Dodd, "Wilsonism," *Political Science Quarterly* 38:1 (March 1923): 115–32.

13. Ambrosius, *Wilsonian Statecraft*, p. 1.

14. See, e.g., campaign address in Baltimore, April 30, 1912, *PWW*, vol. 24, pp. 370–79.

15. Ambrosius, *Wilsonian Statecraft*, pp. 3, 10–11, 13; Arthur S. Link, *Woodrow Wilson and the Progressive Era, 1910–1917* (New York: Harper and Row, 1954), p. 82. For his earlier views, see "Religion and Patriotism," July 4, 1902, *PWW*, vol. 12, pp. 474–78.

16. Knock, *To End All Wars*, pp. 27, 29; Thomas A. Bailey, *A Diplomatic History of the American People*, 2nd edn. (New York: F.S. Crofts, 1944), pp. 592–606.

17. William Appleman Williams, *The Tragedy of American Diplomacy*, 2nd rev. edn. (New York: Dell Publishing, 1972), pp. 73–74.

18. Ibid., p. 128; Ambrosius, *Wilsonian Statecraft*, p. 25.

19. U.S. Department of Commerce, Bureau of Foreign and Domestic Commerce, *Foreign Commerce and Navigation of the United States, 1913* (Washington, DC: Government Printing Office, 1914), p. 7.

20. Ibid., table 3 passim.

21. Ibid., pp. 49, 87, 139, 140, 147, 275–76.

22. Ibid., table 6 passim. It is worth noting that while in 1909 the United States had exported $84,574 worth of firearms to Turkey, that figure dropped to $3,053 in 1913. Ibid., p. 496.

23. See, e.g., Josephus Daniels, *The Navy and the Nation* (New York: George H. Doran, 1919), p. 24.

24. S.N. Patten, "The Basis of National Security," *Annals of the American Academy of Political and Social Science* 66 (July 1916): 1–11.
25. Bradley A. Fiske, "Naval Principles," *North American Review* 202 (Nov. 1915): 693.
26. Josephus Daniels, "The Significance of Naval Preparedness," *Annals of the American Academy of Political and Social Science* 66 (July 1916): 147–56.
27. Josephus Daniels, *The Cabinet Diaries of Josephus Daniels, 1913–1921*, E. David Cronon, ed. (Lincoln: University of Nebraska Press, 1963), p. 5.
28. John A. DeNovo, "Petroleum and the United States Navy before World War I," *Mississippi Valley Historical Review* 41 (March 1955): 642–48.
29. Williams, *Tragedy of American Diplomacy*, p. 88.
30. Robert C. Hilderbrand, *Power and the People* (Chapel Hill: University of North Carolina Press, 1981); Alexander L. George and Juliette L. George, *Woodrow Wilson and Colonel House* (New York: John Day Company, 1956); House Diary, Jan. 8, 1913, *PWW*, vol. 27, pp. 20–24.
31. Wilson, "Constitutional Government," March 24, 1908, *PWW*, vol. 18, p. 121; Merle Eugene Curti, *Bryan and World Peace* (New York: Octagon Books, 1969), pp. 165–66; Paolo E. Coletta, *William Jennings Bryan*, vol. 2: *Progressive Politician and Moral Statesman, 1909–1915* (Lincoln: University of Nebraska Press, 1969), pp. 86–87, 92.
32. Coletta, *Bryan*, pp. 86–87, 92, 111–13, 118, 239, 252. For a laudatory commentary on Wilson's Cabinet by a contemporary observer, see James C. Hemphill, "Mr. Wilson's Cabinet," *North American Review* 202 (July 1915): 112–21. Wilson expected the number of consular officers to expand as foreign trade grew. Wilson to Mary Allen Hulbert, Dec. 8, 1913, *PWW*, vol. 29, p. 23.
33. Both quoted in Williams, *Tragedy of American Diplomacy*, p. 84.
34. Curti, *Bryan*, p. 167.
35. Coletta, *Bryan*, p. 112. See also Library of Congress, Division of Manuscripts, Papers of William Jennings Bryan, Letter Books, Box 45, Special Correspondence, Henry W. Elliott, House of Representatives, to Bryan, March 26, 1914.
36. House Diary, Jan. 8, 1913, *PWW*, vol. 27, p. 23.
37. Daniels, *Cabinet Diaries*, "Preface," p. v.
38. John Wilber Jenkins, "Introduction," in Daniels, *Navy and the Nation*, p. v.
39. Daniels, *Cabinet Diaries*, "Preface," p. vi; Benjamin Franklin Cooling, *Gray Steel and Blue Water Navy: The Formative Years of America's Military-Industrial Complex, 1881–1917* (Hamden, CT: Archon Books, 1979), p. 185; Link, *Woodrow Wilson*, p. 28; Kendrick A. Clements, *The Presidency, of Woodrow Wilson* (Lawrence, KS: University Press of Kansas, 1992), p. 34.

40. Clements, *Presidency*, p. 33.
41. Daniels, *Cabinet Diaries*, March 10, 1913, p. 6.
42. Library of Congress, Division of Manuscripts, Papers of Henry Morgenthau, Sr., General Correspondence and Diaries.
43. Morgenthau contributed about $30,000 to Wilson's campaign. See Barbara W. Tuchman, "The Assimilationist Dilemma: Ambassador Morgenthau's Story," in Tuchman, *Practicing History: Selected Essays* (New York: Ballantine Books, 1982), p. 215.
44. House Diary, Dec. 18, 1912, *PWW*, vol. 25, p. 610. See also House Diary, March 25, 1913, ibid., vol. 27, p. 228; House Diary, May 2, 1913, ibid., pp. 384–85.
45. Library of Congress, Division of Manuscripts, Papers of Henry Morgenthau, Sr., General Correspondence, Container 6, Morgenthau to Wilson, June 12, 1913; Morgenthau to Daniels, June 12, 1913. See also *PWW*, vol. 27, p. 513.
46. Bryan Papers, Letter Books, Special Correspondence, Box 45, Wilson to Bryan, Aug. 11, 1913.
47. Morgenthau Papers, General Correspondence, Container 6, McAdoo to Morgenthau, Aug. 14, 1913.
48. Ibid., Daniels to Morgenthau, n.d. [1913].
49. Ibid., Bryan to Morgenthau, Sept. 9, 1913; Library of Congress, Division of Manuscripts, Papers of Henry Morgenthau, Sr., Diaries, May 18, 1915; cited hereafter as Morgenthau Diary; Henry Morgenthau, *All in a Life-Time* (Garden City, NY: Doubleday, 1922), p. 174.
50. Morgenthau Papers, General Correspondence, Container 6, Robert E. Speer to Morgenthau, Oct. 23, 1913.
51. Ibid., Rev. E.W. McDowell, quoted in Robert E. Speer to Morgenthau, Oct. 23, 1913.
52. Morgenthau Diary, Nov. 1, 2, 27, 1913.
53. Ibid., Dec. 1, 1913.
54. Ibid., Dec. 11, 1913.
55. Ibid., Dec. 8, 1913.
56. Ibid., Dec. 23, 1913; Morgenthau Papers, General Correspondence, Container 4, Morgenthau to Josie, Dec. 27, 1913, p. 1.
57. Morgenthau, *Story*, pp. 36–38.
58. Morgenthau Diary, Dec. 27, 1913; Morgenthau Papers, General Correspondence, Container 4, Morgenthau to Josie, Dec. 27, 1913, pp. 9–10.
59. Great Britain, Parliament, *The Treatment of Armenians in the Ottoman Empire, 1915–16: Documents Presented to Viscount Grey of Fallodon, Secretary of State for Foreign Affairs*, Miscellaneous no. 31, 1916, comp. and ed. Arnold J. Toynbee, 3rd edn. (Beirut: G. Doniguian and Sons, 1988 [London: Sir Joseph Causton and Sons, 1916]), p. 661; cited hereafter as *Treatment of Armenians*; Richard G. Hovannisian, *Armenia on the Road to Independence, 1918* (Berkeley and Los Angeles: University of California Press, 1967), pp. 34–37.

60. FO 24204/19208/13/44, O'Beirne to Grey, May 26, 1913; FO 25212/19208/13/44, O'Beirne to Grey, May 27, 1913, *British Documents on the Origins of the War, 1898–1914*, vol. 10: *The Near and Middle East on the Eve of War*, G.P. Gooch and Harold Temperely, eds., (London: H.M.S.O., 1928–1936), pp. 438, 441. See also Hovannisian, *Armenia on the Road to Independence*, p. 32; Firuz Kazemzadeh, *The Struggle for Transcaucasia, 1917–1921* (New York: Philosophical Library, 1951).

61. Roderic H. Davison, "The Armenian Crisis, 1912–1914," *American Historical Review* 53 (April 1948): 486–88. See also FO 58097/49385/13/44 (No. 391), Buchanan to Grey, Dec. 23, 1913, *British Documents*, vol. 10, p. 395.

62. FO 4452/253/13/44, Grey to Goschen, Jan. 27, 1913; FO 24204/19208/13/44, O'Beirne to Grey, May 26, 1913, *British Documents*, vol. 10, pp. 424, 438; Davison, "Armenian Crisis," pp. 488–89.

63. In the aftermath of the Adana massacres, it was rumored that some Europeans had purchased lands from the Armenians, convincing them that the Europeans, particularly the Germans now influential in Constantinople, would welcome disorder in the region to advance their interests. FO 19328/173/13/44, Lowther to Grey, April 24, 1913, *British Documents*, vol. 10, p. 426.

64. Davison, "Armenian Crisis," p. 503.

65. Morgenthau Papers, General Correspondence, Container 6, Horton to Morgenthau, Jan. 24, 1914.

66. See the preliminary draft, FO 43989/19208/13/44, Marling to Grey, Sept. 26, 1913, *British Documents*, vol. 10, p. 517.

67. Hovannisian, "Armenian Question," pp. 237–38; Simon Vratzian, *Hayastani Hanrapetutiun* [Republic of Armenia] (Paris: Armenian Revolutionary Federation, Central Committee of America, 1928; repr., Erevan: Hayastan, 1993), pp. 5–6.

68. T.P. Conwell-Evans, *Foreign Policy from a Back Bench, 1904–1918: A Study Based on the Papers of Lord Noel-Buxton* (London: Oxford University Press, 1932), pp. 25–26; Davison, "Armenian Crisis," pp. 501–02; *Treatment of Armenians*, pp. 635–36.

69. Djemal Pasha, *Memories of a Turkish Statesman, 1913–1919* (New York: George H. Doran, 1922), p. 276.

70. House to Wilson, May 29, 1914, *PWW*, vol. 30, pp. 108–09.

71. *New York Times*, May 29, 1914, reprinted in ibid., pp. 93–96.

72. Morgenthau Diary, Jan. 10, Feb. 5, 22, 23, March 4, 1914; Morgenthau, *Story*, pp. 39–40. Morgenthau and Schmavonian visited Komitas on March 9, 1914. Morgenthau Diary, March 9, 1914.

73. Morgenthau Diary, Jan. 22, Feb. 10, 16, 21, March 10, 11, 1914.

74. Ibid., Jan. 26, 1914.

75. Otto Liman von Sanders, *Five Years in Turkey* (Baltimore: Williams and Wilkins, 1928), p. 8.

76. Morgenthau Diary, Jan. 17, 1914.

77. Ibid., Jan. 20, 28, Feb. 16, 1914. In his *All in a Life-Time* (p. 196), Morgenthau notes: "The total failure of this party proved again the impossibility of true reform among the Turks. This was evident to careful observers long before my arrival at Constantinople, but I was so ardent in my desire to help that it took me nearly a year to become wholly disillusioned."

78. Morgenthau Diary, Feb. 28, 1914. See also Morgenthau, *Life-Time*, p. 198.

79. The text of this speech appears in Morgenthau, *Life-Time*, pp. 198–202.

80. Ibid., p. 203. See also Morgenthau, *Story*, pp. 35–36.

81. U.S. Department of Commerce, Bureau of Foreign and Domestic Commerce, *Foreign Commerce and Navigation of the United States for the Year Ending June 30, 1914* (Washington, DC: Government Printing Office, 1915), summary tables, table 3, pp. xii–xiii.

82. Ibid., table 5, passim.

83. Morgenthau Diary, June 10, 11, 12, 13, 15, 1914; Morgenthau, *Story*, pp. 49–51.

84. Morgenthau Diary, June 15, 16, 18, 19, 23, 25, 26, 1914.

85. On the *Sultan Osman*, see John Keegan, *The First World War* (New York: Vintage Books, 1998), p. 216.

86. Morgenthau Diary, June 15, 1914.

87. Ibid., July 2, 9, 1914; Morgenthau, *Story*, pp. 55–56.

88. Morgenthau Diary, June 15, 1914.

89. Ibid., June 30, Aug. 15, 29, 1914.

90. Ibid., July 22, 30, 1914.

4 War and Wilsonian Neutrality

1. Thomas J. Knock, *To End All Wars: Woodrow Wilson and the Quest for a New World Order* (Princeton, NJ: Princeton University Press, 1992), p. 32; Merle Eugene Curti, *Bryan and World Peace* (New York: Octagon Books, 1969), pp. 194–96.

2. Library of Congress, Division of Manuscripts, Papers of Henry Morgenthau, Sr., Diary, Aug. 17, 24, 1914; cited hereafter as Morgenthau Diary; U.S. Department of State, *Foreign Relations of the United States, 1914* (Washington, DC: Government Printing Office, 1922), Supp., *The World War*, 763.72111/348, Morgenthau to Secretary of State, Aug. 25, 1914, and Secretary of State to Morgenthau, Aug. 26, 1914, p. 77; 711.0012/538/540a, Secretary of State to Morgenthau, Oct. 5, 1914, and Morgenthau to Secretary of State, Oct. 7, 1914, pp. 9–10. Bryan to Wilson, Sept. 19, 1914, in Arthur S. Link, ed., *The Papers of Woodrow Wilson*, 69 vols. (Princeton, NJ: Princeton University Press, 1966–1994), vol. 31, p. 56; cited hereafter as *PWW*.

3. Paolo E. Coletta, *William Jennings Bryan*, vol. 2: *Progressive Politician and Moral Statesman, 1909–1915* (Lincoln: University of Nebraska Press, 1969), p. 260. And again on October 24, 1914, Carr met with Lansing regarding forwarding money to Turkey. Library of Congress, Division of Manuscripts, Papers of Robert Lansing, Lansing Diaries, Oct. 24, 1914.

4. U.S. National Archives, Department of State, Record Group 59 (cited hereafter as RG 59), 367.116/205, Snyder to Secretary of State, Oct. 13, 1914. See also, e.g., Morgenthau Diary, Sept. 3–5, 1914.

5. RG 59, 367.116/211, Finsley to Lansing, Oct. 16, 1914. Osborne sent a copy of this letter to the Department of the Treasury. Osborne to the Secretary of the Treasury, Oct. 23, 1914.

6. See, e.g., RG 59, 367.116/234/241, Arthur J. Brown to Secretary of State, Nov. 11, 28, 1914; RG 59, 367.116/233, B. Bowman to Secretary of State, Nov. 15, 1914; RG 59, 367.116/247, J.C. Way to Secretary of State, Dec. 7, 1914.

7. Morgenthau Diary, Aug. 18, 25, 1914; RG 59, 367.116/219, James Barton to Secretary of State, Oct. 24, 1914.

8. Morgenthau Diary, Aug. 28, 1914.

9. RG 59, 367.116/217, Morris, U.S. Vice Consul-General in Charge, Smyrna, to Secretary of State, Sept. 19, 1914.

10. RG 59, 367.116/219, James Barton to Secretary of State, Oct. 24, 1914.

11. RG 59, 367.116/219, Lansing to Barton, Oct. 27, 1914.

12. Library of Congress, Division of Manuscripts, Papers of Henry Morgenthau, Sr., General Correspondence, Container 6, Sept. 13, 1914.

13. Ibid., Morgenthau to Secretary of State, Sept. 15, 1914.

14. RG 59, 367.116/187, Snyder to Secretary of State, Sept. 16, 1914; RG 59, 367.116/222, John Osborne, Assistant Secretary for the Acting Secretary of State, to O.B. Snyder, Sept. 24, 1914; RG 59, 367.116, Snyder to Secretary of State, Oct. 13, 1914.

15. RG 59, 367.116/205, Lansing to American Consul, Harput, Oct. 21, 1914. Lansing informed Snyder of this communication.

16. Ibid., Reed to Riggs, Sept. 25, 1914.

17. Landing Papers, Box 4, A.H. Burrows to Lansing, Sept. 2, 1914.

18. Ibid., Lansing to A.H. Burrows, Sept. 3, 1914.

19. Henry Morgenthau, *Ambassador Morgenthau's Story* (New York: Doubleday, 1918), pp. 302–03; File Nos. 711.673/33/34, Morgenthau to Secretary of State, Sept. 10, 1914; Turkish Ambassador, Rustem, to Secretary of State, Sept. 10, 1914, in U.S. Department of State, *Papers Relating to the Foreign Relations of the United States, 1914* (Washington, DC: Government Printing Office, 1922), pp. 1090–91.

20. Morgenthau protested to the grand vizier that Turkey did not have the right to close the straits. Morgenthau Diary, Sept. 27, 1914. Haigazn G. Ghazarian, *Tseghaspan Turke* [The Genocidal Turk]

(Beirut: Hamazkayin Press, 1968), p. 112. The annulment of the Capitulations instigated hostilities toward all foreigners and foreign institutions. RG 59, 367.116/219, James Barton to Secretary of State, Oct. 24, 1914.

21. File No. 711.673/62a, Secretary of State to Morgenthau, Sept. 16, 1914, ibid., p. 1093.

22. Morgenthau Diary, Aug. 25, 1914.

23. Ibid., Sept. 9, 20, 21, 23, Oct. 22, 1914.

24. Ibid., Oct. 19, 1914.

25. Morgenthau Papers, General Correspondence, Container 7, Morgenthau to Secretary of State, Nov. 7, 1914; Ulrich Trumpener, *Germany and the Ottoman Empire, 1914–1918* (Princeton, NJ: Princeton University Press, 1968), p. 55; M.S. Anderson, *The Eastern Question, 1774–1923: A Study in International Relations* (London: Macmillan, 1966), p. 314; John Keegan, *The First World War* (New York: Vintage Books, 1998), p. 217.

26. Morgenthau Diary, Nov. 1, 2, 1914.

27. Ibid., Nov. 15, 1914.

28. Morgenthau Papers, General Correspondence, Container 7, Morgenthau to Secretary of State, Nov. 7, 1914.

29. Morgenthau Papers, Containers 40–41, Nov. 25, 1914.

30. RG 59, 867.00/766, Morgenthau to Secretary of State, May 14, 1915.

31. Morgenthau, *Story*, pp. 162–66.

32. Ibid., pp. 169–70.

33. RG 59, 367.116/222, John E. Osborne, Assistant Secretary, to Snyder, Sept. 24, 1914; and RG 59, 367.116/219, Lansing to Barton, Oct. 27, 1914.

34. RG 59, 867.00/724, Hollis to Bryan, Nov. 16, 1914.

35. RG 59, 867.00/723, Morgenthau to Bryan, Dec. 12, 1914; Morgenthau Diary, Dec. 28, 1914.

36. RG 59, 867.00/723, Morgenthau to Bryan, Dec. 12, 1914.

37. RG 59, 867.00/723, Morgenthau to Secretary of State, Dec. 12, 1914.

38. Morgenthau Papers, General Correspondence, Container 7, Morgenthau to Secretary of State, Nov. 7, 1914.

39. RG 59, 367.116/247, John C. Way to Bryan, Dec. 7, 1914.

40. RG 59, 367.116/205, Lansing to U.S. Consul, Oct. 21, 1914; RG 59, 367.116/219, Lansing to Barton, Oct. 27, 1914; RG 59, 367.116/227, Bryan to Barton, Nov. 9, 1914.

41. See, e.g., RG 59, 367.116/219, Lansing to Barton, Oct. 27, 1914; RG 59, 367.116/227, Bryan to Barton, Nov. 9, 1914; RG 59, 367.116/234, Lansing to Brown, Nov. 21, 1914; and RG 59, 367.116/241, Lansing to Brown, Dec. 3, 1914. See also RG 59, 367.116/247, Counselor (State Department) to John C. Way, Dec. 16, 1914.

42. Thomas A. Bryson, *American Diplomatic Relations with the Middle East, 1784–1975* (Metuchen, NJ: Scarecrow Press, 1977), p. 59; Morgenthau Diary, Nov. 17, 1914.

43. Lansing Diaries, Nov. 18, 19, 21, 1914.
44. Ibid., Dec. 4, 5, 1914.
45. Vahakn N. Dadrian, "Genocide as a Problem of National and International Law: The World War I Armenian Case and Its Contemporary Legal Ramifications," *Yale Journal of International Law* 14:2 (Summer 1989): 260.
46. Henry Morgenthau, *All in a Life-Time* (Garden City, NY: Doubleday, 1922), p. 196; RG 59, 867.00/723, Morgenthau to Bryan, Dec. 12, 1914.
47. *FRUS, 1914, Supp. WWI*, Morgenthau to Secretary of State, Dec. 12, 1914, pp. 776–77.
48. House Diary, Dec. 16, 1914, *PWW*, vol. 31, pp. 468–69.
49. RG 59, 367.116/261a, Bryan to Morgenthau, Dec. 20, 1914; Morgenthau Diary, Dec. 22, 1914.
50. Morgenthau Diary, Dec. 22, 1914.
51. Library of Congress, Division of Manuscripts, Papers of William Jennings Bryan, Special Correspondence, Box 45, Bryan to Wilson, Dec. 26, 1914.
52. Gregory P. Nowell, *Mercantile States and the World Oil Cartel, 1900–1939* (Ithaca and London: Cornell University Press, 1994), p. 127, referring to France, Archives du Ministère des Affaires Etrangères, Levant, Syrie-Liban, 1918–1929, no. 344, A: Syrie-Pétroles; letter from Aublé to Saint-Quentin, Feb. 14, 1928.
53. Richard G. Hovannisian, *Armenia on the Road to Independence, 1918* (Berkeley and Los Angeles: University of California Press, 1967), pp. 45–47; Christopher J. Walker, *Armenia: The Survival of a Nation* (London: Croom Helm, 1980), p. 199; Keegan, *First World War*, pp. 221–22.
54. W.E.D. Allen and Paul Muratoff, *Caucasian Battlefields: A History of the Wars on the Turco-Caucasian Border, 1828–1921* (Cambridge: Cambridge University Press, 1953), pp. 247, 250–52, 283n2, 284; S.L.A. Marshall, *World War I* (Boston: Houghton Mifflin, 1964; repr. Boston and New York: Mariner Books, 2001), pp. 116–17; Morgenthau Diary, Aug. 15, 1914; Keegan, *First World War*, p. 222; Great Britain, Parliament, *The Treatment of Armenians in the Ottoman Empire, 1915–16: Documents Presented to Viscount Grey of Fallodon, Secretary of State for Foreign Affairs*, Miscellaneous no. 31, 1916, comp. and ed. Arnold J. Toynbee, 3rd edn. (Beirut: G. Doniguian and Sons, 1988 [London: Sir Joseph Causton and Sons, 1916]), p. 637; cited hereafter as *Treatment of Armenians*.
55. Allen and Muratoff, *Caucasian Battlefields*, pp. 253, 261–62, 270, 271, 284; Walker, *Armenia*, p. 199; *Treatment of Armenians*, p. 638; Morgenthau Diary, Nov. 29, Dec. 28, 1914, Jan. 4, 19, 1915.
56. Allen and Muratoff, *Caucasian Battlefields*, pp. 245–47; Morgenthau Diary, Dec. 12, 1914; *Treatment of Armenians*, Doc. 21.

57. Sebuh Akuni, *Milion me Hayeru Jardi Patmutiune* [The Story of the Massacre of a Million Armenians] (Constantinople: Hayastan, 1921), p. 29; Hovannisian, *Armenia on the Road to Independence*, p. 53.

58. Zaven Der Yeghiayan, *My Patriarchal Memoirs*, translated from the Armenian by Ared Misirliyan, annotated by Vatche Ghazarian (Barrington, RI: Mayreni Publishing, 2002), p. 63.

59. Morgenthau Diary, Jan. 23, 1915; Allen and Muratoff, *Caucasian Battlefields*, p. 286.

60. Keegan, *First World War*, pp. 219–21; Donald M. McKale, *War by Revolution: Germany and Great Britain in the Middle East in the Era of World War 1* (Kent, OH: Kent State University Press, 1998), pp. 86, 97–98, 100; "Battle of the Suez Canal: A First-Hand Account of the Unsuccessful Turkish Invasion," *Times* (London), Feb. 19, 1915, reprinted in *Current History* 2 (April 1915): 85–88.

61. Morgenthau Diary, Dec. 27, 28, 1914, Jan. 19, 1915.

62. William L. Langer, *The Diplomacy of Imperialism, 1890–1902*, 2nd edn. (New York: Alfred A. Knopf, 1951), pp. 162, 202–10.

63. *Treatment of Armenians*, p. 638.

64. Morgenthau Diary, Jan. 15, 1915.

65. Bryan Papers, Box 45, Special Correspondence, Bryan to Wilson, Jan. 12, 1915.

66. "A Jackson Day Address in Indianapolis," Jan. 8, 1915, *PWW*, vol. 32, pp. 34, 35.

67. Morgenthau Papers, General Correspondence, Container 7, Morgenthau to Elkus, April 13, 1915. In March, Elkus wrote to Morgenthau that "People are now beginning to talk about Presidential possibilities, but it is a little early." Elkus to Morgenthau, March 15, 1915.

68. Edward M. Sait and Lewis Mayers, "Record of Political Events," *Political Science Quarterly* 30:2 (June 1915): 354, 356, 356; Dec. 8, 1914, *PWW*, vol. 31, pp. 414–24. See also William J. Williams, *The Wilson Administration and the Shipbuilding Crisis of 1917* (Lewiston, NY: Edwin Mellen Press, 1992), pp. 17–45.

69. "An Address to the United States Chamber of Commerce," Feb. 3, 1915, *PWW*, vol. 32, pp. 184–85; May 24, 1915, vol. 33, pp. 245–47.

70. William C. Redfield, "America's International Trade as Affected by the European War," *Annals of the American Academy of Political and Social Science* 60 (July 1915): 14–15. See also David M. Kennedy, *Over Here: The First World War and American Society* (New York: Oxford University Press, 1980), pp. 37–38.

5   Power and Its Promises

1. Library of Congress, Division of Manuscripts, Papers of Henry Morgenthau, Sr., Diary, Jan. 23, 1915, cited hereafter as Morgenthau Diary.

2. Ibid., Jan. 4, 28, 1915.

3. Levon Chormisian, *Hamapatker Arevmtahai Mek Daru Patmutian* [A Panorama of One Century of Western Armenian History], 3 vols. (Beirut: Sevan, 1975), vol. 3, pp. 357–58.

4. See Zaven Der Yeghiayan, *My Patriarchal Memoirs*, trans. Ared Misirliyan, and annotated, Vatche Ghazarian (Barrington, RI: Mayreni Publishing, 2002), pp. 99–100.

5. Morgenthau Diary, Jan. 18, Feb. 22, 23, 27, 1915. Bertha B. Morley, *Marsovan 1915: The Diaries of Bertha B. Morley*, Hilmar Kaiser, ed. (Ann Arbor, MI: Gomidas Institute, 1999), pp. 2–3; Rafael de Nogales, *Four Years Beneath the Crescent*, translated from the Spanish, Muna Lee (New York and London: Charles Sribner's Sons, 1926), p. 22; Morgenthau Diary, March 15, 1915.

6. Chormisian, *Hamapatker*, p. 359; Great Britain, Parliament, *The Treatment of Armenians in the Ottoman Empire, 1915–16: Documents Presented to Viscount Grey of Fallodon, Secretary of State for Foreign Affairs*, Miscellaneous no. 31, 1916, comp. and ed. Arnold Toynbee, 3rd edn. (Beirut: G. Doniguian and Sons, 1988; London: Sir Joseph Causton and Sons, 1916), Docs. 29, 30, 31, 36; cited hereafter as *Treatment of Armenians*.

7. Johannes Lepsius, *Rapport secret sur les massacres d'Arménie* (Paris: Payot, 1918; repr. Beirut: Edition Hamazkayin, Association Culturelle Arménienne, 1980), pp. 227–28. On the treatment of Armenian soldiers in Baghdad, see United States, National Archives, Record Group 59 (cited hereafter as RG 59), 867.00/760, U.S. Consul Charles F. Brissel to Secretary of State, April 1, 1915.

8. RG 59, 367.116/298, Morgenthau to Secretary of State, Feb. 20, 1915, U.S. Department of State, *Papers Relating to the Foreign Relations of the United States, 1915*, Supp., *The World War* (Washington, DC: Government Printing Office, 1928), pp. 979–80, cited hereafter as *FRUS, 1915*, Supp.; *Current History* 2 (May 1915): 405.

9. Clarence D. Ussher, *An American Physician in Turkey: A Narrative of Adventures in Peace and War* (Boston: Houghton Mifflin, 1917), p. 221.

10. Ibid., pp. 221–25; Maria Jacobsen, *Oragrutiun 1907–1919: Kharpert* [Diary 1907–1919: Kharpert], translated from Danish by Bishop Nerses Bakhtikian and Mihran Simonian (Antelias: Catholicosate of Cilicia, 1979), p. 67; Lepsius, *Rapport secret*, p. 114. On Clarence Ussher, see Samuel Rshtuni, "Doctor Ussheri Mahe" [The Death of Dr. Ussher], and letter, dated February 25, 1955, from Ussher: "General Society of Vasbouragan," *Varag* 3:12 (Jan. 1956): 20–21, 21–22.

11. Ussher, *American Physician*, p. 226n1.

12. Sebuh Akuni, *Milion me Hayeru Jardi Patmutiune* [The Story of the Massacre of a Million Armenians] (Constantinople: Hayastan, 1921), pp. 26–28; Chormisian, *Hamapatker*, pp. 343–45. See also Nuri Bey to Jemal Bey, Feb. 18, 1915, in Aram Antonian, *Mets Vojire* [The

Colossal Crime] (Boston: Bahak, 1921; repr. Erevan: Arevik, 1990), pp. 129–30, 133; Vahakn N. Dadrian, "The Secret Young-Turk Ittihadist Conference and the Decision for the World War I Genocide of the Armenians," *Holocaust and Genocide Studies* 7:2 (Fall 1993); reprinted with revisions in "The Armenian Genocide in Official Turkish Records," a special issue of the *Journal of Political and Military Sociology* 22:1 (Summer 1994): 173–201.

13. Chormisian, *Hamapatker*, pp. 343–45.

14. See Armenian translation of the letter of February 18, 1915, in Antonian, *Mets Vojire*, pp. 129–33.

15. James J. Reid, "Total War, the Annihilation Ethic, and the Armenian Genocide, 1870–1918," in Richard G. Hovannisian, ed., *The Armenian Genocide: History, Politics, Ethics* (New York: St. Martin's Press, 1992), pp. 21–52; James J. Reid, "Philosophy of State-Subject Relations, Ottoman Concepts of Tyranny, and the Demonization of Subjects: Conservative Ottomanism as a Source of Genocidal Behavior, 1821–1918," in Zoryan Institute, *Problems of Genocide* (Toronto: Zoryan Institute of Canada, 1997), pp. 280–319.

16. "Chronology of the War," *Current History* 2 (April 1915): 197; *Treatment of Armenians*, Doc. 31.

17. *Treatment of Armenians*, Docs. 27, 28, 31, 36. See also *Current History* 2 (May 1915): 405.

18. *Treatment of Armenians*, Docs. 29, 30, 36; Christopher J. Walker, *Armenia: Survival of a Nation* (London: Croom Helm, 1980), p. 205; Henry Barby, *Au pays de l'épouvante: L'Arménie martyre* (Beirut: Edition Hamazkayin, Association Culturelle Arménienne, 1972; first published, 1917), pp. 131–32.

19. *Treatment of Armenians*, Docs. 28, 29, 30, 31, 36.

20. Bibliothèque Nubar (Paris), Boghos Nubar, "The War and the Armenians of Cilicia," Memorandum, 918–923, Cairo, Feb. 3, 1915, in *Boghos Nubar's Papers and the Armenian Question, 1915–1918*, trans. and ed. Vatche Ghazarian (Waltham, MA: Mayrnei Publishing, 1996), pp. 3–5, cited hereafter as Boghos Nubar Papers.

21. Akuni, *Milion*, p. 295; Lepsius, *Rapport secret*, pp. 33–34; Haikaz M. Poghosyan, *Zeituni Patmutiune, 1409–1921 tt.* [The History of Zeitun, 1409–1921] (Erevan: Hayastan, 1969), p. 387; *Treatment of Armenians*, Doc. 122.

22. Khoren K. Davidson, *Odyssey of an Armenian of Zeitoun* (New York: Vantage Press, 1985), p. 65; Zakaria Pztikian, comp., *Kilikian Kskitsner: Vaveragrer Kilikioy Katoghikosakan Divanen, 1903–1915* [Cilician Pains: Documents from the Archives of the Cilician Catholicosate] (Beirut: Hrazdan, 1927), p. 136; Buzand Eghiayan, *Zhamanakakits Patmutiun Katoghikosutian Hayots Kilikioy, 1914–1972* [Contemporary History of the Catholicosate of Cilician Armenians, 1914–1972] (Antelias: Catholicosate of Cilicia, 1975),

pp. 43–44; Chormisian, *Hamapatker*, pp. 440–41. On Jemal Pasha, see also Lepsius, *Rapport secret*, p. 274.

23. Catholicos Sahak to Der Yeghiayan, April 7, 1915, in Pztikian, *Kilikian Kskitsner*, pp. 14–45.

24. RG 59, 867.4016/373, Jackson to Secretary of State, March 4, 1918; Lepsius, *Rapport secret*, pp. 28–29, 38–39, 194; *Treatment of Armenians*, Docs. 29, 30, 31, 36, 137. See also Morgenthau Diary, Feb. 10, 1915.

25. RG 59, 867.00/761, Jackson to Secretary of State, April 21, 1915, encl., a report by Jackson and a report by J.E. Merrill to Jackson, dated April 20, 1915, on the conditions in the Marash region; RG 59, 867.4016/80, Morgenthau to Secretary of State, June 26, 1915, encl., J.E. Merrill, report on the situation in the Zeitun-Marash region, June 14, 1915. See also *Treatment of Armenians*, Docs. 16, 128, 137, 138.

26. RG 59, 867.4016/59, Morgenthau to Secretary of State, April 30, 1915; RG 59, 867.4016/60, Bryan to Bakhméteff, May 3, 1915; Morgenthau Papers, General Correspondence, Container 7, Bryan to Morgenthau, April 29, 1915; Akuni, *Milion*, pp. 303–05; France, Archives du Ministère des Affaires Étrangères (A.M.A.E.), Guerre 1914–1918, *Turquie*, Kévork V, Catholicos de tous les Arméniens, à Sa Majesté Victor-Emmanuel, Roi d'Italie, April 22, 1915, in Arthur Beylerian, ed. and comp., *Les grandes puissances, l'empire ottoman et les arméniens dans les archives françaises (1914–1918)* (Paris: Panthéon-Sorbonne, 1983), p. 14; Catholicos Kevork V to Boghos Nubar, April 22, 1915, Boghos Nubar Papers, p. 17.

27. For the minutes of the meeting, see Der Yeghiayan, *Memoirs*, pp. 62–63. It has been argued that the Allied campaign at Gallipoli may have instigated the wholesale arrests of Armenian leaders in Constantinople. Walker, *Armenia*, pp. 209–10; Grigoris Palakian, *Hai Goghgotan* [The Armenian Calvary] (Vienna: Mkhitarist Press, 1922; repr. Erevan: Hayastan, 1991), pp. 78–79.

28. Palakian, *Hai Goghgotan*, pp. 46–109; Lepsius, *Rapport secret*, pp. 48, 228–29, 231, 233–34. According to Barby, *Au pays de l'épouvante*, pp. 9n2, 56, the Armenian population in Constantinople numbered about 200,000.

29. Morgenthau Papers, General Correspondence, Container 7, Morgenthau to Secretary of State, April 30, 1915; RG 59, 867.4016/59, Morgenthau to Secretary of State, April 30, 1915.

30. Morgenthau Papers, General Correspondence, Container 7, Morgenthau to Secretary of State, April 30, 1915; also in RG 59, 867.4016/59, Morgenthau to Secretary of State, April 30, 1915.

31. RG 59, 867.4016/58, Bryan to Morgenthau, Constantinople, April 27, 1915, sent on April 29; Morgenthau Papers, General Correspondence, Container 7, Bryan to Morgenthau, April 27, 29, 1915; RG 59, 867.4016/61, Bryan to Morgenthau, May 4, 1915.

32. RG 59, 867.4016/60, Bryan to Bakhméteff, May 3, 1915; RG 59, 867.4016/64, Morgenthau to Secretary of State, May 6, 1915.

33. A.N. Mnatsakanyan, "Hay Zhoghovrdi Mets Egherne ev Azgayin Veratsnunte" [The Colossal Calamity of the Armenian People and the National Revival], and V. Kesaratsi, "Kesario ev Shrjakayits Arian Turke Hayots Mets Eghernin" [The Blood Debt of Cesarea and Its Environs During the Colossal Catastrophe], in Gersam Aharonian, ed. and comp., *Hushamatian Mets Egherni, 1915–1965* [Memorial Volume of the Colossal Crime, 1915–1965] (Beirut: Atlas, 1965), pp. 33–34, 339.

34. Der Yeghiayan, *Memoirs*, pp. 63–65; Antonian, *Mets Vojire*, pp. 81–82; Morgenthau Diary, April 26, 27, 1915.

35. Der Yeghiayan, *Memoirs*, p. 58.

36. Morgenthau Diary, May 15, 16, 17, 1915.

37. Ibid., March 26, 1915.

38. Gregory P. Nowell, *Mercantile States and the World Oil Cartel, 1900–1939* (Ithaca and London: Cornell University Press, 1994), pp. 96–97; S.L.A. Marshall, *World War I* (Boston: Houghton Mifflin, 1964; repr. Mariner Books, 2001), pp. 149–53; Niall Ferguson, *The Pity of War* (London: Penguin Press, 1998; New York: Basic Books, 1999), pp. 290–91; Jean Giraudoux, "The Dardanelles," *North American Review* 206 (Aug. 1917): 285–91.

39. Text of Churchill's speech in the House of Commons on November 15, 1915, after his resignation from the Cabinet. *Current History* 3 (Jan. 1916): 697.

40. Quoted in Martin Gilbert, *The First World War: A Complete History* (New York: Henry Holt, 1994), p. 105.

41. Feb. 20, 1915, *PWW*, vol. 32, p. 266; Marshall, *World War I*, pp. 149–53; Ferguson, *Pity of War*, pp. 290–91; Henry Morgenthau, *Ambassador Morgenthau's Story* (New York: Doubleday, 1918), pp. 184–85, 194; on Enver, see pp. 197–99, 202–04. Enver expressed confidence that Turkey could defend the Dardanelles, while Talaat seemed less sure. Morgenthau Diary, March 8, 16, 1915.

42. Donald M. McKale, *War by Revolution: Germany and Great Britain in the Middle East in the Era of World War I* (Kent, OH: Kent State University Press, 1998), pp. 101–02; Brigadier General Cecil Faber Aspinall-Oglander, comp., *Military Operations, Gallipoli* (London: W. Heinemann, 1929–1932); Alan Moorehead, *Gallipoli* (London: H. Hamilton, 1956); *Current History* 2 (May 1915): 400.

43. RG 59, 867.00/428, Jackson to Secretary of State, Nov. 19, 1912.

44. RG 59, 867.00/762, Morgenthau to Secretary of State, May 11, 1915, encl., Jackson to Morgenthau, April 8, 1915, "Seditious pamphlet circulated by Germans."

45. "A Universal Proclamation to All the People of Islam," published by the National Society of Defense, The Seat of the Caliphate, printed in

the Mutba'at el-Haireyet (1333), in RG 59, 867.00/762, Morgenthau to Secretary of State, May 11, 1915, encl., Jackson to Morgenthau, April 8, 1915.
46. Ibid.
47. Chormisian, *Hamapatker*, pp. 439–40.
48. Onnik Mkhitarian, *Vani Herosamarte* [The Heroic Struggle of Van] (Sofia: P. Palegchian, 1930), p. 53; Anahide Ter Minassian, "Van 1915," in Richard G. Hovannisian, ed., *Armenian Van/Vaspurakan* (Costa Mesa, CA: Mazda Publishers, 2000), p. 225; G. Froian, "Karmir Aprile" [The Red April], *Varag* 3:9 (April 1955): 56.
49. Barby gives April 13 as the date when the fighting began. Barby, *Au pays de l'epouvante*, p. 134.
50. Ibid., pp. 237–38, 275.
51. Ibid., pp. 252, 263, 277–79, 286.
52. W.E.D. Allen and Paul Muratoff, *Caucasian Battlefields: A History of the Wars on the Turco-Caucasian Border, 1828–1921* (Cambridge: Cambridge University Press, 1953), p. 299; Morgenthau Diary, May 8, 1915.
53. Lepsius, *Rapport secret*, pp. 130–32; Ter Minassian, "Van 1915," p. 239; Allen and Muratoff, *Caucasian Battlefields*, pp. 300–01.
54. RG 59, 367.11/569a, Bryan to Morgenthau, May 8, 1915.
55. RG 59, 367.11/570, Morgenthau to Bryan, May 10, 1915.
56. "The Petrograd Plan," [Handed to Boghos Nubar by Dr. Zavriev], 1065–1068, [May 1915], in Boghos Nubar Papers, pp. 19–20. See also Jon Kirakosyan, comp., *Hayastane Mijazgayin ev Sovetakan Artakin Kaghakakanutian Pastatghterum, 1828–1923* [Armenia in the Documents of International and Soviet Foreign Policy, 1828–1923] (Erevan: Hayastan, 1972), pp. 371–74.
57. "The Petrograd Plan," pp. 19–20.
58. Lepsius, *Rapport secret*, pp. 34–35; Chormisian, *Hamapatker*, p. 479; Akuni, *Milion*, p. 310.
59. RG 59, 867.4016/72, Jackson to Secretary of State, May 12, 1915, encl., Jackson to Morgenthau, May 12, 1915. This report appeared in part as Doc. 139 in *Treatment of Armenians*; see also Docs. 6, 16, 123, 124, 125, 129, 130, 133.
60. RG 59, 867.4016/97, Hollis to Secretary of State, July 6, 1915; RG 59, 867.4016/104, Morgenthau to Secretary of State, July 21, 1915, encl., report on the situation in Zeitun. See also a report by William S. Dodd of the American Hospital at Konia, Morgenthau Papers, General Correspondence, Container 7, Dodd to Morgenthau, Aug. 15, 1915, p. 6; *Treatment of Armenians*, Docs. 120, 123–125, 128, 129, 130, 133, 138.
61. Morgenthau Papers, General Correspondence, Container 7, Bryan to Morgenthau, May 5, 1915; RG 867.4016/64, Morgenthau to Secretary of State, May 6, 1915; RG 59, 867.00/762, Morgenthau to

Secretary of State, May 11, 1915; RG 59, 867.00/766, Morgenthau
to Secretary of State, May 14, 1915.

62. Morgenthau Papers, General Correspondence, Container 7,
Morgenthau to Secretary of State, May 25, 1915.

63. *Treatment of Armenians*, Docs. 12, 22, 23, 33, 34, 35, 77, 126. The
postwar parliament repealed the Temporary Law of Deportation on
November 4, 1918. Vahakn N. Dadrian, *The History of the Armenian
Genocide: Ethnic Conflict from the Balkans to Anatolia to the Caucasus*
(Providence: Berghahn Books, 1995), pp. 221–22.

64. RG 59, 867.4016/67, Secretary of State to American Embassy,
Constantinople, May 29, 1915; A.M.A.E., Guerre 1914–1918,
Turquie, "Communication de l'Ambassade de Russie au
Département," May 11, 1915, "Communication de l'Ambassade de
Grande-Bretagne au Département," May 19, 1915, "Communication
de l'Ambassade de Grande-Bretagne au Département," May 21,
1915, "Note du Département à l'Agence Havas," May 24, 1915, and
M. William Sharp, Ambassadeur des États-Unis à Paris, à M. Declassé,
Ministre des Affaires étrangères, May 28, 1915, in Beylerian, *Les
grandes puissances*, pp. 23, 25–26, 27–28, 29, 31.

65. Hikmet Yusuf Bayur, *Türk İnkılâbı Tarihi*, vol. 3: *1914–1918
Genel Savaşı*, pt. 3, *1915–1917 Vuruşmaları ve Bunların Siyasal Tepkileri*
[History of the Turkish Revolution, vol. 3: The 1914–1918 World War,
the Battles of 1915–1917 and Their Political Effects] (Ankara: Türk Tarih
Kurumu, 1957), pp. 37–38, as quoted in Richard G. Hovannisian,
Armenia on the Road to Independence, 1918 (Berkeley and Los Angeles:
University of California Press, 1967), p. 50.

66. Gilbert, *First World War*, p. 166.

67. Morgenthau Diary, June 7, 1915.

68. Morgenthau Papers, Container 7, American Ambassador to Secretary
of State, June 18, 1915; RG 59, 867.4016/70, Morgenthau to
Secretary of State, June 18, 1915, *FRUS, 1915*, Supp., p. 982.

69. Bibliothèque Nubar (Paris), 1090–1091, Boghos Nubar to Lieutenant-
Colonel G.M. Gregory, May 25, 1915, Boghos Nubar Papers, p. 54.

70. Ibid., 1107–1110, Levon Meguerditchian to Boghos Nubar, May 28,
1915, Boghos Nubar Papers, p. 65.

71. Makich Arzumanyan, *Hayastan, 1914–1917* [Armenia, 1914–1917]
(Erevan: Hayastan, 1969), p. 446.

72. Ibid., p. 447.

73. RG 59, 867.4016/92, Morgenthau to Secretary of State, July 13,
1915; encls., Jackson to Morgenthau, June 28, 1915, and report on
the atrocities in Urfa by Rev. F.H. Leslie, June 14, 1915. See also
Arzumanyan, *Hayastan*, pp. 446–47.

74. RG 59, 867.4016/92, Morgenthau to Secretary of State, July 13,
1915; encls., Jackson to Morgenthau, June 28, 1915. See also
Treatment of Armenians, Doc. 133.

75. The U.S. embassy staff, however, did not relay this report to the State Department until February 17, 1916. RG 59, 867.4016/269, Hoffman Philip, Chargé d'Affaires, to Secretary of State, Feb. 17, 1916, encl., Davis to Morgenthau, June 30, 1915.
76. Leslie A. Davis, *The Slaughterhouse Province: An American Diplomat's Report on the Armenian Genocide, 1915–1917*, ed. with introduction and notes by Susan K. Blair (New Rochelle, NY: Aristide D. Caratzas Publisher, 1989), p. 7.

6 THE PRIMACY OF REALISM AND LEGALISM

1. Lansing to Wilson, Feb. 5, 1915, encl., "A Draft Note to Germany"; Bryan to Gerard, Feb. 10, 1915, encl., note to the German government, in Arthur S. Link, ed., *The Papers of Woodrow Wilson*, 69 vols. (Princeton: Princeton University Press, 1966–1994), vol. 32, pp. 193–95; 207–10; cited hereafter as *PWW*.
2. Wilson to Hardwick, May 9, 1915, ibid., vol. 33, p. 134.
3. House, May 9, 1915, ibid., vol. 33, p. 134.
4. Bryan to Wilson, May 9, 1915, Wilson to Bryan, May 12, 1915, Bryan to Wilson, June 2, 1915, Bryan to Wilson, June 3, 1915, Bryan to Wilson, June 5, 1915, Wilson to Bryan, June 5, 1915, Bryan to Wilson, June 7, 1915, Bryan to Wilson, June 9, 1915, Wilson to Bryan, June 9, 1915, ibid., vol. 33, pp. 134–35, 174–78, 310–13, 321–26, 326–31, 342–43, 351–60, 375–76; Library of Congress, Division of Manuscripts, Papers of William Jennings Bryan, Letter Book, Box 59, Special Correspondence, Bryan to Wilson, June 3, 1915; Secretary of State to President Wilson, May 10, 1915, encl., Counselor for the Department of State (Lansing) to the Secretary of State, May 9, 1915, U.S. Department of State, *Foreign Relations of the United States: Lansing Papers, 1914–1920*, 2 vols. (Washington, DC: Government Printing Office, 1939), vol. 1, pp. 385–436. See also Editor, "The Revolt of Bryan," *North American Review* 202 (July 1915): 1–6.
5. Page to President and Secretary, May 8, 1915, *PWW*, vol. 33, pp. 129–30.
6. Bibliothèque Nubar (Paris), 1008–1009, Lord Bryce to Boghos Nubar, May 9, 1915, in *Boghos Nubar's Papers and the Armenian Question, 1915–1918*, trans. and ed. Vatche Ghazarian (Waltham, MA: Mayrni Publishing, 1996), p. 23, cited hereafter as Boghos Nubar Papers.
7. Library of Congress, Division of Manuscripts, Papers of Henry Morgenthau, Sr., General Correspondence, Container 14, Morgenthau to Wise, Aug. 3, 1915, p. 2.
8. Wilson to Bryan, June 7, 1915, *PWW*, vol. 33, p. 349.
9. Lloyd E. Ambrosius, *Wilsonian Statecraft: Theory and Practice of Liberal Internationalism during World War I* (Wilmington: Scholarly Resource Books, 1991), p. xv.

10. Library of Congress, Division of Manuscripts, Papers of Robert Lansing, Lansing Diaries, June 23, 1915. Frank L. Polk succeeded Lansing as counselor for the Department of State.

11. Ibid., Lansing Diary, May 3, 1915, Blue Boxes, Box 2, Confidential Memoranda and Notes, April 15, 1915–Dec. 30, 1918; cited hereafter as Lansing Diary.

12. Ibid. See also Library of Congress, Division of Manuscripts, Papers of William Jennings Bryan, Box 59, Lansing, Memorandum on Reply to British Note and Order in Council of March 15, 1915, March 24, 1915.

13. Lansing Diary, May 25, 1915.

14. Ibid.

15. United States, National Archives, Record Group 59 (hereafter RG 59), 367.116/341, Lansing to Barton, July 19, 1915, U.S. Department of State, *Papers Relating to the Foreign Relations of the United States, 1915*, Supp., *The World War* (Washington, DC: Government Printing Office, 1928), pp. 984–85, cited hereafter as *FRUS, 1915*, Supp.

16. The Diary of Colonel Edward M. House, Yale University Library, July 24, 1915, and Lansing Diary, May 25, 1915, quoted in James F. Willis, *Prologue to Nuremberg: The Politics and Diplomacy of Punishing War Criminals of the First World War* (Westport, CT: Greenwood Press, 1982), p. 41.

17. Library of Congress, Division of Manuscripts, Papers of Henry Morgenthau, Sr., Containers 40/41, Henry Wood, "Interview with His Excellency Enver Pasha, Minister of War and Vice-Generalissimo of the Ottoman Army and Navy," p. 3, [n.d.].

18. He was satisfied with Morgenthau's reports which, in response to his inquiries concerning the well-being of American citizens, stated that the "Embassy has not heard of any injuries to native or naturalized citizens of the United States." RG 59, 867.4016/79, Morgenthau to Lansing, July 20, 1915, *FRUS, 1915*, Supp., p. 985.

19. Great Britain, Parliament, *The Treatment of Armenians in the Ottoman Empire, 1915–16: Documents Presented to Viscount Grey of Fallodon, Secretary of State for Foreign Affairs*, Miscellaneous no. 31, 1916, comp. and ed. Arnold Toynbee, 3d ed. (Beirut: G. Doniguian and Sons, 1988; London: Sir Joseph Causton and Sons, 1916), Docs. 4, 12, 22, 25, 53, 57, 76, 94, 120, 121, 126, 139; cited hereafter as *Treatment of Armenians*. See also RG 59, 867.4016/104, Morgenthau to Secretary of State, July 21, 1915.

20. See text of letter, dated June 30/July 13, 1915, in Zaven Der Yeghiayan, *My Patriarchal Memoirs*, trans. Ared Misirliyan, and annotated, Vatche Ghazarian (Barrington, RI: Mayreni Publishing, 2002), pp. 85–87.

21. RG 59, 867.4016/77, Jackson to Secretary of State, June 5, 1915, encl., Jackson to Morgenthau, June 5, 1915.

22. Zakaria Pztikian, comp., *Kilikian Kskitsner: Vaveragrer Kilikioy Katoghikosakan Divanen, 1903–1915* [Cilician Pains: Documents from the Archives of the Cilician Catholicosate] (Beirut: Hrazdan, 1927), pp. 182, 191–92.

23. Morgenthau Diary, June 17, 1915.

24. Morgenthau Papers, General Correspondence, Container 7, American Ambassador to Secretary of State, June 18, 1915.

25. Morgenthau Diary, June 19, 1915.

26. "Turks are Evicting Native Christians," *New York Times*, July 12, 1915, p. 4.

27. *Current History* 2 (Aug. 1915): 1017.

28. *Treatment of Armenians*, p. 615.

29. Makich Arzumanyan, *Hayastan, 1914–1917* [Armenia, 1914–1917] (Erevan: Hayastan, 1969), p. 389; Vartkes Yeghiayan, ed. and comp., *British Foreign Office Dossiers on Turkish War Criminals* (La Verne, CA: American Armenian International College, 1991), pp. 305, 308, 309, 310.

30. Johannes Lepsius, *Rapport secret sur les massacres d'Arménie* (Paris: Payot, 1918; repr. Beirut: Edition Hamazkayin, Association Culturelle Arménienne, 1980), pp. 151–53.

31. Sebuh Akuni, *Milion me Hayeru Jardi Patmutiune* [The Story of the Massacre of a Million Armenians] (Constantinople: Hayastan, 1921), pp. 163, 164; RG 59, 867.4016/241, Morgenthau to Secretary of State, Nov. 17, 1915, encl., "Miss Alma Johanson's Report."

32. *Treatment of Armenians*, editor's note, "Vilayet of Bitlis," p. 79.

33. Arzumanyan, *Hayastan*, pp. 391–94; *Treatment of Armenians*, Doc. 23; RG 59, 867.4016/241, Morgenthau to Secretary of State, Nov. 17, 1915, encl., "Miss Alma Johanson's Report"; W.E.D. Allen and Paul Muratoff, *Caucasian Battlefields: A History of the Wars on the Turco-Caucasian Border, 1828–1921* (Cambridge: Cambridge University Press, 1953), pp. 303–05.

34. Arzumanyan, *Hayastan*, pp. 394, 400–01, 403; Allen and Muratoff, *Caucasian Battlefields*, pp. 305, 308, 310; Grace H. Knapp, *The Tragedy of Bitlis* (New York: Fleming H. Revell, 1919), p. 144.

35. Edward M. Sait, "Record of Political Events," *Political Science Quarterly* 30:4 (Dec. 1915): 705.

36. Martin Gilbert, *The First World War: A Complete History* (New York: Henry Holt, 1994), pp. 202, 211–12.

37. James L. Stokesbury, *A Short History of World War I* (New York: William Morrow, 1981), pp. 115–20; "Battle of the Dardanelles," *Current History* 2 (May 1915): 219–22; *Current History* 3 (Oct. 1915): 203; Sait, "Record of Political Events" (Dec. 1915): 704, 706; Marshall, *World War I*, p. 154.

38. Henry Morgenthau, *Ambassador Morgenthau's Story* (New York: Doubleday, 1918), p. 195.

39. Sait and Mayers, "Record of Political Events" (June 1915): 348.
40. Morgenthau, *Story*, p. 274.
41. Lewis Einstein, *A Diplomat Looks Back* (New Haven and London: Yale University Press, 1968), pp. 118, 133. See also Joseph L. Grabill, *Protestant Diplomacy and the Near East: Missionary Influence on American Policy, 1810–1927* (Minneapolis: University of Minnesota Press, 1971), p. 63.
42. Maria Jacobsen, *Oragrutiun 1907–1919: Kharpert* [Diary 1907–1919: Kharpert], translated from Danish by Bishop Nerses Bakhtikian and Mihran Simonian (Antelias: Catholicosate of Cilicia, 1979), p. 80.
43. RG 59, 867.00/797, Morgenthau to Lansing, Nov. 4, 1915, pp. 5, 6.

7   Ambassador Morgenthau's Policy Recommendations

1. Henry Morgenthau, *Ambassador Morgenthau's Story* (New York: Doubleday, 1918), p. 314.
2. *Horizon* Armenian daily, Tiflis, Aug. 21, 1915, as reported by Henry Barby, *Au pays de l'épouvante: L'Arménie martyre* (Beirut: Edition Hamazkayin, Association Culturelle Arménienne, 1972; first published, 1917), pp. 186–90; Great Britain, Parliament, *The Treatment of Armenians in the Ottoman Empire, 1915–16: Documents Presented to Viscount Grey of Fallodon, Secretary of State for Foreign Affairs*, Miscellaneous no. 31, 1916, comp. and ed. Arnold Toynbee, 3rd edn. (Beirut: G. Doniguian and Sons, 1988; London: Sir Joseph Causton and Sons, 1916), Docs. 46, 48, 49, 50; cited hereafter as *Treatment of Armenians*.
3. Christopher J. Walker, *Armenia: Survival of a Nation* (London: Croom Helm, 1980), p. 226; Johannes Lepsius, *Rapport secret sur les massacres d'Arménie* (Paris: Payot, 1918; repr. Beirut: Edition Hamazkayin, Association Culturelle Arménienne, 1980), p. 40.
4. U.S. National Archives, Record Group 59 (hereafter RG 59) 867.4016/126, Morgenthau to Secretary of State, Aug. 18, 1915, encl., Jackson to Morgenthau, Aug. 3, 1915. See also *Treatment of Armenians*, Docs. 9, 88, 90, 92, 99, 102, 103, 139.
5. RG 59, 867.4016/148, Morgenthau to Secretary of State, Aug. 30, 1915, encl., Jackson to Morgenthau, Aug. 19, 1915. See also *Treatment of Armenians*, Section C of Doc. 139; Zaven Der Yeghiayan, *My Patriarchal Memoirs*, trans. Ared Misirliyan, and annotated, Vatche Ghazarian (Barrington, RI: Mayreni Publishing, 2002), p. 96; Sebuh Akuni, *Milion me Hayeru Jardi Patmutiune* [The Story of the Massacre of a Million Armenians] (Constantinople: Hayastan, 1921), pp. 126–35.
6. RG 59, 867.4016/74, Morgenthau to Secretary of State, July 10, 1915.

7. RG 59, 867.4016/76, Morgenthau to Secretary of State, July 16, 1915. For a different version of this telegram, see Library of Congress, Division of Manuscripts, Papers of Henry Morgenthau, Sr., General Correspondence, Container 7, Morgenthau to Secretary of State, July 16, 1915.

8. RG 59, 867.4016/74, Lansing to American embassy, July 16, 1915; U.S. Department of State, *Papers Relating to the Foreign Relations of the United States, 1915*, Supp., *The World War* (Washington, DC: Government Printing Office, 1928), pp. 984–85, cited hereafter as *FRUS, 1915*, Supp. For a different version of this telegram, see Morgenthau Papers, General Correspondence, Container 7, Lansing to American Embassy, July 16, 1915. RG 59, 367.116/341, Lansing to Barton, July 19, 1915.

9. Library of Congress, Division of Manuscripts, Papers of Henry Morgenthau, Sr., Diary, July 29, Aug. 2, 30, 1915; cited hereafter as Morgenthau Diary.

10. Ibid., Aug. 5, 1915.

11. Ibid., Aug. 8, 1915.

12. Ibid., July 10, Aug. 17, 1915.

13. Ulrich Trumpener, *Germany and the Ottoman Empire, 1914–1918* (Princeton: Princeton University Press, 1968), p. 122.

14. Morgenthau Diary, July 29, 1915.

15. Trumpener, *Germany and the Ottoman Empire*, p. 123.

16. U.S. Department of States, *Papers Relating to the Foreign Relations of the United States: Lansing Papers, 1914–1920*, 2 vols. (Wasington, DC: Government Printing Office, 1939), vol. 1, 763.72/2275½, Gerard to Secretary of State, Nov. 9, 1915, p. 667.

17. Morgenthau Diary, July 24, 1915.

18. RG 59, 867.00/797, Morgenthau to Lansing, Nov. 4, 1915, p. 7.

19. RG 59, 867.4016/90, Morgenthau to Secretary of State, Aug. 11, 1915; *FRUS, 1915*, Supp., p. 986.

20. RG 59, 867.4016/91, Morgenthau to Secretary of State, Aug. 12, 1915; Morgenthau Papers, General Correspondence, Container 7, Morgenthau to Secretary of State, Aug. 12, 1915, Lansing to American Embassy, Aug. 18, 1915; Morgenthau, *Story*, pp. 292, 374. See also Vahakn N. Dadrian, *German Responsibility in the Armenian Genocide: A Review of the Historical Evidence of German Complicity* (Watertown: Blue Crane Books, 1996), pp. 21–22.

21. Morgenthau, *Story*, p. 383 (emphasis in original). Similarly, Lord Bryce (on October 15) argued that among the major powers, only Germany could stop the Armenian atrocities. *Current History* 3 (Nov. 1915): 208.

22. Morgenthau Diary, Oct. 15, 1915.

23. Morgenthau, *Story*, pp. 374–75.

24. Dadrian, *German Responsibility*, pp. 11–12.

25. RG 59, 867.4016/90, Morgenthau to Lansing, Aug. 11, 1915; *FRUS, 1915*, Supp., p. 987.

26. See, e.g., Louise Nalbandian, *The Armenian Revolutionary Movement: The Development of Armenian Political Parties* (Berkeley and Los Angeles: University of California Press, 1963), pp. 75–76; Richard G. Hovannisian, *Armenia on the Road to Independence, 1918* (Berkeley and Los Angeles: University of California Press, 1967), pp. 15–17; Thomas A. Bryson, *American Diplomatic Relations with the Middle East, 1784–1975* (Metuchen, NJ: Scarecrow Press, 1977), pp. 32–33; Joseph L. Grabill, *Protestant Diplomacy and the Near East: Missionary Influence on American Policy, 1810–1927* (Minneapolis: University of Minnesota Press, 1971), pp. 45–47.

27. RG 59, 867.4016/70, Morgenthau to Secretary of State, June 18, 1915; *FRUS, 1915*, Supp., p. 982; James B. Gidney, *A Mandate for Armenia* (Kent, OH: Kent State University Press, 1967); Thomas A. Bryson, "Woodrow Wilson, the Senate, Public Opinion, and the Armenian Mandate Question, 1919–1920," Ph.D. Diss. (University of Georgia, 1965); Richard G. Hovannisian, *The Republic of Armenia*, 4 vols. (Berkeley and Los Angeles: University of California Press, 1971–1996), vol. 1, pp. 133–34, 300–01, 303; vol. 2, pp. 316–403; vol. 3, pp. 434–38; vol. 4, pp. 1–44.

28. Morgenthau Diary, Aug. 13, 1915.

29. Grabill, *Protestant Diplomacy*, pp. 70–73. See also Robert L. Daniel, *American Philanthropy in the Near East, 1820–1960* (Athens: Ohio State University, 1970), p. 150; *New York Times*, July 15, 1915.

30. Papers of James L. Barton, Papers and Correspondence, James L. Barton, "Autobiographical Notes," p. 250, Box 12, 12:2, American Board of Commissioners for Foreign Missions, Manuscript Collection, Houghton Library, Harvard University; W.W. Peet to Enoch Bell, April 28, 1937, Barton Papers, Papers and Correspondence, Box 12, 12:8, ABCFM.

31. Barton, "Autobiographical Notes," p. 250; "A Chronicle of Dr. Barton's Life," Barton Papers, Papers and Correspondence, Box 12, 12:6, ABCFM.

32. Barton, "Autobiographical Notes," p. 251.

33. Grabill, *Protestant Diplomacy*, pp. 70–73; Daniel, *American Philanthropy*, p. 150; James L. Barton, *Story of Near East Relief, 1915–1930* (New York: Macmillan, 1930).

34. RG 59, 367.11/851, Morgenthau to Secretary of State, Oct. 15, 1915, encl., U.S. Embassy, Note Verbale, to the Sublime Porte, Ministry of Foreign Affairs, Aug. 31, 1915; RG 59, 367.11/851, Morgenthau to Secretary of State, Oct. 15, 1915, encl., the Sublime Porte, Ministry of Foreign Affairs, Note Verbale, to the U.S. Embassy, Oct. 12, 1915; RG 59, 367.11/851, John Osborne, for the Secretary of State, to Morgenthau, Nov. 23, 1915; RG 59, 367.11/851, Adee

to Singer Sewing Machine Company, Nov. 23, 1915, encls., Morgenthau to Secretary of State, Oct. 15, 1915.

35. RG 367.11/1002, Nathan to Secretary of State, Nov. 2, 1915; Secretary of State to International Harvester Company, Jan. 20, 1916; Secretary of State to Messrs, Rumsey and Company, Jan. 20, 1916; Secretary of State to the Goulds Manufacturing Company, Jan. 20, 1916; RG 59, 367.11/1147, Secretary of State, May 24, 1916.

36. RG 59, 367.11/1127, Nathan to Secretary of State, March 16, 1916.

37. RG 59, 367.11/1140, Allen to Secretary of State, May 2, 1916, encls., Allen to Imperial Ottoman Bank, and Allen to Consul Nathan, May 2, 1916.

38. RG 59, 367.11/1164, Nathan to Secretary of State, May 2, 1916.

39. Morgenthau Diary, Oct. 18, 30, Nov. 15, 1915.

40. Der Yeghiayan, *Memoirs*, p. 111.

41. Trumpener, *Germany and the Ottoman Empire*, p. 124. Morgenthau Papers, General Correspondence, Container 27, "Interview of Ambassador Morgenthau with Halil Bey, Minister for Foreign Affairs, on Nov. 12, 1915, at the American Embassy," p. 1.

42. "Interview of Ambassador Morgenthau with Halil Bey," p. 2; Morgenthau Diary, Nov. 12, 1915. See also Esther Mugerditchian, *From Turkish Toils: The Narrative of an Armenian Family's Escape* (New York: George H. Doran, 1918), p. 26.

43. Morgenthau Diary, Nov. 23, 1915, Jan. 22, 1916.

44. RG 59, 867.4016/78, Catholicos Gevorg V to President Wilson, July 18, 1915.

45. RG 59, 867.4016/119, Page to Secretary of State, Aug. 24, 1915, encl., "Letter received from Constantinople on the situation of the Armenians in Asiatic Turkey," July 13, 1915. See the full text in Der Yeghiayan, *Memoirs*, pp. 85–87.

46. RG 59, 867.4016/158, Arnold to Secretary of State, Sept. 2, 1915, encls., Bishop Torkom to Arnold, Aug. 23, 1915; and [Zaven Der Yeghiayan] to Archbishop Ghevont Turian, July 13, 1915.

47. RG 59, 867.4016/81, Bryan to Lansing, July 9, 1915, encl., Cardashian to Bryan, July 8, 1915.

48. RG 59, 867.4016/81, Lansing to Bernstorff, July 14, 1915; RG 59, 867.4016/93, Morgenthau to Secretary of State, July 13, 1915, encl., Heizer to Morgenthau, June 30, 1915; Morgenthau to Lansing, Aug. 11, 1915, RG 59, 867.4016/91, Morgenthau to Lansing, Aug. 12, 1915; Lansing to Morgenthau, Aug. 18, 1915; RG 59, 867.4016/101, Morgenthau to Secretary of State, Aug. 20, 1915; RG 59, 867.4016/118, Bernsdorff to Lansing, Aug. 31, 1915, encl., Imperial German Consulate, Trebizond, July 9, 1915, *FRUS, 1915*, Supp., pp. 985–87.

49. RG 59, 867.4016/197, Copley to Lansing, Nov. 5, 1915, and Lansing to Copley, Nov. 9, 1915.

50. RG 867.4016/141, Richard W. Austin to Secretary of State, Sept. 23, 1915, encl., Armenian National Defence Union of America to Richard W. Austin.

51. RG 59, 867.4016/144, Polk to Austin, Sept. 25, 1915.

52. RG 59, 867.4016/151, Adee to Sevasly, Oct. 14, 1915.

53. Library of Congress, Division of Manuscripts, Papers of Robert Lansing, Lansing Diaries, Oct. 4, 13, 14, 16, 1915. On October 7, Lansing entered in his diary: "Armenian troubles." Lansing Diaries, Oct. 7, 1915.

54. Morgenthau Papers, Container 7, Lansing to Morgenthau, Oct. 4, 1915; *FRUS, 1915*, Supp., p. 988.

55. Library of Congress, Division of Manuscripts, Papers of Woodrow Wilson, Presidential Papers, Lansing to Tumulty, Oct. 26, 1915, with enclosed "form letter."

56. France, Archives du Ministère des Affaires Étrangères (A.M.A.E.), Guerre 1914–1918, *Turquie*, Gevorg V, Catholicos of All Armenians, to Viviani, President of the Council, Minister of Foreign Affairs, Oct. 5/18, 1915, in Arthur Beylerian, ed. and comp., *Les grandes puissances l'empire ottoman et les arméniens dans les archives* françaises (1914–1918) (Paris: Panthéon-Sorbonne, 1983), pp. 126–27.

57. House to Wilson, Oct. 1, 1915, in Arthur S. Link, ed., *The Papers of Woodrow Wilson*, 69 vols. (Princeton: Princeton University Press, 1966–1994), vol. 35, pp. 3–4; cited hereafter as *PWW*.

58. Morgenthau Diary, Sept. 6, 1915. Morgenthau mentioned this to John Reed.

59. Papers of Woodrow Wilson, Presidential Papers, Wilson to Joseph P. Tumulty, Secretary to the President, Sept. 27, 1915, Wilson to Tumulty, Oct. 5, 1915. Topakyan to Wilson, Oct. 22, 1915, Wilson to Topakyan, Oct. 28, 1915, *PWW*, vol. 35, pp. 104–05, 119.

60. "An Annual Message on the State of the Union," Dec. 7, 1915, *PWW*, vol. 35, pp. 293–310.

61. Ibid., pp. 299, 301, 302, 306–7.

62. U.S. Department of Commerce, Bureau of Foreign and Domestic Commerce, *Foreign Commerce and Navigation of the United States* (Washington, DC: Government Printing Office, 1917), pp. xii–xiii, Table III. The data for imports and exports appear in Table 3, p. 293, and Table 5, p. 766. Edward M. Sait, "Record of Political Events," *Political Science Quarterly* 30 (Dec. 1915): 714; Sait and Moon, "Record of Political Events," *Political Science Quarterly* 31 (Sept. 1916): 23.

63. Morgenthau Papers, General Correspondence, Container 7, Barton to Morgenthau, Jan. 17, 1916; Morgenthau Diary, Jan. 27, 1916.

64. Morgenthau Diary, Feb. 1, 1916.

65. RG 59, 867.4016/248, American Embassy, London, to Secretary of State, Jan. 24, 1916; the Department of State to American embassy, London, Jan. 27, 1916.

8 Between Realism and Philanthropy

1. Library of Congress, Division of Manuscripts, Papers of Henry Morgenthau, Sr., Diary, Feb. 23, 1916; cited hereafter as Morgenthau Diary.
2. Library of Congress, Division of Manuscripts, Papers of Robert Lansing, Diaries, Feb. 9, 1916; cited hereafter as Lansing Diaries.
3. Library of Congress, Division of Manuscripts, Papers of Henry Morgenthau, Sr., General Correspondence, Container 7, Lansing to Morgenthau, Feb. 17, 1916.
4. Ibid., Container 8, Morgenthau to Wilson, July 21, 1916.
5. Lansing, Diaries, March 8, 1916; Morgenthau Papers, General Correspondence, Container 7, Morgenthau to Wilson, March 23, 1916, Wilson to Morgenthau, March 23, 1916; Wilson to Morgenthau, May 23, 1916, *The Papers of Woodrow Wilson*, Arthur Link, ed., 69 vols. (Princeton, NJ: Princeton University Press, 1966–94), vol. 37, pp. 96–97, cited hereafter as *PWW*; Morgenthau Diary, April 29, 1916.
6. Morgenthau Diary, Dec. 5, 1913, Feb. 19, 1914. Hoffman Philip later served as U.S. minister to Columbia. Henry Morgenthau, *Ambassador Morgenthau's Story* (New York: Doubleday, 1918), p. 249.
7. Leslie A. Davis, *The Slaughterhouse Province*, ed. with introduction and notes by Susan K. Blair (New Rochelle, NY: Aristide D. Caratzas Publisher, 1989), p. 46.
8. Morgenthau Papers, General Correspondence, Container 7, Philip to Morgenthau, March 5, 1916.
9. U.S. National Archives, File 711.673/69, Philip to Secretary of State, March 9, 1916; encl., Note verbale, the American Embassy to the Minister of Foreign Affairs, Feb. 19, 1916; and the Ministry of Foreign Affairs to the American Embassy, March 7, 1916, U.S. Department of State, *Foreign Relations of the United States, 1916* (Washington, DC: Government Printing Office, 1925), pp. 963–64.
10. 711.673/70, Philip to Secretary of State, April 24, 1916, ibid., pp. 964–65.
11. U.S. National Archives, Record Group 59 (hereafter RG 59), 867.48/271, Jackson to Morgenthau, Feb. 8, 1916; Great Britain, Parliament, *The Treatment of Armenians in the Ottoman Empire, 1915–16: Documents Presented to Viscount Grey of Fallodon, Secretary of State for Foreign Affairs*, Arnold Toynbee, comp. and ed., 3rd edn. (Beirut: G. Doniguian and Sons, 1988; London: Sir Joseph Causton and Sons, 1916), Doc. 139, cited hereafter as *Treatment of Armenians*; Henry H. Riggs, *Days of Tragedy in Armenia: Personal Experiences in Harpoot, 1915–1917* (Ann Arbor: Gomidas Institute, 1997), p. 176.
12. Aram Antonian, *Mets Vojire* [The Colossal Crime] (Boston: Bahak, 1921; repr. Erevan: Arevik, 1990), pp. 63, 169.

13. Levon Chormisian, *Hamapatker Arevmtahai Mek Daru Patmutian* [A Panorama of One Century of Western Armenian History], 3 vols. (Beirut: Sevan, 1975), vol. 3, p. 505.

14. Zaven Der Yeghiayan, *My Patriarchal Memoirs*, trans. from the Armenian by Ared Misirliyan, copyedited and annotated by Vatche Ghazarian (Barrington, RI: Mayreni Publishing, 2002; Cairo: Nor Astgh, 1947), pp. 114–15; Stanley E. Kerr, *The Lions of Marash* (Albany: State University of New York Press, 1973), pp. 24, 28.

15. Antonian, *Mets Vojire*, pp. 101, 105; Chormisian, *Hamapatker*, p. 506.

16. Christopher J. Walker, *Armenia: Survival of a Nation* (London: Croom Helm, 1980), pp. 226–29.

17. Der Yeghiayan, *My Patriarchal Memoirs*, pp. 116–17, 276n159.

18. Babgen I. Guleserian, *Patmutiun Katoghikosats Kilikioy (1441-en minchev Mer Orere)* [History of the Catholicoses of Cilicia (from 1441 until Our Days)] (Antelias: Catholicosate of Cilicia, 1939, 2d pr., 1990), pp. 925–26, 929–30.

19. Der Yeghiayan, *Memoirs*, pp. 121–22, 123, 125, 129–75.

20. Guleserian, *Patmutiun Katoghikosats Kilikioy*, p. 924; Der Yeghiayan, *Memoirs*, pp. 112–13.

21. Excerpt of letter in Der Yeghiayan, *Memoirs*, p. 113.

22. Guleserian, *Patmutiun Katoghikosats Kilikioy*, pp. 925–26; Buzand Eghiayan, *Zhamanakakits Patmutiun Katoghikosutian Hayots Kilikioy, 1914–1972* [Contemporary History of the Catholicosate of Cilician Armenians, 1914–1972] (Antelias: Catholicosate of Cilicia, 1975), pp. 33, 34.

23. Chormisian, *Hamapatker*, p. 508.

24. Papers of James L. Barton, Papers and Correspondence, Box 12, "Autobiographical Notes," p. 224, American Board of Commissioners for Foreign Missions, Manuscript Collection, Houghton Library, Harvard University.

25. Morgenthau Papers, General Correspondence, Container 7, Barton to Morgenthau, March 30, 1916.

26. RG 38, Chief of Naval Operations, Intelligence Division, Naval Attache Reports, 1880–1939, C-6-C, Box 420, Reg. No. 7434, W.W. Peet, Treasurer of the Constantinople Chapter of the American National Red Cross, to Director of Naval Intelligence, U.S.S. Scorpion, Nov. 29. 1916.

27. James L. Barton, *Story of Near East Relief, 1915–1930* (New York: Macmillan, 1930), p. 54.

28. Morgenthau Diary, April 7, 24, 1916; Morgenthau Papers, General Correspondence, Container 8, Morgenthau to Wilson, May 4, 1916; and letters by the American Committee for Armenian and Syrian Relief, the Laymen's Missionary Movement, and the International Committee of Young Men's Christian Associations, to Morgenthau and others, May 11, 16, 18, and June 2, 1916.

29. Morgenthau Papers, General Correspondence, Container 8, Morgenthau to Wilson, May 4, 1916.
30. Library of Congress, Division of Manuscripts, Papers of Robert Lansing, Lansing Papers, vol. 19, Tumulty to Lansing, June 21, 1916, and Lansing to Tumulty, June 21, 1916. Elkus remained at his post until May 29, 1917. U.S. Department of State, Historical Office, Bureau of Public Affairs, *United States Chiefs of Mission, 1778–1982* (Washington, DC: Government Printing Office, 1982), pp. 238–239n7.
31. RG 38, Chief of Naval Operations, Intelligence Division, Naval Attache Reports, 1880–1939, C-10-B, Box 479, Reg. No. 7435, translation from French of an editorial in the Constantinople daily newspaper *Hilal*, Sept. 1, 1916.
32. Elkus interview, "Amérique et Turquie: Déclarations du nouvel ambassadeur des Etats-Unis," *Hilal*, Sept. 15, 1916.
33. RG 59, 867.4016/299, Elkus to Secretary of State, Oct. 17, 1916.
34. House to Wilson, May 9, 1916, *PWW*, vol. 37, pp. 6–7.
35. Lansing to Wilson, May 25, 1916, ibid., pp. 106–07.
36. Lloyd E. Ambrosius, *Wilsonian Statecraft* (Wilmington: Scholarly Resource Books, 1991), p. 71.
37. Thomas J. Knock, *To End All Wars* (Princeton: Princeton University Press, 1992), pp. 76–78. Wilson met with Lansing on May 26 to discuss the speech. Lansing Diaries, May 26, 1916.
38. See the text of Wilson's speech in *PWW*, vol. 37, pp. 113–16.
39. Knock, *To End All Wars*, pp. 79, 91.
40. U.S. Department of State, *Papers Relating to the Foreign Relations of the United States, 1918: The World War* (Washington, DC: Government Printing Office, 1933), Supp. 1, p. 892; James B. Gidney, *A Mandate for Armenia* (Kent, OH: Kent State University Press, 1967), p. 45; Richard G. Hovannisian, *Armenia on the Road to Independence, 1918* (Berkeley and Los Angeles: University of California Press, 1967), p. 251; Barton, *Story of Near East Relief*, pp. 381–82.
41. Kendrick A. Clements, *The Presidency of Woodrow Wilson* (Lawrence, KS: University Press of Kansas, 1992), p. 101.
42. Ambrosius, *Wilsonian Statecraft*, p. 76.
43. "A Speech in Long Branch, New Jersey, Accepting the Presidential Nomination," Sept. 2, 1916, *PWW*, vol. 38, pp. 126–39. See also Ambrosius, *Wilsonian Statecraft*, pp. 73, 74.
44. Knock, *To End All Wars*, pp. 86, 89, 106, 110.
45. RG 59, 867.4016/299, Lansing to Ambassador Gerard, Nov. 1, 1916.
46. Lansing to Wilson, Nov. 21, 1916, U.S. Department of State, *Papers Relating to the Foreign Relations of the United States: The Lansing Papers, 1914–1920*, 2 vols. (Washington, DC: Government Printing Office, 1939–1940), Lansing Papers, vol. 1, pp. 42–43; also in *PWW*, vol. 40, pp. 24–27; RG 38, Chief of Naval Operations,

Intelligence Division, Naval Attaché Reports, 1880–1939, C-10-B, Box 479, Reg. No. 7435, translation from French, the daily Constantinople newspaper *Hilal,* Jan. 31, 1916.

47. Lansing to Wilson, Nov. 21, 1916, Lansing Papers, vol. 1, pp. 42–43; also in *PWW,* vol. 40, pp. 24–27.

48. Walter Hines Page to Wilson, Nov. 24, Dec. 29, 1916, *PWW,* vol. 40, pp. 65–66, 357; House Diary, Nov. 26, Dec. 14, 1916, Jan. 3, 12, 1917, *PWW,* vol. 40, pp. 85, 241, 403, 463.

49. House to Wilson, Dec. 31, 1916, ibid., pp. 374–75.

50. House, Diary, Jan. 2, 1917, ibid., p. 403.

51. Gregory P. Nowell, *Mercantile States and the World Oil Cartel, 1900–1939* (Ithaca and London: Cornell University Press, 1994), pp. 101, 125–26; Gerald D. Nash, *United States Oil Policy, 1890–1964* (Pittsburgh, PA: University of Pittsburgh Press, 1968), pp. 24–37; George Sweet Gibb and Evelyn K. Knowlton, *The History of the Standard Oil Company (New Jersey): The Resurgent Years, 1911–1927* (New York: Harper and Row, 1956), pp. 237–41; J. Leonard Bates, *The Origins of Teapot Dome* (Urbana: University of Illinois Press, 1963), pp. 99–100.

52. Nash, *United States Oil Policy,* pp. 24–25.

53. Daniels to Wilson, May 13, 1916, Lane to Wilson, June 1, 1916, House to Wilson, May 17, June 1, 18, 1916, *PWW,* vol. 37, pp. 41, 64, 134, 142, 265–66; Tillman to Wilson, Jan. 6, 1917, *PWW,* vol. 40, p. 420.

54. Clements, *Presidency of Woodrow Wilson,* p. 151.

55. See text in *PWW,* vol. 37, pp. 190–200.

56. "An Address to the Joint Session of Congress," April 2, 1917, ibid., vol. 41, pp. 519–27; House, Diary, Jan. 3, 1917, ibid., vol. 40, p. 404. See also "A Flag Day Address," June 14, 1917, ibid., vol. 42, pp. 499–503.

57. Robert L. Daniel, *American Philanthropy in the Near East, 1820–1960* (Athens: Ohio State University, 1970), p. 154; RG 59, 867.00/793, Elkus to Secretary of State, Feb. 16, and March 2, 1917, Lansing Papers, vol. 1, p. 787.

58. Barton, *Story of Near East Relief,* pp. 55, 64.

59. Daniel, *American Philanthropy,* pp. 154–55.

60. Gidney, *Mandate for Armenia,* pp. 60–61.

61. Lansing to Wilson, May 2, 1918, Lansing Papers, vol. 2, p. 121 ff; Library of Congress, Division of Manuscripts, Papers of Woodrow Wilson, Elkus to Tumulty, March 30, 1917. See also Daniel, *American Philanthropy,* p. 154.

62. Clements, *Presidency of Woodrow Wilson,* p. 146; Emily S. Rosenberg, *Spreading the American Dream* (New York: Hill and Wang, 1982), pp. 75, 76; Frank M. Surface, *The Grain Trade during the World War* (New York: Macmillan, 1928), pp. 4, 7–8, and Appendix B, pp. 517–19. See also Wilson, May 19, 1917, excerpt in Edith

Guerrier, *We Pledged Allegiance* (Stanford and London: Stanford University Press, 1941), p. 3.

63. Guerrier, *We Pledged Allegiance*, pp. 6, 7, 8, 10, 15, 17–18.

64. Quoted in ibid., p. 84.

65. Morgenthau Papers, General Correspondence, Container 8, American Committee for Armenian and Syrian Relief, May 19, 1917, italics in original.

66. Barton, *Story of Near East Relief*, p. 64; Davis, *Slaughterhouse Province*, pp. 119–20; Riggs, *Days of Tragedy*, pp. 201–02, 203–04, 209.

67. Davis, *Slaughterhouse Province*, pp. 120, 121; Riggs, *Days of Tragedy*, pp. 203, 205, 210, 213, 214–15.

9   SEPARATION AND PEACE

1. Library of Congress, Division of Manuscripts, Papers of Robert Lansing, Diary, May 16, 1917; *The Papers of Woodrow Wilson*, Arthur Link, ed., 69 vols. (Princeton, NJ: Princeton University Press, 1966–1994), vol. 42, pp. 317–18n1; cited hereafter as *PWW*.

2. Alsberg had left Constantinople on April 6 or 7, 1917. Lansing to Wilson, May 17, 1917, *PWW*, vol. 42, pp. 315–16. Lansing Papers, Memoranda and Notes, June 10, 1917, Diary, Blue Boxes, Box 2, Confidential Memoranda and Notes, April 15, 1915–Dec. 30, 1918. On Alsberg's plan, see also Suzanne E. Moranian, "The American Missionaries and the Armenian Question, 1915–1927," Ph.D. Dissertation (University of Wisconsin-Madison, 1994).

3. Lansing Papers, Memoranda and Notes, June 10, 1917, Diary, Blue Boxes, Box 2, Confidential Memoranda and Notes, April 15, 1915–Dec. 30, 1918.

4. Ibid.

5. Lansing to Wilson, May 17, 1917, *PWW*, vol. 42, pp. 316–17; Lansing Diary, May 16, 1917; Lansing Papers, Memoranda and Notes, June 10, 1917, Diary, Blue Boxes, Box 2, Confidential Memoranda and Notes, April 15, 1915–Dec. 30, 1918.

6. Lansing Papers, Memoranda and Notes, June 10, 1917, Diary, Blue Boxes, Box 2, Confidential Memoranda and Notes, April 15, 1915–Dec. 30, 1918.

7. Lansing Diary, May 22, 1917; Kendrick A. Clements, *The Presidency of Woodrow Wilson* (Lawrence, KS: University Press of Kansas, 1992), p. 66. See also Louis D. Brandeis to Jacob deHaas, June 7, 1917, in Melvin I. Urofsky and David W. Levy, eds., *Letters of Louis D. Brandeis* (New York: State University of New York Press, 1975), vol. 4, pp. 296–97n1.

8. Lansing Diary, May 28, June 1, 5, 8, 10, 11, 12,15, 1917, Lansing Papers, Memoranda and Notes, Blue Boxes, Box 2, Confidential Memoranda and Notes, April 15, 1915–Dec. 30, 1918. See also

William Yale, "Ambassador Henry Morgenthau's Special Mission of 1917," *World Politics* 1 (April 1949): 308–20; Laurence Evans, *United States Policy and the Partition of Turkey, 1914–1924* (Baltimore, MD: Johns Hopkins Press, 1965), pp. 43–45.

9. Lloyd E. Ambrosius, *Wilsonian Statecraft* (Wilmington: Scholarly Resource Books, 1991), p. 113; Lansing Diary, Dec. 20, 1917.

10. Thomas J. Knock, *To End All Wars* (Princeton: Princeton University Press, 1992), p. 138.

11. "A Flag Day Address," June 14, 1917, *PWW*, vol. 42, pp. 498–504.

12. Quote in Ambrosius, *Wilsonian Statecraft*, p. 115.

13. Ibid., p. 112.

14. Library of Congress, Division of Manuscripts, Papers of Henry Morgenthau, Sr., General Correspondence, Container 8, Morgenthau to President Wilson, Sept. 15, 1917, and Boghos Nubar to Morgenthau, Aug. 27, 1917; Lansing Diary, Sept. 19, Oct. 5, 1917.

15. Morgenthau Papers, General Correspondence, Container 8, Morgenthau to Wilson, Sept. 15, 1917.

16. Ibid., Morgenthau to Wilson, Nov. 26, 1917.

17. Ibid.

18. Ibid., Schmavonian to Morgenthau, Jan. 16, 1918.

19. Ibid., Morgenthau to Long, Jan. 9, 1918.

20. See "Ambassador Morgenthau's Story," *World's Work* 36 (May 1918): 42–73; (June 1918): 154–84; (July 1918): 262–83; (Aug. 1918): 376–92; (Sept. 1918): 479–95; (Oct. 1918): 648–60.

21. See, e.g., Morgenthau Papers, General Correspondence, Container 8, Nicholas Butler, Carnegie Endowment for International Peace, to Morgenthau, April 23, 1918; Preston, Hamilton National Bank at Chatanooga, to Morgenthau, April 30, 1918; Louis Gibbs, Judge of the County Court, Bronx, to Morgenthau, June 14, 1918.

22. Ibid., W.L. Launders to Morgenthau, May 9, 1918.

23. Ibid., M. Vartan Malcom to Morgenthau, Oct. 29, 1918.

24. Ibid., Wilson to Morgenthau, June 14, 1918. See also Moranian, "The American Missionaries and the Armenian Question," p. 221.

25. Morgenthau Papers, General Correspondence, Container 8, Morgenthau to Wilson, Sept. 24, Oct. 7, 1918; Henry Morgenthau, *Ambassador Morgenthau's Story* (New York: Doubleday, 1918).

26. Ambrosius, *Wilsonian Statecraft*, p. 107.

27. "An Annual Message on the State of the Union," *PWW*, vol. 45, pp. 194–202.

28. Robert L. Daniel, *American Philanthropy in the Near East, 1820–1960* (Athens: Ohio State University, 1970), p. 155; Ambrosius, *Wilsonian Statecraft*, pp. 106–07.

29. Morgenthau Papers, General Correspondence, Container 8, Barton to Lodge, Dec. 10, 1917.

30. Ibid., Barton to Morgenthau, Dec. 15, 1917, encl., letter, Barton to Lodge, Dec. 10, 1917; Lansing Diaries, May 10, July 9, 1918.

31. "An Address to a Joint Session of Congress," Jan. 8, 1918, *PWW*, vol. 45, pp. 535–39.
32. Clements, *Presidency of Woodrow Wilson*, p. 164.
33. Quoted in Arno J. Mayer, *Political Origins of the New Diplomacy, 1917–1918* (New Haven, CT: Yale University Press, 1959), pp. 247–48.
34. "An Address to a Joint Session of Congress," Jan. 8, 1918, *PWW*, vol 45, p. 538.
35. House Diary, Jan. 9, 1918, ibid., p. 553.
36. Morgenthau Papers, General Correspondence, Container 8, Ambassador Page to Arthur, Jan. 19, 1918.
37. "An Address to a Joint Session of Congress," Jan. 8, 1918, *PWW*, vol. 45, p. 537.
38. Carl P. Parrini, *Heir to Empire: United States Economic Diplomacy, 1916–1923* (Pittsburgh: University of Pittsburgh Press, 1969), pp. 12–14, 15–16. See also Emily S. Rosenberg, *Spreading the American Dream* (New York: Hill and Wang, 1982), p. 70. Lansing disagreed with Wilson on the utility of the Fourteen Point program. See Lansing Papers, Memoranda and Notes, Jan. 10, and Dec. 30, 1918, Diary, Blue Boxes, Box 2, Confidential Memoranda and Notes, April 15, 1915–Dec. 30, 1918.
39. Lansing Papers, Memoranda and Notes, May 2, 1918, Diary, Blue Boxes, Box 2, Confidential Memoranda and Notes, April 15, 1915–Dec. 30, 1918.
40. Sen. Brandegee quoted in *Cong. Record*, 65 Cong., 2d Sess., p. 5473, April 23, 1918. See Daniel, *American Philanthropy*, p. 155.
41. Morgenthau Papers, General Correspondence, Container 8, Poindexter to Morgenthau, Sept. 18, 1918.
42. See Richard G. Hovannisian, *The Republic of Armenia*, 4 vols. (Berkeley and Los Angeles: University of California Press, 1971–1996); Richard G. Hovannisian, *Armenia on the Road to Independence, 1918* (Berkeley and Los Angeles: University of California Press, 1967), pp. 67, 70; Simon Vratzian, *Hayastani Hanrapetutiun* [Republic of Armenia] (Paris: A.R.F. Central Committee of America, 1928; repr., Erevan: Hayastan, 1993), p. 17.
43. Vratzian, *Hayastani Hanrapetutiun*, pp. 28–30, 35–36; Hovannisian, *Armenia on the Road to Independence*, pp. 70–71, 73, 78–80, 81–82.
44. Hovannisian, *Armenia on the Road to Independence*, pp. 95, 97.
45. Aleksandr Khatisian, *Hayastani Hanrapetutian Tsagumn u Zargatsume* [The Creation and Development of the Republic of Armenia], 2nd pr. (Beirut: Hamazkayin Press, 1968), p. 31; W.E.D. Allen and Paul Muratoff, *Caucasian Battlefields: A History of the Wars on the Turco-Caucasian Border, 1828–1921* (Cambridge: Cambridge University Press, 1953), pp. 458–59, 460–63; Peter Hopkirk, *Like Hidden Fire: The Plot to Bring Down the British Empire* (New York: Kodansha, 1994), p. 258. On the conditions in Erzerum and difficulties

confronted by General Andranik, see Levon Tutunjian, "Karno Ankumin Voghbergutiune" [The Tragedy of the Fall of Karin], in Gersam Aharonian, comp. and ed., *Hushamatian Mets Egherni, 1915–1965* [Memorial Volume of the Colossal Crime, 1915–1965] (Beirut: Atlas, 1965), pp. 811–27; Vratzian, *Hayastani Hanrapetutiun*, pp. 67–68, 92–93, 152–53; Hovannisian, *Armenia on the Road to Independence*, pp. 98–102, 104, 121–24, 191; idem, *Republic of Armenia*, vol. 1, p. 24.

46. Vratzian, *Hayastani Hanrapetutiun*, p. 96; Khatisian, *Hayastani Hanrapetutian Tsagumn u Zargatsume*, p. 64; Hovannisian, *Republic of Armenia*, vol. 1, pp. 27–28.
47. Hayastani Hanrapetutiun, Patmutian Kentronakan Petakan Arkhiv (HH PKPA), 57/3/176, no. 1–2, Hambartsum Arakelian to Gevorg V, Catholicos of All Armenians, March 23, 1918, in *Vaveragrer Hai Ekeghetsu Patmutyan*, girk 5: *Mair Ator S. Echmiatsine Arajin Hanrapetutyan Tarinerin (1918–1920 tt.)* [Documents of the History of the Armenian Church, Bk 5: The Mother See St. Echmiadzin during the Years of the First Republic (1918–1920)], comp. Sandro Behbudyan (Erevan: Voskan Erevantsi, 1999), pp. 18–20.
48. Ibid., 57/2/481, no. 12–13, Gevorg V, Catholicos of All Armenians, April 10, 1918, pp. 25–26.
49. Lansing Papers, Memoranda and Notes, Sept. 21, 1918, Diary, Blue Boxes, Box 2, Confidential Memoranda and Notes, April 15, 1915–Dec. 30, 1918.
50. "An Address in the Metropolitan Opera House," Sept. 27, 1918, *PWW*, vol. 51, pp. 127–33.
51. See Knock, *To End All Wars*, pp. 163, 165.
52. Josephus Daniels, *The Navy and the Nation: War-Time Addresses* (New York: George H. Doran, 1919), pp. 262–63.
53. Lansing Papers, Memoranda and Notes, Oct. 12, 1918, Diary, Blue Boxes, Box 2, Confidential Memoranda and Notes, April 15, 1915–Dec. 30, 1918.
54. Morgenthau Papers, General Correspondence, Container 8, MacCraken, President of Vassar College, to Morgenthau, Oct. 10, 1918; Orville Reed to Morgenthau, Oct. 25, 1918.
55. Ibid., Short to Morgenthau, Oct. 25, 1918.
56. Ibid., Katrina Ely Tiffany to Morgenthau, Nov. 21, 1918; Charles M. Mayne to Morgenthau, Nov. 21, 1918.
57. Clements, *Presidency of Woodrow Wilson*, pp. 160–61.
58. Adamantios Th. Polyzoides, "The Passing of Turkey," *Current History* 15 (Oct. 1921): 33; Vahakn N. Dadrian, "Genocide as a Problem of National and International Law: The World War I Armenian Case and Its Contemporary Legal Ramifications," *Yale Journal of International Law* 14:2 (Summer 1989): 221–334.
59. Daniels, *Navy and the Nation*, p. 269.
60. Polyzoides, "Passing of Turkey," p. 34.

61. James L. Barton, *Story of Near East Relief, 1915–1930* (New York: Macmillan, 1930), p. 107; Polyzoides, "Passing of Turkey," p. 34.

62. Hovannisian, *Republic of Armenia*, vol. 1, pp. 55–56, 60–62.

63. Morgenthau Papers, General Correspondence, Container 8, Trowbridge to Vickrey, Dec. 24, 1918; FO 382/2032, WO 95/4372, WO 95/4372, Sykes to GOC, GHQ, Egypt, and FO 371/3657, FO 371/4177, as cited in T.H. Greenshields, "The Settlement of Armenian Refugees in Syria and Lebanon, 1915–1939," Ph.D. Diss. (Durham University, 1978), pp. 55–57; Stanley E. Kerr, *The Lions of Marash* (Albany: State University of New York Press, 1973), pp. 43–48.

64. Levon Chormisian, *Hamapatker Arevmtahai Mek Daru Patmutian* [A Panorama of One Century of Western Armenian History], 3 vols. (Beirut: Sevan, 1975), vol. 3, p. 513.

65. Morgenthau Papers, General Correspondence, Container 8, Morgenthau to Hoover, Nov. 15, 1918; Barton, *Story of Near East Relief*, pp. 109–10n1.

66. Morgenthau Papers, General Correspondence, Container 8, Vickrey to the Members of the Executive Committee, Nov. 15, 1918.

67. Barton, *Story of Near East Relief*, pp. 110, 111.

68. Morgenthau Papers, General Correspondence, Container 8, Morgenthau to Daniels, Dec. 27, 1918; encls., cables from Caleb Gates, President of Robert College and Chairman of the Committee in Constantinople; Howard Bliss, President of American College, Beirut; Bayard Dodge and James Nicol of the American Committee for Armenian and Syrian Relief, New York.

69. Morgenthau Papers, General Correspondence, Container 8, Morgenthau to Wilson, Nov. 20, 1918.

70. Ibid., Guy Emerson, Director of Publicity, Liberty Loan Committee, to Morgenthau, Oct. 1, 1918; Arthur Loasby to Morgenthau, Oct. 4, 1918; Henry Rosenfelt, Assistant Director, the American Jewish Relief Committee, to Morgenthau, Oct. 26, Nov. 20, 1918.

71. Ibid., Strauss to Jacob Billikoff, Dec. 11, 1918.

72. Library of Congress, Division of Manuscripts, Papers of Henry Morgenthau, Sr., Diary, Jan. 4, 1919.

73. State of Oregon, Senate, 13th Legislative Assembly, Sen. J. Res. 5, U.S. Department of State, *Records of the Department of State Relating to Internal Affairs of Armenia, 1910–1929*, Division of Near Eastern Affairs, File 860j.01/19 (Washington, DC: National Archives Microfilm Publications, 1975), roll 1, no. T1192.

10   THE PERVERSION OF PEACE

1. Kendrick A. Clements, *The Presidency of Woodrow Wilson* (Lawrence, KS: University Press of Kansas, 1992), pp. 143–44, 158, 174.

232 NOTES

2. Thomas, J. Knock, *To End All Wars: Woodrow Wilson and the Quest for a New World Order* (Princeton, NJ: Princeton University Press, 1992), pp. 194–96.
3. Clements, *Presidency of Woodrow Wilson*, pp. 174, 205, 208.
4. Knock, *To End All Wars*, pp. 189, 190.
5. Ibid., pp. 124, 164–65, 166, 170–71; James B. Gidney, *A Mandate for Armenia* (Kent, OH: Kent State University Press, 1967), p. 70.
6. See House to Wilson, Oct. 30, 1918, Wilson to House, Oct. 30, 1918, *The Papers of Woodrow Wilson*, Arthur Link, ed., 69 vols. (Princeton: Princeton University Press, 1966–1994), vol. 51, pp. 511–17; cited hereafter as *PWW*. See also Clements, *Presidency of Woodrow Wilson*, p. 166; Knock, *To End All Wars*, p. 200.
7. Josephus Daniels, *The Navy and the Nation: War-Time Addresses* (New York: George H. Doran, 1919), pp. 295–301.
8. Gerald D. Nash, *United States Oil Policy 1890–1964* (Pittsburgh, PA: University of Pittsburgh Press, 1968), pp. 40–41, 43–44, 45.
9. Ibid., p. 50.
10. Ibid., p. 44; Emily S. Rosenberg, *Spreading the American Dream: American Economic and Cultural Expansion, 1890–1945* (New York: Hill and Wang, 1982), p. 128.
11. Levon Chormisian, *Hamapatker Arevmtahai Mek Daru Patmutian* [A Panorama of One Century of Western Armenian History], 3 vols. (Beirut: Sevan, 1975), vol. 3, pp. 515, 516–17, 522.
12. Ibid., pp. 514, 518, 528, 530, 534.
13. Ibid., pp. 531–34; James L. Barton, *Story of Near East Relief, 1915–1930* (New York: Macmillan, 1930), p. 220.
14. Chormisian, *Hamapatker*, pp. 534–36.
15. Gregory P. Nowell, *Mercantile States and the World Oil Cartel, 1900–1939* (Ithaca and London: Cornell University Press, 1994), p. 129.
16. Abraham H. Hartunian, *Neither to Laugh Nor to Weep: A Memoir of the Armenian Genocide* (Boston: Beacon Press, 1968), pp. 116–17; Stanley E. Kerr, *The Lions of Marash* (Albany: State University of New York Press, 1973), p. 35.
17. Chormisian, *Hamapatker*, pp. 544–47.
18. Library of Congress, Division of Manuscripts, Papers of Henry Morgenthau, Sr., General Correspondence, Container 9, Bryce to Morgenthau, April 19, 1919.
19. Boghos Nubar (1851–1930) was the son of Nubar Pasha (1825–1899) who had served as prime minister of Egypt. For a succinct background on Boghos Nubar and the Armenian National Delegation, see *Boghos Nubar's Papers and the Armenian Question, 1915–1918: Documents*, ed. and trans. Vatche Ghazarian (Waltham, MA: Mayreni Publishing, 1996), "Preface," pp. xvii–xxxiii.
20. Richard G. Hovannisian, *The Republic of Armenia*, 4 vols. (Berkeley and Los Angeles: University of California Press, 1971–1996), vol. 1, pp. 265n46, 265–69, 294.

21. Library of Congress, Division of Manuscripts, Papers of Henry Morgenthau, Sr., Diary, March 26, 27, April 19, June 4, 1919; cited hereafter as Morgenthau Diary.

22. Hovannisian, *Republic of Armenia*, vol. 1, pp. 134–35.

23. Admiral Bristol was appointed as senior representative in Constantinople in January 1919 and succeeded Gabriel Bie Ravendal as U.S. High Commissioner to Turkey in August 1919, who in turn had replaced Lewis Heck in May 1919. Heck had served as U.S. Commissioner in Constantinople from November 1918 to May 1919.

24. Barton, *Story of Near East Relief*, pp. 110–16, 120.

25. Ibid., pp. 118–19.

26. Gregory P. Nowell, *Mercantile States and the World Oil Cartel 1990–1939*, (Ithaca and London: Cornell University Press, 1994), pp. 126–27; Benjamin Gerig, *The Open Door and the Mandates System* (London: George Allen and Unwin, 1930), p. 143.

27. Frank M. Surface, *The Grain Trade during the World War: Being a History of the Food Administration Grain Corporation and the United States Grain Corporation* (New York: Macmillan, 1928), pp. 156–57; Hovannisian, *Republic of Armenia*, vol. 2, pp. 367–72, 401.

28. Beginning in January 1919, ACRNE extended its activities to Western Armenia only to realize that there were no Armenian refugees left in the region. Hovannisian, *Republic of Armenia*, vol. 1, pp. 134–35. In August 1919, Congress incorporated the Near East Relief. Barton, *Story of Near East Relief*, pp. 432–34.

29. Hovannisian, *Republic of Armenia*, vol. 1, p. 141.

30. Barton, *Story of Near East Relief*, pp. 124–25, 240, 268; Hovannisian, *Republic of Armenia*, vol. 2, p. 402.

31. *New Near East* 7 (June 1922): 6, as quoted in Robert L. Daniel, *American Philanthropy in the Near East, 1820–1960* (Athens: Ohio State University, 1970), pp. 158–59.

32. Barton, *Near East Relief*, pp. 383–88, 389–90.

33. Ibid., pp. 390n1, 397, 402–03.

34. Ibid., pp. 411–12.

35. Ibid., pp. 175–76.

36. Haskell, report, 1919, excerpt in ibid., p. 179n1.

37. Ibid., pp. 180–81, 185, 216, 408.

38. Clements, *Presidency of Woodrow Wilson*, p. 37.

39. Barton, *Story of Near East Relief*, pp. 215–16.

40. Surface, *Grain Trade*, pp. 416–17.

41. Rosenberg, *Spreading the American Dream*, p. 117.

42. Emily S. Rosenberg, *Financial Missionaries to the World: The Politics and Culture of Dollar Diplomacy, 1900–1930* (Cambridge, MA: Harvard University Press, 1999), p. 99.

43. Clements, *Presidency of Woodrow Wilson*, p. 51.

44. See, e.g., Gidney, *Mandate for Armenia*; Hovannisian, *Republic of Armenia*, vol. 2, pp. 316–403; vol. 4, pp. 1–44; Thomas A. Bryson,

"Woodrow Wilson and the Armenian Mandate: A Reassessment," *Armenian Review* 21 (Autumn 1968): 10–29; Bryson, "John Sharp Williams: An Advocate for the Armenian Mandate," *Armenian Review* 26 (Fall 1973): 10–25; Bryson, "Mark Lambart Bristol, U.S. Navy, Admiral-Diplomat: His Influence on the Armenian Mandate Question," *Armenian Review* 21 (Winter 1968): 3–22.

45. Gerig, *Open Door*, pp. 85–86.

46. See the text in *PWW*, vol. 55, pp. 65–66. See also Tumulty to Wilson, March 5, 1919, encl., James W. Gerard to Wilson, ibid., p. 446.

47. Dodge to Wilson, Feb. 25, 1919, ibid., p. 265.

48. "Remarks to Members of the Democratic National Committee," Feb. 28, 1919, ibid., pp. 321–22.

49. Library of Congress, Division of Manuscripts, Papers of Robert Lansing, Memoranda and Notes, June 20, 1919, Diary, Blue Boxes, Box 2, Confidential Memoranda and Notes, Jan. 2–Dec. 27, 1919; cited hereafter as Lansing Diary.

50. Hovannisian, *Republic of Armenia*, vol. 2, pp. 317–18.

51. Morgenthau Papers, General Correspondence, Container 9, A. Galajikian, Secretary, and Hagopos H. Djedjizian, Chairman of the Association of Armenian Alumni and Former Students of Robert College, to Morgenthau, May 10, 1919.

52. John Hope Simpson, *The Refugee Problem: Report of a Survey* (London: Oxford University Press, 1939), pp. 172–80, 184–85; Morgenthau Papers, General Correspondence, Container 9, Vickrey to Morgenthau, n.d., 1919. This letter was dated either June 9 or 10, 1919.

53. Morgenthau Papers, General Correspondence, Container 9, Morgenthau and Hemphill, to Barton, Peet, and Smith, June 3, 1919; Bristol to Morgenthau, June 4, 1919; Morgenthau, to Arnold, June 5, 1919; Morgenthau and John Kingsbury to American Relief, Constantinople, June 6, 1919.

54. Ibid., Morgenthau to Rickard, AMREFA, New York, June 6, 1919; Morgenthau to Rickard and Vickery, June 9, 1919; Vickrey to Morgenthau, n.d., 1919. This letter was dated either June 9 or 10, 1919; AMREFA, signed Dodge and MacCallum, to Morgenthau, June 20, 1919.

55. Ibid., Morgenthau to AMERFA, New York, June 11, 1919; Hoover, AMREFA for Rickard, June 14, 1919; Dodge and MacCallum to ARA, June 15, 1919; Hemphill and Morgenthau to Barton, June 23, 1919; AMREFA, signed Dodge and MacCallum, to Morgenthau, June 20, 1919.

56. Ibid., Morgenthau to Harbord, June 25, 1919. In one draft of this letter, Morgenthau stated that he and Hoover were prepared to undertake the return of Armenian refugees to their homeland, "Armenia proper." Morgenthau met with Wilson on June 26, 1919. Morgenthau Diary, June 26, 1919.

NOTES   235

57. Ibid., Harbord to Morgenthau, June 25, 1919; Morgenthau Diary, June 28, 1919.
58. Morgenthau Papers, General Correspondence, Container 9, Barton and Peet to Morgenthau, June 25, 1919; Bristol to Hoover and Morgenthau, June 28, 1919.
59. Ibid., Kingsbury to Morgenthau, June 25, 1919; Phillips to Ammission, Paris, June 28, 1919.
60. Ibid., Phillips to Ammission, Paris, June 28, 1919. This message was sent to Wilson on June 22, 1919. Morgenthau Diary, June 30, 1919. The quotation marks inserted manually in the original.
61. Morgenthau Diary, July 1, 1919. See also Baker to Wilson, July 15, 1919, encl., American Mission, July 5, 1919, *PWW*, vol. 61, pp. 485–87.
62. Morgenthau Diary, June 11, 1919.
63. Morgenthau Papers, General Correspondence, Container 9, Harbord to Morgenthau, Paris, June 28, 1919.
64. Harry N. Howard, *The King–Crane Commission: An American Inquiry in the Middle East* (Beirut: Khayat, 1963), p. 32; Hovannisian, *Republic of Armenia*, vol. 2, p. 323.
65. Gidney, *Mandate for Armenia*, pp. 143, 150, 151.

11   Unsustainable Divisions

1. Kendrick A. Clements, *The Presidency of Woodrow Wilson* (Lawrence, KS: University Press of Kansas, 1992), p. 189; Lloyd E. Ambrosius, *Wilsonian Statecraft: Theory and Practice of Liberal Internationalism during World War I* (Wilmington: Scholarly Resource Books, 1991), p. 133.
2. William C. Widenor, *Henry Cabot Lodge and the Search for an American Foreign Policy* (Berkeley: University of California Press, 1980), pp. 297, 316.
3. Clements, *Presidency of Woodrow Wilson*, pp. 192–93; Cary T. Grayson, *Woodrow Wilson: An Intimate Memoir* (New York: Holt, Rinehart and Winston, 1960), pp. 94–95.
4. Thomas J. Knock, *To End All Wars: Woodrow Wilson and the Quest for a New World Order* (Princeton, NJ: Princeton University Press, 1992), p. 260; Library of Congress, Division of Manuscripts, Papers of Robert Lansing, Diary, Nov. 22, 1919; cited hereafter as Lansing Diary.
5. "A Luncheon Address to the St. Louis Chamber of Commerce," Sept. 5, 1919, *The Papers of Woodrow Wilson*, Arthur Link, ed., 69 vols. (Princeton: Princeton University Press, 1966–1994), vol. 63, pp. 33–42; cited hereafter as *PWW*.
6. "An Address in the St. Louis Coliseum," Sept. 5, 1919, ibid., pp. 43–51.
7. "An Address in Convention Hall in Kansas City," and "An Address in the Des Moines Coliseum," Sept. 6, 1919, ibid., pp. 66–75, 76–88.

See also "An Address in the Auditorium in Omaha," Sept. 8, 1919;
"An Address in the Coliseum in Sioux Falls," Sept. 8, 1919, "An
Address in St. Paul to a Joint Session of the Legislature of
Minnesota," Sept. 9, 1919, "An Address in the Minneapolis Armory,"
Sept. 9, 1919, ibid., pp. 97–107, 107–17, 125–31, 131–38.

8. "An Address in the Auditorium in Omaha," Sept. 8, 1919, ibid.,
   pp. 97–107; "An Address in the Coliseum in Sioux Falls," Sept. 8,
   1919, ibid., pp. 107–17; "An Address in St. Paul to a Joint Session of
   the Legislature of Minnesota," Sept. 9, 1919, ibid., pp. 125–31;
   "An Address in the Minneapolis Armory," Sept. 9, 1919, ibid.,
   pp. 131–38.

9. "An Address in the St. Paul Auditorium," Sept. 9, 1919, ibid., p. 140;
   "An Address in the Portland Auditorium," Sept. 15, 1919, ibid.,
   pp. 291–92; "An Address in the City Auditorium in Pueblo,
   Colorado," Sept. 25, 1919, ibid., pp. 500–13.

10. See John Milton Cooper, Jr., *Breaking the Heart of the World: Woodrow
    Wilson and the Fight for the League of Nations* (Cambridge: Cambridge
    University Press, 2001), pp. 341–42.

11. "An Address at Bismarck," Sept. 10, 1919, *PWW*, vol. 63, p. 157.

12. See, e.g., speech by Senator William S. Kenyon (R., Iowa), Sept. 10,
    1919, *Cong. Record*, 66th Cong., 1st sess., pp. 5149–55.

13. *Cong. Record*, 66th Cong., 1st sess., p. 5067; Richard G. Hovannisian,
    The Republic of Armenia, 4 vols. (Berkeley and Los Angeles: University
    of California Press, 1971–1996), vol. 2, pp. 374–75.

14. Wilson to Phillips, Sept. 16, 1919, *PWW*, vol. 63, p. 304.

15. Library of Congress, Division of Manuscripts, Papers of Henry
    Morgenthau, Sr., General Correspondence, Containers 9/10, Eliot to
    Morgenthau, Nov. 8, 1919.

16. Phillips to Wilson, Sept. 20, 1919, Wilson to Phillips, Sept. 23, 1919,
    PWW, vol. 63, pp. 423, 464.

17. U.S. National Archives, Record Group 59 (hereafter RG 59),
    860J.01/90, Polk to Secretary of State, Sept. 22, 1919, mentioned in
    Phillips to Wilson, Sept. 23, 1919, *PWW*, vol. 63, p. 466.

18. Hovannisian, *Republic of Armenia*, vol. 2, pp. 372–90.

19. Harry N. Howard, *The King–Crane Commission: An American
    Inquiry in the Middle East* (Beirut: Khayat, 1963), pp. 235, 311;
    Hovannisian, *Republic of Armenia*, vol. 2, pp. 55–57, 332–33.

20. After his return to Washington, Harbord hoped to write articles on
    Armenia and a book. Morgenthau Papers, General Correspondence,
    Container 9/10, Harbord to Morgenthau, Nov. 28, 1919.

21. See text in Hovannisian, *Republic of Armenia*, vol. 2, pp. 357,
    358–360.

22. Ibid., pp. 358, 360, 364–65; Edward M. House and Charles Seymour,
    What Really Happened at Paris: The Story of the Paris Peace Conference
    (New York: Charles Scribner's Sons, 1921), pp. 178–80, 227.

23. See Henry Morgenthau, "Mandates or War," *New York Times*, Magazine section, Nov. 9, 1919; Hovannisian, *Republic of Armenia*, vol. 2, pp. 371, 431–33. The Senate rejected the treaty again on March 19, 1920. Ibid., vol. 3, p. 73.

24. Clements, *Presidency of Woodrow Wilson*, p. 200.

25. Hovannisian, *Republic of Armenia*, vol. 1, p. 294; Press conference, July 10, 1919, in *The Papers of Woodrow Wilson: The Complete Press Conferences, 1913–1919*, ed. Robert C. Hilderbrand (Princeton: Princeton University Press, 1985), vol. 50, p. 793.

26. Hovannisian, *Republic of Armenia*, vol. 1, pp. 298–99.

27. Ibid., vol. 2, p. 390.

28. Morgenthau Papers, General Correspondence, Containers 9/10, Barton to Morgenthau, Dec. 24, 1919.

29. Ibid., Morgenthau to Barton, Dec. 26, 1919.

30. Ibid., Barton to Morgenthau, Dec. 29, 1919.

31. Ibid., Barton to Morgenthau, Feb. 26, 1920.

32. Ibid., Grayson to Morgenthau, Feb. 27, 1920, Morgenthau to Barton, Feb. 28, 1920; Morgenthau to Barton, [n.d., but "March 16, 1920" written on top of letter. Barton's reply indicates that this letter was dated March 16, 1920]. Ibid., Barton to Morgenthau, March 19, 1920.

33. Hovannisian, *Republic of Armenia*, vol. 2, pp. 450–52, 453.

34. Colby to Wilson, April 23, 1920, *PWW*, vol. 65, p. 222; Colby to Pastermadjian, April 23, 1920, in U.S. Department of State, *Foreign Relations of the United States, 1920* (Washington, DC: Government Printing Office, 1925), vol. 3, p. 778. See also Hovannisian, *Republic of Armenia*, vol. 2, pp. 486, 509–10, 512, 518. On the debate within the Wilson administration regarding U.S. policy toward Armenia in general and support for the Armenians in Transcaucasia as a buffer against Bolshevik Russia in particular, see Lloyd E. Ambrosius, "Wilsonian Diplomacy and Armenia: The Limits of Power and Ideology," in Jay Winter, ed., *America and the Armenian Genocide of 1915* (Cambridge, UK: Cambridge, UK Cambridge University Press, 2003), pp. 113–45, esp. 116–17.

35. Clements, *Presidency of Woodrow Wilson*, p. 103.

36. Lansing, Desk Diaries, Feb. 8, 1920.

37. Lansing Diary, Jan. 7, 1920, in Lansing Papers, Blue Boxes, Box 2, Confidential Memoranda and Notes, Jan. 1, 1920–May 23, 1922.

38. Lansing Diary, Feb. 9, 1920. Emphasis in original.

39. Ibid., Feb. 13, 1920.

40. Lansing, Desk Diaries, Feb. 24, 1920.

41. Knock, *To End All Wars*, pp. 263–65; Clements, *Presidency of Woodrow Wilson*, pp. 190–91.

42. Clements, *Presidency of Woodrow Wilson*, pp. 191, 193.

43. See, e.g., Arthur M. Schlesinger, Jr., *The Imperial Presidency* (Boston: Houghton Mifflin, 1973).

44. Morgenthau Papers, General Correspondence, Barton to Morgenthau, March 19, 1920.

45. Polk to Wilson, March 6, 1920, and Wilson to Polk, March 8, 1920, *PWW*, vol. 65, pp. 64–65, 72–73, encl., Draft, Amembassy, Paris, RG 59, 763.72119/10040. See also, Polk to Wilson, March 22, 1920, *PWW*, vol. 65, pp. 111–12, encl.; Lansing Diary, Jan. 16, 1919, Blue Boxes, Box 2, Confidential Memoranda and Notes, Jan. 2–Dec. 27, 1919.

46. Wilson to Polk, March 17, 1920, *PWW*, vol. 65, p. 91.

47. William Appleman Williams, *The Tragedy of American Diplomacy*, 2nd rev. edn. (New York: Dell Publishing, 1972), pp. 110–12. See also Lansing Diary, Jan. 4, 1919.

48. Dodge to Wilson, April 29, 1920, *PWW*, vol. 65, pp. 234–35.

49. Gerard to Wilson, May 14, 1920, ibid., pp. 287–88. Sen. Res. 359, adopted on May 13, 1920. *Cong. Record*, 66th Cong., 2d sess., p. 6978.

50. Gerard to Wilson, May 18, 1920, *PWW*, vol. 65, p. 298.

51. Swem to Colby, and Colby to Wilson, May 20, 1920, encl., ibid., pp. 299–312.

52. "To the United States Congress," May 24, 1920, ibid., pp. 320–23.

53. Henry Fountain Ashurst, Diary, May 24, 1920, ibid., pp. 323–24.

54. Colby to Wilson, July 20, 1920, ibid., p. 532.

55. Nowell, *Mercantile States*, pp. 129–32. See the text of the agreement in Benjamin Gerig, *The Open Door and the Mandates System* (London: George Allen and Unwin, 1930), pp. 227–29.

56. Gerig, *Open Door*, pp. 135–36.

57. Daniels Diary, June 8, 1920, *PWW*, vol. 65, p. 380.

58. Gerald D. Nash, *United States Oil Policy 1890–1964* (Pittsburgh: University of Pittsburgh Press, 1968), pp. 40–41, 50, 52; Emily S. Rosenberg, *Spreading the American Dream: American Economic and Cultural Expansion, 1890–1945* (New York: Hill and Wang, 1982), p. 128; John A. DeNovo, "The Movement for a More Aggressive Oil Policy Abroad," *American Historical Review* 61 (1955–56): 857–58.

59. Nash, *Oil Policy*, p. 44; Hovannisian, *Republic of Armenia*, vol. 2, pp. 90–91.

60. RG 38, Chief of Naval Operations, Intelligence Division, Naval Attache Reports, 1880–1939, U-1-i, Box 1345, Mark L. Bristol, July 12, 1919. On Bristol, see Hovannisian, *Republic of Armenia*, vol. 1, pp. 298–9, 325–26n114; Laurence Evans, *United States Policy and the Partition of Turkey, 1914–1924* (Baltimore, MD: Johns Hopkins Press, 1965), pp. 292–322.

61. RG 45, Naval Records Collection of the Office of Naval Records and Library, Subject File 1911–1927, Box 831, Bristol to Secretary of State, May 7, 1920, pp. 1–6.

62. Gerig, *Open Door*, pp. 143–44.

63. *Manchester Guardian Commercial*, July 6, 1922, p. 255, quoted in ibid., p. 144n2.
64. United States, Department of Commerce, Bureau of Foreign and Domestic Commerce, *Foreign Commerce and Navigation of the United States for the Calendar Year 1921* (Washington, DC: Government Printing Office, 1922), summary tables, No. III, pp. x–xi; *Calendar Year 1919* (1920), summary tables, No. III, pp. xii–xiii; *Calendar Year 1924* (1925), summary tables, No. IV, p. xi, Table 13, p. 634; *Calendar Year 1925* (1926), summary tables, Nos. III and IV, pp. xliii, xlvii.
65. Gerig, *Open Door*, p. 146.
66. James B. Gidney, *A Mandate for Armenia* (Kent, OH: Kent State University Press, 1967), pp. 233–37; Hovannisian, *Republic of Armenia*, vol. 4, pp. 3–24.
67. Hovannisian, *Republic of Armenia*, vol. 4, p. 303; Robert L. Daniel, *American Philanthropy in the Near East, 1820–1960* (Athens: Ohio State University, 1970), p. 165.

12 THE REMNANTS OF WILSONISM

1. M.S. Anderson, *The Eastern Question, 1774–1923: A Study in International Relations* (London: Macmillan, 1966), pp. 361–64.
2. Ibid., pp. 363–66; Richard G. Hovannisian, *The Republic of Armenia*, 4 vols. (Berkeley and Los Angeles: University of California Press, 1971–1996), vol. 1, pp. 434–37; James B. Gidney, *A Mandate for Armenia* (Kent, OH: Kent State University Press, 1967), p. 254.
3. Anderson, *Eastern Question*, pp. 367–68.
4. Library of Congress, Division of Manuscripts, Papers of Henry Morgenthau, Sr., General Correspondence, Containers 9/10, Department of State, press release, Nov. 30, 1920, text of letter, Hymans to Wilson, Nov. 26, 1920.
5. Ibid., text of letter, Wilson to Hymans, Nov. 30, 1920.
6. Ibid., Richard Strong, Director, Harvard University Medical School, to Morgenthau, Dec. 1, 1920.
7. Ibid., George R. Montgomery to Morgenthau, Dec. 23, 1920.
8. Hovannisian, *Republic of Armenia*, vol. 3, p. 254.
9. Ibid., vol. 4, pp. 350–51, 354–55.
10. See text in ibid., pp. 361, 364.
11. Ibid., p. 368.
12. Ibid., pp. 369, 379, 385–87; Mary K. Matossian, *The Impact of Soviet Policies in Armenia* (Leiden: E.J. Brill, 1962), p. 28.
13. Hovannisian, *Republic of Armenia*, vol. 4, pp. 391, 400–01.
14. Bernard Lewis, *The Emergence of Modern Turkey*, 2nd edn. (London: Oxford University Press, 1968), p. 254.

15. Morgenthau Papers, General Correspondence, Containers 9/10, Caldwell to Morgenthau, Dec. 3, 1920. For a similar letter from Barton, see ibid., Barton to Morgenthau, Dec. 3, 1920.

16. Ibid., Barton to Morgenthau, Dec. 11, 1920.

17. Ibid., Stanley White, Armenia America Society, to Morgenthau, Dec. 16, 1920.

18. Ibid., Jessup to Morgenthau, Dec. 30, 1920. Emphasis in original.

19. Ibid., encl., "A Memorandum to the Honorable, Warren G. Harding, President-Elect of the United States of America," by a Subcommittee of the Executive Committee of the American Committee for the Independence of Armenia, presented on December 17, 1920, at Marion, Ohio, pp. 5–6; cited hereafter as ACIA Memorandum.

20. Ibid., pp. 5–6.

21. They included Charles Evans Hughes, Elihu Root, Henry Cabot Lodge, John Sharp Williams, James W. Gerard, Alfred Smith, Frederic C. Penfield, and Charles W. Eliot. Ibid., p. 8.

22. Ibid., pp. 7–8.

23. Ibid., Morgenthau to Colby, Sept. 1, 1921.

24. Morgenthau Papers, General Correspondence, Containers 9/10, Brig. Gen. E.F. McGlachlin, Jr., to Morgenthau, Nov. 8, 1921.

25. Library of Congress, Division of Manuscripts, Papers of Robert Lansing, Confidential Memoranda and Notes, Feb. 16, 1922, Diary, Blue Boxes, Box 2, Jan. 1, 1920–May 23, 1922.

26. Leland James Gordon, *American Relations with Turkey, 1830–1930: An Economic Interpretation* (Philadelphia: University of Pennsylvania Press, 1932), pp. 132–36.

27. John A. DeNovo, *American Interests and Policies in the Middle East, 1900–1939* (Minneapolis: University of Minnesota Press, 1963), pp. 186–88. On efforts to improve the image of Turkey in the United States in the 1920s and 1930s, see Roger R. Trask, *The United States Response to Turkish Nationalism and Reform, 1914–1939* (Minneapolis: University of Minnesota Press, 1971), pp. 65–93 passim.

28. Gregory P. Nowell, *Mercantile States and the World Oil Cartel, 1900–1939* (Ithaca and London: Cornell University Press, 1994), p. 184.

29. DeNovo, *American Interests*, p. 235n13.

30. Ibid., pp. 229–30.

31. *Preliminary Report of the Near East Survey*, April 1927, Papers of James L. Barton, Papers and Correspondence, Box 14, 14:1, American Board of Commissioners for Foreign Missions, Manuscript Collection, Houghton Library, Harvard University.

32. Ibid., Section I, p. 6.

33. Ibid., pp. 10–11.

34. Ibid., Section II, p. 1.

35. Ibid., p. 7.

36. Ibid., pp. 24, 27, 39–41.
37. Levon Marashlian, "Finishing the Genocide: Cleansing Turkey of Armenian Survivors, 1920–1923," in Richard G. Hovannisian, ed., *Remembrance and Denial: The Case of the Armenian Genocide* (Detroit: Wayne State University Press, 1999), pp. 113–45.
38. On Smyrna, see Marjorie Housepian Dobkin, *Smyrna 1922: The Destruction of a City* (Kent, OH: Kent State University Press, 1988).
39. George R. Montgomery, "Mangling Asia Minor," *Current History* 15 (Oct. 1921): 93–101.
40. Clarence D. Ussher, *An American Physician in Turkey: A Narrative of Adventures in Peace and War* (Boston: Houghton Mifflin, 1917), pp. 331–32.

BIBLIOGRAPHY

PUBLISHED AND UNPUBLISHED PRIMARY SOURCES

American Board of Commissioners for Foreign Missions. Manuscript Collection. Houghton Library, Harvard University, Cambridge, Massachusetts.

Beylerian, Arthur, ed. and comp. *Les grandes puissances l'empire ottoman et les arméniens dans les archives françaises (1914–1918)*. Paris: Université de Paris I, Panthéon-Sorbonne, 1983.

Bibliothèque Nubar (Paris). *Boghos Nubar's Papers and the Armenian Question, 1915–1918*. Trans. and ed. Vatche Ghazarian. Waltham, MA: Mayrnei Publishing, 1996.

Daniels, Josephus. *The Cabinet Diaries of Josephus Daniels, 1913–1921*. Ed. E. David Cronon. Lincoln: University of Nebraska Press, 1963.

Great Britain. *British Documents on the Origins of the War, 1898–1914*, vol. 10: *The Near and Middle East on the Eve of War*. Ed. G.P. Gooch and Harold Temperely. London: H.M.S.O., 1928–1936.

Great Britain. Parliament. *The Treatment of Armenians in the Ottoman Empire, 1915–1916*. Documents Presented to Viscount Grey of Fallodon, Secretary of State for Foreign Affairs. Arnold Toynbee, ed. and comp. 3rd edn. Beirut: G. Doniguian and Sons, 1988 [London: Sir Joseph Causton and Sons, 1916].

Hayastani Hanrapetutiun, Patmutian Kentronakan Petakan Arkhiv (HH PKPA). *Vaveragrer Hai Ekeghetsu Patmutyan, Girk 5: Mair Ator S. Echmiatsine Arajin Hanrapetutyan Tarinerin (1918–1920 tt.)* [Documents of the History of the Armenian Church, Bk 5: The Mother See St. Echmiadzin during the Years of the First Republic (1918–1920)]. Comp. Sandro Behbudyan. Erevan: Voskan Erevantsi, 1999.

Kirakosyan, Jon, comp. *Hayastane Mijazgayin ev Sovetakan Artakin Kaghakakanutian Pastatghterum, 1828–1923* [Armenia in the Documents of International and Soviet Foreign Policy, 1828–1923]. Erevan: Hayastan, 1972.

Link, Arthur, ed. *The Papers of Woodrow Wilson*. 69 vols. Princeton: Princeton University Press, 1966–1994.

U.S. Congress. *Circular Letters of Congressmen to Their Constituents, 1789–1829*. Ed. Noble E. Cunningham, Jr. 3 vols. Chapel Hill: University of Carolina Press, 1978.

————. *Congressional Record* [various years].

U.S. Department of Commerce. Bureau of Foreign and Domestic Commerce. *Foreign Commerce and Navigation of the United States.* Washington, DC: Government Printing Office [various years].

U.S. Department of Commerce and Labor. Bureau of Statistics. *Foreign Commerce and Navigation of the United States.* Washington, DC: Government Printing Office [various years].

U.S. Department of State. *Papers Relating to the Foreign Relations of the United States.* Washington, DC: Government Printing Office [various years].

————. *Papers Relating to the Foreign Relations of the United States: The Lansing Papers, 1914–1920.* 2 vols. Washington, DC: Government Printing Office, 1939–1940.

————. *Records of the Department of State Relating to Internal Affairs of Armenia, 1910–1929.* Washington, DC: National Archives Microfilm Publications, 1975. Microfilm, 8 reels.

————. *Records of the Department of State Relating to Political Relations Between Armenia and Other States, 1910–1929.* Washington, DC: National Archives Microfilm Publications, 1975. Microfilm, 2 reels.

————. *Despatches from United States Ministers to Turkey, 1818–1906.* Washington, DC: National Archives, 1952. Microfilm, 77 reels.

U.S. Department of State. Historical Office, Bureau of Public Affairs. *United States Chiefs of Mission, 1778–1982.* Washington, DC: Government Printing Office, 1982.

U.S. Department of the Treasury. Bureau of Statistics. *The Foreign Commerce and Navigation of the United States.* Washington, DC: Government Printing Office [various years].

U.S. National Archives
Record Group 59: General Records of the Department of State.
Record Group 38: Records of the Office of the Chief of Naval Operations.
Record Group 45: Naval Records Collection of the Office of Naval Records and Library.

Library of Congress, Division of Manuscripts, Washington, DC

Papers of William Jennings Bryan, Manuscript Division, Library of Congress, Washington, DC.

Papers of Robert Lansing, Manuscript Division, Library of Congress, Washington, DC.

Papers of Henry Morgenthau, Sr., Manuscript Division, Library of Congress, Washington, DC.

Papers of Woodrow Wilson, Manuscript Division, Library of Congress, Washington, DC.

SECONDARY SOURCES

Books

Aharonian, Gersam, ed. and comp. *Hushamatian Mets Egherni, 1915–1965* [Memorial Volume of the Colossal Crime, 1915–1965]. Beirut: Atlas, 1965.

Akuni, Sebuh. *Milion me Hayeru Jardi Patmutiune* [The Story of the Massacre of a Million Armenians]. Constantinople: Hayastan, 1921.

Allen, W.E.D. and Paul Muratoff. *Caucasian Battlefields: A History of the Wars on the Turco-Caucasian Border, 1828–1921.* Cambridge: Cambridge University Press, 1953.

Ambrosius, Lloyd E. *Wilsonian Statecraft: Theory and Practice of Liberal Internationalism during World War I.* Wilmington: Scholarly Resource Books, 1991.

Anderson, M.S. *The Eastern Question, 1774–1923: A Study in International Relations.* London: Macmillan, 1966.

Arzumanyan, Makich. *Hayastan, 1914–1917* [Armenia, 1914–1917]. Erevan: Hayastan, 1969.

Astourian, Stephan. *The Armenian Genocide: An Interpretation.* Glendale: ARF Shant Committee, 1995.

Atkinson, Tacy. *"The German, the Turk and the Devil Made a Triple Alliance": Harpoot Diaries, 1908–1917.* Princeton, NJ: Gomidas Institute, 2000.

Bacqué-Grammont, Jean-Louis and Paul Dumont, eds. *Contributions à l'histoire économique et sociale de l'Empire ottoman.* Leuven, Belgium: Édition Peeters, 1983.

Bailey, Thomas A. *A Diplomatic History of the American People.* 2nd edn. New York: F.S. Crofts, 1944.

Barby, Henry. *Au pays de l'épouvante: L'Arménie martyre.* Beirut: Hamazkayin, Association Culturelle Arménienne, 1973; first published, 1917.

Barton, James L. *Story of Near East Relief, 1915–1930.* New York: Macmillan, 1930.

———, comp. *"Turkish Atrocities": Statements of American Missionaries on the Destruction of Christian Communities in Ottoman Turkey, 1915–1917.* Ann Arbor, MI: Gomidas Institute, 1998.

Beach, Harlan. *A Geography and Atlas of Protestant Missions,* vol. 1: *Geography.* New York: Student Volunteer Movement for Foreign Missions, 1901.

———. *A Geography and Atlas of Protestant Missions,* vol. 2: *Statistics and Atlas.* New York: Student Volunteer Movement for Foreign Missions, 1903 [1906].

Beach, Harlan and Burton St. John, eds. *World Statistics of Christian Missions.* New York: Foreign Missions Conference of North America, 1916.

Beach, Harlan and Charles H. Fahs, eds. *World Missionary Atlas.* New York: Institute of Social and Religious Research, 1925.

Becker, William H., and Samuels F. Wells, Jr., eds. *Economics and World Power: An Assessment of American Diplomacy since 1789.* New York: Columbia University, 1984.

Blum, John Morton. *Woodrow Wilson and the Politics of Morality*. Boston: Little, Brown, 1956.

Bryson, Thomas A. *American Diplomatic Relations with the Middle East, 1784–1975*. Metuchen, NJ: Scarecrow Press, 1977.

———. *Tars, Turks, and Tankers: The Role of the United States Navy in the Middle East, 1800–1979*. Metuchen, NJ: Scarecrow Press, 1980.

Chizmechian, Manuk G. *Patmutiun Amerikahay Kaghakakan Kusaktsutiants, 1890–1925* [History of American Armenian Political Parties, 1890–1925]. Fresno: Nor Or, 1930.

Chormisian, Levon. *Hamapatker Arevmtahai Mek Daru Patmutian* [A Panorama of One Century of Western Armenian History], vol. 3. Beirut: Sevan, 1975.

Christensen, Torben, and William R. Hutchison, eds. *Missionary Ideologies in the Imperialist Era: 1880–1920*. Aarhus, Denmark: Aros, 1982.

Clements, Kendrick A. *The Presidency of Woodrow Wilson*. Lawrence, KS: University Press of Kansas, 1992.

———. *Woodrow Wilson: World Statesman*. Rev. edn. Chicago: Ivan R. Dee, 1999.

Clements, Kendrick A. *William Jennings Bryan: Missionary Isolationist*. Knoxville: University of Tennessee Press, 1982.

Coletta, Paolo E. *William Jennings Bryan*, vol. 2: *Progressive Politician and Moral Statesman, 1909–1915*. Lincoln: University of Nebraska Press, 1969.

Cooling, Benjamin Franklin. *Gray Steel and Blue Water Navy: The Formative Years of America's Military-Industrial Complex, 1881–1917*. Hamden, CT: Archon Books, 1979.

Cooper, John Milton, Jr. *Breaking the Heart of the World: Woodrow Wilson and the Fight for the League of Nations*. Cambridge: Cambridge University Press, 2001.

Curti, Merle. *American Philanthropy Abroad: A History*. New Brunswick, NJ: Rutgers University Press, 1963.

Curti, Merle Eugene. *Bryan and World Peace*. New York: Octagon Books, 1969.

Dadrian, Vahakn N. *The History of the Armenian Genocide: Ethnic Conflict from the Balkans to Anatolia to the Caucasus*. Providence: Berghahn Books, 1995.

———. *German Responsibility in the Armenian Genocide: A Review of the Historical Evidence of German Complicity*. Watertown: Blue Crane Books, 1996.

Daniel, Robert L. *American Philanthropy in the Near East, 1820–1960*. Athens: Ohio State University, 1970.

Daniels, Josephus. *The Navy and the Nation: War-Time Addresses*. New York: George H. Doran, 1919.

Davenport, E.H., and Sidney Russell Cooke. *The Oil Trusts and Anglo-American Relations*. New York: Macmillan, 1924.

Davidson, Khoren K. *Odyssey of an Armenian of Zeitoun*. New York: Vantage Press, 1985.

Davis, Leslie A. *The Slaughterhouse Province: An American Diplomat's Report on the Armenian Genocide, 1915–1917.* Ed. with Introduction and Notes by Susan K. Blair. New Rochelle, NY: Aristide D. Caratzas Publisher, 1989.

DeConde, Alexander. *A History of American Foreign Policy.* New York: Charles Scribner's Sons, 1963.

Dennis, Alfred L.P. *Adventures in American Diplomacy, 1896–1906.* New York: E.P. Dutton, 1928.

Dennis, James S., Harlan P. Beach, Charles H. Fahs, eds. *World Atlas of Christian Missions.* New York: Student Volunteer Movement for Foreign Missions, 1911.

DeNovo, John A. *American Interests and Policies in the Middle East, 1900–1939.* Minneapolis: University of Minnesota Press, 1963.

Der Yeghiayan, Zaven. *My Patriarchal Memoirs.* Translated from the Armenian by Ared Misirliyan, annotated by Vatche Ghazarian. Barrington, RI: Mayreni Publishing, 2002.

Djemal Pasha. *Memories of a Turkish Statesman, 1913–1919.* New York: George H. Doran, 1922.

Dobkin, Marjorie Housepian. *Smyrna 1922: The Destruction of a City.* Kent, OH: Kent State University Press, 1988.

Dwight, Henry Otis, H. Allen Tupper, Edwin Munsell Bliss, eds. *The Encyclopedia of Missions.* 2nd edn. New York and London: Funk and Wagnalls, 1904.

Eghiayan, Buzand. *Zhamanakakits patmutiun katoghikosutian Hayots Kilikioy, 1914–1972* [Contemporary History of the Catholicosate of Cilician Armenians, 1914–1972]. Antelias: Catholicosate of Cilicia, 1975.

Einstein, Lewis. *A Diplomat Looks Back.* New Haven and London: Yale University Press, 1968.

Evans, Laurence. *United States Policy and the Partition of Turkey, 1914–1924.* Baltimore, MD: Johns Hopkins Press, 1965.

Eysenbach, Mary Locke. *American Manufactured Exports, 1879–1914: A Study of Growth and Comparative Advantage.* New York: Arno, 1976.

Fairbank, John K. ed. *The Missionary Enterprise in China and America.* Cambridge, MA: Harvard University Press, 1974.

Faroqhi, Suraiya, Bruce McGowan, Donald Quataert, Şevket Pamuk. *An Economic and Social History of the Ottoman Empire,* vol. 2: *1600–1914.* Cambridge: Cambridge University Press, 1994.

Ferguson, Niall. *The Pity of War.* New York: Basic Books, 1999.

Field, James A. *America and the Mediterranean World, 1776–1882.* Princeton, NJ: Princeton University Press, 1969.

Galustian, Grigor H. comp. and ed. *Marash kam Germanik ev heros Zeitun* [Marash or Germanica and Heroic Zeitun]. 2nd edn. New York: Compatriotic Union of Marash, 1934; Long Island City, NY: Union of Marash Armenians, 1988.

George, Alexander L., and Juliette L. George. *Woodrow Wilson and Colonel House: A Personality Study.* New York: John Day, 1956.

Gerig, Benjamin. *The Open Door and the Mandates System*. London: Allen and Unwin, 1930.

Ghazarian, Haigazn G. *Tseghaspan Turke* [The Genocidal Turk]. Beirut: Hamazkayin Press, 1968.

Gibb, George Sweet and Evelyn K. Knowlton. *The History of the Standard Oil Company (New Jersey): The Resurgent Years, 1911–1927*. New York: Harper and Row, 1956.

Gidney, James B. *A Mandate for Armenia*. Kent, OH: Kent State University Press, 1967.

Gilbert, Martin. *The First World War: A Complete History*. New York: Henry Holt, 1994.

Gordon, Leland James. *American Relations with Turkey, 1830–1930: An Economic Interpretation*. Philadelphia: University of Pennsylvania Press, 1932.

Gould, Lewis L. *The Presidency of Theodore Roosevelt*. Lawrence, KS: University Press of Kansas, 1991.

Grabill, Joseph L. *Protestant Diplomacy and the Near East: Missionary Influence on American Policy, 1810–1927*. Minneapolis: University of Minnesota Press, 1971.

Grayson, Cary T. *Woodrow Wilson: An Intimate Memoir*. New York: Holt, Rinehart and Winston, 1960.

Greene, Joseph K. *Leavening the Levant*. Boston: Pilgrim Press, 1916.

Guleserian, Babgen I. *Patmutiun Katoghikosats Kilikioy (1441-en minchev Mer Orere)* [History of the Catholicoses of Cilicia (from 1441 until Our Days)]. Antelias: Catholicosate of Cilicia, 1939, 2nd pr., 1990.

Hartunian, Abraham H. *Neither to Laugh Nor to Weep: A Memoir of the Armenian Genocide*. Boston: Beacon Press, 1968.

Headland, Isaac Taylor. *Some By-Products of Missions*. New York and Cincinnati: Methodist Book Concern, 1912.

Heyd, Uriel. *Foundations of Turkish Nationalism: The Life and Teachings of Ziya Gökalp*. London: Luzac, 1950.

Hidy, Ralph W., and Muriel E. Hidy. *Pioneering in Big Business, 1882–1911*. New York: Harper and Brothers, 1955.

Hilderbrand, Robert C. *Power and the People: Executive Management of Public Opinion in Foreign Affairs, 1897–1921*. Chapel Hill: University of North Carolina Press, 1981.

Hopkirk, Peter. *Like Hidden Fire: The Plot to Bring Down the British Empire*. New York: Kodansha, 1994.

House, Edward M., and Charles Seymour. *What Really Happened at Paris: The Story of the Paris Peace Conference*. New York: Charles Scribner's Sons, 1921.

Hovannisian, Richard G., *Armenia on the Road to Independence, 1918*. Berkeley and Los Angeles: University of California Press, 1967.

———. *The Republic of Armenia*. 4 vols. Berkeley and Los Angeles: University of California Press, 1971–1996.

Hovannisian, Richard G., ed. *The Armenian Genocide in Perspective*. New Brunswick, NJ: Transaction Books, 1986.

Hovannisian, Richard G., ed. *The Armenian Genocide: History, Politics, Ethics.* New York: St. Martin's Press, 1992.

———. *The Armenian People from Ancient to Modern Times,* vol. 2: *Foreign Dominion to Statehood: The Fifteenth Century to the Twentieth Century.* New York: St. Martin's Press, 1997.

———. *Remembrance and Denial: The Case of the Armenian Genocide.* Detroit: Wayne State University Press, 1999.

———. *Armenian Van/Vaspurakan.* Costa Mesa, CA: Mazda Publishers, 2000.

———. *Armenian Karin/Erzerum.* Costa Mesa, CA: Mazda Publishers, 2003.

Howard, Harry N. *The King-Crane Commission: An American Inquiry in the Middle East.* Beirut: Khayat, 1963.

Jacobsen, Maria. *Oragrutiun 1907–1919: Kharpert* [Diary 1907–1919: Kharpert]. Translated from the Danish, Bishop Nerses Bakhtikian and Mihran Simonian. Antelias: Catholicosate of Cilicia, 1979.

Kazemzadeh, Firuz. *The Struggle for Transcaucasia, 1917–1921.* New York: Philosophical Library, and Oxford: George Ronald, 1951.

Keegan, John. *The First World War.* New York: Vintage Books, 1998.

Kennedy, David M. *Over Here: The First World War and American Society.* New York: Oxford University Press, 1980.

Kennedy, Paul M. *The Rise and Fall of British Naval Mastery.* London: Ashfield Press, 1983.

Kerr, Stanley E. *The Lions of Marash.* Albany, NY: State University of New York Press, 1973.

Khatisian, Aleksandre. *Hayastani Hanrapetutian Tsagumn u Zargatsume* [The Creation and Development of the Republic of Armenia]. 2nd pr. Beirut: Hamazkayin Press, 1968.

Kirakosyan, Jon S. *Arajin Hamashkharayin Paterazme ev Arevmtahaiutiune 1914–1916 tt.* [The First World War and the Western Armenians, 1914–1916]. Erevan: Hayastan, 1967.

Knapp, Grace H. *The Tragedy of Bitlis.* New York: Fleming H. Revell, 1919.

Knock, Thomas J. *To End All Wars: Woodrow Wilson and the Quest for a New World Order.* Princeton, NJ: Princeton University Press, 1992.

LaFeber, Walter. *The New Empire: An Interpretation of American Expansion, 1860–1898.* Ithaca and London: Cornell University Press, 1963.

———. *The Cambridge History of American Foreign Relations,* vol. 2: *The American Search for Opportunity, 1865–1913.* Cambridge: Cambridge University Press, 1993.

Landau, Jacob M. *Pan-Turkism: From Irredentism to Cooperation.* 2nd rev. edn. Bloomington: Indiana University Press, 1995.

Langer, William L. *The Diplomacy of Imperialism, 1890–1902.* 2nd edn. New York: Alfred A. Knopf, 1951.

Lepsius, Johannes. *Armenia and Europe: An Indictment.* Trans. and ed. J. Rendel Harris. London: Hodder and Stoughton, 1897.

———. *Rapport secret sur les massacres d'Armenie.* Beirut: Edition Hamazkayin, Association Culturelle Arménienne, 1980; first published, Paris: Payot, 1918.

Lewis, Bernard. *The Emergence of Modern Turkey.* 2nd edn. London: Oxford University Press, 1968.

Liman von Sanders, Otto. *Five Years in Turkey.* Baltimore, MD: Williams and Wilkins, 1928.

Link, Arthur S. *Woodrow Wilson and the Progressive Era, 1910–1917.* New York: Harper and Row, 1954.

Mahan, Alfred Thayer. *The Influence of Sea Power upon History, 1660–1783.* Boston: Little, Brown, 1890; repr. Mineola, NY: Dover, 1987.

Malcom, Vartan M. *The Armenians in America.* Boston: Pilgrim Press, 1919.

Marshall, S.L.A. *World War I.* Boston: Houghton Mifflin, 1964; repr. Boston and New York: Mariner Books, 2001.

Matossian, Mary K. *The Impact of Soviet Policies in Armenia.* Leiden: E.J. Brill, 1962.

May, Ernest R. *Imperial Democracy: The Emergence of America as a Great Power.* New York: Harcourt, Brace, 1961.

McKale, Donald M. *War by Revolution: Germany and Great Britain in the Middle East in the Era of World War I.* Kent, OH, and London: Kent State University Press, 1998.

Mirak, Robert. *Torn Between Two Lands: Armenians in America, 1890 to World War I.* Cambridge, MA: Harvard University Press, 1983.

Mkhitarian, Onnik. *Vani Herosamarte* [The Heroic Struggle of Van]. Sofia: P. Palegchian, 1930.

Mohr, Anton. *The Oil War.* New York: Harcourt, Brace, 1926.

Moorehead, Alan. *Gallipoli.* London: H. Hamilton, 1956.

Morgenthau, Henry. *Ambassador Morgenthau's Story.* New York: Doubleday, 1918.

———. *All in a Life-Time.* Garden City, NY: Doubleday, 1922.

Morley, Bertha B. *Marsovan 1915: The Diaries of Bertha B. Morley.* Ed. Hilmar Kaiser. Ann Arbor, MI: Gomidas Institute, 1999.

Mugerditchian, Esther. *From Turkish Toils: The Narrative of an Armenian Family's Escape.* New York: George H. Doran, [1918].

Nalbandian, Louise. *The Armenian Revolutionary Movement: The Development of Armenian Political Parties.* Berkeley and Los Angeles: University of California Press, 1963.

Nash, Gerald D. *United States Oil Policy 1890–1964.* Pittsburgh: University of Pittsburgh Press, 1968.

Nassibian, Akaby. *Britain and the Armenian Question, 1915–1923.* London: Croom Helm, 1984.

Nogales, Rafael de. *Four Years Beneath the Crescent.* Translated from the Spanish, Muna Lee. New York and London: Charles Sribner's Sons, 1926.

Nowell, Gregory P. *Mercantile States and the World Oil Cartel, 1900–1939.* Ithaca and London: Cornell University Press, 1994.

Okyar, Osman and Halil İnalcık, eds. *Türkiye'nin Sosyal ve Ekonomik Tarihi (1071–1920)* [Social and Economic History of Turkey, 1071–1920]. Ankara: Mateksan Limited Şirketi, 1980.

Palakian, Grigoris. *Hai Goghgotan* [The Armenian Calvary]. Vienna: Mkhitarist Press, 1922; repr. Erevan: Hayastan, 1991.

Parker, Joseph I., ed. *Interpretative Statistical Survey of the World Mission of the Christian Church.* New York and London: International Missionary Council, 1938.

Parla, Taha. *The Social and Political Thought of Ziya Gökalp, 1876–1924.* Leiden: E.J. Brill, 1985.

Parrini, Carl P. *Heir to Empire: United States Economic Diplomacy, 1916–1923.* Pittsburgh: University of Pittsburgh Press, 1969.

Paullin, Charles O. *Diplomatic Negotiations of American Naval Officers, 1778–1883.* Baltimore, MD: Johns Hopkins Press, 1912.

Permanent Peoples' Tribunal. *A Crime of Silence: The Armenian Genocide.* London: Zed Books, 1985.

Phillips, Clifton Jackson. *Protestant America and the Pagan World: The First Half Century of the American Board of Commissioners for Foreign Missions, 1810–1860.* Cambridge, MA: Harvard University, East Asian Research Center, 1969.

Poghosyan, Haikaz M. *Zeituni Patmutiune, 1409–1921 tt.* [The History of Zeitun, 1409–1921]. Erevan: Hayastan, 1969.

Price, Maurice T. *Christian Missions and Oriental Civilizations: A Study in Culture Contact.* Shanghai, China: n.p., 1924.

Pztikian, Zakaria, comp. *Kilikian Kskitsner: Vaveragrer Kilikioy Katoghikosakan Divanen* [Cilician Pains: Documents from the Archives of the Cilician Catholicosate]. Beirut: Hrazdan, 1927.

Quataert, Donald. *Social Disintegration and Popular Resistance in the Ottoman Empire, 1881–1908: Reactions to European Economic Penetration.* New York and London: New York University Press, 1983.

———. *Manufacturing and Technology Transfer in the Ottoman Empire, 1800–1914.* Istanbul and Strasbourg: Isis Press, 1992.

Quataert, Donald, ed. *Consumption Studies and the History of the Ottoman Empire, 1550–1922.* Albany, NY: State University of New York Press, 2000.

Redwood, Boverton. *Petroleum: A Treatise on the Geographical Distribution and Geological Occurrence of Petroleum and Natural Gas.* 3 vols. 3rd. edn. London: Charles Griffin, 1913.

Riggs, Henry H. *Days of Tragedy in Armenia: Personal Experiences in Harpoot, 1915–1917.* Ann Arbor, MI: Gomidas Institute, 1997.

Rosenberg, Emily S. *Spreading the American Dream: American Economic and Cultural Expansion, 1890–1945.* New York: Hill and Wang, 1982.

———. *Financial Missionaries to the World: The Politics and Culture of Dollar Diplomacy, 1900–1930.* Cambridge, MA: Harvard University Press, 1999.

Sander, Oral, and Kurthan Fişek. *Türk-ABD Silah Ticaretinin İlk Yüzyılı, 1829–1929.* [The First Century of Turkish-U.S. Arms Trade, 1829–1929]. İstanbul: Çağdaş Yayınları, 1977.

Schlesinger, Arthur M. Jr. *The Imperial Presidency.* Boston: Houghton Mifflin, 1973.

Scholes, Walter V., and Marie V. Scholes. *The Foreign Policies of the Taft Administration.* Columbia: University of Missouri Press, 1970.

Simpson, John Hope. *The Refugee Problem: Report of a Survey.* London: Oxford University Press, 1939.

Smith, Adam. *An Inquiry into the Nature and Causes of the Wealth of Nations.* 2 vols. Gen. eds. R.H. Campbel and A.S. Skinner. Textual ed. W.B. Todd. Indianapolis: Liberty Fund, 1981.

Spykman, Nicholas J. *America's Strategy in World Politics.* New York: Harcourt, Brace, 1942.

Still, William N., Jr. *American Sea Power in the Old World: The United States Navy in European and Near Eastern Waters, 1865–1917.* Westport, CT: Greenwood Press, 1980.

Stokesbury, James L. *A Short History of World War I.* New York: William Morrow, 1981.

Strong, William Ellsworth. *The Story of the American Board.* Boston: Pilgrim Press, 1910; rep. New York: Arno Press and the New York Times, 1969.

Surface, Frank M. *The Grain Trade during the World War: Being a History of the Food Administration Grain Corporation and the United States Grain Corporation.* New York: Macmillan, 1928.

Taylor, A.J.P. *The Struggle for Mastery in Europe, 1848–1918.* Oxford: Oxford University Press, 1954.

Trask, Roger R. *The United States Response to Turkish Nationalism and Reform, 1914–1939.* Minneapolis: University of Minnesota Press, 1971.

Trumpener, Ulrich. *Germany and the Ottoman Empire, 1914–1918.* Princeton, NJ: Princeton University Press, 1968.

Ussher, Clarence D. *An American Physician in Turkey: A Narrative of Adventures in Peace and War.* Boston: Houghton Mifflin, 1917.

Vartooguian, Aramayis P. *Armenia's Ordeal: A Sketch of the Main Features of the History of Armenia, and an Inside Account of the Work of American Missionaries among Armenians, and Its Ruinous Effect.* New York: n.p., 1896.

Vratzian, Simon. *Hayastani Hanrapetutiun* [Republic of Armenia]. Paris: A.R.F. Central Committee of America, 1928; repr., Erevan: Hayastan, 1993.

Walker, Christopher J. *Armenia: The Survival of a Nation.* London: Croom Helm, 1980.

Widenor, William C. *Henry Cabot Lodge and the Search for an American Foreign Policy.* Berkeley: University of California Press, 1980.

Wilkins, Mira. *The Emergence of Multinational Enterprises: American Business Abroad from the Colonial Era to 1914.* Cambridge and London: Harvard University Press, 1970.

Williams, William Appleman. *The Tragedy of American Diplomacy.* 2nd rev. edn. New York: Dell Publishing, 1972.

Williams, William J. *The Wilson Administration and the Shipbuilding Crisis of 1917.* Lewiston, NY: Edwin Mellen Press, 1992.

Williamson, Harold F., and Arnold R. Daum. *The American Petroleum Industry: The Age of Illumination 1859–1899*. Evanston, IL: Northwestern University Press, 1959.

Willis, James F. *Prologue to Nuremberg: The Politics and Diplomacy of Punishing War Criminals of the First World War*. Westport, CT: Greenwood Press, 1982.

Wilson, F.M. Huntington. *Memoirs of an Ex-Diplomat*. Boston: Bruce Humphries, 1945.

Winter, Jay, ed. *America and the Armenian Genocide of 1915*. Cambridge, UK: Cambridge University Press, 2003.

Yeghiayan, Vartkes, ed. and comp. *British Foreign Office Dossiers on Turkish War Criminals*. La Verne, CA: American Armenian International College, 1991.

Articles

Barton, James L. "What America Has Done for Armenia." *Armenia* 1:3 (Dec. 1904): 3–10.

Bryson, Thomas A. "Woodrow Wilson and the Armenian Mandate: A Reassessment." *Armenian Review* 21 (Autumn 1968): 10–29.

———. "Mark Lambart Bristol, U.S. Navy, Admiral-Diplomat: His Influence on the Armenian Mandate Question." *Armenian Review* 21 (Winter 1968): 3–22.

———. "John Sharp Williams, An Advocate for the Armenian Mandate." *Armenian Review* 26 (Fall 1973): 10–25.

Carson, John M. "Trade in the Near East." *Levant Trade Review* 1:1 (June 1911): 16–17.

Cohen, Naomi W. "Ambassador Straus in Turkey, 1909–1910: A Note on Dollar Diplomacy," *Mississippi Valley Historical Review* 45:4 (March 1959): 632–42.

Dadrian, Vahakn N. "Genocide as a Problem of National and International Law: The World War I Armenian Case and Its Contemporary Legal Ramifications." *Yale Journal of International Law* 14:2 (Summer 1989): 221–334.

———. "The Secret Young-Turk Ittihadist Conference and the Decision for the World War I Genocide of the Armenians." *Holocaust and Genocide Studies* 7:2 (Fall 1993). Reprinted with revisions in *Journal of Political and Military Sociology (The Armenian Genocide in Official Turkish Records)* 22:1 (Summer 1994): 173–201.

Daniel, Robert L. "The Armenian Question and American-Turkish Relations, 1914–1927." *Mississippi Valley Historical Review* 46 (Sept. 1959): 252–75.

Daniels, Josephus. "The Significance of Naval Preparedness." *Annals of the American Academy of Political and Social Science* 66 (July 1916): 147–56.

Davison, Roderic H. "The Armenian Crisis, 1912–1914." *American Historical Review* 53 (April 1948): 481–505.

DeNovo, John A. "Petroleum and the United States Navy before World War I." *Mississippi Valley Historical Review* 41 (March 1955): 641–56.

———. "The Movement for a More Aggressive Oil Policy Abroad." *American Historical Review* 61 (1955–56): 854–76.

———. "A Railroad for Turkey: The Chester Project, 1908–1913." *Business History Review* 33:3 (Autumn 1959): 300–29.

Dodd, William E. "Wilsonism." *Political Science Quarterly* 38:1 (March 1923): 115–32.

Fiske, Bradley A. "Naval Principles." *North American Review* 202 (Nov. 1915): 693.

Froian, G. "Karmir Aprile" [The Red April]. *Varag* 3:9 (April 1955): 56.

Gaddis, John Lewis. "The Corporatist Synthesis: A Skeptical View." *Diplomatic History* 10 (Fall 1986): 357–62.

Ghevond, George. "Conditions in Armenia." *Levant Trade Review* 1:1 (June 1911):114, 116.

Giraudoux, Jean. "The Dardanelles." *North American Review* 206 (Aug. 1917): 285–91.

Hogan, Michael J. "Corporatism: A Positive Appraisal." *Diplomatic History* 10 (Fall 1986): 363–72.

Karo (Garo), Armen. "Aprvats Orer" [Days Lived]. *Hairenik Amsagir* 1:9 (July 1923): 93–96.

Kutvirt, Thomas Otakar. "The Emergence and Acceptance of Armenia as a Legitimate American Missionary Field." *Armenian Review* 37 (Autumn 1984): 7–32.

McCormick, Thomas J. "Drift or Mastery? A Corporatist Synthesis for American Diplomatic History." *Review in American History* 10 (Dec. 1982): 318–30.

McKillen, Beth. "The Corporatist Model, World War I, and the Public Debate over the League of Nations." *Diplomatic History* 15 (Spring 1991): 171–97.

Merguerian, Barbara J. "The American Response to the 1895 Massacres." *Genocide and Human Rights: Lessons from the Armenian Experience.* Special issue, *Journal of Armenian Studies* 4:1–2 (1992): 53–83.

Minassian, Gaidz F. "Les Relations entre le Comité Union et Progrès et la Fédération Révolutionnaire Arménienne à la veille de la Premiere Guerre Mondiale d'après les sources arméniennes." *Revue d'Histoire Arménienne Contemporaine* 1 (1995): 45–99.

Montgomery, George R. "Mangling Asia Minor." *Current History* 15 (Oct. 1921): 93–101.

Patten, S.N. "The Basis of National Security." *Annals of the American Academy of Political and Social Science* 66 (July 1916): 1–11.

Polyzoides, Adamantios Th. "The Passing of Turkey." *Current History* 15 (Oct. 1921): 34–36.

Redfield, William C. "America's International Trade as Affected by the European War." *Annals of the American Academy of Political and Social Science* 60 (July 1915): 7–15.

Walker, Christopher J. "From Sassun to the Ottoman Bank: Turkish Armenians in the 1890s." *Armenian Review* 30 (March 1979): 227–64.
Williams, William Appleman. "The Age of Mercantilism: An Interpretation of the American Political Economy, 1763–1828." *William and Mary Quarterly* 15 (Oct. 1958): 419–37.
Woodhouse, Henry. "American Oil Claims in Turkey." *Current History* 15:6 (March 1922): 953–59.
Yale, William. "Ambassador Henry Morgenthau's Special Mission of 1917." *World Politics* 1 (April 1949): 308–20.

Ph.D. Dissertations

Bryson, Thomas A. "Woodrow Wilson, the Senate, Public Opinion, and the Armenian Mandate Question, 1919–1920." Ph.D. Dissertation. University of Georgia, 1965.
Cook, Ralph Elliott. "The United States and the Armenian Question, 1884–1924." Ph.D. Dissertation. Fletcher School of Law and Diplomacy, 1957.
Greenshields, T.H. "The Settlement of Armenian Refugees in Syria and Lebanon, 1915–1939." Ph.D. Dissertation. Durham University, 1978.
Moranian, Suzanne E. "The American Missionaries and the Armenian Question, 1915–1927." Ph.D. Dissertation. University of Wisconsin-Madison, 1994.

INDEX

Untermeyer, Samuel, 104, 186
Urfa, 71, 78, 188
Urmia, 37, 61, 67, 81, 151
Urmia, Lake, 60, 61
U.S. Chamber of Commerce, 3, 30, 42, 56; in Turkey, 22
U.S. Congress, 6, 7, 18, 45, 56, 96, 100, 104, 114, 117–19 *passim*, 128, 130–1, 133, 136–7, 139, 142–3, 149, 152–3, 158, 160, 162, 165, 168–9, 173–5, 177–8, 181; congressional elections of 1918, 129; declaration of war (April 1917), 129; (Dec. 1917), 130
U.S. Department of Agriculture, 115, 120
U.S. Department of Army, 158
U.S. Department of Commerce, 30, 31, 42
U.S. Department of Justice, 153
U.S. Department of State, 5, 6, 8, 17, 22, 24, 30, 35, 36, 38, 44, 47, 48, 49, 50, 63, 74, 84, 85, 89, 90, 91, 95, 96–7, 98, 99–100, 103, 106, 111, 112, 120, 139, 144, 153, 166, 175, 176, 185, 186
U.S. Department of the Navy, 2, 5, 6, 7, 10, 17, 23, 26, 27, 32, 33, 35, 49, 51, 118, 144, 151, 158, 176
U.S. Department of the Treasury, 3, 17, 46, 153; Liberty Loan Committee of (Buffalo), 140
U.S. Department of War, 118, 151, 158
U.S. Food Administration, 120–1, 149
U.S. Grain Corporation, 149, 152–3
U.S. House of Representatives, 20, 35, 183; House Naval Affairs Committee, 144
U.S. Navy Fuel Oil Board, 26, 33
U.S. Rubber Company, 45
U.S. Senate, 5, 6, 33, 143, 161–2, 168–70, 172–3, 178, 180; rejection of the Armenian mandate, 167; rejection of the Versailles Treaty, 167; Senate Foreign Relations

Committee, 132, 137, 165; Senate Joint Res. 106, 164–5; Senate Res. 359, 174, 175
U.S. Shipping Board, 117; *See also* Teagle, Walter; Standard Oil
Ussher, Clarence, 59, 60, 67, 188
U.S. Steel, 153
U.S. Supreme Court, 25
U.S.-Turkish commerce treaty (1830), 2; (1862), 2
Uhl, Edwin F., 5

Van, city and *vilayet*, 4, 8, 39, 40, 54, 59, 61, 63, 66–8 *passim*, 70, 78–81 *passim*, 86, 93, 108, 148, 154, 166, 171, 182
Van, Lake, 26, 61, 67, 71, 80, 81
Van Buren, Martin, 2
Varak Monastery, 67
Varak Mountain, 67
Verakazmial (Reformed) Hnchakian Party, 16; *See also* Hnchakian Revolutionary Party
Verdun, 127
Vickrey, Charles V., 140, 156
Vladivostock, 26
Volk, Douglas, 150
Vramian, Arshak, 93
Vratzian, Simon, 181, 182

Wangenheim, Baron Hans von, 64, 88
Wanger, Irving P., 20
Warwick Iron Company (Pottstown), 41
Way, John, 51
Westenenk, Louis, 40
Westermann, William L., 175
Western Asian Division, 147
White, Henry, 143
White, Stanley, 148, 183
Wilhelm II, Kaiser, 88
Willard, Frances E., 15
Williams, John Sharp, 164–5
Williams, William A., 33, 173
Williamson, Harold F., 25
Wilson, F.M. Huntington, 24

Printed in the United States
69979LV00001BD/1